D0535317

America's Best QUILTING PROJECTS

Edited by Mary V. Green

Written by Marianne Fons and Liz Porter

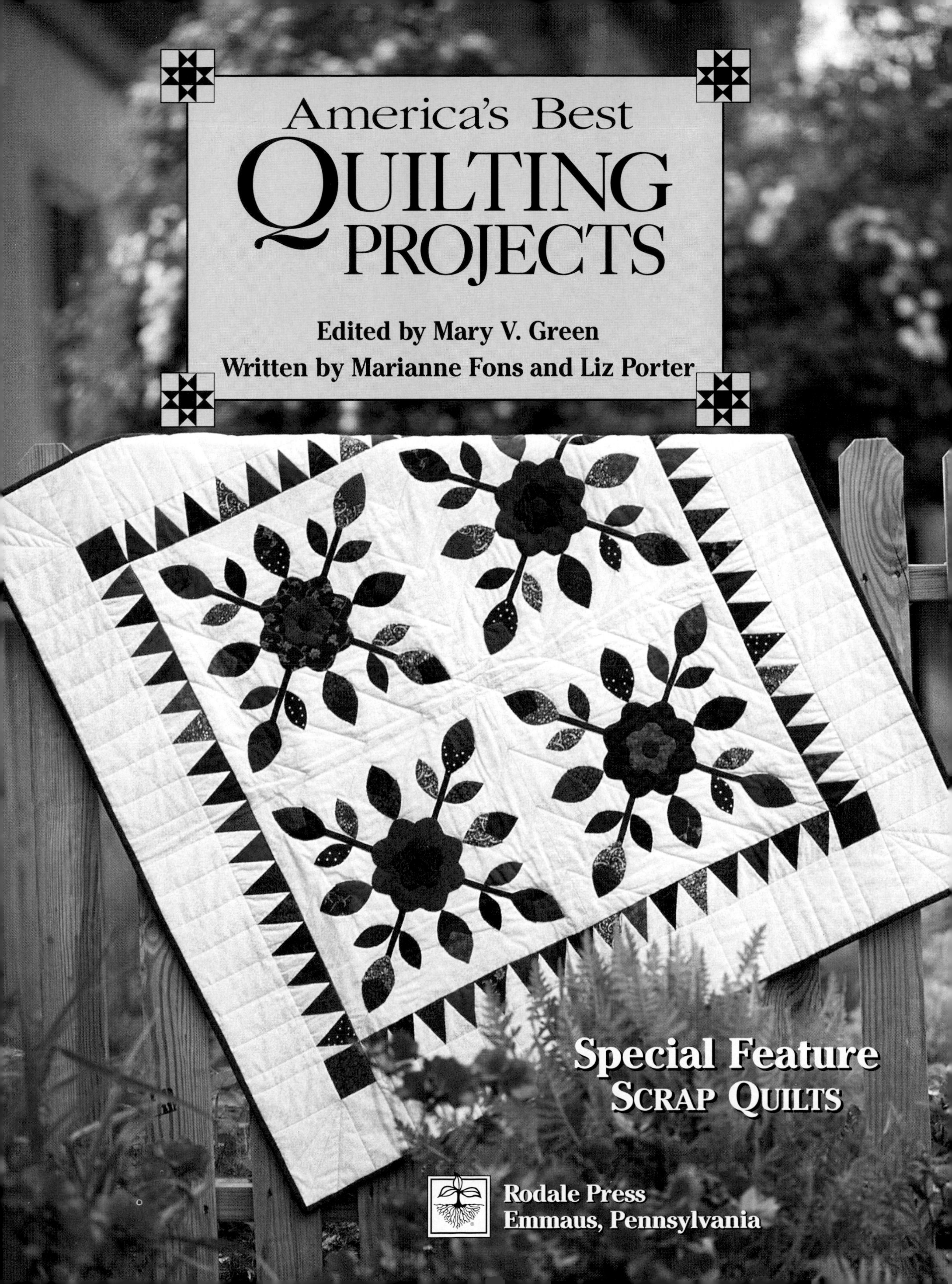

Special Feature
SCRAP QUILTS

Rodale Press
Emmaus, Pennsylvania

Our Mission

We publish books that empower people's lives.

RODALE BOOKS

Printed in the United States of America on acid-free ∞, recycled ♻ paper, containing 10 percent post-consumer waste

Executive Editor: Margaret Lydic Balitas

Senior Editor: Suzanne Nelson

Senior Associate Editor: Mary V. Green

Copy Manager: Dolores Plikaitis

Copy Editor: Carolyn R. Mandarano

Technical Writers: Marianne Fons and Liz Porter

Administrative Assistant: Susan Nickol

Editorial assistance: Deborah Weisel

Office Manager: Karen Earl-Braymer

Cover and Book Designer: Denise M. Shade

Book Layout: Lisa Palmer

Photographer: Mitch Mandel

Photo Stylist: Marianne G. Laubach

Project Illustrator: Sandy Freeman

Tips and Techniques Illustrator: Charles Metz

Logo Designer: Denise M. Shade

On the Cover: The quilt shown is Jim's Scrappy Nine Patch and may be found on page 87. The fabric shown is Country Fantasies, pattern number 7835-10, by Springmaid Fabrics.

If you have any questions or comments concerning this book, please write to:

Rodale Press
Book Readers' Service
33 East Minor Street
Emmaus, PA 18098

Library of Congress Cataloging-in-Publication Data

Fons, Marianne.

America's best quilting projects / edited by Mary V. Green : Written by Marianne Fons and Liz Porter.
p. cm.

On cover: "Featuring scrap quilts."

ISBN 0–87596–604–7 : hardcover 1. Patchwork–United States–Patterns. 2. Patchwork quilts–United States. I. Porter, Liz. II. Green, Mary V. III. Title. IV. Title: Quilting projects.

TT835.F64 1994
746.46–dc20 93–33166

Distributed in the book trade by St. Martin's Press

2 4 6 8 10 9 7 5 3 1 hardcover

Contents

Acknowledgments

Stars at Sea by Becky Herdle, Rochester, New York. Becky has been quilting since the early 1980s and is a National Quilting Association certified quilt judge. Her sparkling interpretation of the traditional Storm at Sea pattern received an Honorable Mention at the National Quilting Association show in 1991, and was awarded Second Place in the Schweinfurth Art Center "Quilts=Art=Quilts" exhibit in Auburn, New York, in 1991. In addition, the quilt was included in the "Quilt Art '93 Calendar."

Double Irish Chain by Barbara Lantz, Charleston, West Virginia. This quilt was exhibited at the American Quilter's Society show in 1990, the Quilters' Heritage Celebration in 1990, and the Creative Quilters Show in Huntington, West Virginia in 1992, where it received a First Place award. In addition, it was featured as an Editor's Choice in *Lady's Circle Patchwork Quilts,* no. 14, 1990. Barbara has been quilting for about ten years and favors traditional designs. She especially enjoys appliqué and hand quilting.

Bleeding Heart by Yvonne Rock, Moorhead, Minnesota. Although she does lots of sewing, Yvonne had never before made a large quilt. Her efforts earned her First Place in the combination (pieced and appliquéd) category at the 1991 Indian Summer Quilt Show in Fargo, North Dakota. She was also awarded the Viewers Choice award and the Judges Award for Workmanship at that show.

Generations by Kathleen Etherington-Schiano, Nanuet, New York. Kathleen combined two traditional blocks in a contemporary design to create this quilt, which won the First Quilt Award at the American Quilter's Society show in 1991 and was featured in the fall 1991 issue of *American Quilter.*

Burgoyne Surrounded by Sharlotte Johnston, Detroit Lakes, Minnesota. Sharlotte likes to make traditional quilts, trying to reproduce quilts that our ancestors made. This classic quilt was exhibited at the American Quilter's Society show in 1992, and it was awarded Second Place at the 1991 Indian Summer Quilt Show in Fargo, North Dakota.

Blossoms and Buds by Mollie Fish, Corvallis, Oregon. Mollie is a busy quilter and designer who markets her quilt designs through her business, The Garden Patch. She loves creating traditional-looking designs, especially floral designs, in fresh new colors. This design was created especially for this book.

Totable Totes by Judy Curtis, Humble, Texas. Judy is an award-winning quiltmaker who began designing quilt patterns at the same time she started quilting in 1984. Her quilts have been exhibited at the International Quilt Festival in Houston, Texas, the American Quilter's Society show in Paducah, Kentucky, and a number of local quilt shows. She favors contemporary interpretations of traditional patterns, particularly geometric shapes, and translates her designs into rugs and cross-stitch projects as well as wallhangings. Judy's designs are available under the name Simple Treasures.

Midnight Rainbows by Donna Svoboda, Lincoln, Nebraska. Donna began quilting in 1981 as therapy for the "empty nest." Her unusual and sophisticated wallhanging was the result of a guild challenge. It has won numerous awards and honors, including a First Place ribbon in the Nebraska State Fair in 1990 and Second Place in the National Quilting Association show in 1991. It was also featured in the January/February 1991 issue of *Lady's Circle Patchwork Quilts.*

Roses in a Ruby Vase by Virginia Carman Dambach, Fargo, North Dakota. Virginia found the block design for her quilt in the 1986 issue of *Editor's Choice Patchwork Quilts.* Twenty of the quilt's 32 blocks were made by members of the Friendship BlockClub III and other friends. The quilt was part of a juried exhibit at the New England Quilt Museum in Lowell, Massachusetts. It was also exhibited at the 1991 Indian Summer Quilt Show in Fargo, North Dakota, where it was awarded Best of Show and First Prize, Pieced Quilts.

Nectar by Joanna Evans, Montague, Massachusetts. Joanna is a member of the Hands Across the Valley Quilters Guild and the New England Quilters Guild. She enjoys both traditional and contemporary designs, and she likes to experiment with using traditional patchwork patterns in nontraditional settings. In this wallhanging, the traditional pineapple pattern is interpreted in an original, contemporary color scheme. The quilt was exhibited in the Hands All Around III show in Amherst, Massachusetts, in 1991.

Brick Wall by Tina M. Gravatt, Philadelphia, Pennsylvania. Tina is a teacher, lecturer, and author whose historically accurate miniatures have appeared in many exhibitions and publications. This miniature is a reproduction of the full-size antique, which was found in an antique shop in upstate New York. The miniature was exhibited at the Museum of the American Quilter's Society in 1992 and was featured at the Quilter's Heritage Celebration in 1992 as part of an invited special exhibit entitled "Reconstructing the Past."

A Dozen Roses for You by Marty Freed, Winterset, Iowa. Marty took her first quilting class in 1982. This quilt, her first appliqué quilt, was funded through the Iowa Arts Council's Folk Art Apprenticeship

Program. The quilt was exhibited at the Iowa State Fair in 1992, where it was awarded First Place, Appliqué; Best of Show; and *Better Homes and Gardens* Blue Ribbon Award for Appliqué.

Plaid Spools by Kim Baird, Fargo, North Dakota. Kim has been quilting since 1978. Her favorite quilts are strong, graphic designs; she likes antique scrap quilts as well as contemporary art pieces. Kim lets her quilts "evolve," starting with a pattern and some color ideas and just making blocks until there are enough. From 1983 to 1985, Kim headed the North Dakota Quilt Project, which documented over 3,500 quilts. Plaid Spools was exhibited at the 1991 Indian Summer Quilt Show in Fargo, North Dakota, and appeared in the 1991 American Quilter's Society "Quilt Art Engagement Calendar."

Patchwork Pillows by Cyndi Hershey, Lansdale, Pennsylvania. Cyndi is a busy quilt shop owner who enjoys developing new projects for her classes. She generally teaches either original designs or traditional designs with unusual or original construction techniques. Her favorite part of quiltmaking is designing a project and choosing the colors. Cyndi's been quilting since 1978 and teaching since 1983. She is a founding member of the County Line Quilters.

Jim's Scrappy Nine Patch by Gloria Greenlee, Tulsa, Oklahoma. Gloria likes traditional quilts best, as this scrap quilt demonstrates. And although she enjoys the hand quilting process, she also does a lot of machine quilting in order to complete more quilts. This quilt was exhibited at the Green Country Quilter's Guild show in 1991; A Celebration of Quilts in Oklahoma City in 1991, where it was awarded Third Place in the Traditional Pieced category; and the Tulsa State Fair in 1990, where it was awarded First Place in the Machine Pieced/Machine Quilted category.

Scrap Baskets by Kris Merkens, Ada, Minnesota. Kris prefers hand piecing and hand quilting traditional designs. The pattern she used for this quilt is by Susan Bartlett of The Quilted Cottage in Erie, Pennsylvania. Scrap Baskets was exhibited at the 1991 Indian Summer Quilt Show in Fargo, North Dakota, where it was awarded First Place in the Small Quilts category.

Diamond Charms by Pat Yamin, Brooklyn, New York. Pat has been a quiltmaker since 1970, when she started making quilts as a break from her graduate-school studies. She likes traditional patterns best and considers a well-executed red-and-white schoolhouse one of her favorites. This quilt was made as a sample to demonstrate the templates that Pat markets nationwide as part of her business, Come Quilt with Me, Inc.

Broken Hearts for Daddy by Elsie Campbell, Arkansas City, Kansas. Though she's done all kinds of needlework since childhood, Elsie states that she's only been seriously quilting for five years. Her favorite quilts are pieced scrap quilts. This quilt is based on "My Quilted Heart," a St. Nicole pattern designed by Marilyn Ginsburg. The quilt appeared in the American Quilter's Society show in 1992 and the Dallas Quilt Show, and was a finalist in the *Better Homes and Gardens*/Land's End Search for the Great American Quilt.

Stars and Stripes Picnic Set by Marianne Laubach, Easton, Pennsylvania. Marianne is a designer and a photo stylist who has been doing needlework all her life. She especially enjoys designing projects, choosing the fabrics, then watching it all come together. Her picnic set is a fun project to make for yourself or to give as a gift.

Halloween Mini Quilts by Barbara Vassler, Banks, Oregon. Barbara has been an avid designer and quiltmaker for 12 years. She started her own pattern business ten years ago in response to numerous requests for her designs. These fun Halloween quilts are just one example. Barbara's patterns are available nationally under the name Little Brown House Patterns.

Oak Leaf Wreath by Mollie Fish, Corvallis, Oregon. Mollie is a designer and quilter who markets her designs under the name The Garden Patch. She got her inspiration for this design from the dried flower wreaths she also enjoys making.

Holiday Gift Bags by Kathy Berschneider, Rockford, Illinois. Kathy is a quilter and craft designer who has also taught children's quilting classes. She designed these gift bags to be attractive, useful, and easy to make!

Christmastime by Kathy Munkelwitz, Isle, Minnesota. Kathy has been quilting for 13 years and now sells most of her work. She has also published several of her patterns. Kathy enjoys all aspects of the quiltmaking process, especially sharing ideas with other quiltmakers. Christmastime was exhibited at the Minnesota State Fair, where it won First Place, and at the 1991 Indian Summer Quilt Show in Fargo, North Dakota, where it won First Place in the Household category.

Crazy Quilt Stockings by Lois Richichi, Roslyn, Pennsylvania. Lois has been quilting for five years and has taught classes for three of them. She enjoys developing new projects to teach. When she makes a gift project like these stockings, she tries to match the fabric to the recipient—like the one she made for her son with car prints and toy cars sewn to it.

Stepping Stones by Kathy Munkelwitz, Isle, Minnesota. Kathy designed this quilt using some of her favorite colors. The quilt appeared in the American Quilter's Society show in 1991 and at the Minnesota State Fair in 1992.

Introduction

Welcome to the second volume of *America's Best Quilting Projects.* Once again, we've traveled to quilt shows and events throughout the country to bring you the very best bed quilts, wallhangings, and home accessories we could find.

It's so exciting to able to get out and see what's going on in the world of quiltmaking—to discover the latest trends, the most exciting fabrics, the newest tools and techniques. It's pure delight to visit with quiltmakers from all over and talk about their favorite patterns or colors, what they like best about quiltmaking, and what part of the process they still want to learn more about (don't we all have areas where we want to improve?). Best of all is the chance to see the gorgeous quilts that are being made all over the country. It's never difficult to find projects to include in this book; the hard part is narrowing the many wonderful choices down to the 25 we've included here.

One trend we've noticed is a strong interest in scrap quilts. Old scraps, new scraps, swapped scraps—they're all turning up in stunning traditional patterns and exciting contemporary quilts. In fact, we've seen so many scrap quilts and scrap projects that we selected six of them for our Special Feature.

But the job doesn't end with choosing the quilts. That's when the real work begins. We very carefully measure the quilts, draft the patterns, calculate the number of pieces and the yardages, and draw the diagrams—all to make it as easy as possible for you to create these beautiful quilts at home. Then we make sure the step-by-step directions are clear, complete, and easy to follow. And while that sometimes means long hours at the computer, every minute is worth it. We know from our own experiences as quiltmakers how terribly frustrating it is to find an error or wish that more details had been given.

Since we believe that beautiful photos add to your enjoyment of the book, we go to great lengths to bring you the best possible photos of the quilts. We plan *everything:* from what the photo will look like, to where it will be taken, and what, if any, props will be used. And we think all that hard work pays off because it means the quilts look as good on the pages of the book as they did when we had them here in the office.

We're sure you'll enjoy paging through the book. And once you've spotted a project that you want to make, you'll find that the directions include many features specially tailored to a quiltmaker's needs. Each project features an indication of skill level, a list of all the fabrics and supplies you need, step-by-step directions with lots of diagrams, and full-size patterns so you don't have to waste time with enlargements. At the back of the book, you'll find a "Tips and Techniques" section, which includes all the general information you need to make a quilt, plus lots of valuable tips and handy ideas to guarantee your project is a success. And in the Acknowledgments section you can read about the quilts and their makers: what inspired them, where the patterns came from, what shows the quilts have appeared in. We'd like to thank the quiltmakers for generously sharing their projects with us so that we could bring them to you.

We hope you find that *America's Best Quilting Projects* is a book you come back to again and again—to linger over, be inspired by, and, most of all, to use! Happy quilting!

Mary V. Green
Project Editor

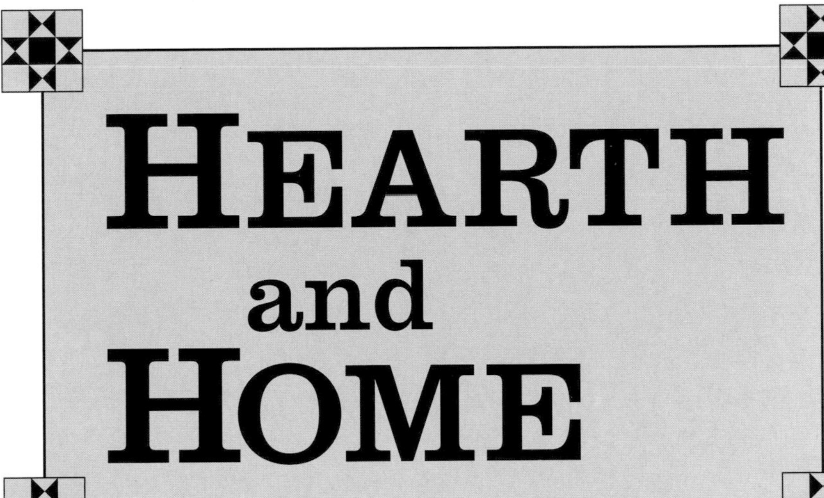

HEARTH and HOME

Stars at Sea

Quiltmaker: Becky Herdle

Using traditional patterns in nontraditional ways is Becky's favorite aspect of quiltmaking. This sparkling adaptation of the Storm at Sea pattern is a good example. The traditional pattern offers almost endless design possibilities through varied color and fabric placement. Experiment with your own fabrics to see what develops.

Skill Level: Intermediate

Size: Finished quilt is 79 × 97 inches

Fabrics and Supplies

The materials listed and the instructions that follow will result in a quilt exactly like the one shown in the photo. If you prefer, design your own Storm at Sea quilt. First, photocopy the diagram of the inner quilt on page 7; then experiment by using colored pencils to create your own variation.

- 4¾ yards of black print fabric for blocks, borders, and binding
- 4¼ yards of black/teal/plum tropical print fabric for blocks
- 4½ yards of teal solid fabric for blocks
- 1¼ yards *each* of light turquoise print, plum solid, and dark pink solid fabrics for blocks
- ½ yard of light pink print fabric for blocks
- 6 yards of fabric for quilt back
- Queen-size quilt batting (90 × 108 inches)
- Rotary cutter, ruler, and mat
- Template plastic
- Colored pencils (optional)

Cutting

All measurements include ¼-inch seam allowances. Measurements for the borders are longer than needed; trim them to the exact length when they are added to the quilt top. Instructions given are for quick-cutting all of the pieces except B, C, and E using a rotary cutter and ruler. Make templates for B, C, and E using the patterns on page 8. If you prefer to cut all of the pieces using the traditional method, then also make templates for patterns A, D, F, G, and H as directed below.

Label the templates. Use the B template label side down to mark the B pieces and label side up to mark the B reverse pieces. Tips for making and using templates are on page 153.

- **A:** Make a 2⅜-inch square; cut the square in half diagonally.
- **D:** Make a 4¼-inch square; cut the square in half diagonally both ways.
- **F:** Make a 3⅞-inch square; cut the square in half diagonally.
- **G:** 3½-inch square
- **H:** 2⅝-inch square

Before You Begin

To prepare the black print fabric, first cut off one 100-inch-long piece.

From the 100-inch-long piece of black print fabric, cut:

- Four 3¾ × 100-inch border strips
- 116 A triangles
  Use Template A
  OR
  Cut six 2⅜-inch strips across the width of the fabric (approximately 27 inches after the borders have been cut). Cut the strips into 2⅜-inch squares; you will need 58 squares. Cut each square in half diagonally to make two triangles.
- 36 C triangles
- 18 D triangles
  Use Template D
  OR
  Cut one 4¼-inch strip across the width of the fabric. From the strip, cut five 4¼-inch squares. Cut each square in half diagonally both ways to make four triangles. You will have two extra triangles.
- 14 E diamonds
- 36 F triangles
  Use Template F
  OR
  Cut three 3⅞-inch strips across the width of the fabric. Cut the strips into 3⅞-inch squares. You will need 18 squares. Cut each square in half diagonally to make two triangles.

From the remaining black print fabric, cut:

- 80 F triangles. (You will have a total of 116 triangles.)
  Use Template F
  OR
  Cut four 3⅞ × 44-inch strips. Cut the strips into 3⅞-inch squares. You will need 40 squares. Cut each square in half diagonally to make two triangles.
- 48 G squares

Use Template G
OR
Cut four 3½ × 44-inch strips. Cut the strips into 3½-inch squares.

- Reserve the remaining fabric for binding

From the black tropical print fabric, cut:

- 140 A triangles
  Use Template A
  OR
  Cut four 2⅜ × 44-inch strips. Cut the strips into 2⅜-inch squares; you will need 70 squares. Cut each square in half diagonally to make two triangles.
- 24 D triangles
  Use Template D
  OR
  Cut one 4¼ × 44-inch strip. From the strip, cut six 4¼-inch squares. Cut each square in half diagonally both ways to make four triangles.
- 128 E diamonds
- 140 F triangles
  Use Template F
  OR
  Cut seven 3⅞ × 44-inch strips. Cut the strips into 3⅞-inch squares. You will need 70 squares. Cut each square in half diagonally to make two triangles.

From the teal solid fabric, cut:

- 152 B and 152 B reverse triangles
- 296 D triangles
  Use Template D
  OR
  Cut eight 4¼ × 44-inch strips. Cut the strips into 4¼-inch squares; you will need 74 squares. Cut each square in half diagonally both ways to make four triangles.
- 22 H squares
  Use Template H
  OR
  Cut two 2⅝ × 44-inch strips. Cut the strips into 2⅝-inch squares.

From the light turquoise print fabric, cut:

- 4 A triangles
  Use Template A
  OR
  Cut two 2⅜-inch squares. Cut each square in half diagonally to make two triangles.
- 80 B and 80 B reverse triangles
- 14 D triangles
  Use Template D
  OR
  Cut one 4¼ × 44-inch strip. Cut the strip into 4¼-inch squares; you will need four squares. Cut each square in half diagonally both ways to make four triangles.
- 10 H squares
  Use Template H
  OR
  Cut one 2⅝ × 44-inch strip. Cut the strip into 2⅝-inch squares.

From the plum solid fabric, cut:

- 64 A triangles
  Use Template A
  OR
  Cut two 2⅜ × 44-inch strips. Cut the strips into 2⅜-inch squares; you will need 32 squares. Cut each square in half diagonally to make two triangles.
- 64 F triangles
  Use Template F
  OR
  Cut three 3⅞ × 44-inch strips. Cut the strips into 3⅞-inch squares. You will need 32 squares. Cut each square in half diagonally to make two triangles.
- 32 G squares
  Use Template G
  OR
  Cut three 3½ × 44-inch strips. Cut the strips into 3½-inch squares.

From the dark pink solid fabric, cut:

- 60 B and 60 B reverse triangles
- 28 H squares
  Use Template H
  OR
  Cut two 2⅝ × 44-inch strips. Cut the strips into 2⅝-inch squares.

From the light pink print fabric, cut:

- 28 B and 28 B reverse triangles
- 3 H squares
  Use Template H
  OR
  Cut three 2⅝-inch squares.

Piecing the Patchwork Units

This pattern is not pieced in a traditional block format but rather in smaller units that are

then assembled into rows. The **Unit Chart** on this page shows the correct fabric placement for each unit and the number of each unit needed. Referring to the **Unit Chart** and the **Fabric Key,** follow the directions below for piecing the units. Keep the completed units grouped according to number, and pin a label on each stack.

Piecing Unit 1

1. Sew pairs of light turquoise and black print A triangles together to form squares.

2. Press the seams toward the black print triangles.

Piecing Units 2 and 3

1. Refer to the **Unit Chart** for correct fabric placement for each unit. To make one unit, sew a B triangle to one short side of a C triangle, as shown in **Diagram 1** on page 6. Press the seam away from the C triangle.

Fabric Key

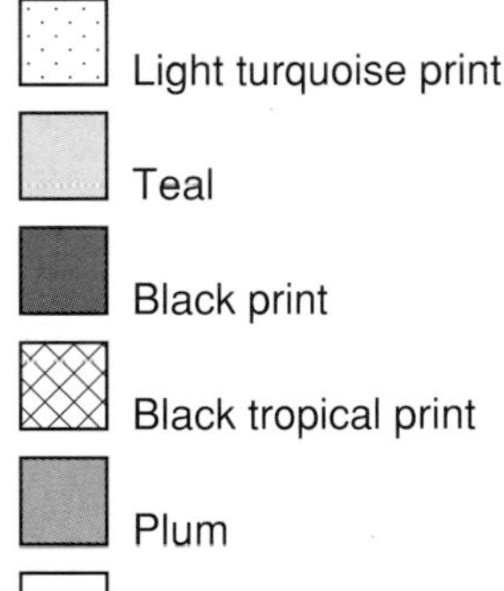

Light turquoise print

Teal

Black print

Black tropical print

Plum

Light pink print

Dark pink

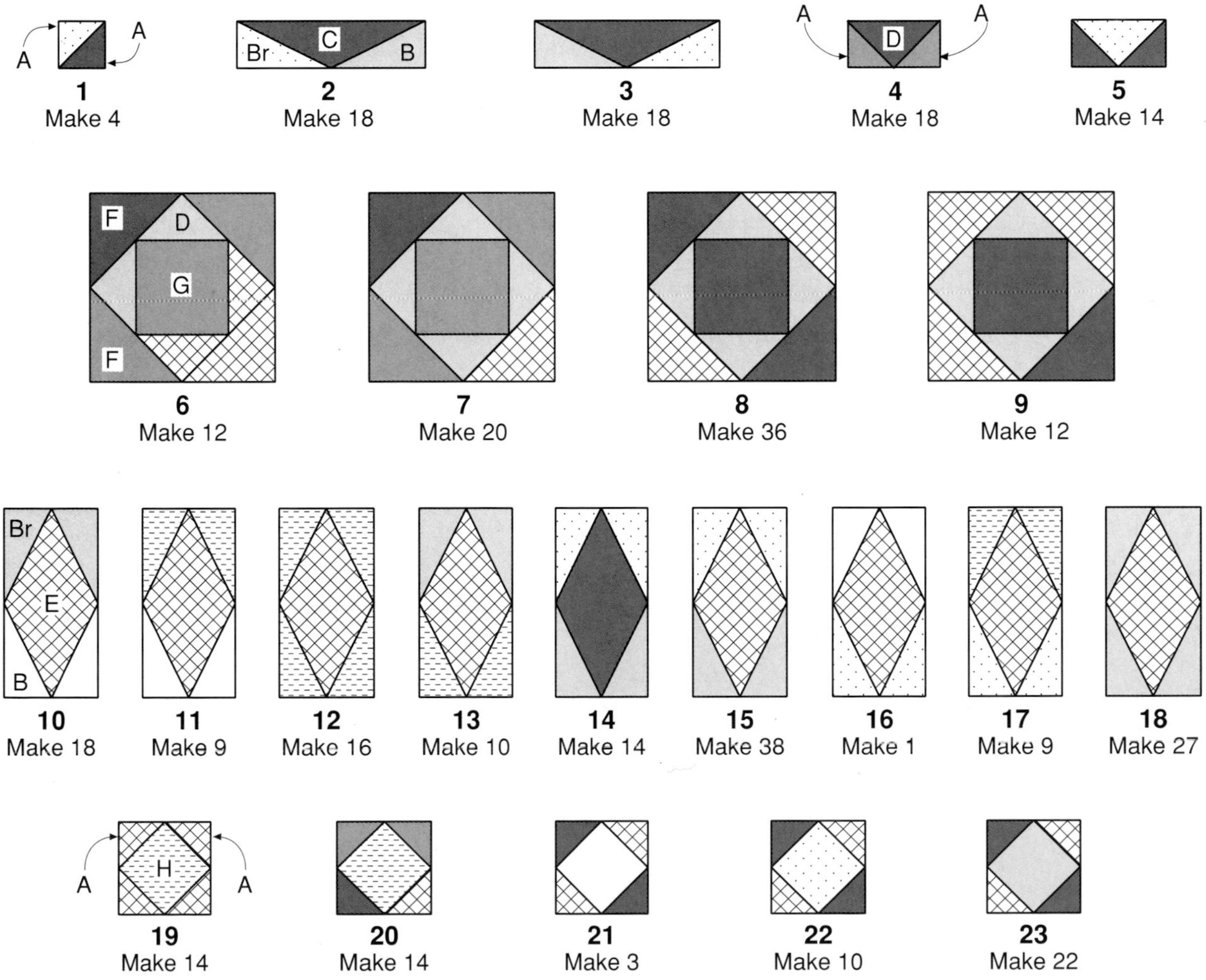

A A 1 Make 4

Br C B 2 Make 18

3 Make 18

A D A 4 Make 18

5 Make 14

F D G F 6 Make 12

7 Make 20

8 Make 36

9 Make 12

Br E B 10 Make 18

11 Make 9

12 Make 16

13 Make 10

14 Make 14

15 Make 38

16 Make 1

17 Make 9

18 Make 27

A H A 19 Make 14

20 Make 14

21 Make 3

22 Make 10

23 Make 22

Unit Chart

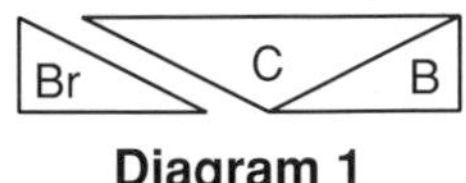

Diagram 1

2. Stitch a B reverse triangle to the other short side of the C triangle. Press the seam away from the C triangle.

Piecing Units 4 and 5

1. Refer to the **Unit Chart** for correct fabric placement for each unit. To make one unit, sew an A triangle to one short side of a D triangle, as shown in **Diagram 2.** Press the seam away from the D triangle.

Diagram 2

2. Stitch a second A triangle to the other short side of the D triangle; press as above.

Piecing Units 6 through 9

1. Refer to the **Unit Chart** for correct fabric placement for each unit. To make one unit, sew a D triangle to two opposite sides of a G square, as shown in **Diagram 3.** Press the seams away from the square.

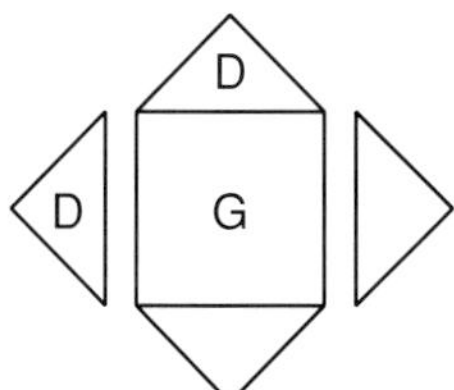

Diagram 3

2. Add a D triangle to the remaining two sides of the square and press as above.

3. Sew an F triangle to two opposite sides of the Step 2 unit, as shown in **Diagram 4.** Press the seams away from the center of the unit.

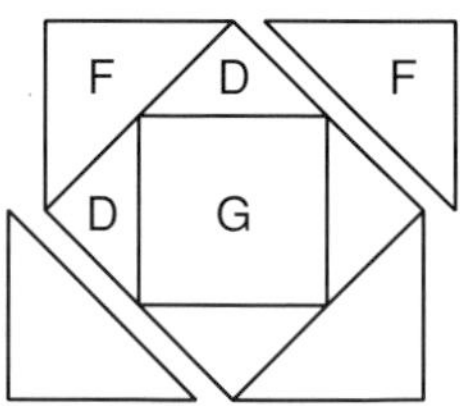

Diagram 4

4. Stitch an F triangle to the remaining two sides of the square. Press the seams away from the center of the unit.

Piecing Units 10 through 18

1. Refer to the **Unit Chart** for correct fabric placement for each unit. To make one unit, sew B triangles to opposite sides of an E diamond, as shown in **Diagram 5.** Press the seams away from the E diamond.

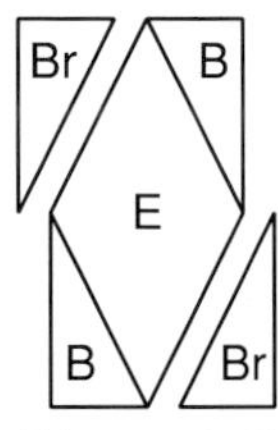

Diagram 5

2. Stitch B reverse triangles to the remaining two sides of the E diamond. Press the seams away from the diamond.

Piecing Units 19 through 23

1. Refer to the **Unit Chart** for correct fabric placement for each unit. To make one unit, sew an A triangle to opposite sides of an H square, as shown in **Diagram 6.** Press the seams away from the square.

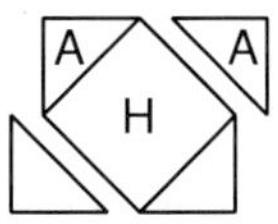

Diagram 6

2. Stitch an A triangle to the remaining two sides of the square and press as above.

Assembling the Quilt Top

1. Referring to the **Unit Placement Diagram** and the photo on page 2, lay out the units for the quilt, rotating units as needed to create the stars and patterns within the quilt.

2. Join the units in horizontal rows, pressing the seams in opposite directions from row to row.

3. Join the rows. The inner quilt should

1	2	4	3	5	2	4	3	5	2	4	3	5	2	4	3	1
3	6	10	6	14	7	13	7	14	7	13	7	14	6	10	6	2
4	10	19	11	20	12	19	12	20	12	19	12	20	11	19	10	4
2	6	11	9	15	8	13	9	18	8	17	9	18	8	11	6	3
5	14	20	15	22	15	23	18	23	15	22	15	23	18	20	14	5
3	7	12	8	15	8	10	8	18	8	15	8	15	9	12	7	2
4	13	19	13	23	10	21	10	23	18	23	15	22	17	19	13	4
2	7	12	9	15	8	10	8	18	8	15	8	15	8	12	7	3
5	14	20	15	22	15	23	18	23	15	22	15	23	18	20	14	5
3	7	17	8	15	8	15	8	18	8	15	8	18	9	17	7	2
4	15	19	15	23	15	22	15	23	18	23	18	23	15	19	15	4
2	7	17	9	18	8	15	8	15	8	18	8	10	8	17	7	3
5	14	20	18	23	18	23	15	22	15	23	10	21	10	20	14	5
3	7	12	8	10	8	18	8	15	8	18	8	16	9	12	7	2
4	13	19	11	21	10	23	18	23	18	23	15	22	17	19	13	4
2	7	12	9	10	8	15	8	18	8	15	8	15	8	12	7	3
5	14	20	18	23	15	22	15	23	15	22	15	23	18	20	14	5
3	6	11	8	18	9	17	8	18	9	17	8	18	9	11	6	2
4	10	19	11	20	12	19	12	20	12	19	12	20	11	19	10	4
2	6	10	6	14	7	13	7	14	7	13	7	14	6	10	6	3
1	3	4	2	5	3	4	2	5	3	4	2	5	3	4	2	1

Unit Placement Diagram

measure approximately 72½ × 90½ inches, including seam allowances.

4. Mark and sew the border strips to the quilt, mitering the border corner seams. See page 160 for instructions for adding borders with mitered corners.

Quilting and Finishing

1. Mark quilting designs as desired.

2. Divide the backing fabric into two equal 108-inch lengths. Trim the selvages and cut one of the pieces in half lengthwise. Sew a half panel

to each side of the full-width panel. Press the seams away from the center panel.

3. Layer the quilt back, batting, and quilt top; baste. Trim the quilt back so it is approximately 3 inches larger than the quilt top on all sides.

4. Quilt all marked designs, and add additional quilting as desired.

5. From the reserved binding fabric, make approximately 370 inches of French-fold binding. See page 164 for suggested binding widths and instructions on making and attaching binding.

6. Sew the binding to the quilt top, mitering the corners. Trim the excess batting and backing, and hand finish the binding on the back side of the quilt.

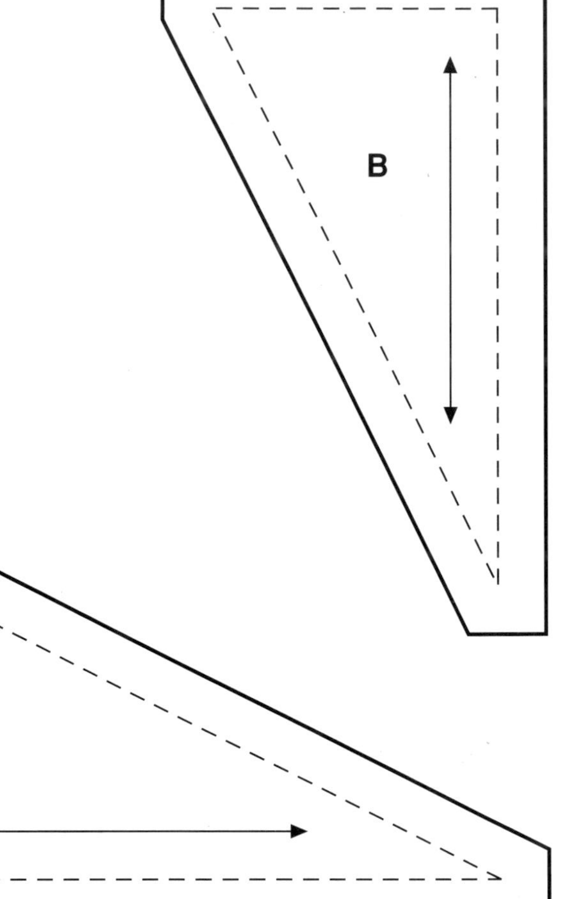

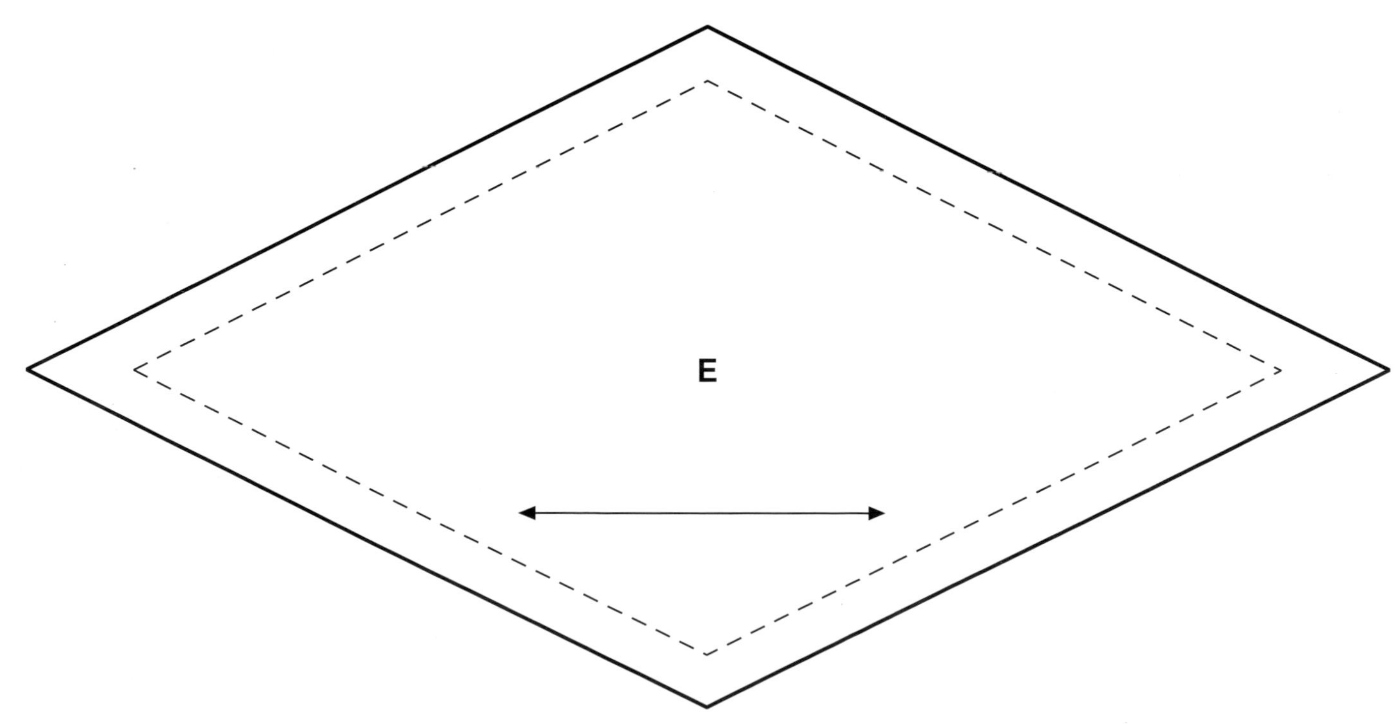

Double Irish Chain

Quiltmaker: Barbara Lantz

"Quiet simplicity" makes this traditional quilt Barbara's favorite. She interprets the Double Irish Chain pattern in soothing shades of blue and cream. In the true spirit of quilting, Barbara used remnants of blue fabric from a bedroom decorating project. This design is ideal for quick-cutting and strip piecing. The large white areas offer ample room in which to showcase fancy quilting.

Skill Level: Easy

Size: Finished quilt is 82 × 102 inches
Finished block is 10 inches square

Fabrics and Supplies

- 5 yards of white fabric for blocks, borders, and binding
- 3½ yards of light blue fabric for blocks and borders
- 2¾ yards of medium blue fabric for blocks and corner blocks
- 7⅞ yards of fabric for quilt back
- King-size quilt batting (120 inches square)
- Rotary cutter, ruler, and mat

Cutting

All measurements include ¼-inch seam allowances. Measurements for the borders are longer than needed; trim them to the exact length when they are added to the quilt top. Instructions given are for quick-cutting the pieces with a rotary cutter and ruler.

Before You Begin

To prepare the white fabric, first cut off a 94-inch-long piece. In the same manner, cut a 94-inch-long piece from the light blue yardage.

From the 94-inch-long piece of white fabric, cut:

- Four 2½ × 94-inch border strips
- Eight 2½ × 47-inch strips for strip sets
  Cut four 2½ × 94-inch strips. Cut each strip in half.
- Sixteen 10½-inch squares
  Cut two 10½ × 94-inch strips. Cut the strips into 10½-inch squares.

From the remaining white fabric, cut:

- Sixteen 10½-inch squares
  Cut four 10½ × 44-inch strips. Cut the strips into 10½-inch squares. (You should have a total of 32 large squares for the quilt.)
- Twenty 2½-inch squares
  Cut two 2½ × 44-inch strips. Cut the strips into 2½-inch squares.
- Reserve the remaining fabric for binding

From the 94-inch-long piece of light blue fabric, cut:

- Eight 2½ × 94-inch border strips
- Sixteen 2½ × 47-inch strips for strip sets
  Cut eight 2½ × 94-inch strips. Cut each strip in half.

From the remaining light blue fabric, cut:

- Two 2½ × 44-inch strips for strip sets
- Sixteen 2½-inch squares
  Cut one 2½ × 44-inch strip. From the strip, cut sixteen 2½-inch squares.

From the medium blue fabric, cut:

- Twenty-four 2½ × 44-inch strips for strip sets
- One hundred twenty-eight 2½-inch squares
  Cut eight 2½ × 44-inch strips. Cut the strips into 2½-inch squares.

Piecing the Blocks

Two types of blocks are needed to complete the Double Irish Chain design. **Diagram 1** shows the two types of blocks. You will need 31 Block 1 blocks and 32 Block 2 blocks. Refer to the **Fabric Key** when making the strip sets and piecing the blocks.

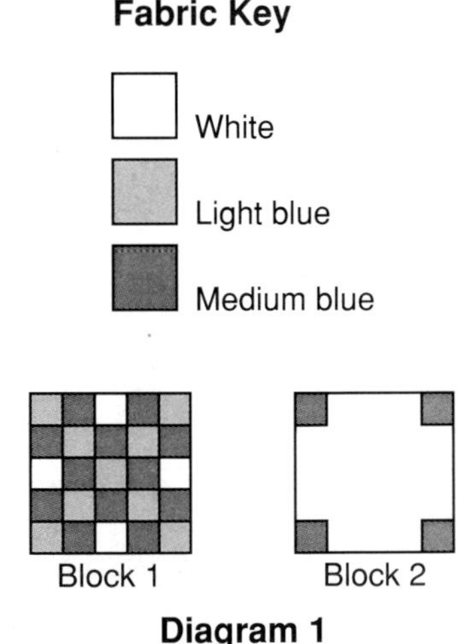

Diagram 1

Block 1

1. Referring to **Diagram 2,** make a strip set by sewing 2½-inch-wide strips together in the following order: light blue, medium blue, white, medium blue, and light blue. Press all the seams in one direction. Trim the longer strips even with the shorter ones. Make four of these strip sets.

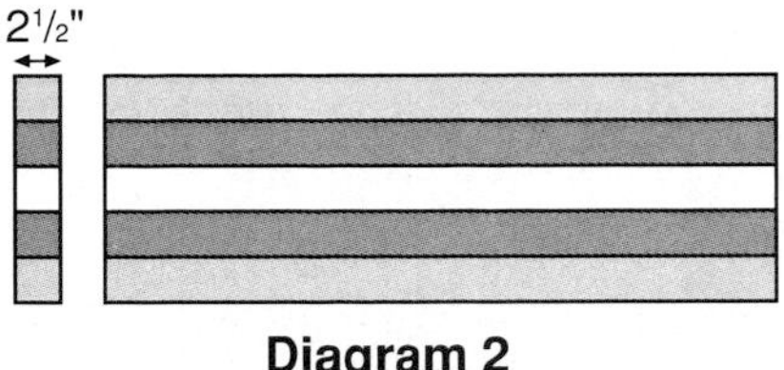

Diagram 2

2. Cut 2½-inch-wide segments from the completed strip sets. You will need a total of 62 segments.

3. Referring to **Diagram 3,** sew 2½-inch-wide strips together in the following order: medium blue, light blue, medium blue, light blue, medium blue. Press all the seams in one direction. Trim the longer strips even with the shorter ones. Repeat to make a total of four strip sets.

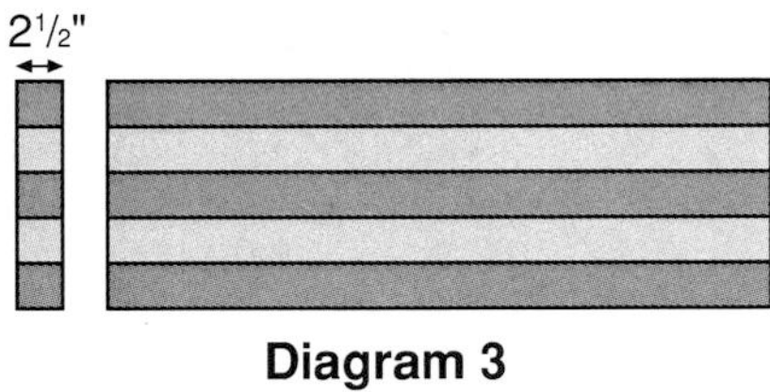

Diagram 3

4. Cut 2½-inch-wide segments from the completed strip sets. You will need a total of 62 segments.

5. In the same manner, sew 2½-inch-wide strips together in the order shown in **Diagram 4:** white, medium blue, light blue, medium blue, and white. Press all the seams in one direction. Trim the longer strips. Make two of these strip sets.

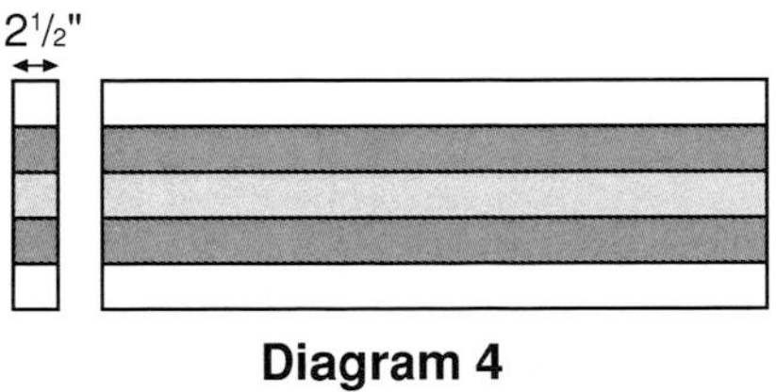

Diagram 4

6. Cut a total of thirty-one 2½-inch-wide segments from the completed Step 5 strip sets.

7. To make one Block 1, lay out two Step 1 segments (Rows 1 and 5), two Step 3 segments (Rows 2 and 4), and one Step 5 segment (Row 3), as shown in **Diagram 5.** For more accurate piecing, turn the segments as necessary to alternate the direction of the seam allowances from row to row. Join the segments. Repeat to make 31 blocks. The completed blocks should measure 10½ inches square.

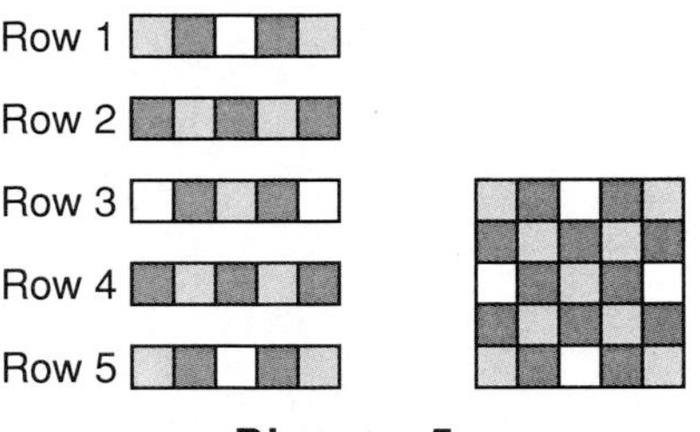

Diagram 5

Block 2

1. To make one Block 2 block, you will need one 10½-inch white square and four 2½-inch medium blue squares. Turn under ¼-inch seam allowances on two adjacent sides of each blue square and baste.

2. Aligning the raw edges of the blue squares with the corners of the white square, appliqué the blue squares to the white square using thread that matches the blue squares. Repeat to make 32 blocks.

Assembling the Quilt Top

1. Referring to the **Quilt Diagram** on page 12, lay out the blocks in nine horizontal rows with seven blocks in each row. Alternate Block 1 with Block 2; be sure there is a Block 2 at each of the four corners of the quilt top.

2. Sew the blocks together in rows; press the seams toward the Block 2 blocks. Join the rows.

3. To make each pieced border, sew a light blue border strip to each side of one white border strip, as shown in the **Quilt Diagram.** Press the seams toward the blue border strips. Make four pieced borders.

4. To make each Nine-Patch corner block, lay out five white and four light blue 2½-inch squares, as shown in the **Quilt Diagram.** Sew the squares together in three rows; press the seams toward the blue squares. Join the rows. Make four border corner squares.

5. Measure the length of the quilt top. Trim two borders to this measurement (approximately 90½ inches) and sew them to the sides of the quilt top. Press the seams toward the borders.

6. Measure the width of the quilt top (not including the two borders you just added). Trim the remaining two borders to this measurement (approximately 70½ inches). Sew a Nine-Patch corner block to each end of the borders. Sew the

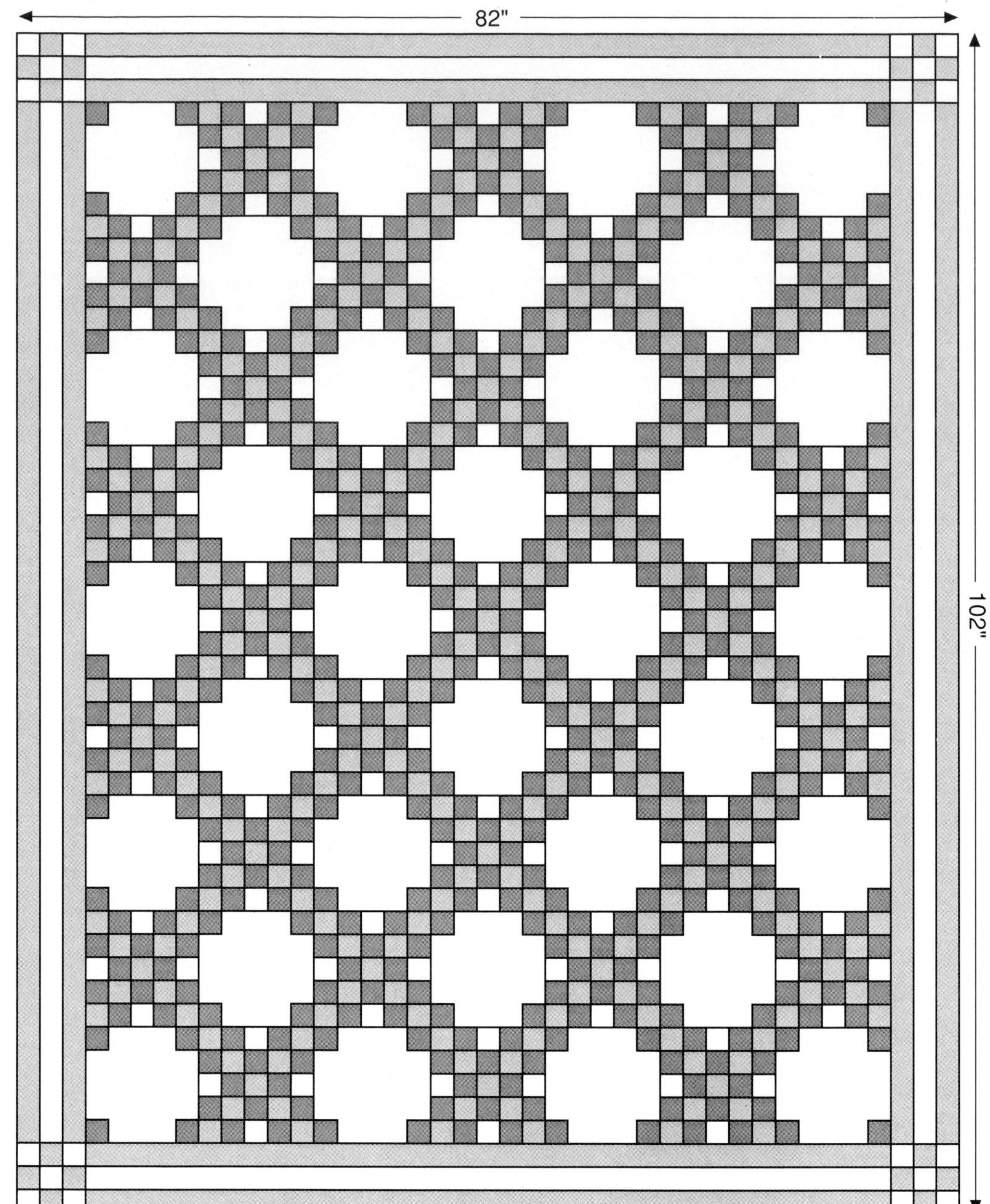

Quilt Diagram

borders to the top and bottom edges of the quilt top. Press the seams toward the borders.

Quilting and Finishing

1. Mark quilting designs. The patterns for the feathered circle, used in the center of Block 2, and the cable design for the borders are on the opposite page.

2. Divide the backing fabric into three equal 94½-inch lengths. Trim the selvages and sew the three pieces together. Press the seams away from the center panel. The seams will run parallel to the top and bottom of the quilt.

3. Layer the quilt back, batting, and quilt top; baste. Trim the quilt back so it is approximately 3 inches larger than the quilt top on all sides.

4. Quilt all marked designs, and add additional quilting as desired. On the quilt shown, each small square was quilted in an X, with diagonal lines of quilting from corner to corner.

5. From the reserved white fabric, make approximately 390 inches of French-fold binding. See page 164 for suggested binding widths and instructions on making and attaching binding.

6. Sew the binding to the quilt top. Trim the excess batting and backing, and hand finish the binding on the back side of the quilt.

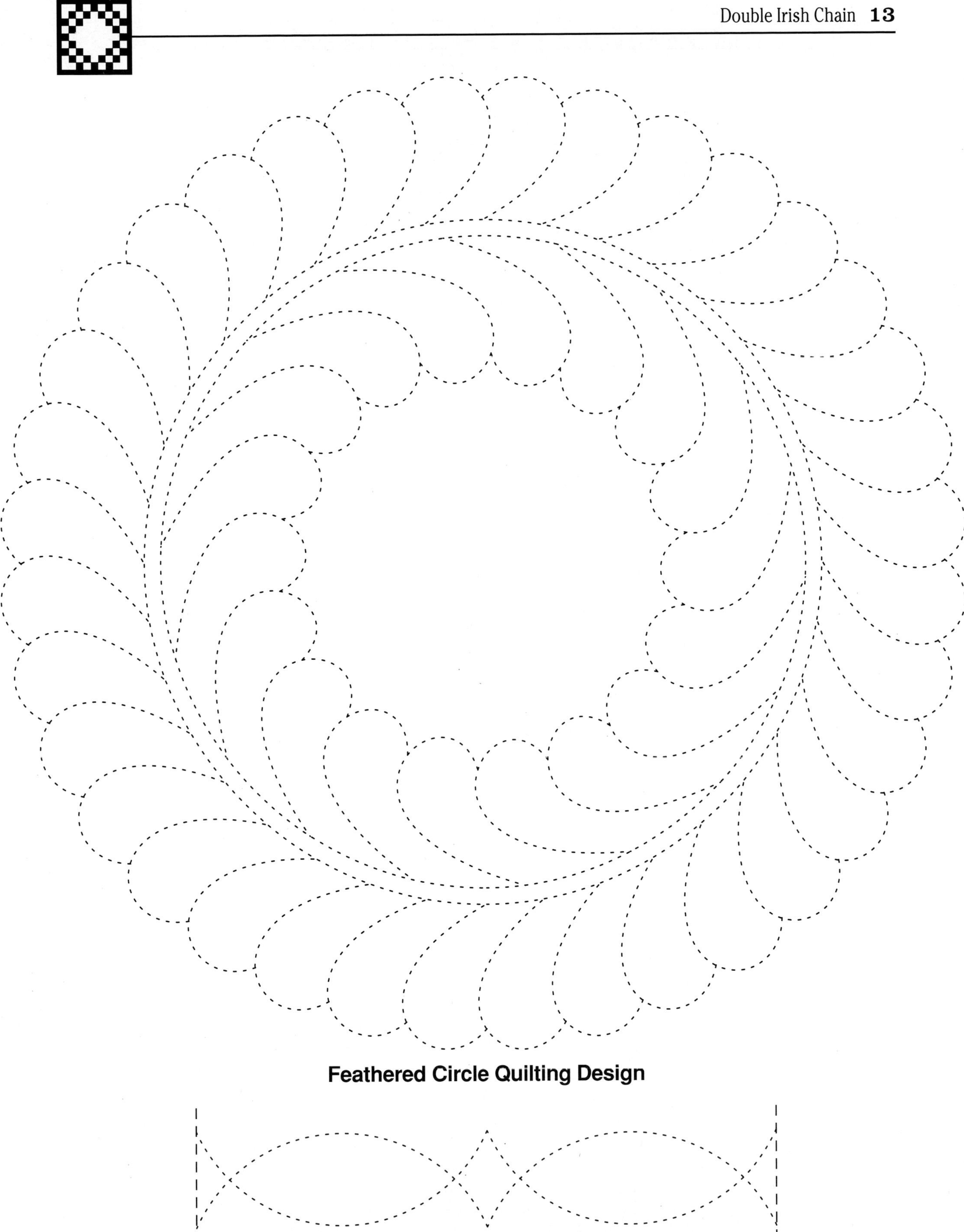

Feathered Circle Quilting Design

Border Cable Quilting Design

Bleeding Heart

Quiltmaker: Yvonne Rock

Yvonne chose this pattern for her first large quilt because it reminds her of the lovely flowering bleeding heart plant in her garden. Taking her cue from nature, Yvonne selected pink and green fabrics that are reminiscent of the flowers and foliage of the garden perennial. Quilters who love hand piecing will enjoy making this project. The border flowers and swags are appliquéd.

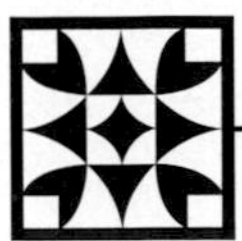

Skill Level: Intermediate to Challenging

Size: Finished quilt is 84 × 108 inches
Finished block is 12 inches square

Fabrics and Supplies

- 10 yards of unbleached muslin or off-white solid fabric for blocks, borders, and binding
- 4 yards of green print fabric for blocks and border swags
- 3½ yards of pink print fabric for blocks and border appliqués
- 7⅞ yards of fabric for quilt back
- King-size quilt batting (120 inches square)
- Rotary cutter, ruler, and mat
- Template plastic

Cutting

All measurements include ¼-inch seam allowances. Measurements for the borders are longer than needed; trim them to the exact length when they are added to the quilt top. Instructions are given for quick-cutting the border pieces with a rotary cutter and ruler.

The instructions provided are for hand piecing the quilt top; refer to page 154 for general tips on hand piecing. The border swags and border flowers are appliquéd. See page 156 for tips on hand appliqué.

Make templates for pattern pieces A through H on pages18–19; include the register marks on the A, B, C, D, and E templates. The patterns are finished size; use the templates to mark sewing lines on the fabric, then add seam allowances when cutting. Transfer the register marks onto the seam allowances of the fabric pieces when marking. The marks will make pinning and stitching the pieces easier. Tips for making and using templates are on page 153.

Before You Begin

To prepare the muslin, first cut off the following pieces: one 36-inch-long piece, one 88-inch-long piece, and one 120-inch-long piece. Set aside the 36-inch-long piece for binding.

From the 88-inch-long piece of muslin, cut:
- Two 12½ × 88-inch border strips

From the 120-inch-long piece of muslin, cut:
- Two 12½ × 120-inch border strips
- 140 B pieces
- 140 F pieces

From the remaining muslin (including fabric leftover from cutting the 88-inch border strips), cut:
- 140 E pieces
- 140 E reverse pieces

From the green print fabric, cut:
- 35 A pieces
- 140 C pieces
- 24 G border swags
- 4 H corner border swags

From the pink print fabric, cut:
- 168 D pieces

Piecing the Blocks

When pinning curved pieces together before stitching, begin by pin-matching corners; then pin at the register marks. Add more pins as needed along the sewing line to distribute fullness evenly. Sew directly on the sewing line, removing pins as you go. When hand piecing, finger press seams as you construct the block. Press the completed block with an iron.

1. Referring to the **Bleeding Heart Block Diagram** on page 16, lay out the following pieces for one block: one A piece, four B pieces, four C pieces, four D pieces, four E and four E reverse pieces, and four F pieces.

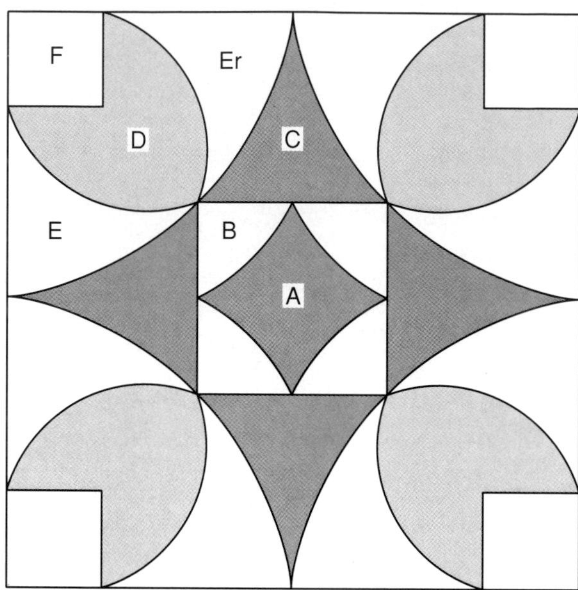

Bleeding Heart Block Diagram

2. To piece one block, begin by sewing the four B pieces to the center A piece.

3. Add a C piece to each of the four sides of the center unit.

4. Make the DEF units. First, add one E and one E reverse piece to opposite sides of a D piece. Then set in the F corner square by pinning one side of the square to one side of the opening in the D piece, pin-matching at an outside corner. Sew into the inner corner, and backstitch to secure the corner. Reposition the fabric pieces so that you can align the adjacent seam, and pin-match. Sew to the outside corner. Make four of these DEF units.

5. Add DEF units to two opposite sides of the center unit. Then add the remaining DEF units to the remaining sides to complete the block.

6. Piece a total of 35 blocks. Press the blocks, pressing the seams toward the darker fabrics when possible or away from planned quilting lines.

Assembling the Quilt Top

1. Lay out the blocks in seven horizontal rows with five blocks in each row, as shown in the **Quilt Diagram.**

2. Sew the blocks together in rows; press the seams in alternate directions from row to row.

3. Join the rows.

Adding the Borders

1. Measure the length and width of the inner quilt top, measuring through the center (approximately 60½ × 84½ inches). Measure and mark the four border strips for mitered corner seams. See page 160 for instructions on marking and adding mitered borders. Sew the borders to the quilt, mitering the corner seams.

2. Prepare 28 pink D pieces, the G border swags, and the H border corner swags for appliqué. Refer to the instructions on page 156 for tips on hand appliqué.

3. Referring to the **Quilt Diagram,** position the flowers and swags on the borders. Place the tips of the flowers approximately 2 inches away from the border seam, with the "V" of the flower shapes opposite the seams that join the blocks. Position the swags between the flowers. Appliqué the flowers and swags in place.

Quilting and Finishing

1. Mark quilting designs. The design for the flower shape is printed on the D pattern piece on page 18.

2. Divide the backing fabric into three equal 94½-inch-long pieces. Trim the selvages and sew the three pieces together. Press the seams away from the center panel. The seams will run parallel to the top and bottom of the quilt.

3. Layer the quilt back, batting, and quilt top; baste. Trim the quilt back and batting so that they are approximately 3 inches larger than the quilt top on all sides.

4. Quilt all marked designs, and add additional quilting as desired. On the quilt shown, the blocks are quilted ¼ inch away from the seams, and the corner squares are also crosshatched. The appliquéd border pieces are quilted in the ditch around the outside edges as well as ¼ inch

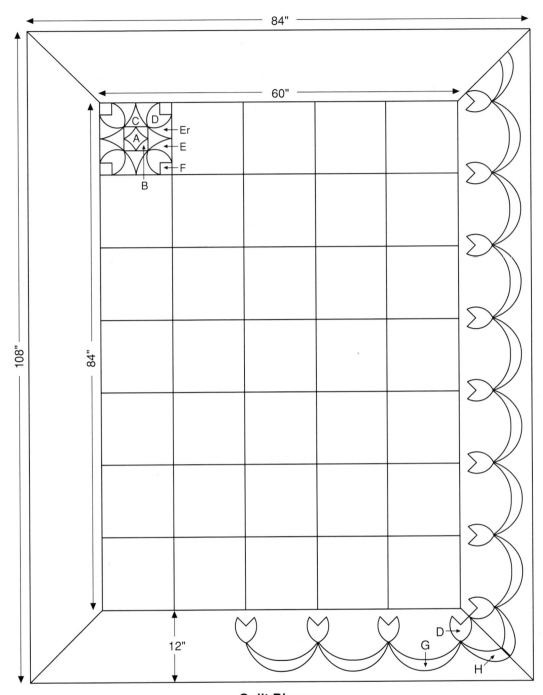

Quilt Diagram

to the inside. The borders have background quilting of straight lines spaced 1 inch apart alternating with two lines spaced ½ inch apart.

5. From the binding fabric, make approximately 400 inches of French-fold binding. See page 164 for suggested binding widths and instructions on making and attaching binding.

6. Sew the binding to the quilt top. Trim the excess batting and backing and hand finish the binding on the back side of the quilt.

A

B

C

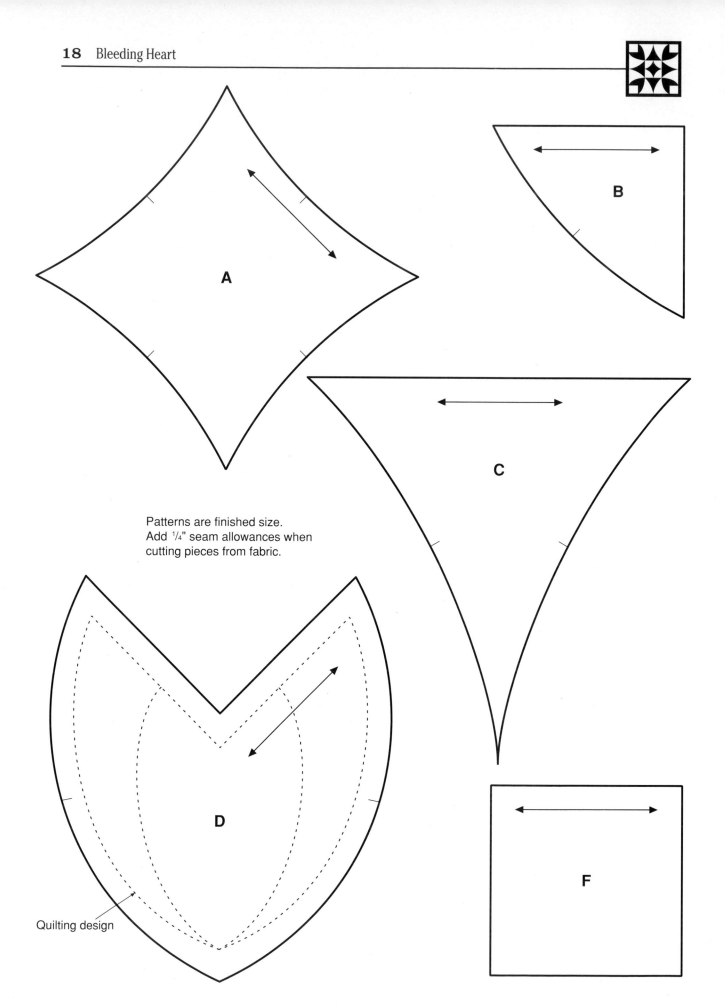

Patterns are finished size.
Add ¼" seam allowances when
cutting pieces from fabric.

D

Quilting design

F

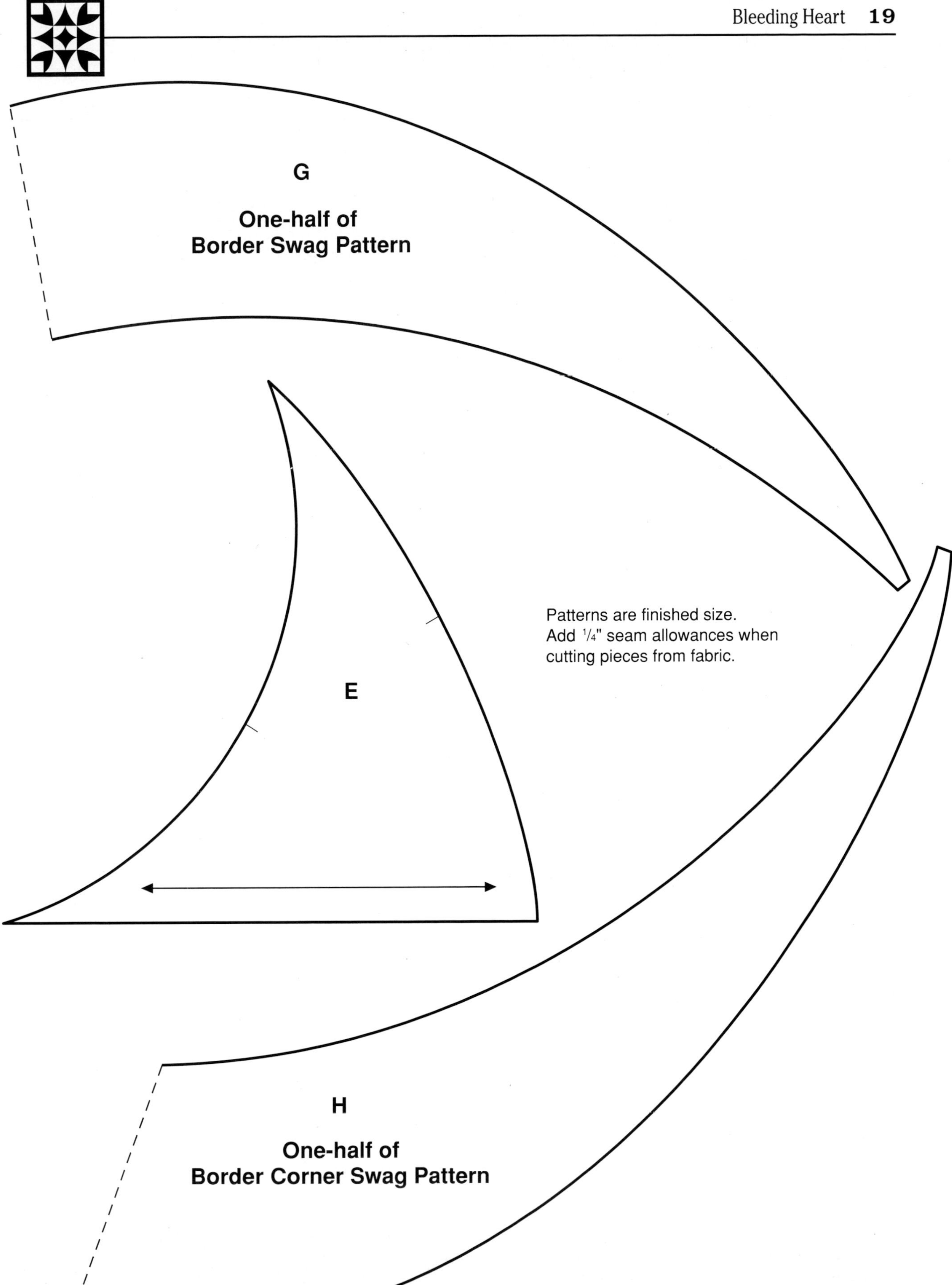
G
One-half of
Border Swag Pattern
E
Patterns are finished size.
Add 1/4" seam allowances when
cutting pieces from fabric.
H
One-half of
Border Corner Swag Pattern

Generations

Quiltmaker: Kathleen Etherington-Schiano

Eight years ago, when Kathleen thought she would only make one quilt in her life, she combined two block patterns to create this colorful design. The Roman Stripe pattern at the bottom of the quilt becomes a basket block variation at the top edge. Clear colors against a black background add to this hand-quilted beauty. Kathleen was so pleased with the way the quilt turned out, she's been quilting ever since.

Skill Level: Intermediate

Size: Finished quilt is 79½ × 92¼ inches
Finished block is 9 inches square

Fabrics and Supplies

- 8 yards of black solid fabric for blocks, setting triangles, borders, and binding
- ½ yard of blue-gray solid fabric for narrow borders
- ½ yard of light gray solid fabric for blocks
- ⅓ yard of dark blue solid fabric for narrow borders
- ¼ yard of dark purple solid fabric for narrow borders
- ¼ yard *each* of the following solid-color fabrics for the Roman Stripe patchwork: green, blue, purple, red, orange, and yellow (6 fabrics total)
- ¼ yard *each* of 3 additional fabrics in *each* of the following colors (prints or solids) for the tops of the basket blocks: green, blue, purple, red, orange, and yellow (18 fabrics total)
- 6 yards of fabric for quilt back
- Queen-size quilt batting (90 × 108 inches)
- Rotary cutter, ruler, and mat
- Template plastic

Cutting

All measurements include ¼-inch seam allowances. Measurements for the borders are longer than needed; trim them to the exact length when they are added to the quilt top. After cutting border strips and setting triangles, label them and set them aside.

Make templates for A, B, C, D, E, F, G, and H using the patterns on pages 26–27. Use a sewing machine needle to make holes in the templates at the corner dots as indicated on the patterns; these marks will help when setting-in pieces. Mark around the templates on the wrong side of the fabric. Mark dots on the fabric pieces through the corner holes. Also make special template I, which is a right-angle triangle with 9⅞-inch legs. Tips for making and using templates are on page 153.

The A diamonds for the basket tops are used in sets of four and sets of eight matching diamonds. The number of matching sets needed in each color is listed below. The basket tops within each color can either be identical or varied. Plan your cutting accordingly.

Before You Begin

Prepare the black fabric by cutting off one 104-inch-long piece and one 84-inch-long piece.

From the 104-inch piece of black fabric, cut:

- Two 11½ × 104-inch outer border strips
- 14 side setting triangles
  Cut four 14-inch squares. Cut each square in half diagonally in both directions to make four triangles. You will have two extra triangles.
- 4 corner setting triangles
  Cut two 7¼-inch squares. Cut each square in half diagonally to make two triangles.
- 7 I triangles
  Use Template I
  OR
  Cut four 9⅞-inch squares. Cut each square in half diagonally to make two triangles. You will have one extra triangle.

From the 84-inch-long piece, cut:

- Two 11½ × 84-inch outer border strips
- Two 1½ × 84-inch inner border strips
- One 2½ × 84-inch border strip

From the remaining black fabric, cut:

- 50 B triangles
- 25 C squares
- 36 D rectangles
- 7 F triangles
- 3 G pieces and 3 G reverse pieces
- 4 H pieces and 4 H reverse pieces
- Three 1½ × 8½-inch strips
- Four 2½ × 8½-inch strips
- Reserve the remaining fabric for binding

From the blue-gray fabric, cut:

- Eight 1¾ × 44-inch border strips

From the light gray fabric, cut:

- 39 E pieces

From the dark blue fabric, cut:

- Eight 1¼ × 44-inch border strips

From the dark purple fabric, cut:

- Eight ¾ × 44-inch border strips

From the solid-color fabrics for the Roman Stripe patchwork, cut:

- Seven 1½ × 15-inch green pieces
- Eleven 1½ × 12½-inch blue pieces
- Fourteen 1½ × 10½-inch purple pieces
- Eighteen 1½ × 8½-inch red pieces
- Twenty-one 1½ × 6½-inch orange pieces
- Twenty-five 2 × 4½-inch yellow pieces

From the solid or print fabrics for the basket tops, cut:

- 128 green A diamonds (8 sets of 8 and 16 sets of 4)
- 48 blue A diamonds (3 sets of 8 and 6 sets of 4)
- 64 purple A diamonds (4 sets of 8 and 8 sets of 4)
- 48 red A diamonds (3 sets of 8 and 6 sets of 4)
- 64 orange A diamonds (4 sets of 8 and 8 sets of 4)
- 48 yellow A diamonds (3 sets of 8 and 6 sets of 4)

Piecing the Blocks

The blocks in the quilt vary from row to row. The rows are labeled in the **Quilt Diagram.** All of the blocks in Rows 1 and 2 are Roman Stripe blocks. All of the blocks in Rows 8 and 9 are basket blocks. In Rows 3 to 7, the blocks gradually transform from Roman Stripe blocks into basket blocks through variations in the lower portion of the blocks. Refer to the **Fabric Key** for correct color placement when making the blocks.

Fabric Key

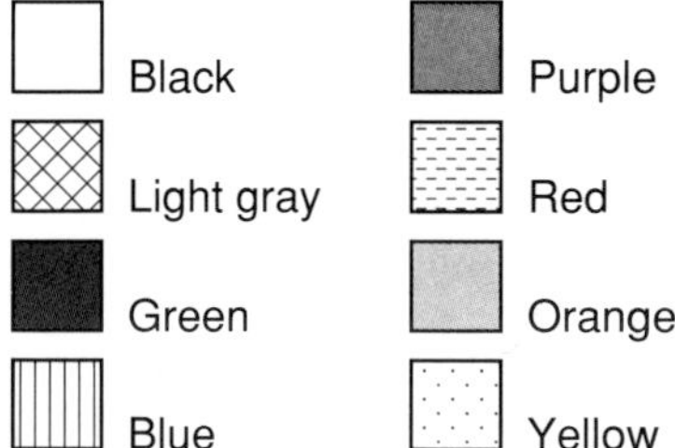

Making the Roman Stripe Blocks for Rows 1 and 2

1. To make one block, begin by centering and sewing together green, blue, purple, red, orange, and yellow strips to form the strip section shown in **Diagram 1.** Press seams toward the yellow strip.

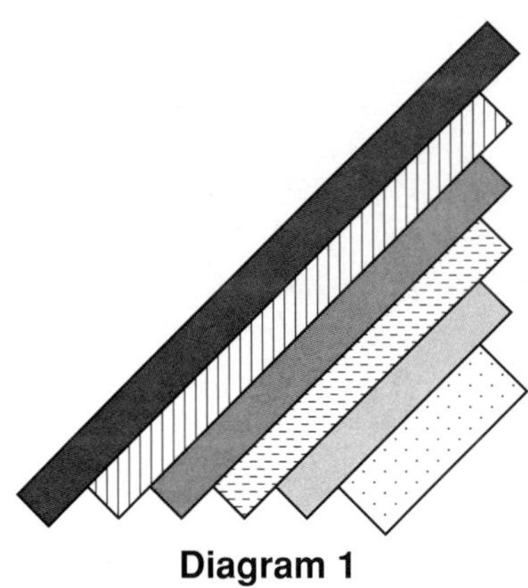

Diagram 1

2. Lay out the strip section, wrong side up, and align the long side of the I triangle template with the long raw edge of the green strip. Mark along the remaining two sides of the template and cut out the triangle.

3. To complete a block, stitch a striped I triangle to a black I triangle along the long sides to make a square. Press the seams toward the black triangle.

4. Repeat to make a total of seven Roman Stripe blocks.

Piecing the Basket Tops

Piece the 25 basket tops for Rows 3 to 9. You will need eight green, three blue, four purple, three red, four orange, and three yellow basket tops. The basket tops of each color will be identical or varied, depending on how you have cut the A diamonds.

1. To make one basket top, you will need two sets of four matching A diamonds and one set of eight matching A diamonds. The two sets of four can be the same fabric or two different fabrics, as long as all the diamonds in each set are the same. Lay out the diamonds, as shown in **Diagram 2.**

Diagram 2

2¼" wide total (3 strips)

C A B D E E F

Row 9

Row 8

Row 7

F

Row 6

Row 5

G G

Row 4

1" black

H H

Row 3

Row 2

Row 1

2" wide black

2¼" wide total (3 strips)

Note: The wide black outer borders are not shown

Quilt Diagram

2. Combine groups of four A diamonds into four larger pieced diamonds, as shown in **Diagram 3.** To make one pieced diamond, begin by joining pairs of diamonds, as shown in **Diagram 4** on page 24; press seams in opposite directions from pair to pair. Join pairs to form pieced diamonds.

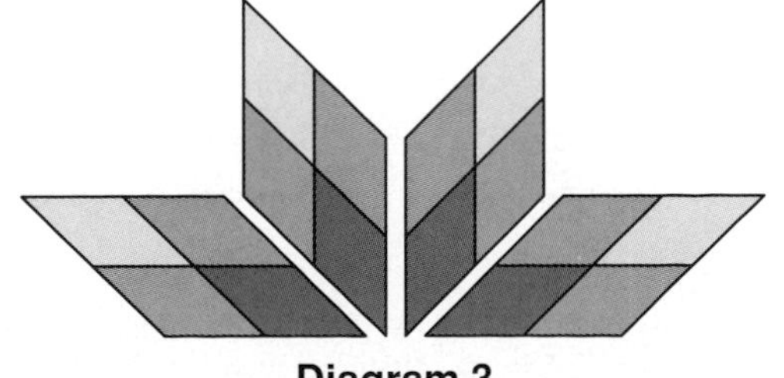

Diagram 3

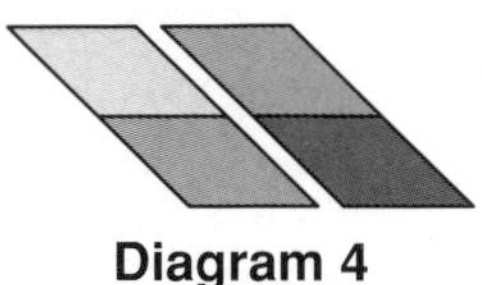

Diagram 4

3. Join four large pieced diamonds to make a half star. Stitch from dot to dot, and backstitch to secure the beginning and end of each seam. Do not sew into the seam allowances at the ends of the seams. Press the seams to one side.

4. Set in two black B triangles and one black C square, as shown in **Diagram 5.** Press seams away from the diamonds.

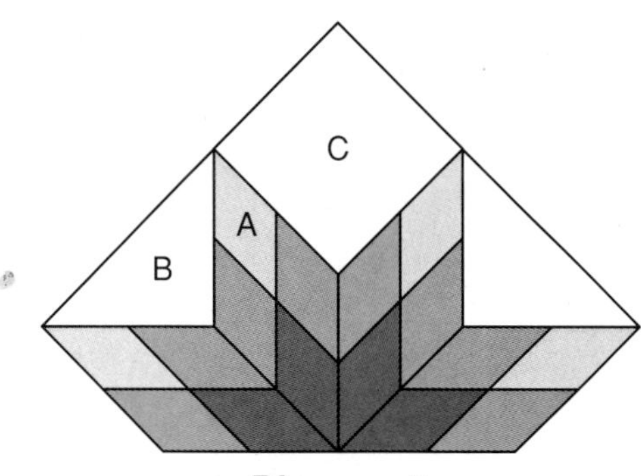

Diagram 5

Making the Blocks for Row 3

1. To make one block, begin by sewing a black H piece to one side of a green basket top and an H reverse piece to the other side, as shown in **Diagram 6.** Press the seams away from the diamonds.

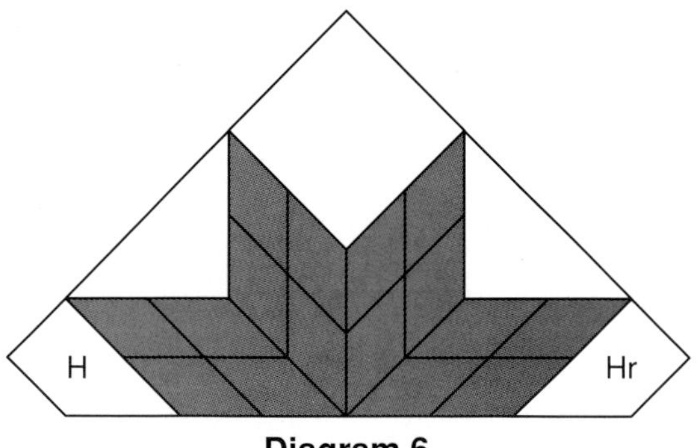

Diagram 6

2. Make a strip section by centering and sewing together a blue, purple, red, orange, and yellow strip as you did for the Roman Stripe blocks.

3. Adjust the I triangle template by trimming a 1-inch-wide section off the long side, as shown in **Diagram 7.** Use the adjusted template to mark and cut a striped triangle from the strip section, aligning the long side of the I triangle with the raw edge of the blue strip.

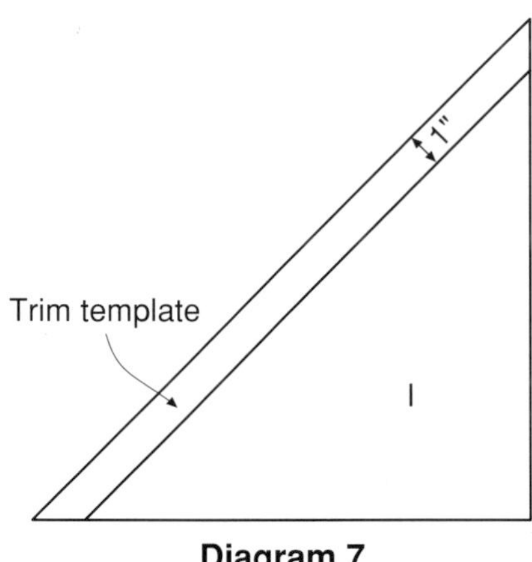

Diagram 7

4. Join the striped triangle to the green basket top to complete the block. Press the seam toward the pieced triangle.

5. Repeat to make a total of four blocks, each with a green basket top.

Making the Blocks for Row 4

1. To make one block, begin by sewing a light gray E piece to the lower edge of a blue basket top, as shown in **Diagram 8.** Press the seam toward the E piece.

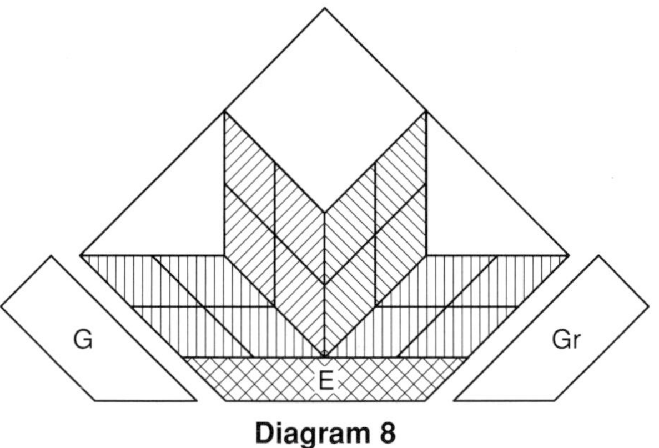

Diagram 8

2. Sew a black G piece to one side of the basket top and a G reverse piece to the other side, as shown in the diagram. Press the seams away from the diamonds.

3. Make a strip section by centering and sewing together a purple, red, orange, and yellow strip as you did for the Roman Stripe blocks.

4. Adjust the I triangle template by trimming

another 1-inch-wide section off the long side. Use the adjusted template to mark and cut a striped triangle from the strip section.

5. Join the striped triangle to the blue basket top to complete the block. Press the seam toward the pieced triangle.

6. Repeat to make a total of three blocks, each with a blue basket top.

Making the Blocks for Row 5

1. To make one block, begin by joining two light gray E pieces along the shorter of the two long edges. Stitch only from dot to dot and not into the seam allowances at the ends of the seam.

2. Sew the pair of E pieces to the lower edge of a purple basket top, as shown in **Diagram 9.** Press the seam away from the basket top.

3. Set in a black D rectangle on each side of the basket top, as shown in the diagram.

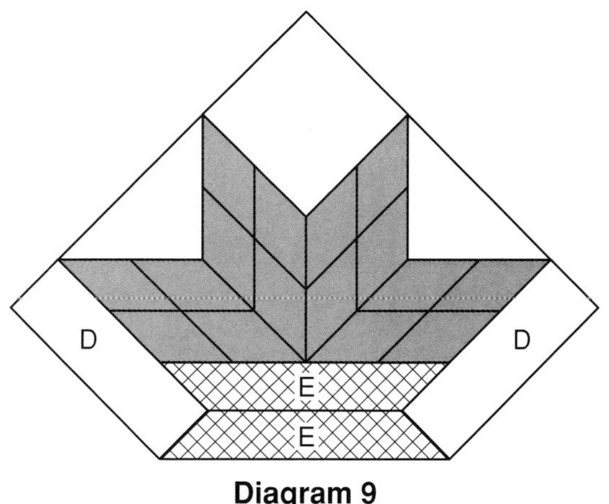

Diagram 9

4. Make a strip section by centering and sewing together a red, orange, and yellow strip as you did for the Roman Stripe blocks.

5. Use triangle template F to mark and cut a triangle from the strip section.

6. Join the striped triangle to the purple basket top to complete the block. Press the seam toward the pieced triangle.

7. Repeat to make a total of four blocks, each with a purple basket top.

Making the Blocks for Row 6

1. To make one block, follow Steps 1, 2, and 3 under "Making the Blocks for Row 5," but use a red basket top.

2. Make a strip section by centering and sewing together a $1\frac{1}{2} \times 8\frac{1}{2}$-inch black strip, an orange strip, and a yellow strip.

3. Use triangle template F to mark and cut a triangle from the strip section.

4. Join the striped triangle to the red basket top to complete a block. Press the seam toward the pieced triangle.

5. Repeat to make a total of three blocks, each with a red basket top.

Making the Blocks for Row 7

1. To make one block, follow Steps 1, 2, and 3 under "Making the Blocks for Row 5," but use an orange basket top.

2. Make a strip section by centering and sewing together a $2\frac{1}{2} \times 8\frac{1}{2}$-inch black strip and a yellow strip.

3. Use triangle template F to mark and cut a triangle from the strip section.

4. Join the striped triangle to the orange basket top to complete the block. Press the seam toward the pieced triangle.

5. Repeat to make a total of four blocks, each with an orange basket top.

Making the Blocks for Rows 8 and 9

For Row 8, make three blocks with yellow basket tops. For Row 9, make four blocks with green basket tops.

1. To make each of the blocks, follow Steps 1, 2, and 3 under "Making the Blocks for Row 5," using either a yellow or green basket top.

2. To complete each block, sew a black F triangle to the lower edge of the basket section. Press the seam toward the black triangle.

Assembling the Quilt Top

1. Lay out the completed blocks in rows, as shown in the **Quilt Diagram** on page 23. Fill in the sides with the black side setting triangles and the corners with the black corner setting triangles.

2. Sew the blocks and setting pieces together in diagonal rows, pressing the seams in opposite directions from row to row. Join the rows.

3. Measure the length of the completed inner quilt top (approximately 64¼ inches including seam allowances), measuring through the center of the quilt. Trim the two 1½ × 84-inch black border strips to this measurement. Sew the strips to the two sides of the inner quilt top.

4. Measure the width of the quilt top (approximately 53½ inches including seam allowances). Trim the 2½ × 84-inch black border to this measurement. Sew the strip to the bottom of the quilt top.

5. Sew two 1¾ × 44-inch blue-gray border strips end to end to make one long strip. Make four of these long strips. In the same manner, make four long border strips from the 1¼ × 44-inch dark blue strips and four from the ¾ × 44-inch dark purple strips.

6. Center and sew sets of border strips together to make multiple-fabric borders. First, sew a dark blue strip to a blue-gray strip. Then add a purple strip to the dark blue strip. Finally, center and sew an 11½-inch-wide black border to the purple strip. Repeat to make four borders.

7. Using the methods described on page 160 for adding mitered borders, measure, mark, and add the multiple borders to the four sides of the quilt top. Make sure the blue-gray strip is against the edge of the inner quilt and the black strip is on the outside edge.

Quilting and Finishing

1. Mark quilting designs.

2. Divide the backing fabric into two equal 108-inch-long pieces. Trim the selvages and cut one of the pieces in half lengthwise. Sew a half to each side of the full-width panel. Press the seams away from the center panel.

3. Layer the quilt back, batting, and quilt top; baste. Trim the quilt back so it is approximately 3 inches larger than the quilt top on all sides.

4. Quilt all marked designs, and add additional quilting as desired. The quilt shown has in-the-ditch quilting next to patchwork seams.

5. From the binding fabric, make approximately 360 inches of French-fold binding. See page 164 for suggested binding widths and instructions on making and attaching binding.

6. Sew the binding to the quilt top. Trim the excess batting and backing, and hand finish the binding on the back side of the quilt.

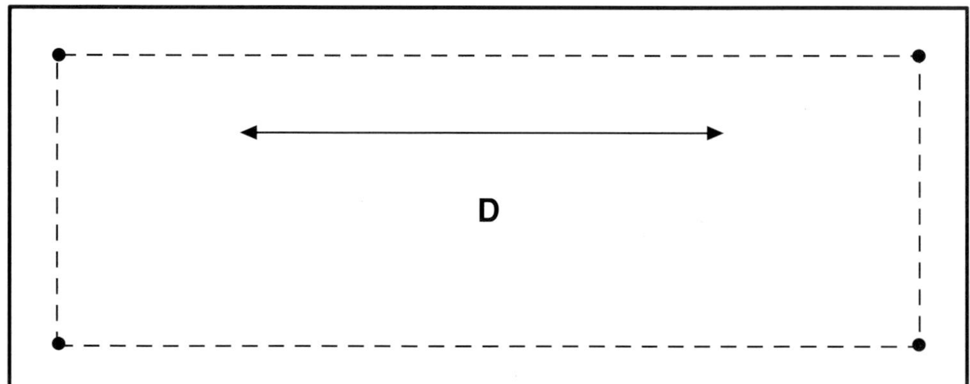

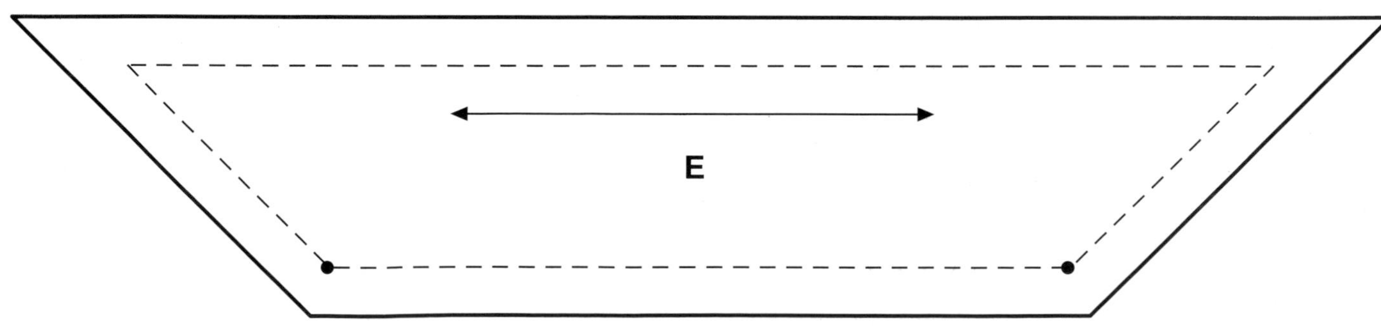

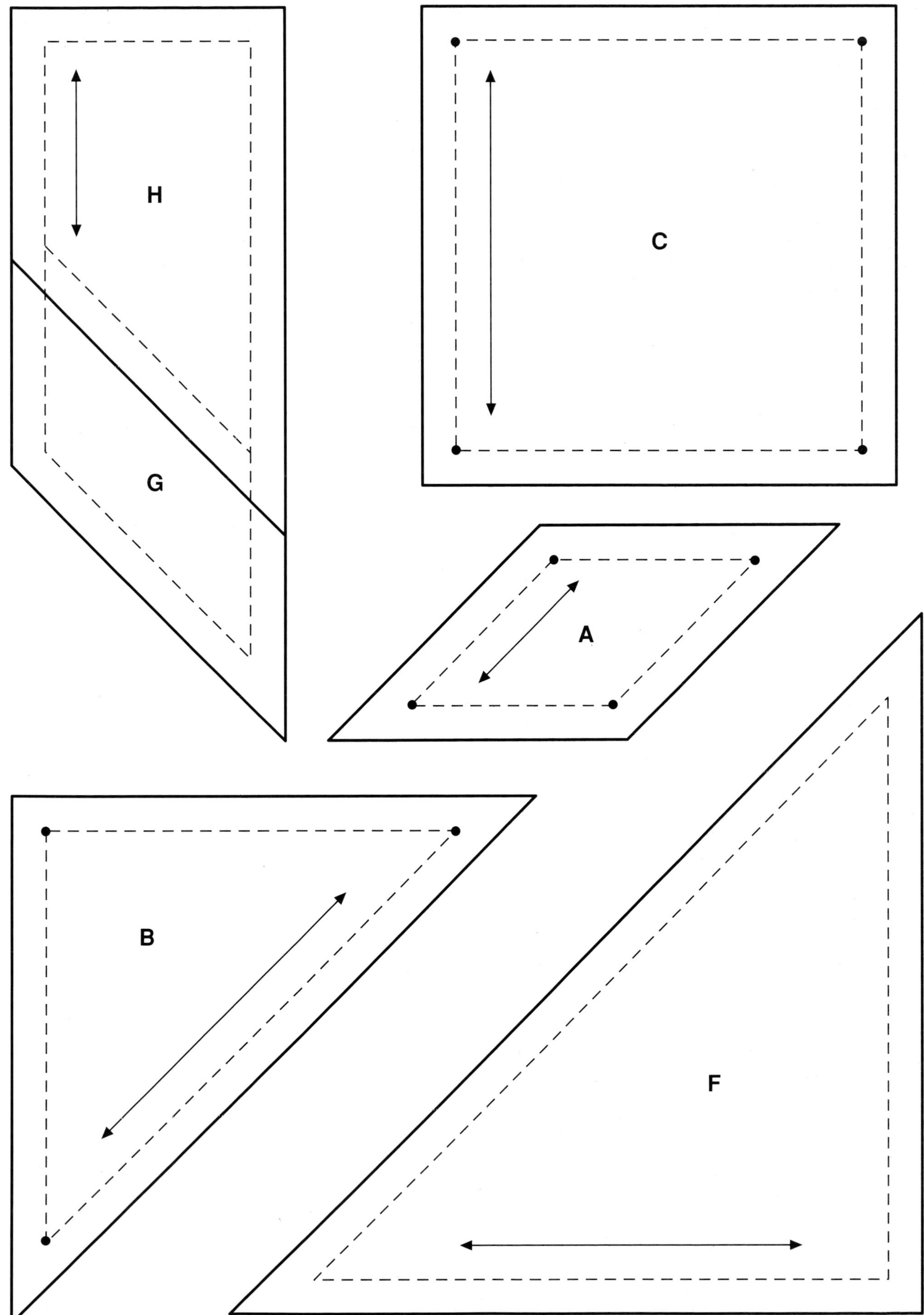

H
C
G
A
B
F

Burgoyne Surrounded

Quiltmaker: Sharlotte Johnston

The Persian Gulf War was in the news while Sharlotte was quilting this patriotic-looking quilt. The 12 patchwork blocks are separated with sashing strips and Nine-Patch sashing squares in a classic setting for Burgoyne Surrounded blocks. The pieced sashing squares merge with the pieced blocks to create an overall design reminiscent of an antique woven coverlet.

Skill Level: Easy

Size: Finished quilt is 79 × 96 inches
Finished block is 15 inches square

Fabrics and Supplies

- 7 yards of white fabric for blocks, borders, and sashing strips
- 2 yards of navy print fabric for blocks and borders
- 1¾ yards of red print fabric for blocks, sashing squares, and border
- 1 yard of fabric for binding
- 7⅛ yards of fabric for quilt back
- King-size quilt batting (120 inches square)
- Rotary cutter, ruler, and mat

Cutting

All measurements include ¼-inch seam allowances. Measurements for the borders are longer than needed; trim them to the exact length when they are added to the quilt top. Instructions given are for quick-cutting the pieces with a rotary cutter and ruler.

Before You Begin

To prepare the white fabric, first cut off one 100-inch-long piece.

From the 100-inch-long piece of white fabric, cut:

- Two 4 × 100-inch strips for the inner top and bottom borders
- Two 4½ × 100-inch strips for the inner side borders
- Four 2¼ × 100-inch strips for the outer borders
- Twenty-four 3½ × 15½-inch sashing strips
  Cut four 3½ × 100-inch strips. From the strips, cut 15½-inch-long sashing strips.

From the remaining white fabric, cut:

- Seven 3½ × 15½-inch sashing strips
  Cut four 3½ × 44-inch strips. From these strips, cut seven 3½ × 15½-inch sashing strips. (You will have a total of 31 sashing strips.)
- Twenty 1½ × 44-inch strips for strip sets
- Six 2½ × 44-inch strips for strip sets
- 96 A rectangles
  Cut eight 2½ × 44-inch strips. Cut the strips into 2½ × 3½-inch rectangles.
- 48 B rectangles
  Cut seven 3½-inch-wide strips. Cut the strips into 3½ × 5½-inch rectangles.
- 224 border triangles
  Cut six 4⅛ × 44-inch strips. Cut the strips into 4⅛-inch squares. You will need 56 squares. Cut each square in half diagonally both ways to make four triangles.

From the navy print fabric, cut:

- Ten 3 × 44-inch strips for middle borders
- 16 border squares
  Cut one 2½ × 44-inch strip. Cut the strip into 2½-inch squares.
- Eight 1½ × 44-inch strips for strip sets
- Four 2½ × 44-inch strips for strip sets

From the red print fabric, cut:

- 92 border squares
  Cut six 2½ × 44-inch strips. Cut the strips into 2½-inch squares.
- Fourteen 1½ × 44-inch strips for strip sets
- Four 2½ × 44-inch strips for strip sets

Piecing the Blocks

The Burgoyne Surrounded block is made by cutting apart strip sets and sewing them together in sections. Refer to the **Fabric Key** and **Block Diagram** on page 30 to piece the blocks.

Fabric Key

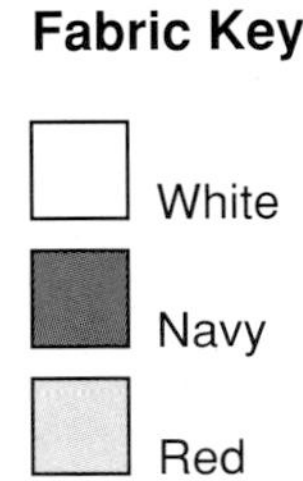

1. Sew a 1½ × 44-inch red print strip to a 1½ × 44-inch white strip, as shown in **Diagram 1.** Press the seam toward the red strip. Repeat to make a total of four strip sets.

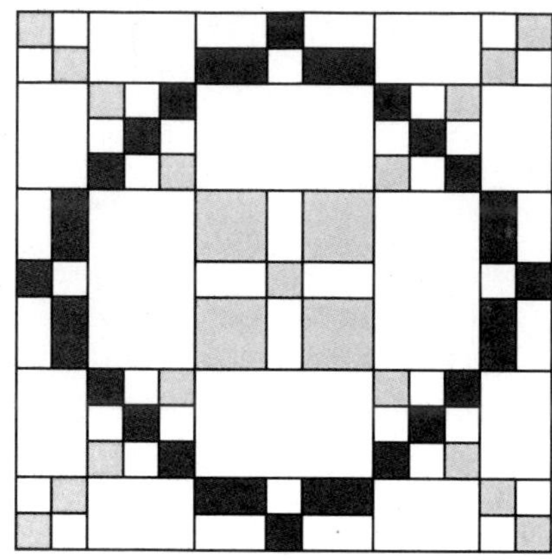

Block Diagram

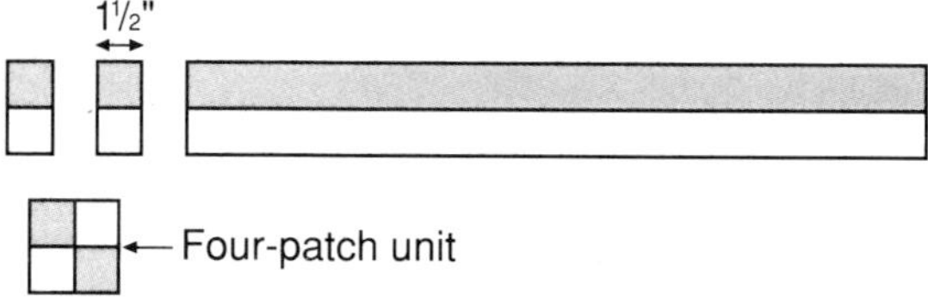

Diagram 1

2. Cut 1½-inch-wide segments from the strip sets. You will need a total of 96 segments. Referring to the diagram, assemble the segments into 48 four-patch units.

3. Make a strip set using 1½ × 44-inch navy print, white, and red print strips, as shown in **Diagram 2.** Press the seams away from the white strip. Make a total of four of these strip sets.

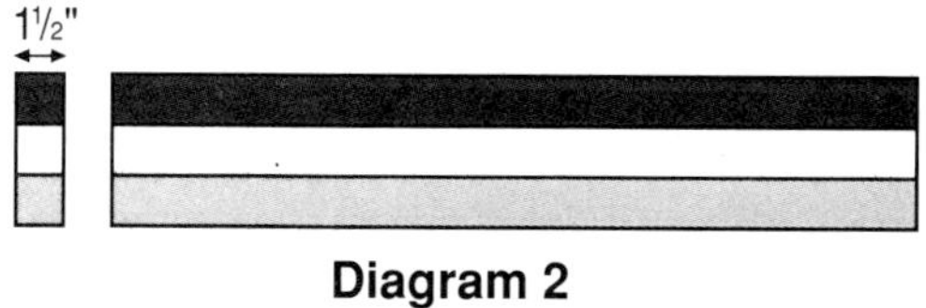

Diagram 2

4. Cut the strip sets into 1½-inch-wide segments. You will need a total of 96 segments.

5. Referring to **Diagram 3,** stitch together a set of two white and one navy print 1½ × 44-inch strips. Press the seams toward the navy strip. Make two of these strip sets. Cut the strip sets into forty-eight 1½-inch-wide segments.

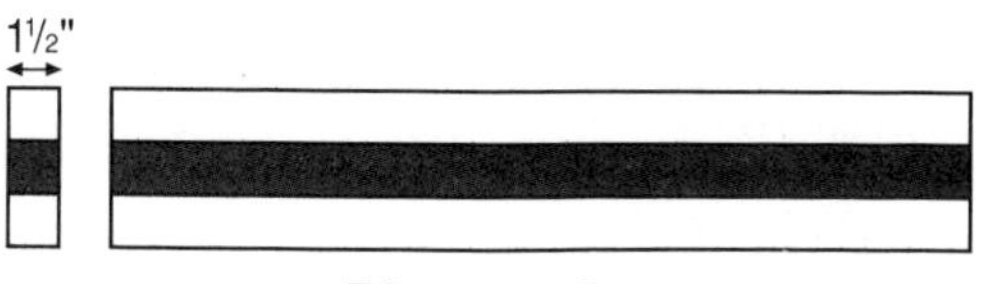

Diagram 3

6. Make 48 Nine-Patch units by joining two Step 4 segments and one Step 5 segment, as shown in **Diagram 4.** Press the seams away from the center segment.

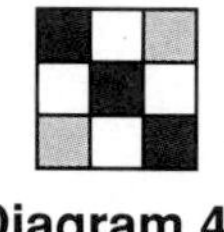

Diagram 4

7. Referring to **Diagram 5,** stitch together two 2½ × 44-inch navy print strips and one 1½ × 44-inch white strip. Press the seams away from the white strip. Make two of these strip sets.

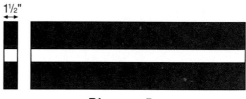

Diagram 5

8. Cut the strip sets into 1½-inch-wide segments. You will need a total of 48 segments.

9. Referring to **Diagram 6,** stitch together two 2½ × 44-inch white strips and one 1½ × 44-inch navy print strip. Press the seams toward the navy strip. Make two of these strip sets. Cut the strips into forty-eight 1½-inch-wide segments.

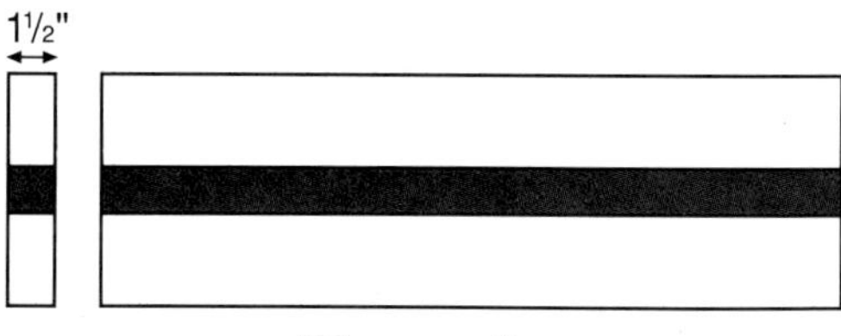

Diagram 6

10. Sew a Step 8 segment to a Step 9 segment, as shown in **Diagram 7.** Press the seams toward the Step 8 segment. Make a total of 48 of these units.

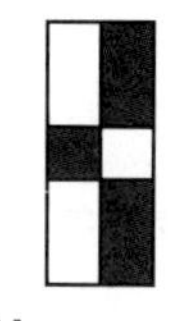

Diagram 7

11. Stitch together two 2½ × 44-inch red print strips and one 1½ × 44-inch white strip, as shown in **Diagram 8.** Press the seams away from the white strip. Make two of these strip sets. Cut the strip sets into 2½-inch-wide segments. You will need a total of 24 segments.

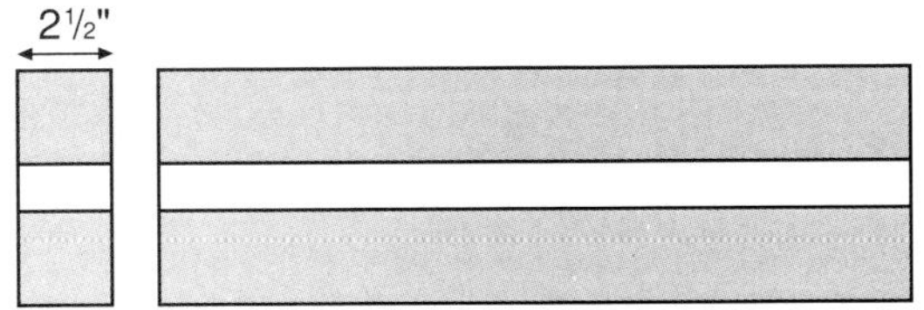

Diagram 8

12. Referring to **Diagram 9,** join two 2½ × 44-inch white strips and one 1½ × 44-inch red print strip. Press the seams toward the red strip. Cut twelve 1½-inch-wide segments from the strip set.

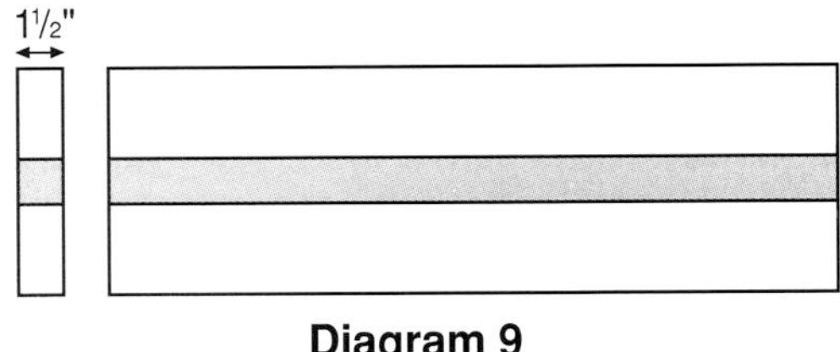

Diagram 9

13. Join two Step 11 segments and one Step 12 segment, as shown in **Diagram 10.** Press the seams toward the Step 12 segment. Make a total of 12 of these units.

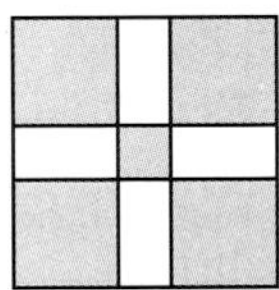

Diagram 10

14. Referring to **Diagram 11,** lay out the white A and B rectangles and the pieced units for one block. Pay attention to the placement of the red and blue in the Nine Patch units. Join the pieces in vertical rows. Press the seams toward the A and B rectangles. Join the rows to complete the block. Repeat to make a total of 12 blocks.

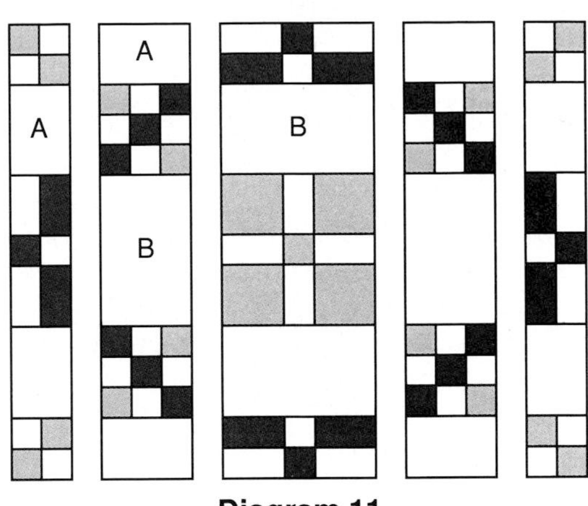

Diagram 11

Piecing the Nine-Patch Sashing Squares

1. Referring to **Diagram 12,** stitch together two 1½ × 44-inch red print strips and one 1½ × 44-inch white strip. Press the seams away from the white strip. Make two of these strip sets. Cut the strip sets into 1½-inch-wide segments. You will need a total of 40 segments.

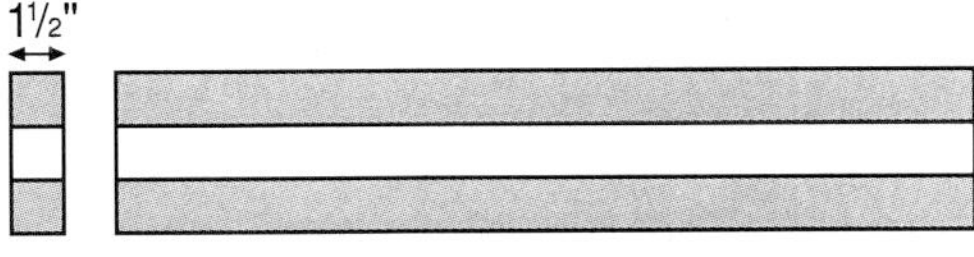

Diagram 12

2. Stitch together two 1½ × 44-inch white strips and one 1½ × 44-inch red strip, as shown in **Diagram 13.** Press the seams toward the red strip. Cut 1½-inch-wide segments from the strip set. You will need 20 segments.

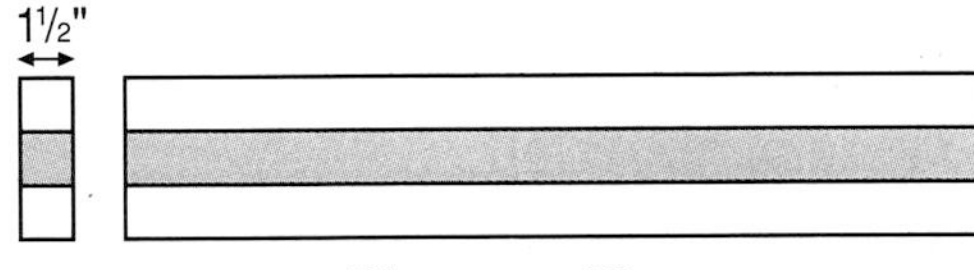

Diagram 13

3. Join two Step 1 segments and one Step 2 segment to make 20 Nine-Patch units, as shown in **Diagram 14.** Press the seams away from the center segment.

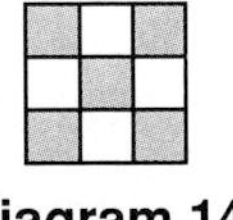

Diagram 14

Assembling the Quilt Top

1. The quilt top is composed of two types of rows. In the first type, pieced blocks alternate with 3½ × 15½-inch sashing strips. In the second type, Nine-Patch units alternate with 3½ × 15½-inch sashing strips. Referring to the photo on page 28, make four of the pieced block/sashing rows and five of the Nine Patch/sashing rows. Press all seams toward the sashing strips.

2. Join the rows, alternating block/sashing rows with Nine-Patch/sashing rows. Press the seams toward the Nine-Patch/sashing rows.

3. Measure the length of the inner quilt top. Trim the two 4½ × 100-inch border strips to this length (approximately 75½ inches). Sew the borders to the sides of the quilt top. Press the seams toward the borders.

4. Measure the width of the inner quilt top including the side borders. Trim the two 4 × 100-inch border strips to this length (approximately 65½ inches). Sew the borders to the top and bottom edges of the quilt top. Press the seams toward the borders.

5. To make the pieced borders, begin by sewing a white border triangle to two opposite sides of all the red and navy border squares, as shown in **Diagram 15.** Press the seams toward the triangles.

Diagram 15
Border Unit

6. Referring to the photograph on page 28, make one side border by joining 13 red border units, 3 navy border units, and 13 red border units. Add a white border triangle to each end of the border. Using a rotary cutter and ruler, trim off the white triangles at the ends of the borders, as shown in **Diagram 16,** leaving ¼ inch for seam allowance. Sew the border to the side of the quilt. Press the seam toward the white inner border. Repeat to make a border for the other side of the quilt.

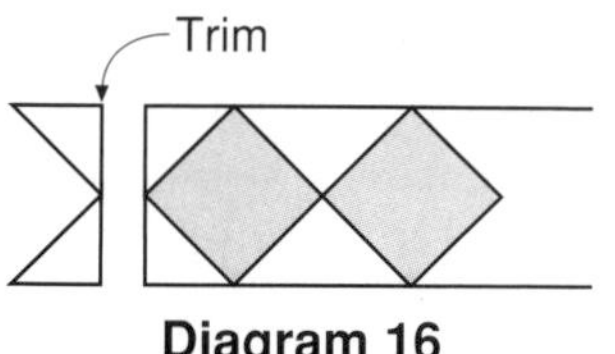

Diagram 16

7. In a similar manner, join ten red border units, five navy border units, and ten red border units for each top and bottom border. Add triangles to the ends of the borders; trim as directed in Step 6. Sew the borders to the top and bottom edges of the quilt top. Press the seams toward the white inner borders.

8. Cut two of the 3 × 44-inch navy print border strips in half crosswise. To make each side border, join two full-length navy strips and one half strip. Measure the length of the quilt top. Trim the borders to this length, and sew them to the sides of the quilt. Press the seams toward the navy borders.

9. Join two 3 × 44-inch navy print border strips to make each top and bottom border. Measure the width of the quilt top. Trim the borders to this length, and sew them to the top and bottom edges of the quilt top. Press the seams toward the navy borders.

10. Again measure the length of the quilt top and trim two 2¼-inch-wide white borders to this length. Sew the borders to the sides of the quilt top. Press the seams toward the navy borders. Measure the width of the quilt top, and trim two 2¼-inch-wide white borders to this length. Sew the borders to the top and bottom edges of the quilt top. Press the seams toward the navy borders.

Quilting and Finishing

1. Mark quilting designs as desired. Patterns for the feather quilting designs for the B rectangles, sashing strips, border corners, and inner white border are provided on pages 33–34.

2. Divide the backing fabric into three equal 85½-inch-long pieces. Trim the selvages and sew the pieces together. The seams will run parallel to the top and bottom of the quilt. Press the seams away from the center panel.

3. Layer the quilt back, batting, and quilt top; baste. Trim the quilt back so that it is approximately 3 inches larger than the quilt top on all sides.

4. Outline quilt in the ditch around all patchwork pieces. Quilt all marked designs, and add additional quilting as desired.

5. From the white binding fabric, make approximately 370 inches of French-fold binding. See page 164 for suggested binding widths and instructions on making and attaching binding.

6. Sew the binding to the quilt top. Trim the excess batting and backing, and hand finish the binding on the back side of the quilt.

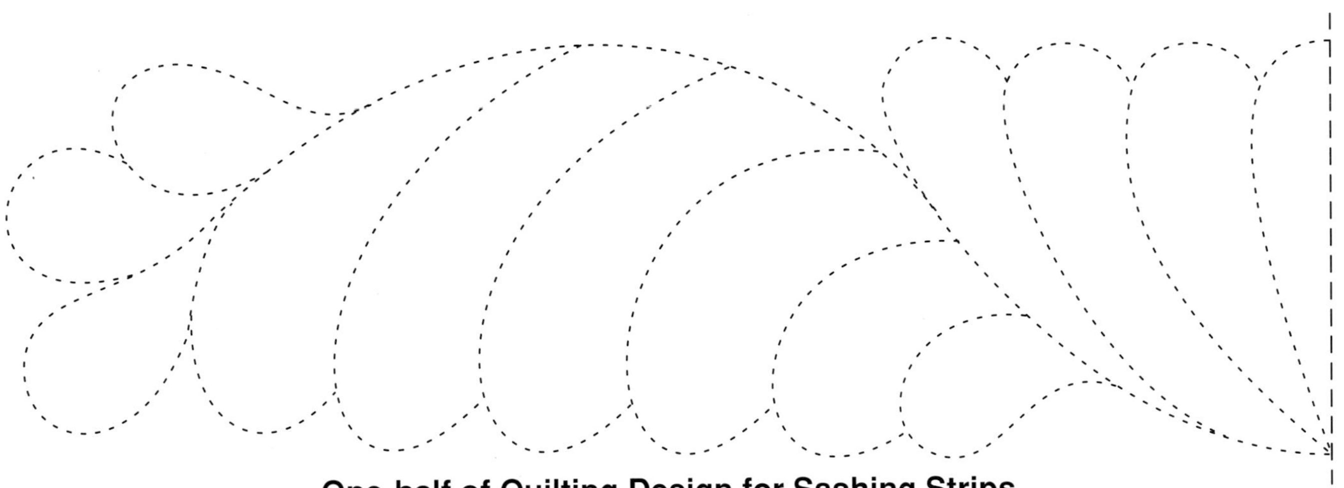

One-half of Quilting Design for Sashing Strips

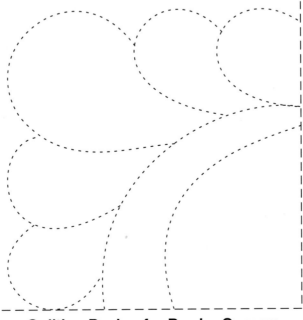

Quilting Design for Border Corners

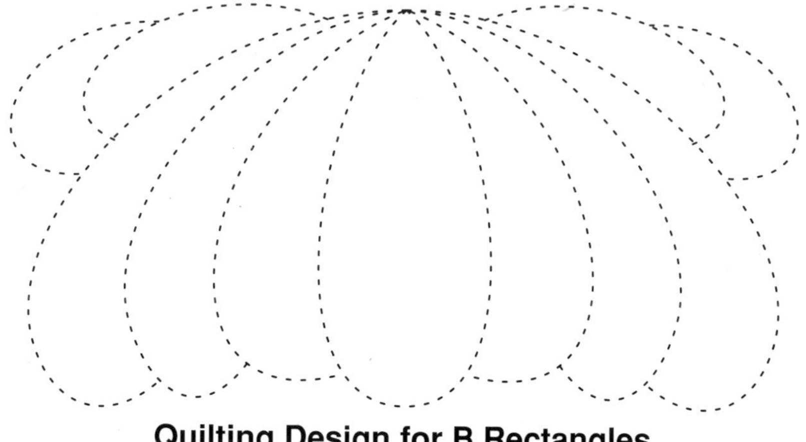

Quilting Design for B Rectangles

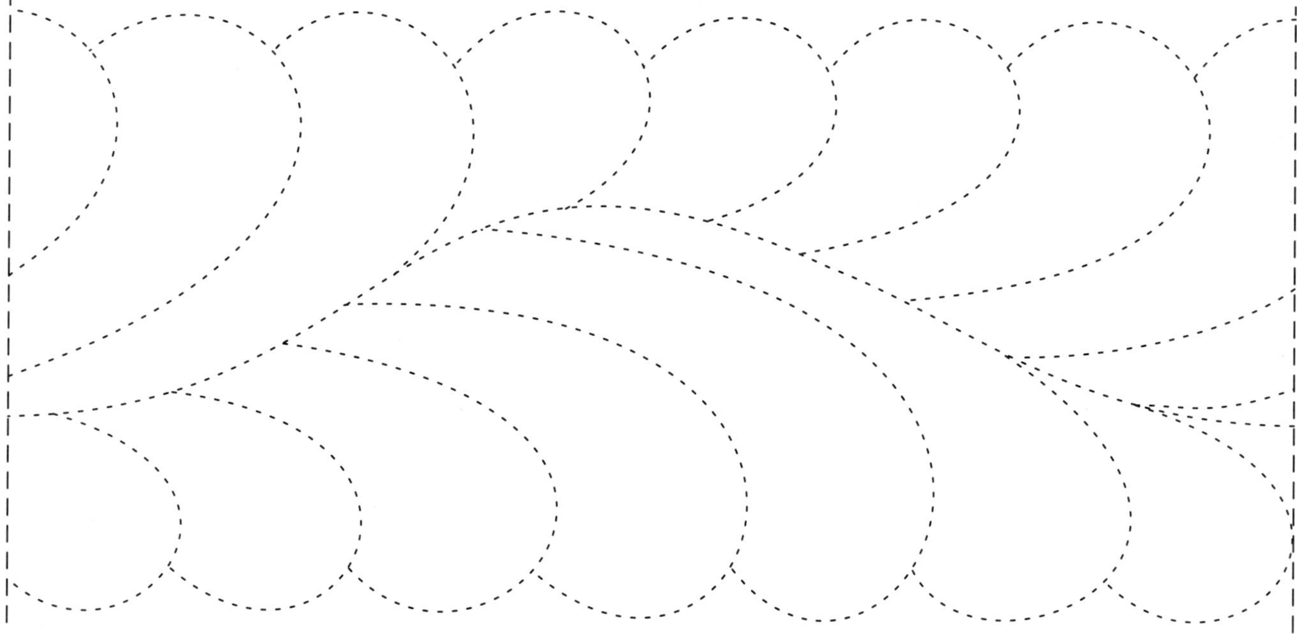

Quilting Design for Side Borders

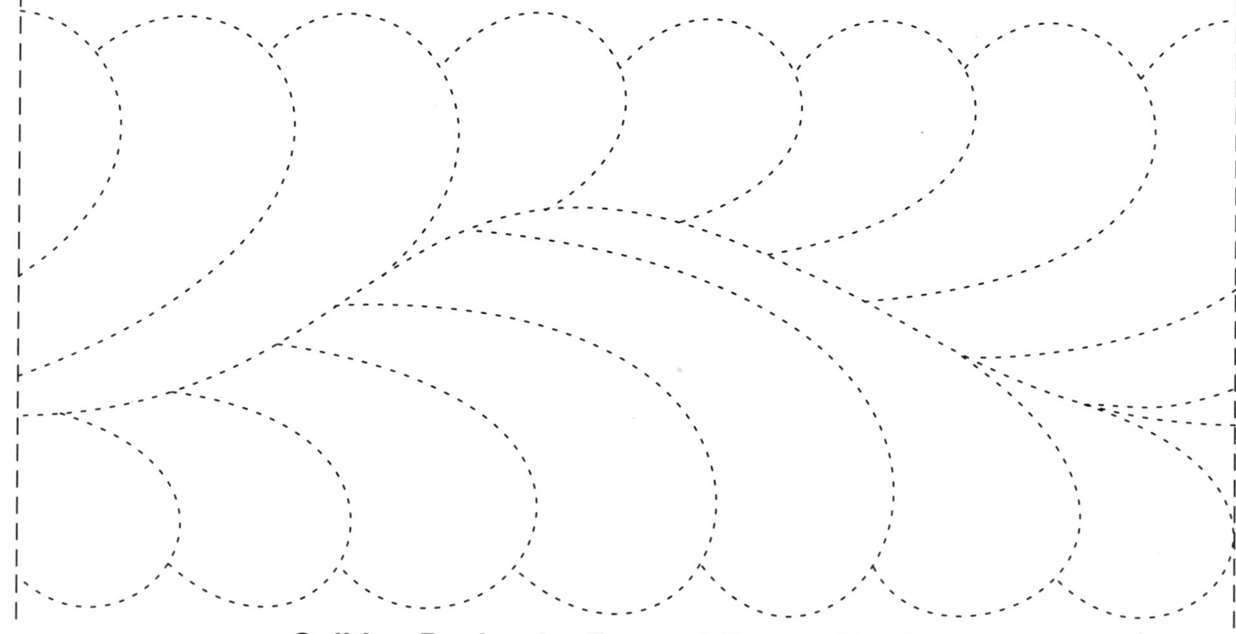

Quilting Design for Top and Bottom Borders

Blossoms and Buds

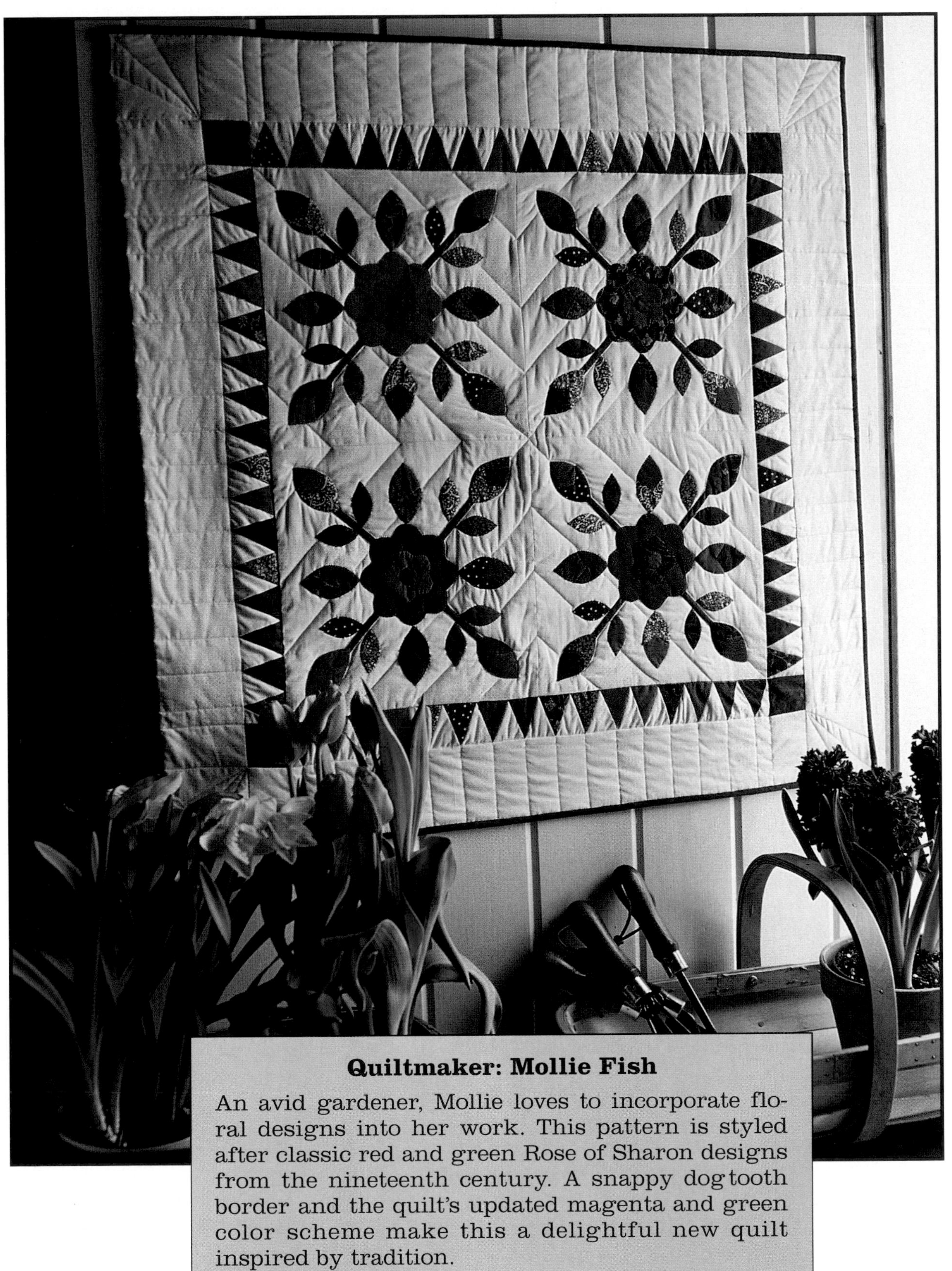

Quiltmaker: Mollie Fish

An avid gardener, Mollie loves to incorporate floral designs into her work. This pattern is styled after classic red and green Rose of Sharon designs from the nineteenth century. A snappy dogtooth border and the quilt's updated magenta and green color scheme make this a delightful new quilt inspired by tradition.

Skill Level: Easy

Size: Finished quilt is 35 inches square
Finished block is 12 inches square

Fabrics and Supplies

- 1¾ yards of printed muslin fabric for blocks and borders
- ½ yard of dark green fabric for appliqués and binding
- Scraps (9 × 22-inch "fat eighths") of approximately eight different magenta and purple print fabrics for appliqués and pieced border
- Scraps (9 × 22 inches) of approximately eight different dark green print fabrics for appliqués and pieced border
- 1⅛ yards of fabric for quilt back
- Crib-size quilt batting (45 × 60 inches)
- Rotary cutter, ruler, and mat
- Template plastic or freezer paper
- Tracing paper
- Black, fine-point, permanent marking pen
- Index or recipe card

Cutting

All measurements include ¼-inch seam allowances. Measurements for the borders are longer than needed; trim them to the exact length when they are added to the quilt top. Instructions given are for quick-cutting the border strips, background squares for blocks, stem strips, and border corner squares.

Make templates for the appliqués using the pattern pieces on page 39. Appliqué patterns are finished size; add seam allowances when you cut the pieces from fabric. Read through the tips in "Hand Appliqué," beginning on page 156, and choose an appliqué method. See "Making Crisp Appliqué Circles" on page 37 for tips on making the flower centers.

From the printed muslin fabric, cut:
- Four 4 × 44-inch strips for outer borders
- Four 13-inch squares for the appliqué blocks
- 68 border triangles

From the dark green fabric, cut:
- One ⅞ × 44-inch strip for stems
- Reserve the remaining fabric for binding

From the assorted magenta fabrics, cut:
- Four large blossoms
- Four small blossoms
- 32 bud tips
- 32 border triangles
- Two 2½-inch border corner squares

From the assorted dark green fabrics, cut:
- 32 buds
- 32 leaves
- 32 border triangles
- Two 2½-inch border corner squares

Appliquéing the Blocks

1. For each block, prepare one large blossom, one small blossom, eight bud tips, eight buds, and eight leaves for appliqué. See page 156 for tips on appliqué.

2. See page 157 for tips on making bias strips for stems. Fold and press the ⅞-inch-wide green strip lengthwise in thirds. The prepared strip will be about 5/16 inch wide. Cut four 2½-inch-long stem segments for each block.

3. Make a master pattern of the appliqué design to use as a guide for positioning the appliqué pieces on the background squares. Fold a 12½-inch square of tracing paper in half vertically, horizontally, and diagonally in both directions to form guidelines. Referring to **Diagram 1** for correct placement, use the templates and a pencil to draw outlines for the appliqués on the paper pattern. To make sure the outlines are in exactly the same position in all areas of the pattern, refold the paper and see if the shapes are in perfect alignment. Darken the pattern outlines with the permanent marking pen.

4. Fold a background square in half vertically, horizontally, and diagonally both ways, creasing lightly.

5. Center the background block over the master pattern (the darkened lines should show through the fabric). Center the prepared stems over the diagonal crease lines so that the center blossom and buds will overlap the raw ends; pin in place and appliqué.

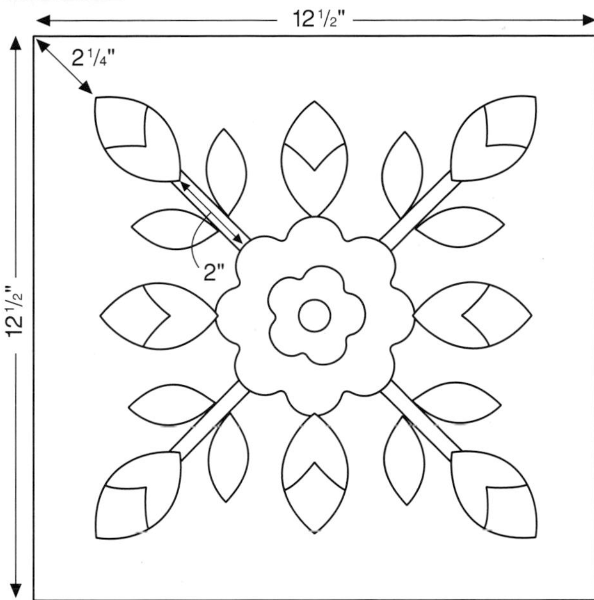

Diagram 1

6. Using the master pattern as a guide, position a large blossom in the center of the block and appliqué in place. Turn the block to the wrong side and trim away the background fabric from behind the appliqué, leaving a scant ¼-inch seam allowance. Position and appliqué a small blossom on top of the large blossom; trim the fabric from behind as described above. Wait to add the center circle.

7. Position and appliqué bud tips, buds, and leaves.

8. See "Making Crisp Appliqué Circles" on this page for tips on making and adding the flower centers. Make these circles a scant ¾ inch in diameter. Use magenta fabric for the flower centers.

9. Make a total of four blocks.

MAKING CRISP APPLIQUÉ CIRCLES

Begin by making a stiff paper circle template from an index card. Cut out the template and use it to mark the size of the desired finished circle. Use this template to mark a circle on the wrong side of the fabric. Cut out the circle, adding a scant ¼-inch seam allowance.

Run a basting thread around the fabric circle, sewing in the area between the drawn line and the raw edge. Position the paper template on the wrong side of the fabric circle. Pull on the thread to gather the fabric over the paper template. Tighten, then make a few stitches to secure the gathers.

Appliqué the circle in place. Turn the block to the wrong side, and make a cut in the base fabric. Remove and discard the paper template. ♦

Assembling the Quilt Top

1. Referring to the photograph on page 35, lay out the four blocks in two rows. Join the blocks, then join the rows.

2. To piece the dogtooth borders, lay out 17 printed muslin triangles, 8 magenta triangles, and 8 green triangles for each border. Begin and end each strip with a muslin triangle, and alternate the magenta and green triangles. Sew the triangles together, making four border strips. Referring to **Diagram 2,** trim the ends of the pieced borders. Cut ¼ inch away from the inside point of the muslin end triangles to allow for seams.

3. Sew two trimmed border strips to the sides of the quilt top. Press the seams toward the quilt top. Sew a magenta corner square to one end of each remaining border strip and a green corner square to the other end of each strip. Sew the strips to the quilt top so that the opposite diagonal corners will be the same color.

4. Measure the width of the bordered quilt top (approximately 28½ inches), measuring through the center rather than along the edges, which may have stretched. Trim two of the 4 × 44-inch outer borders to this length. Sew the

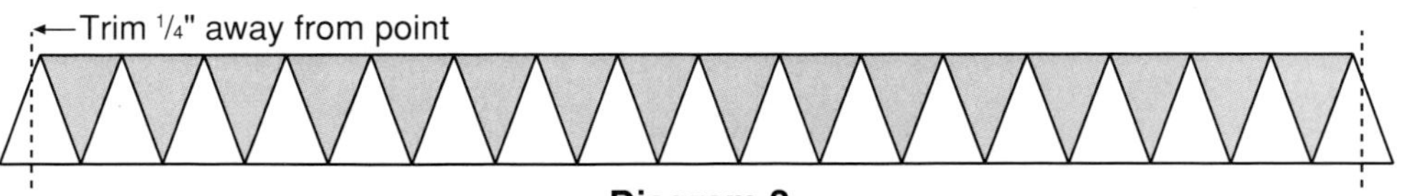

Diagram 2

trimmed borders to the sides of the quilt top. Press the seams toward the border strips.

5. Measure the quilt top again, through the center, from the raw edge of one border to the raw edge of the other (approximately 35 ½ inches). Trim the two remaining border strips to this length, and add them to the quilt top.

Quilting and Finishing

1. Mark quilting designs. The wallhanging shown was quilted with diagonal lines in the background area of the blocks and straight lines in the outer border.

2. Layer the quilt back, batting, and quilt top; baste. Trim the quilt back so it is approximately 3 inches larger than the quilt top on all sides.

3. Quilt in the ditch around the appliquéd pieces. Quilt all marked designs, and add additional quilting as desired.

4. From the binding fabric, make approximately 150 inches of French-fold binding. See page 164 for suggested binding widths and instructions on making and attaching binding.

5. Sew the binding to the quilt top. Trim the excess batting and backing, and hand finish the binding on the back side of the quilt. Add a hanging sleeve, if desired, following the instructions on page 167.

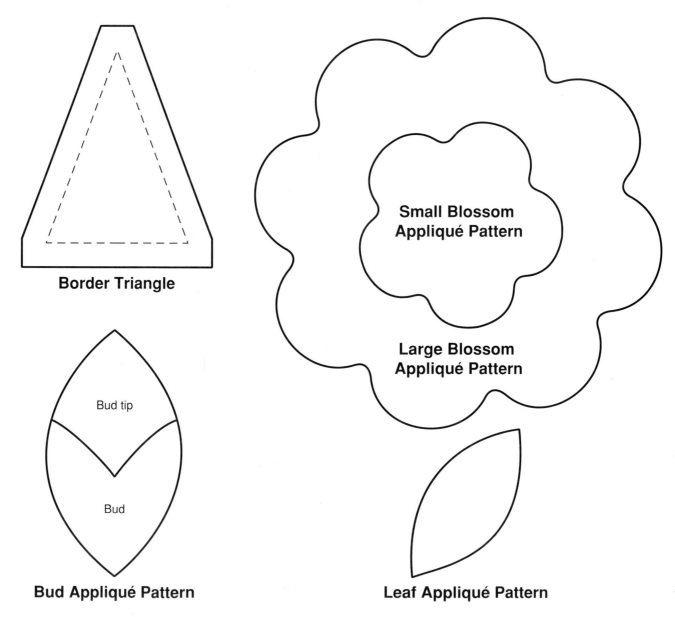

Border Triangle

Small Blossom Appliqué Pattern

Large Blossom Appliqué Pattern

Bud tip

Bud

Bud Appliqué Pattern

Leaf Appliqué Pattern

Totable Totes

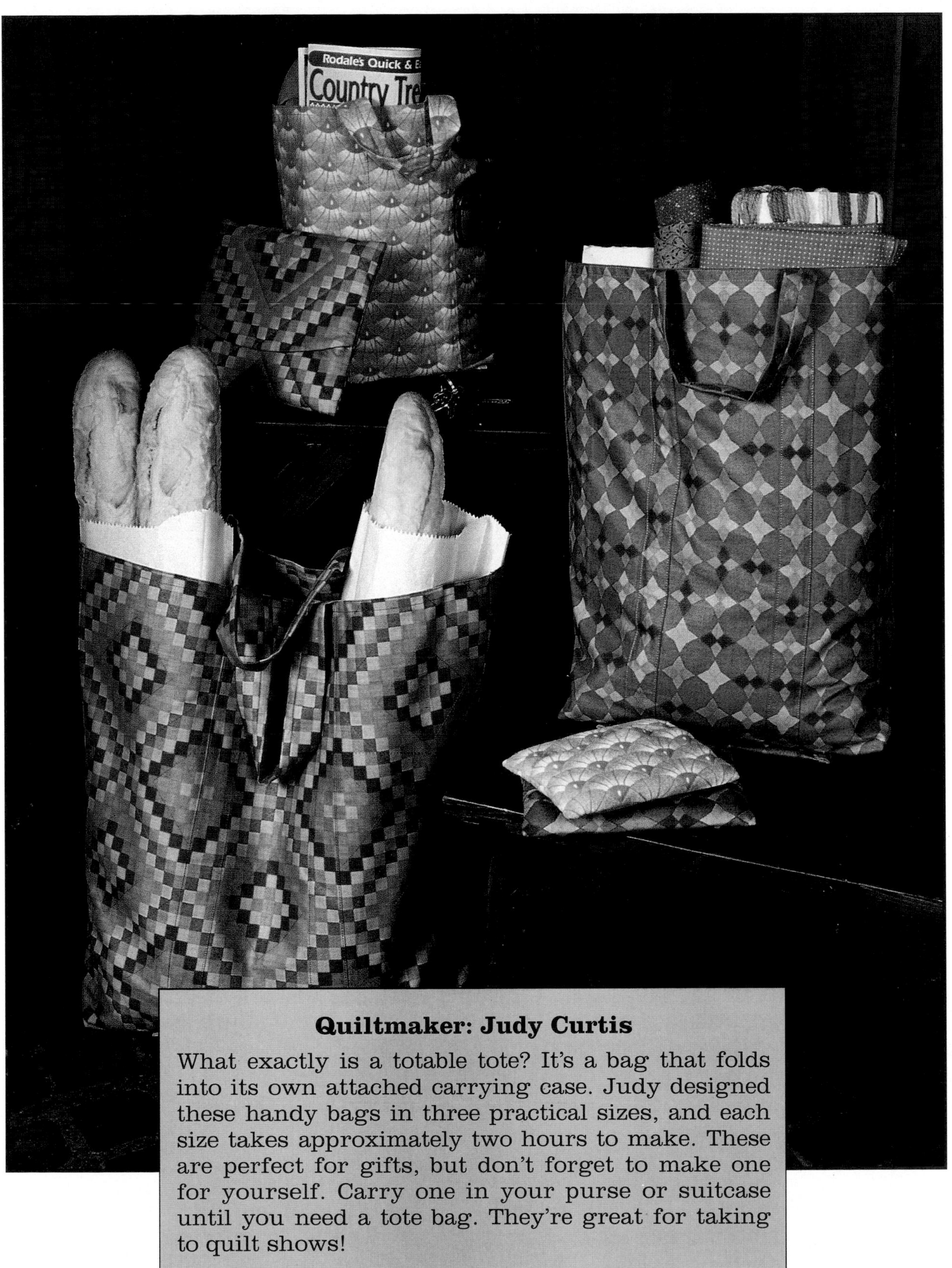

Quiltmaker: Judy Curtis

What exactly is a totable tote? It's a bag that folds into its own attached carrying case. Judy designed these handy bags in three practical sizes, and each size takes approximately two hours to make. These are perfect for gifts, but don't forget to make one for yourself. Carry one in your purse or suitcase until you need a tote bag. They're great for taking to quilt shows!

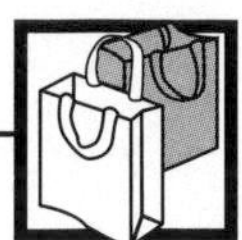

Skill Level: Easy

Size: Small tote bag is 7 inches wide, 10 inches tall, and 3 inches deep
Medium tote bag is 10 inches wide, 14 inches tall, and 3 ½ inches deep
Large tote bag is 13 inches wide, 16 inches tall, and 5 inches deep

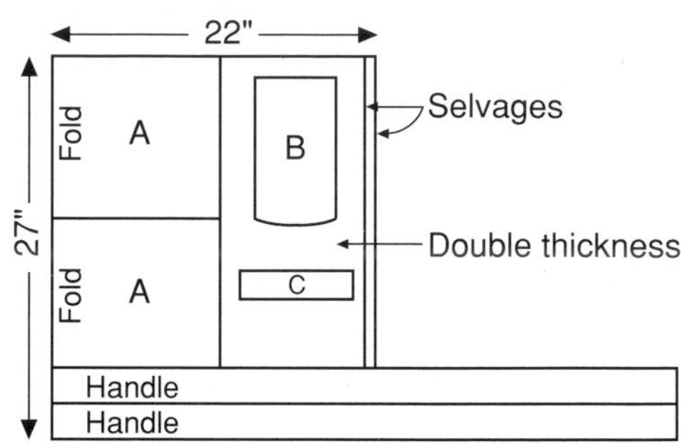

Small Bag Cutting Diagram

Fabrics and Supplies

- ¾ yard of fabric for small bag
- 1 yard of fabric for medium bag
- 1 ½ yards of fabric for large bag
- One sheet of poster board for templates
- Chalk marker or water-soluble pen
- Rotary cutter, ruler, and mat

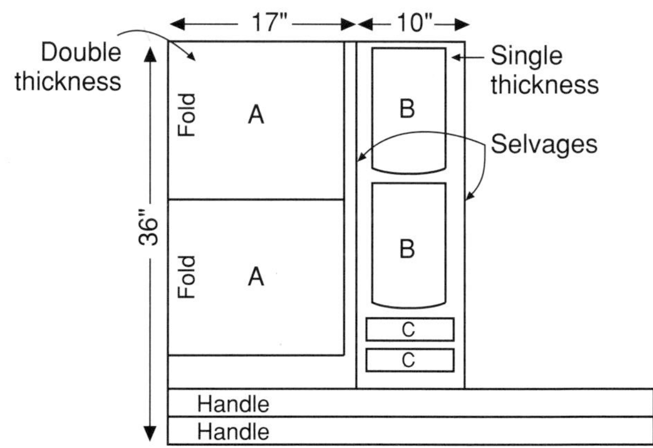

Medium Bag Cutting Diagram

Cutting

All measurements include ¼-inch seam allowances. From poster board, make templates for A, B, C, and D, according to the dimensions listed in the table below. Make a template for the E triangle using the pattern on page 44. Tips for making and using templates are on page 153.

Write "place on fold" along one short side of template A. Using the curve patterns on page 44, trace and cut the appropriate curve onto one short end of template B. Mark horizontal and vertical centerlines on templates B and D.

Referring to the **Cutting Diagrams,** cut the A, B, and C pieces and the handles from the tote bag fabric. Transfer the center markings on template B onto the fabric. Do not cut a fabric piece for template D. For the small and medium bags, cut two 2 ½ × 44-inch handle strips. For the large bag, cut two 3 × 44-inch handle strips.

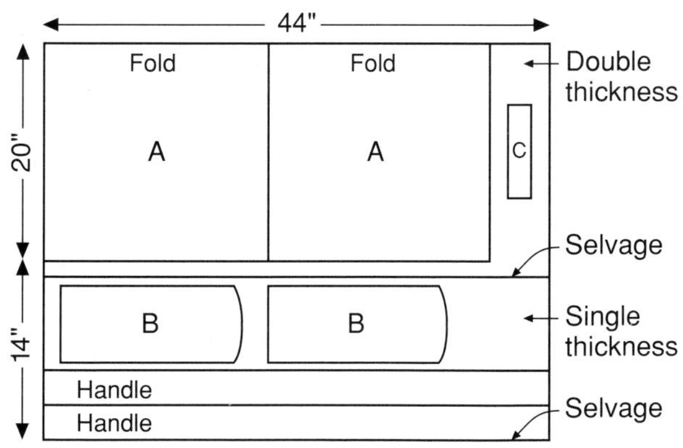

Large Bag Cutting Diagram

TOTE BAG PATTERN DIMENSIONS

Pattern Piece	Small Bag	Medium Bag	Large Bag
A (tote body)	10 ½ × 11 ¾	14 × 16	18 ½ × 18 ¾
B (case)	5 ¾ × 10	6 ¾ × 11 ⅛	7 ¾ × 15 ⅞
C (case binding)	2 × 8	2 × 8	2 × 8
D (case placement template)	3 × 4	3 ½ × 5	6 × 5

Making the Bags

Instructions for the three sizes of bags are written together. The instructions for the small bag appear first, with the instructions for the medium bag and the large bag in parentheses.

1. Fold each handle strip in half lengthwise, right sides together, and sew the long edges together. Do not sew across the ends. Turn the

handles right side out, center the seam on the back, and press flat.

2. With right sides facing, sew two A rectangles together along one short side to form a long rectangle.

3. Fold the long fabric rectangle in half lengthwise, and crease to form a center guideline. Lay the rectangle right side up on a table, and use chalk to mark the following placement lines on the fabric rectangle, as shown in **Diagram 1.** For the handle top placement lines, draw a crosswise line 11½ (15¾, 18½) inches away from each side of the center seam. For the handle side placement lines, draw a lengthwise line 2 (2½, 3) inches to each side of the center crease. For the case placement lines, draw a crosswise line 1½ (1¾, 2½) inches to each side of the center seam.

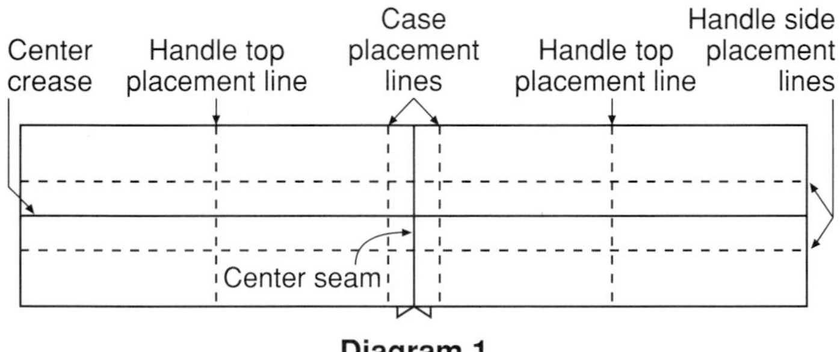

Diagram 1

4. Starting at the center seam, place a handle strip, seam side down, along a handle side placement line. Align the outside edge of the strip with the line; the inside edge of the strip should be toward the center crease. Referring to **Diagram 2,** pin along the strip from the center seam to the handle top placement line. Measure 11 or 12 inches along the strip; leave this part loose for a handle. Resume pinning the handle down the other side to the center seam, aligning the strip with the side placement line. Trim off excess handle strip. Repeat for the other handle.

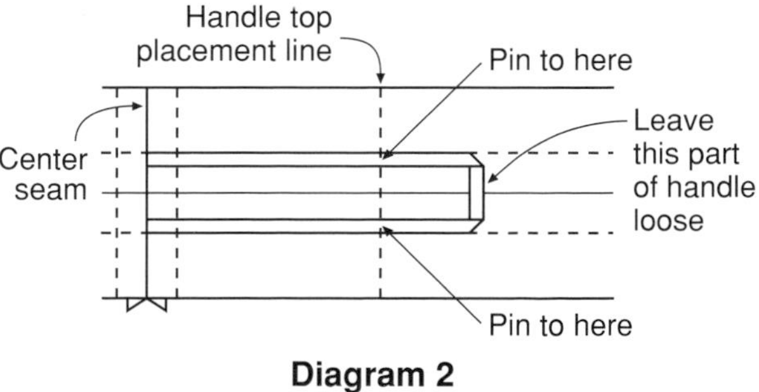

Diagram 2

5. Topstitch the handles to the bag rectangle, stitching from the center seam to the handle top placement line. Do not sew beyond the handle top placement line.

6. Pin the two B case pieces together with right sides facing. Sew along the two short sides. Clip seams as needed and turn right side out. Topstitch ¼ inch away from the seams, leaving the long sides open.

7. Place template D on piece B (the case), matching up the centerlines drawn on template D with the centerlines marked on B. Referring to **Diagram 3,** use chalk to draw around the template to mark the case placement lines. You will sew the case to the tote along these lines. Also mark overlap marks ½ inch from each end along the unsewn sides of the case.

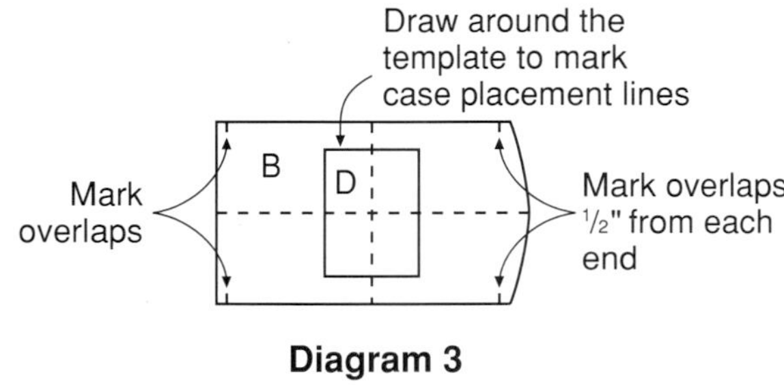

Diagram 3

8. With the marked side of the case facing up, place the case on the right side of the tote rectangle. Pin-match the placement lines on the case to the center seam and the center crease on the tote rectangle. Sew the case to the tote rectangle, following the guidelines marked in Step 7 and stitching through all three layers. See **Diagram 4.**

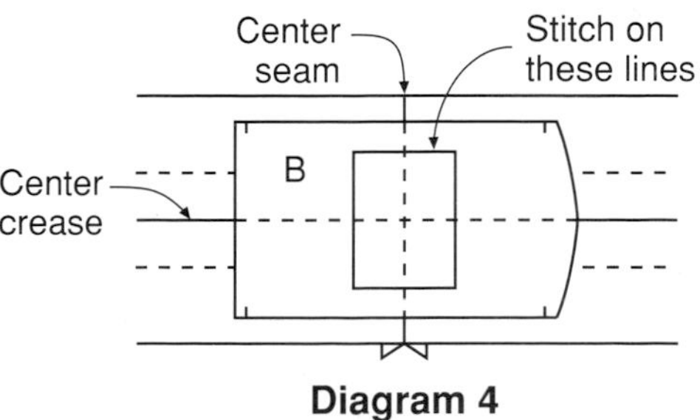

Diagram 4

9. Fold the curved edge of the case over, and align the overlap marks with the center seam on the tote. Repeat on the other side, folding the straight edge over and aligning the overlap marks with the center seam. With all marks

aligned, pin the raw edges together at both sides of the case, as shown in **Diagram 5.**

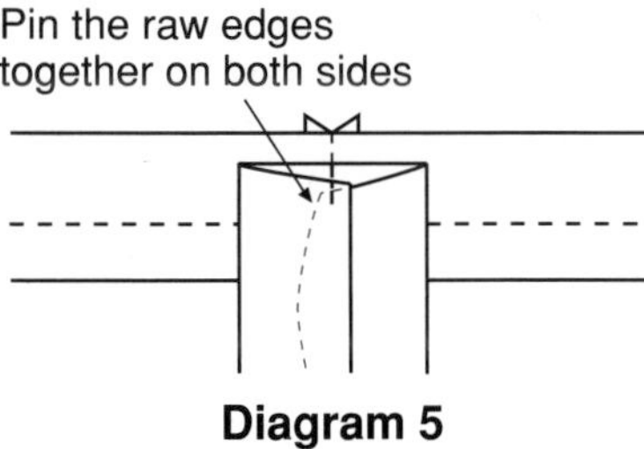

Diagram 5

10. Press each binding strip in half lengthwise with wrong sides facing. Referring to **Diagram 6,** sew the binding to the sides of the case. First, fold ½ inch of the binding to the back side on one end of the case, as shown. Align the raw edge of the binding with the raw edges of the case and pin. Fold ½ inch of binding to the back side at the other end, and trim the excess binding strip. Sew the binding to the edge of the case, as shown in the diagram, taking care not to catch the tote fabric in the stitching.

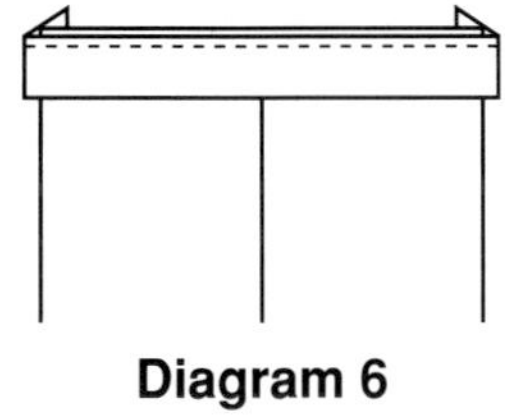

Diagram 6

11. To finish the binding, turn its folded edge to the back side of the case and pin. From the right side, stitch in the ditch, catching the fold of the binding in the stitching on the back side of the case. See **Diagram 7.** Repeat to bind the other side.

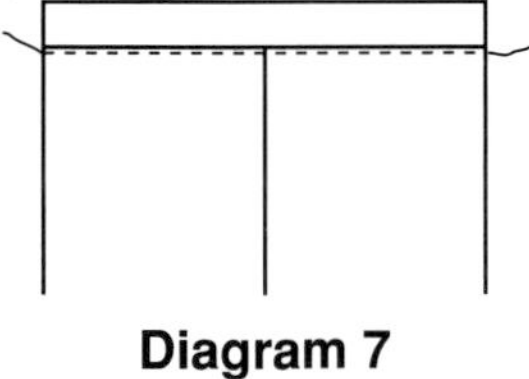

Diagram 7

12. With right sides facing, fold the tote rectangle in half crosswise, matching short ends. The case will be inside the fold. Stitch the short ends together, leaving a 6-inch opening in the center for turning.

13. Fold the tote in half again, matching short ends. Pin the four layers of fabric together along one side of the bag and stitch, as shown in **Diagram 8.** Repeat for the other side.

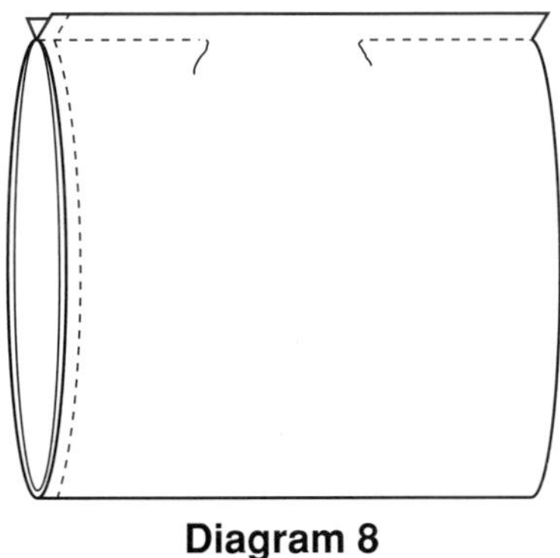

Diagram 8

14. Turn the tote right side out through the opening. You will be looking at the lining side of an inside-out tote bag. Hand stitch the opening closed.

15. With the tote bag still inside out, poke the corner out and match the side seam to the bottom seam. Place the appropriate E template over the corner, and draw along the base of the triangle to mark the stitching guideline. Sew the layers together along the line, backstitching at the beginning and end of the seam. Repeat for the other corner, as shown in **Diagram 9.**

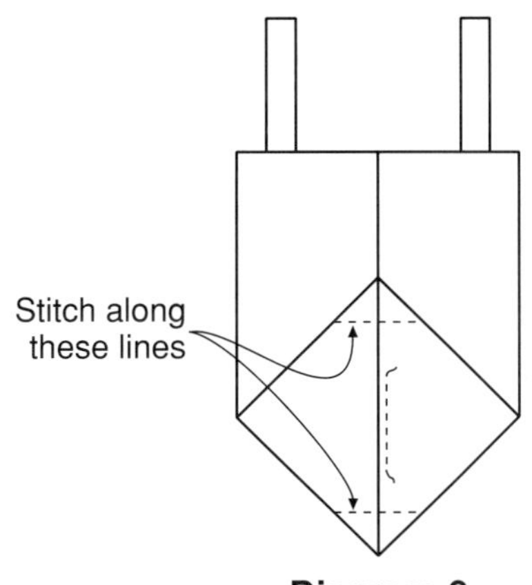

Diagram 9

16. Turn the bag right side out. Press the top edge of the bag. Topstitch around the top edge close to the fold and again ¼ inch away, sewing over the handles to reinforce them.

Pressing the Bag and Folding It into the Case

1. Lay the tote on an ironing board and press the main body flat. Fold the bottom up so that the case is facing you, as shown in **Diagram 10,** and press.

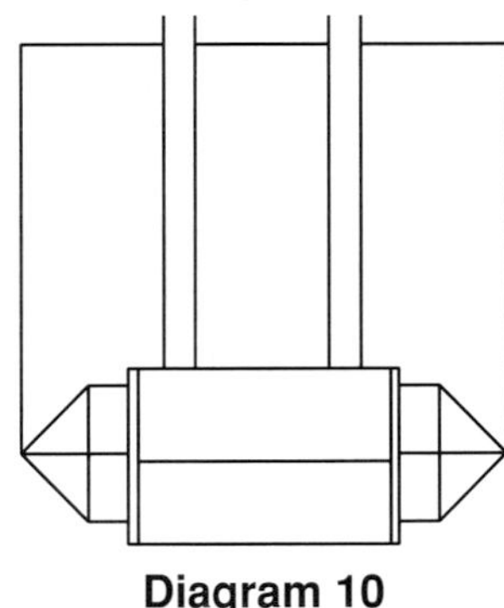

Diagram 10

2. Turn the tote over so that the case is facing away from you. Fold the right side of the bag toward the center, using the outer edge of the handle as a fold line. Repeat for the left side, as shown in **Diagram 11.**

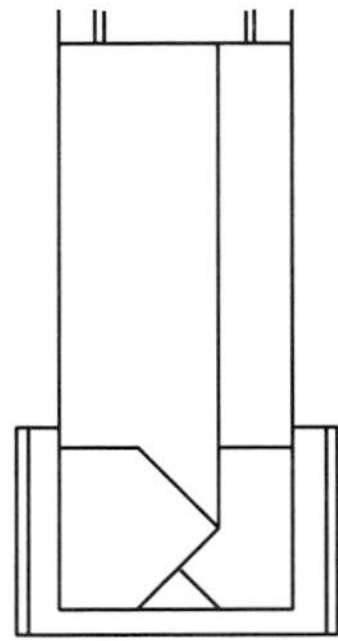

Diagram 11

3. Rotate the tote so that the handles are closest to you. Fold the handles toward the case. (Fold the top edge of the medium tote 3 inches toward the case before proceeding.) Fold the top edge of the tote in half so that it meets the top edge of the case, as shown in **Diagrams 12** and **13.** Fold the top edge in half again, bringing the folded edge even with the other side of the case.

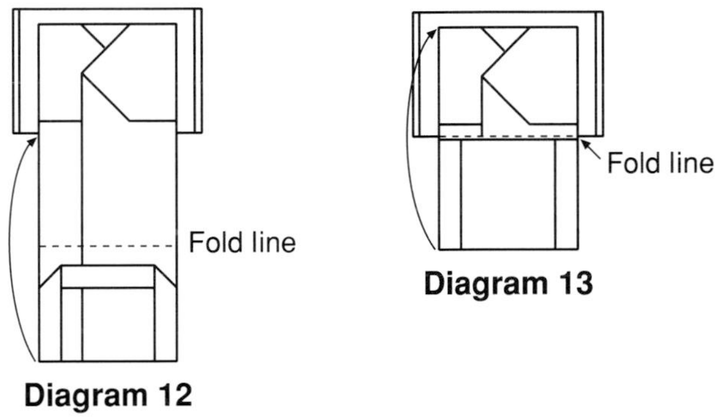

Diagram 12

Diagram 13

4. Holding the package in your hand so that the tote does not unfold, turn the package over so that the case is facing you, as shown in **Diagram 14.**

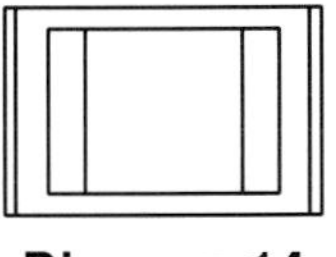

Diagram 14

5. To enclose the tote in the case, turn and flip each side of the case around the folded tote. The curved side of the case will be on the outside.

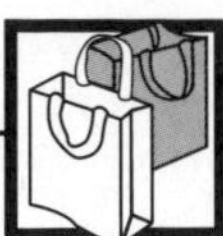

Large

Medium

E

Small

Small

Medium

Large

Curve Pattern for Template B

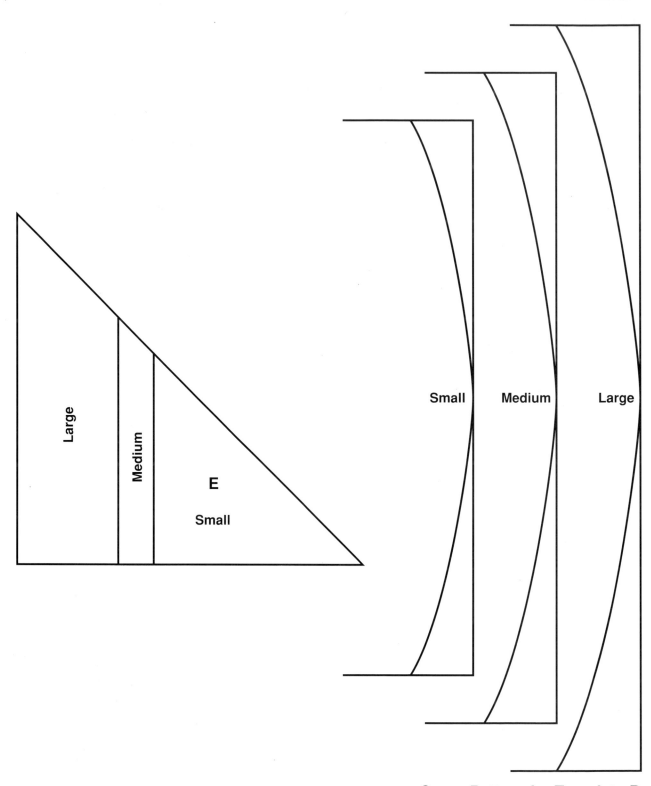

Midnight Rainbows

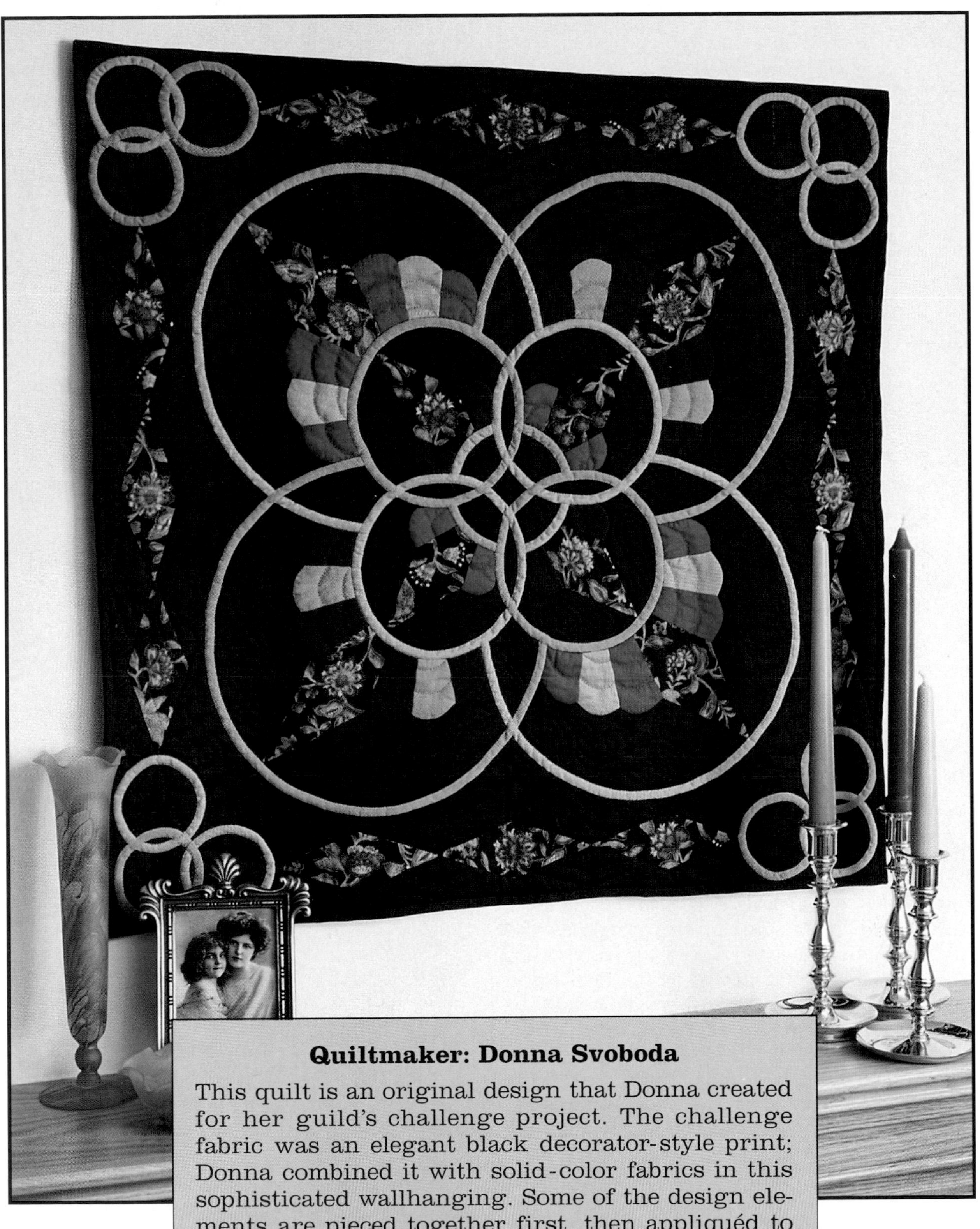

Quiltmaker: Donna Svoboda

This quilt is an original design that Donna created for her guild's challenge project. The challenge fabric was an elegant black decorator-style print; Donna combined it with solid-color fabrics in this sophisticated wallhanging. Some of the design elements are pieced together first, then appliquéd to the large background square. Bias strips form the colored rings. This is an ideal project for the quiltmaker who loves hand piecing and appliqué.

Skill Level: Intermediate

Size: Finished quilt is 26½ inches square

Fabrics and Supplies

- 1 yard of black solid fabric for background square and binding
- ½ yard of black/mauve/green/blue floral print fabric
- ½ yard *each* of mauve and light turquoise solid fabrics
- ¼ yard *each* of burgundy and medium turquoise solid fabrics
- 1 yard of fabric for quilt back
- Crib-size quilt batting (45 × 60 inches)
- Rotary cutter, ruler, and mat
- Template plastic
- Tracing paper
- Black permanent felt-tip pen
- ¼-inch-wide bias pressing bar
- Chalk pencil or other marker for dark fabric

Cutting

This quilt is constructed by hand piecing sections of patchwork together and then appliquéing those sections to the background fabric. The background square is cut oversize and trimmed to the exact size when the appliqué is complete. Make finished-size templates for pieces A, B, C, D, E, F, and G using the patterns on page 49. Label the templates on the right side. Refer to page 153 for tips on making and using templates.

When marking and cutting pieces A, B, C, D, E, and F, mark on the wrong side of the fabric; add ¼-inch seam allowances when cutting out the pieces. Use the template label side up to mark reverse pieces, label side down to mark regular pieces. Later, you will use the templates again to mark fold-over lines on the right side of sections to prepare them for appliqué. Mark on the right side of the fabric for the G diamond pieces. (See page 156 for tips on hand appliqué.)

Use a rotary cutter to cut the bias strips. Tips on cutting bias strips appear on page 157.

From the black solid fabric, cut:
- One 28-inch background square
- Reserve the remaining fabric for binding

From the floral print fabric, cut:
- 4 A pieces
- 4 C pieces
- 12 G diamonds (mark on right side of fabric)

From the mauve fabric, cut:
- Three ⅞ × 18-inch bias strips
- 2 E and 2 E reverse pieces

From the light turquoise fabric, cut:
- Three ⅞ × 18-inch bias strips
- 2 E and 2 E reverse pieces

From the burgundy fabric, cut:
- 2 B and 2 B reverse pieces
- 2 D and 2 D reverse pieces
- 2 F and 2 F reverse pieces

From the medium turquoise fabric, cut:
- 2 B and 2 B reverse pieces
- 2 D and 2 D reverse pieces
- 2 F and 2 F reverse pieces

Preparing the Background Square

1. Fold the black fabric background square in half horizontally, vertically, and diagonally in both directions, and lightly crease.

2. Use a photocopy machine to enlarge the **Bias Appliqué Placement Diagram** 200 percent. Copy-shop personnel can help you copy the design onto 11 × 17-inch sheets of paper. You will probably have to copy it in sections and tape the sections together to get the whole design. When complete, the enlarged pattern will equal one 13¼-inch quadrant of the quilt top. If necessary, darken the lines on the copy so that they are highly visible.

3. Working at a light table or a window, place the black background square over the master pattern, aligning the inside corner dashed lines on the pattern with the center of the fabric square. Secure the paper pattern with tape. Pin or tape the fabric over the pattern to keep it from slipping.

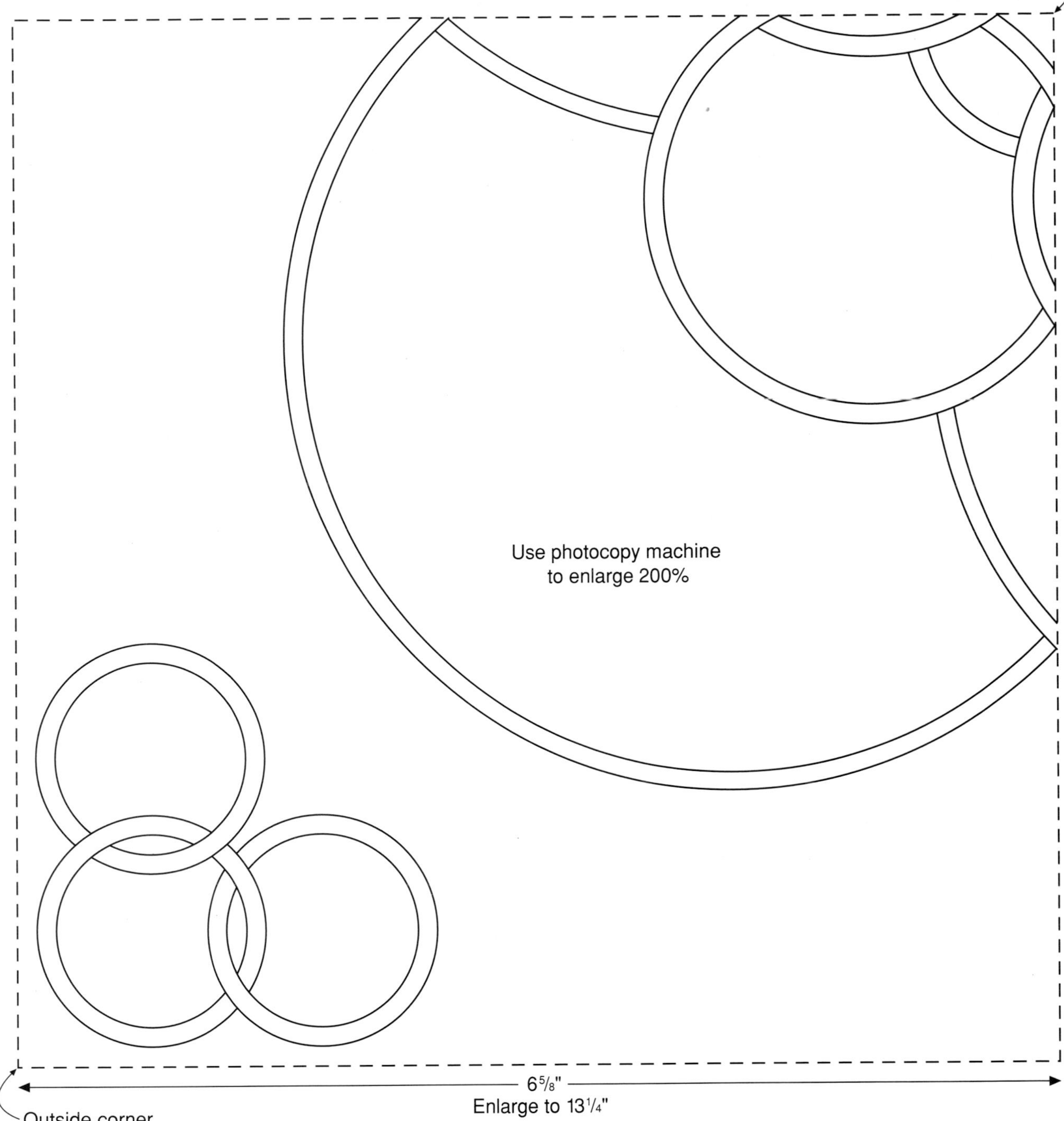

One-quarter of Bias Appliqué Placement Diagram

4. With a chalk pencil or other marker that will show on dark fabric, trace placement lines for the bias appliqué circles onto one quadrant of the fabric. Pay close attention to sections that overlap or underlap.

5. Rotate the fabric square one-quarter turn and mark the second quadrant. Continue turning and marking in this manner until the circle placement lines are complete.

Preparing Bias Strips for Appliqué

1. To prepare one bias strip, fold it in half, *wrong* sides together, and machine stitch ⅛ inch from the raw edges, forming a long tube.

2. Insert a ¼-inch-wide bias pressing bar into the tube. Bring the seam to the center of one flat side of the bar.

3. Steam press on both sides. Push the bar farther into the tube and press. Continue pushing the bar through the tube until all of the bias strip is pressed. Repeat to prepare all of the mauve and light turquoise bias strips.

Appliquéing the Bias Strips

1. Referring to the **Fabric Key** and **Diagram 1** for color placement, thread baste the prepared mauve and light turquoise bias strips to the background square. Conceal the raw ends of the strips under overlapping circles.

Fabric Key

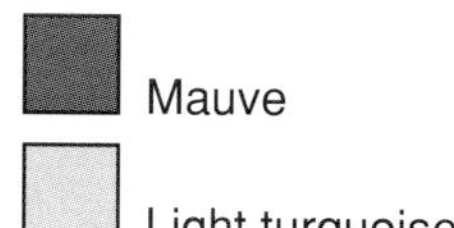

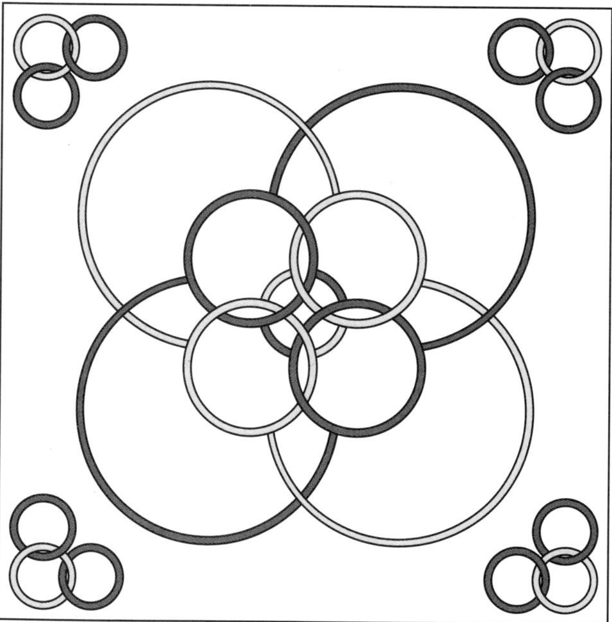

Diagram 1

2. Using thread that matches the fabrics, appliqué the strips in place. Appliqué inner curves first, then outer curves, so that the bias will lie flat.

3. Gently steam press the bias pieces once the appliqué is complete.

Adding the Patchwork/Appliqué Sections

1. Referring to **Diagram 2** and the photo on page 45, sew one B and one B reverse piece to opposite sides of each of the four A pieces. Sew burgundy B pieces to two of the A pieces and medium turquoise B pieces to the remaining two A pieces. Press the seams toward the B pieces.

2. Using the A and B templates, mark foldover lines on the right sides of the AB units. Turn the seam allowances back along the marked lines and thread baste.

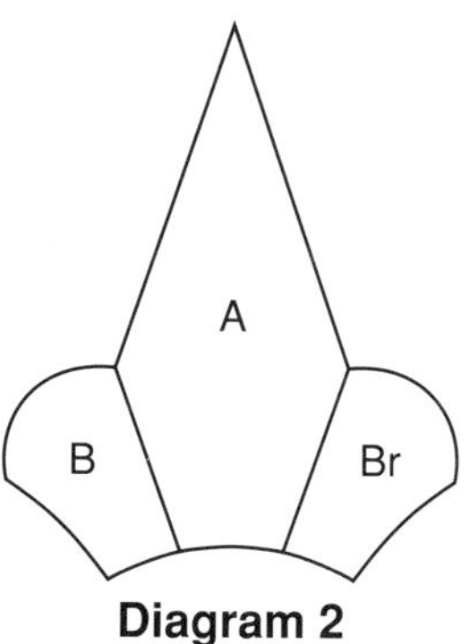

Diagram 2

3. Position, pin, and appliqué the four AB units to the central portion of the quilt top.

4. Referring to **Diagram 3,** construct four CDEF units. Use burgundy and mauve D, E, and F pieces on two units, and light and medium turquoise pieces on the other two units. Pin and appliqué the units to the quilt top, as shown in the photo on page 45.

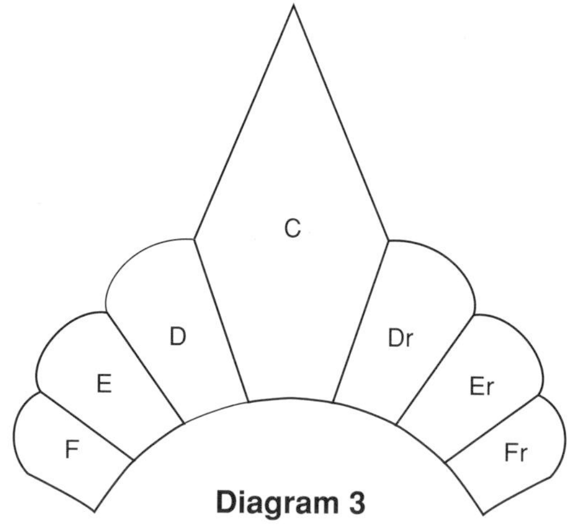

Diagram 3

5. Prepare the 12 G diamonds for appliqué. Position the prepared pieces around the outside edges of the quilt top. Check to make sure the diamonds are an equal distance from the edge on all four sides. Appliqué in place.

6. Trim the completed quilt top to 27 inches square.

Quilting and Finishing

1. Mark quilting designs. Designs for some of the motifs on the quilt shown are indicated on the pattern pieces on this page.

2. Trim the quilt backing fabric to a 35-inch square.

3. Layer the quilt back, batting, and quilt top; baste.

4. Quilt all marked designs, and add additional quilting as desired.

5. From the binding fabric, make approximately 120 inches of French-fold binding. See page 164 for suggested binding widths and instructions on making and attaching binding.

6. Sew the binding to the quilt top. Trim the excess batting and backing, and hand finish the binding on the back side of the quilt. See the instructions on page 167 for making a hanging sleeve.

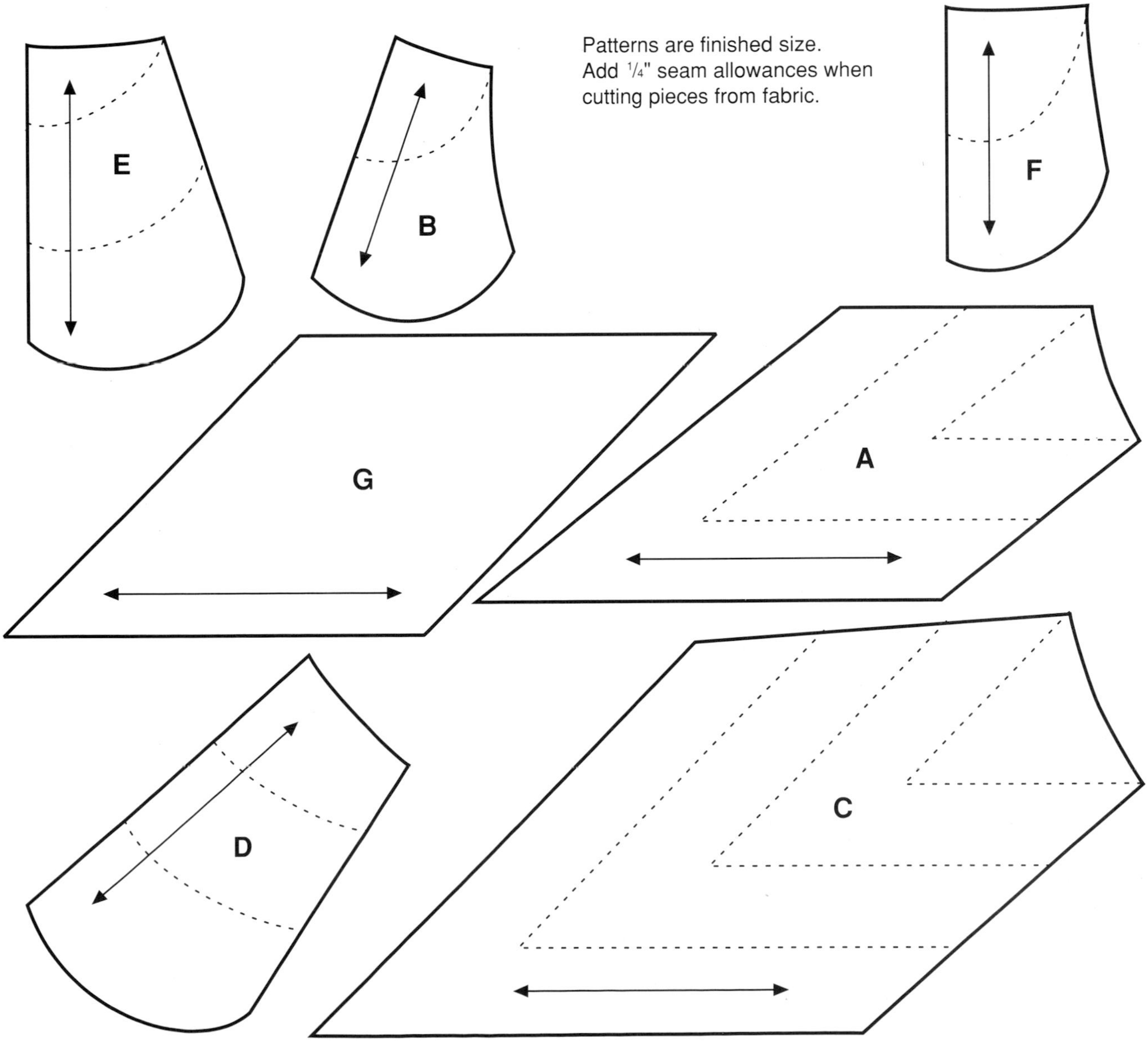

Patterns are finished size.
Add ¼" seam allowances when cutting pieces from fabric.

E

B

F

G

A

D

C

Roses in a Ruby Vase

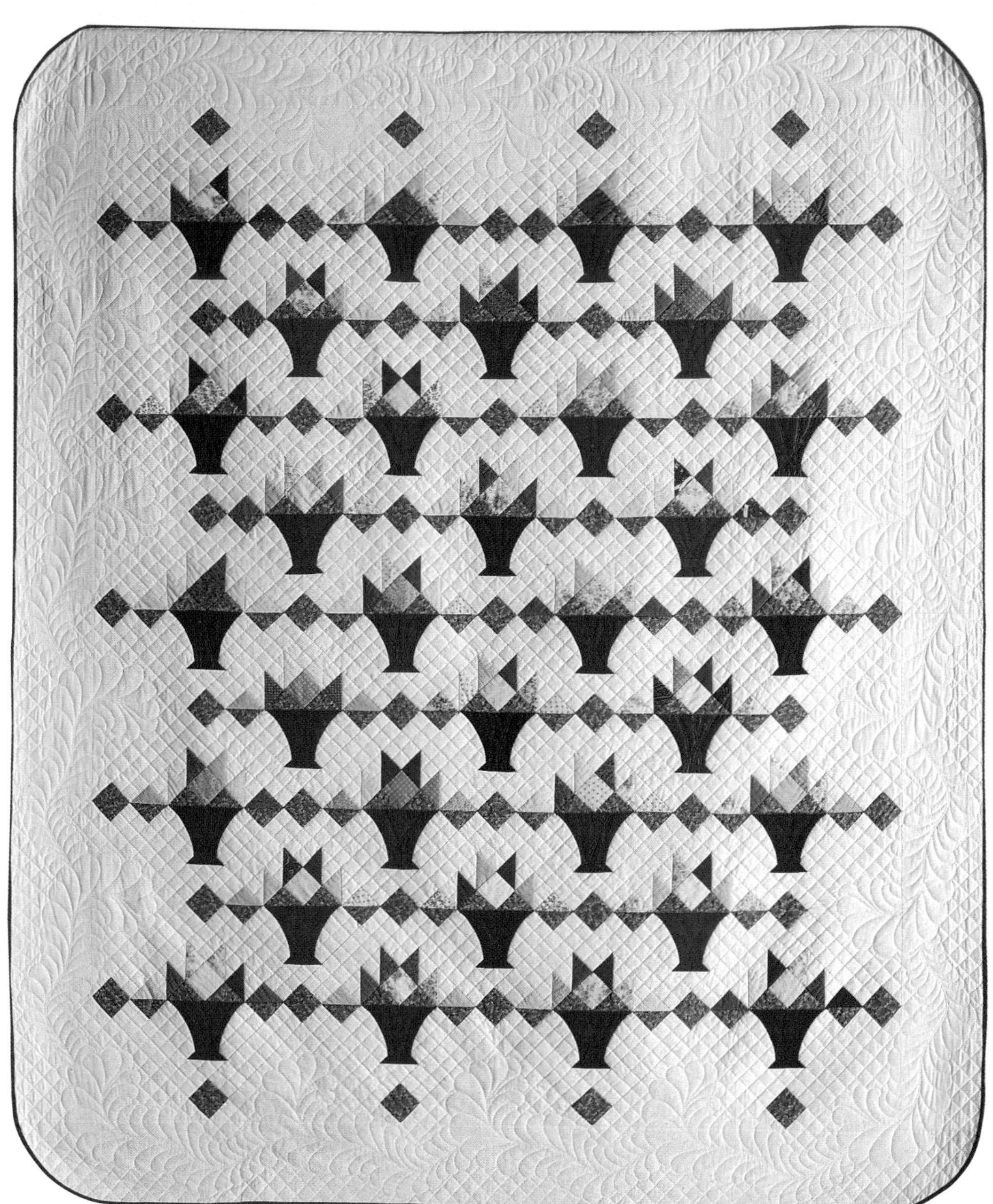

Quiltmaker: Virginia Carman Dambach

Virginia's inspiration for this quilt was an image of a ruby glass pitcher filled with full-blown roses, sitting on a coffee table splashed with sunlight. The block pattern, found in *Editor's Choice Patchwork Quilts,* was perfect for her interpretation of that bouquet. The blocks can be sewn by either hand or machine. Fancy feathered quilting designs add interest to the wide cream borders.

Skill Level: Intermediate

Size: Finished quilt is approximately 89⅛ × 106¾ inches
Finished block is 10 inches square

Fabrics and Supplies

- 8 yards of cream solid fabric for blocks, sashing strips, and borders
- 1¼ yards of dusty green print for blocks and sashing squares
- Approximately 1½ yards total of assorted deep burgundy print and solid fabric scraps for blocks. (Each vase can be cut from a 6 × 9-inch square.)
- Approximately 1½ yards total of assorted pink, mauve, and yellow print and solid fabric scraps for blocks
- 1 yard of burgundy print fabric for binding
- 8¼ yards of fabric for quilt back
- King-size quilt batting (120 inches square)
- Rotary cutter, ruler, and mat
- Template plastic

Cutting

All measurements include ¼-inch seam allowances. Measurements for the borders are longer than needed; trim them to the exact length when they are added to the quilt top. Instructions given are for quick-cutting all of the pieces, except A, B, and C, using a rotary cutter and ruler.

Make templates for A, B, and C using the pattern pieces on page 55. If you prefer to cut all the pieces using the traditional method, then also make templates for patterns D and E, as directed below. The patterns as given include seam allowances. If you will be hand piecing, make finished-size templates, and add the seam allowances when you cut out the pieces. Tips for making and using templates are on page 153.

- **D:** Make a 3⅜-inch square; cut the square in half diagonally.
- **E:** 3-inch square

Before You Begin

Prepare the cream fabric by cutting off one 96-inch-long piece.

From the 96-inch-long piece of cream fabric, cut:

- Four 8 × 96-inch border strips
- 16 C and 16 C reverse pieces

From the remaining cream fabric, cut:

- 16 C and 16 C reverse pieces. (You will have a total of 32 C and 32 C reverse pieces.)
- 160 D triangles
  Use Template D
  OR
  Cut seven 3⅜ × 44-inch strips. Cut the strips into 3⅜-inch squares. You will need 80 squares. Cut each square in half diagonally to make two triangles.
- 32 E squares
  Use Template E
  OR
  Cut three 3 × 44-inch strips. Cut the strips into 3-inch squares.
- 80 sashing strips
  Cut six 10½ × 44-inch strips. Cut the strips into 3 × 10½-inch rectangles.
- 14 side setting triangles
  Cut four 18⅞-inch squares. Cut each square in half diagonally in both directions to make four triangles.
- 4 corner setting triangles
  Cut two 11½-inch squares. Cut each square in half diagonally to make two triangles.

From the green print fabric, cut:

- 128 D triangles
  Use Template D
  OR
  Cut six 3⅜ × 44-inch strips. Cut the strips into 3⅜-inch squares. You will need 64 squares. Cut each square in half diagonally to make two triangles.
- 49 E squares
  Use Template E
  OR
  Cut four 3 × 44-inch strips. Cut the strips into 3-inch squares.

From the assorted deep burgundy fabrics, cut:

- 32 A vases
- 32 B vase bases. (Cut one B base to match each A vase.)

From the assorted pink, mauve, and yellow fabrics, cut:

- 192 D triangles

  Use Template D

  OR

  Cut ninety-six 3⅜-inch squares. Cut each square in half diagonally to make two triangles.

- 32 E squares

  Use Template E

  OR

  Cut 3-inch squares

Piecing the Blocks

1. Referring to the **Fabric Key** and the **Block Diagram,** lay out the following pieces for one block: one A, one matching B, one C and one C reverse, five cream D triangles, one cream E square, four green D triangles, and six D triangles and one E square of assorted pink, mauve, and yellow fabrics.

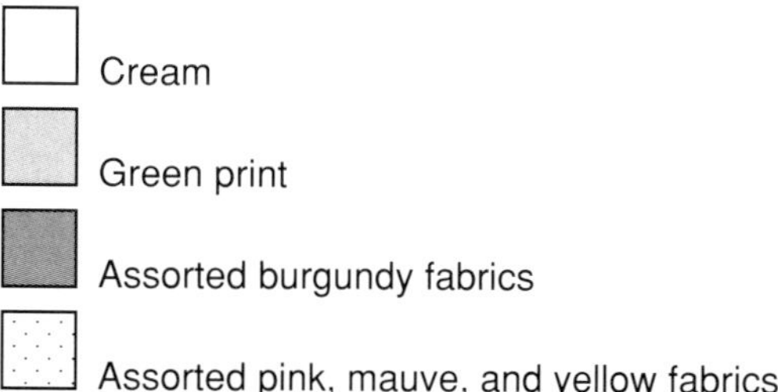

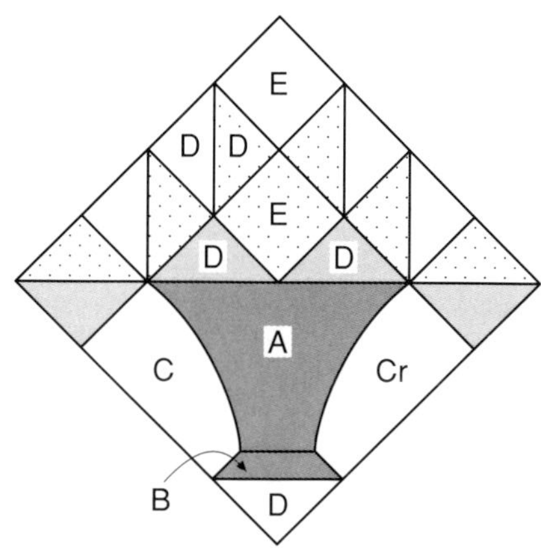

Block Diagram

2. Sew the B base to the bottom edge of the A vase, as shown in **Diagram 1.** Press the seam toward the B base.

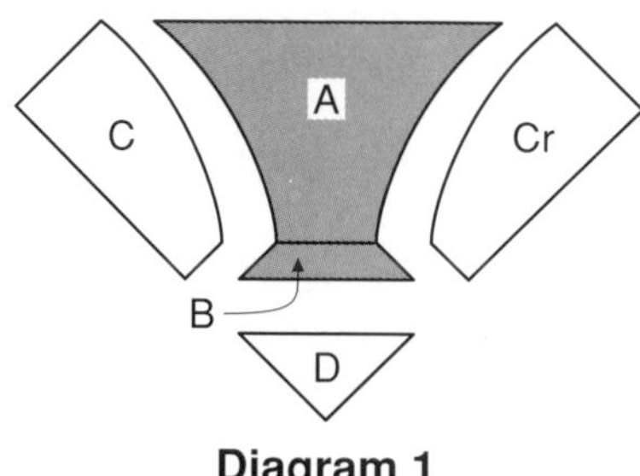

Diagram 1

3. Set a C piece into one curved edge along the side of the vase and a C reverse piece into the other, clipping the curved seam as needed. Refer to page 155 for tips on setting-in. Press the seams toward the C pieces.

4. Stitch a cream D triangle along the bottom edge of the B base. Press seams toward the D triangle.

5. Form a pieced triangle by sewing green D triangles to two adjacent sides of the E square, as shown in **Diagram 2.** Press seams away from the E square. Sew the triangle to the upper edge of the A vase as shown.

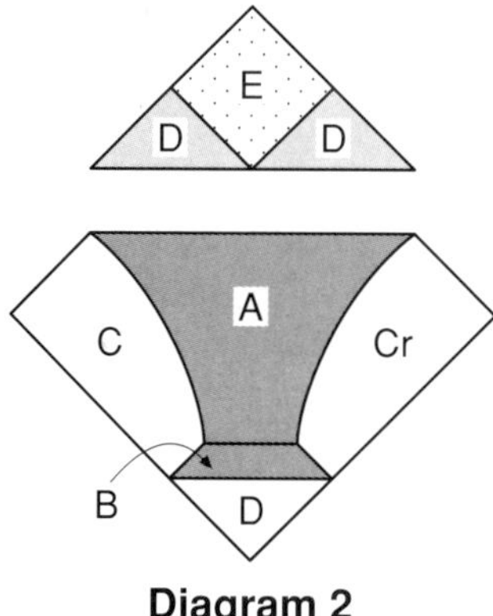

Diagram 2

6. Sew pairs of D triangles together along the long sides to make pieced squares. You will need four pieced squares made with cream and a colored fabric and two pieced squares made with green and a colored fabric. Press the seams toward the darker fabric.

7. Referring to **Diagram 3** for correct positioning, join three pieced squares together into a strip. Press the seams toward the darker fabric. Sew the strip to the top right side of the partial block.

8. Join four pieced squares and one cream E square into a strip, making sure the triangles are positioned as shown in **Diagram 4.** Press the

seams toward the darker fabric. Sew the strip to the top left side of the block.

9. Repeat to make 32 blocks.

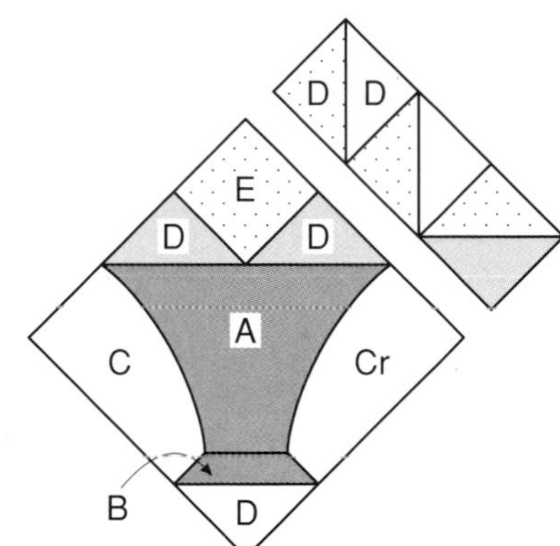

Diagram 3

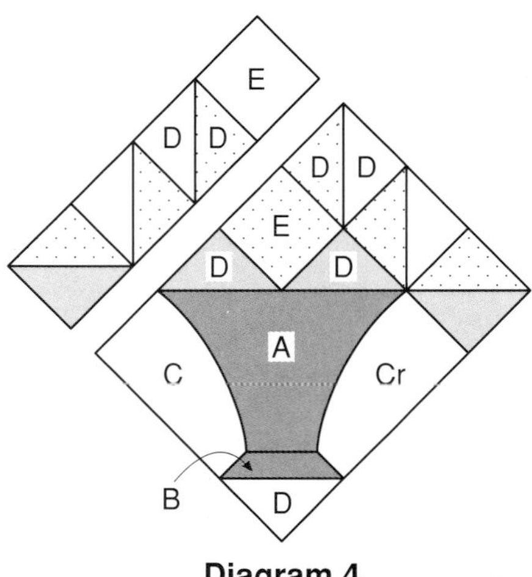

Diagram 4

Assembling the Quilt Top

1. Referring to **Diagram 5,** lay out the blocks on point with all baskets facing in the same direction. The dashed lines on the diagram define the diagonal rows of the quilt top. Place sashing strips and green E sashing squares around the blocks as shown. Fill in along the four sides with side setting triangles. Do not lay out the corner setting triangles at this time.

2. To make assembling the quilt top easier, sew sashing strips and sashing squares to the blocks first, then join the blocks into rows. Referring to **Diagram 6,** sew a sashing strip to the lower left side of all the blocks in Rows 1, 2, 3, and 4. Sew a green E sashing square to the end of a second sashing strip, and sew the unit to the lower right side of the blocks, as shown in the diagram.

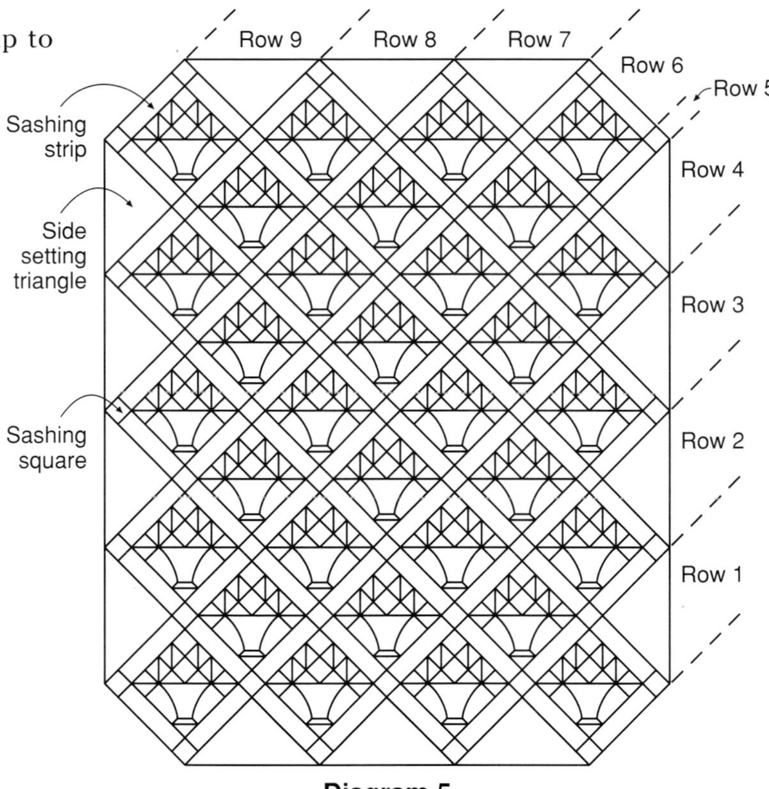

Diagram 5

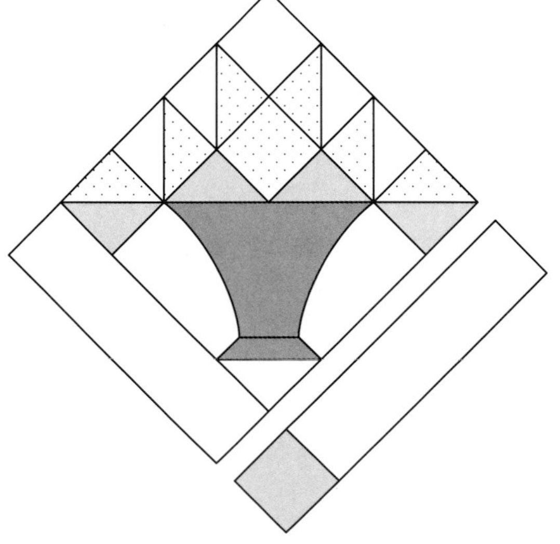
Diagram 6

3. In the same manner, sew a sashing strip to the upper left side of all the blocks in Rows 6, 7, 8, and 9. Sew a green E sashing square to the end of a second sashing strip, and sew the unit to the upper right side of the blocks, as shown in **Diagram 7.**

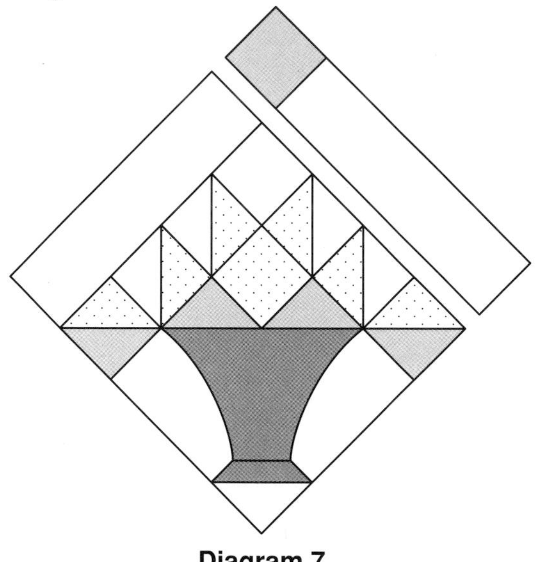

Diagram 7

4. Refer to **Diagram 5** to assemble the rows. To make Row 1, add a sashing strip and sashing square to the top right side of the block. Sew side setting triangles to the top right and lower left sides of the block.

5. To make Row 2, join three blocks. Add a sashing strip and sashing square to the top right side of the top block. Add side setting triangles at each end of the row. Sew Row 1 and Row 2 together.

6. In a similar manner, make and add Rows 3 and 4, adding an extra sashing strip and sashing square to the top block in each row.

7. To make Row 5, join nine sashing squares and eight sashing strips, alternating the pieces as shown. Sew Row 5 to Row 4.

8. To make Row 6, join seven blocks. Add a sashing strip and square and a side setting tringle to the lower left edge of the bottom block in the row. Sew Row 6 to Row 5.

9. In a similar manner, make and add Rows 7, 8, and 9, adding the extra sashing strip, sashing square, and side setting triangle to the bottom block in each row.

10. Stitch a corner setting triangle to each corner of the quilt top.

11. Measure the length of the quilt top. Trim two cream borders to this length (approximately 92¼ inches long). Sew the borders to the sides of the quilt top. Press the seams toward the borders.

12. Measure the width of the quilt top, including the side borders. Trim the remaining two borders to this length (approximately 89⅝ inches long). Sew the borders to the top and bottom edges of the quilt top. Press the seams toward the borders.

13. To round off the corners of the borders as in the quilt shown, draw around a dinner plate or similar-size circular object. Be sure to position the plate in the same place on each of the four corners. Trim the excess border along the drawn line.

Quilting and Finishing

1. Mark quilting designs as desired. The quilt shown was outline quilted around the patchwork pieces. Flower stems were quilted in the A vase pieces, a fancy feather design was quilted in the borders, and all remaining cream areas were quilted with a diagonal grid of 1¼-inch squares.

2. To piece the quilt back, begin by dividing the backing fabric into three equal 99-inch lengths. Trim the selvages and sew the three pieces together. The seams will run parallel to the top and bottom of the quilt.

3. Layer the quilt back, batting, and quilt top; baste. Trim the quilt back so that it is approximately 3 inches larger than the quilt top on all sides.

4. Quilt all marked designs, and add additional quilting as desired.

5. From the binding fabric, make approximately 410 inches of French-fold bias binding. See page 164 for suggested binding widths and instructions on making and attaching binding.

6. Sew the binding to the quilt top. Trim the excess batting and backing, and hand finish the binding on the back side of the quilt.

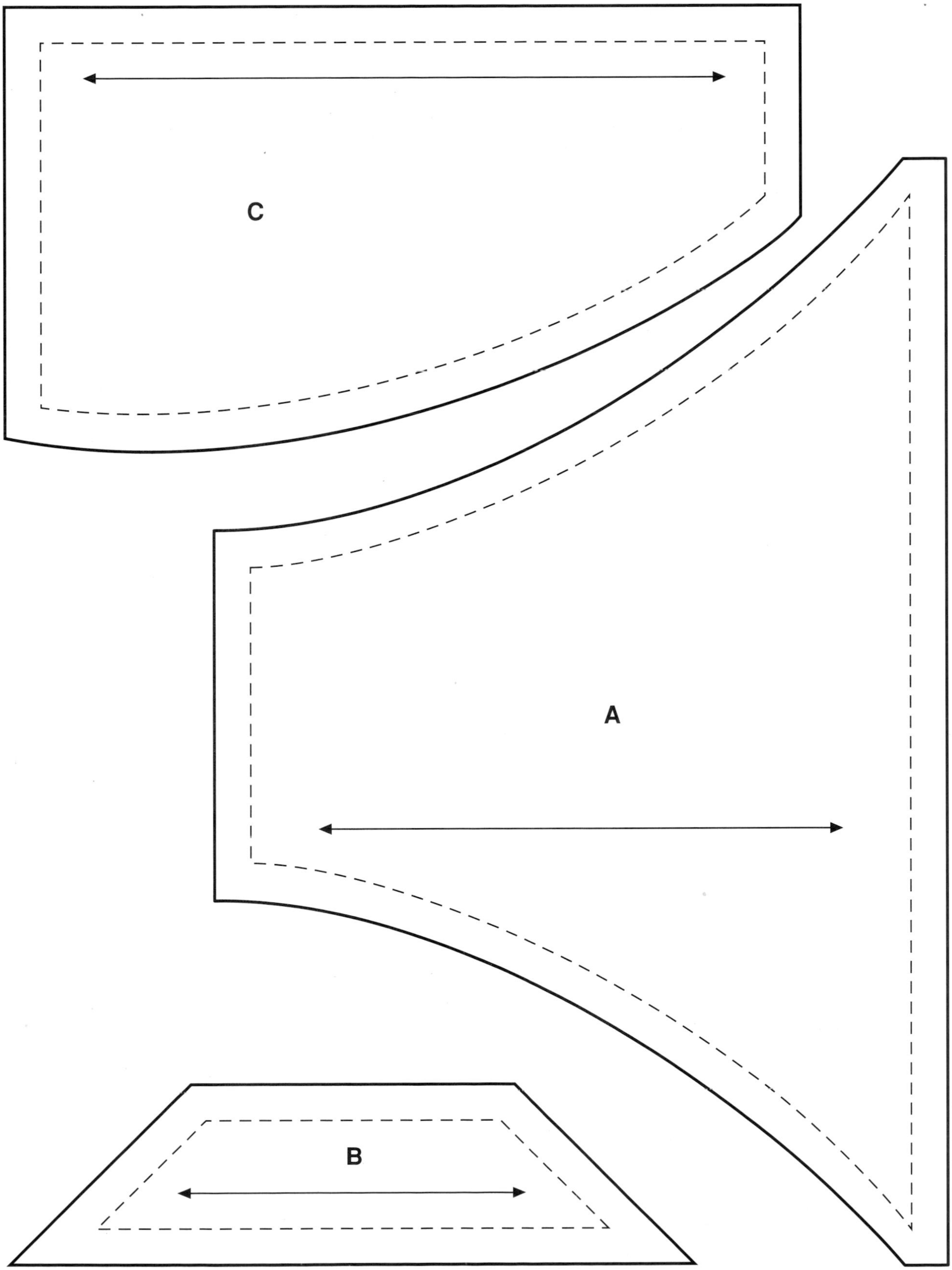

C

A

B

Nectar

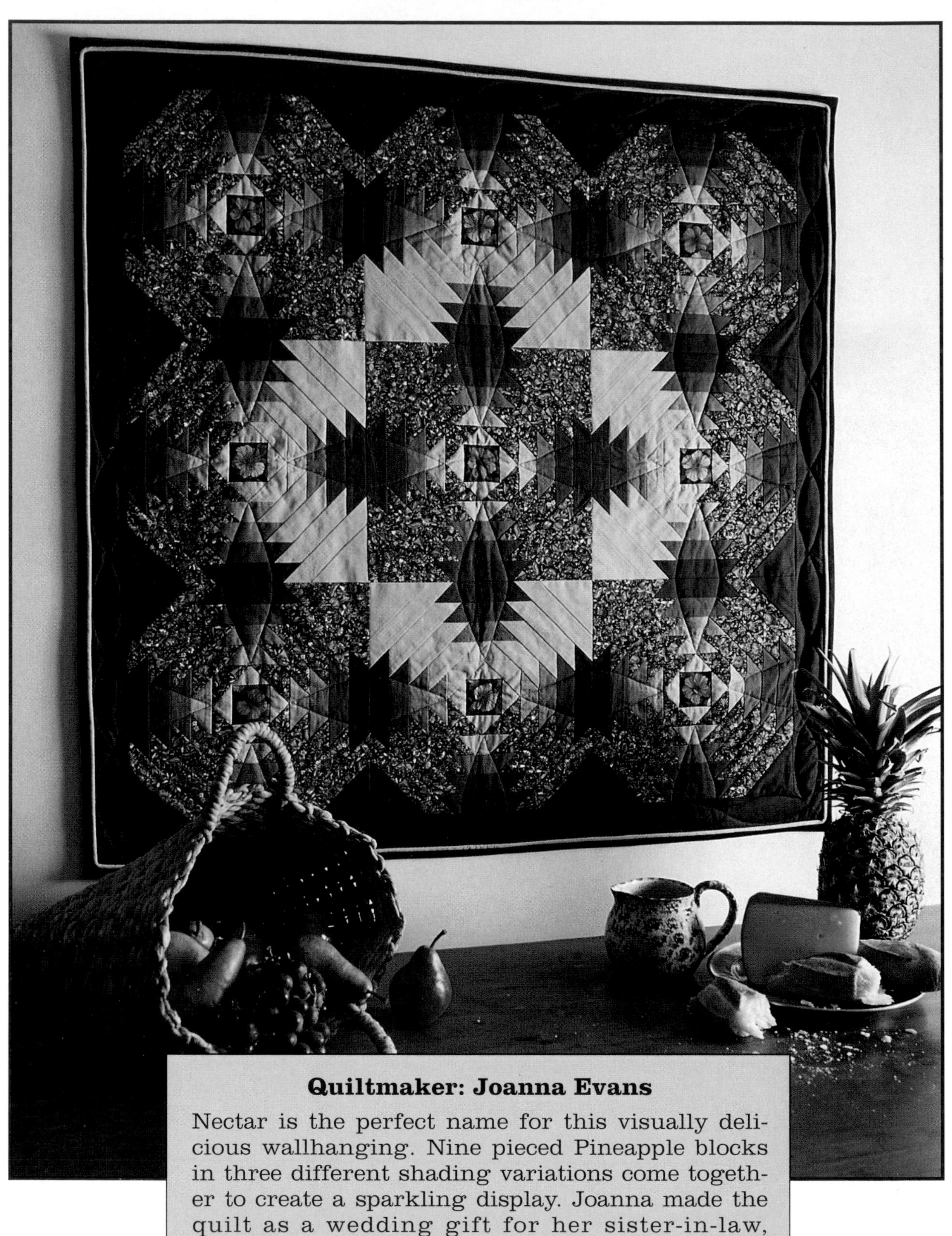

Quiltmaker: Joanna Evans

Nectar is the perfect name for this visually delicious wallhanging. Nine pieced Pineapple blocks in three different shading variations come together to create a sparkling display. Joanna made the quilt as a wedding gift for her sister-in-law, Barbara. Pineapple foundation papers make accurate piecing easy.

Skill Level: Intermediate

Size: Finished quilt is 40 inches square
Finished block is 12 inches square

Fabrics and Supplies

The Pineapple blocks were pieced on paper foundation squares that are printed with the pineapple design. This method results in absolutely accurate patchwork. The printed paper foundation squares are available at quilt shops or through mail-order companies. Or you can make your own paper squares using the pattern on page 60.

- 1¼ yards of blue floral print fabric for blocks
- 1¼ yards of navy blue solid fabric (Blue 5) for blocks, borders, and binding
- ⅞ yard of gold solid fabric for blocks and piping trim
- ¼ yard *each* of four blue solid fabrics. Fabrics should range from very pale blue (Blue 1) to medium dark blue (Blue 4) and coordinate with the navy solid.
- ¼ yard *each* of five purple solid fabrics. Fabrics should range from very pale purple (Purple 1) to very dark purple (Purple 5).
- ⅛ yard of medium- to large-scale blue-and-pink print fabric for block centers
- 1¼ yards of fabric for quilt back
- Crib-size quilt batting (45 × 60 inches)
- Rotary cutter, ruler, and mat
- 4¾ yards of ¼-inch-diameter cord for piping
- Set of nine paper foundation squares for making 12-inch Pineapple blocks. (Available in most quilt shops, or write to: Jane McQuade, Perfectly Simple Paper Patterns, 19 Halsey Drive, Smithfield, RI 02917; or Quilting Techniques, Inc., P.O. Box 7252, Country Club Road, Guilford, NH 03246.)
- Fabric glue stick

Cutting

All measurements include ¼-inch seam allowances. Measurements for the borders are longer than needed; trim them to the exact length when they are added to the quilt top. Instructions given are for quick-cutting the pieces with a rotary cutter and ruler. The number of strips to cut for the blocks is approximate; you may need to cut an additional strip from some fabrics if they are not a full 44 inches wide.

From the blue floral print fabric, cut:
- 8 corner triangles for blocks
  Cut one 4 × 44-inch strip. From the strip, cut four 4-inch squares. Cut each square in half diagonally to make two triangles.
- Sixteen 1¾ × 44-inch strips

From the navy solid (Blue 5), cut:
- Three 1¾ × 44-inch strips
- Four 2½ × 44-inch border strips
- 20 corner triangles for blocks
  Cut one 4 × 44-inch strip. Cut the strip into 4-inch squares. You will need 10 squares. Cut each square in half diagonally to make two triangles.
- Reserve the remaining fabric for binding

From the gold solid fabric, cut:
- 8 corner triangles for blocks
  Cut one 4 × 44-inch strip. From the strip, cut four 4-inch squares. Cut each square in half diagonally to make two triangles.
- Seven 1¾ × 44-inch strips

From Blue 1, cut:
- One 1¾ × 44-inch strip

From each of fabrics Blue 2, 3, and 4 and Purple 1 and 2, cut:
- Two 1¾ × 44-inch strips

From each of fabrics Purple 3 and 4, cut:
- Three 1¾ × 44-inch strips

From Purple 5, cut:
- Four 1¾ × 44-inch strips

From the blue-and-pink print fabric, cut:
- 9 block centers. (A flower is centered in each of the squares on the quilt shown.)
  Cut nine 2¾-inch squares

Piecing the Blocks

If you are making your own foundation papers, use the pattern on page 60. You will need nine 12½-inch-square sheets of white paper. Fold the sheets into quarters and crease to make guidelines. Trace the pattern onto each quadrant of the paper.

If you have purchased foundation papers, follow the block piecing instructions included with them. If your papers did not include instructions, adapt the general guidelines that follow for pinning fabric strips to the *blank* side of the paper foundation and sewing from the *printed* side. This technique ensures accurate piecing.

Pineapple blocks are built from the center outward in rounds of patchwork pieces. In this Pineapple pattern, five rounds of patchwork are added to the center square before the corner triangles are added. Refer to the **Diagram Key** and the diagrams to determine fabric placement. You will need one Block 1 block, four Block 2 blocks, and four Block 3 blocks.

Making the Blocks

Follow the instructions below to make Block 1 for the center of the quilt. Make the Block 2 and Block 3 blocks in the same manner, positioning the different fabrics as indicated in the block diagrams. Refer to the **Diagram Key** for the abbreviations used in the diagrams.

DIAGRAM KEY

Abbreviation	Fabric
CTR	Center
G	Gold
F	Blue floral print
B1 to B5	Blue 1 to Blue 5
P1 to P5	Purple 1 to Purple 5

1. Referring to the **Block 1 Diagram,** position the center 2¾-inch square of print fabric right side up over the center square area on the blank (unprinted) side of the paper foundation. Use a glue stick to lightly secure the square at the four corners.

2. Place a Purple 1 fabric strip right sides together with the center fabric square, aligning the edges. Use a pin to match a point ¼ inch in from one short end of the strip and the corner of the center square printed on the paper. Check the alignment by looking at the printed side of the paper to see that the pin has come through exactly at the corner, and adjust the pin if needed. In a similar manner, pin the strip to the next corner of the center square; trim the excess strip so that ¼ inch extends beyond the pin.

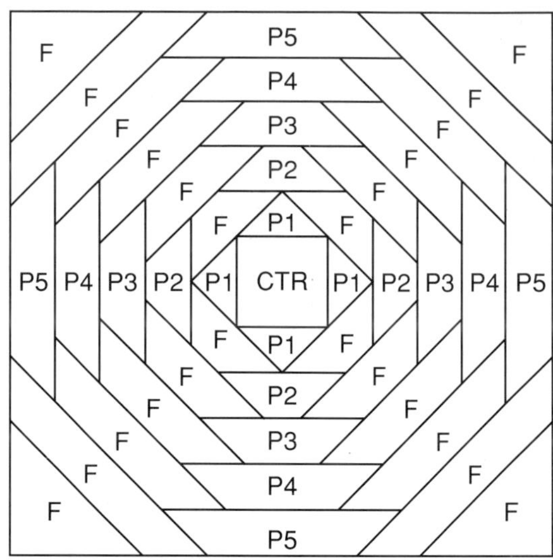

Block 1 Diagram

3. Repeat to pin a second Purple 1 piece to the opposite side of the center square. There will be two strips of the same color pinned in place opposite each other. Both strips should be pinned to the blank (unprinted) side of the paper.

4. Adjust your sewing machine for a short stitch length (12 to 15 stitches per inch). Sewing will be done from the *printed* side of the paper with the fabric pinned to the blank underneath side. This enables you to clearly see the seam line you will be stitching.

5. With the printed side of the paper facing up, attach the first strip by stitching from the first pin to the second pin exactly on the printed line. Repeat to attach the strip on the opposite side of the square.

6. Open out the strips and finger press the seams. To hold the strips in place as you sew, lightly adhere them to the blank side of the paper with a glue stick.

7. With the blank side of the paper facing you, fold the paper along the diagonal line at one end of a strip. Using the folded paper as a guide, trim the excess strip at an angle. Repeat to trim all strip ends.

8. In a similar manner, add Purple 1 strips to the remaining two sides of the center square.

9. Use blue floral print fabric to complete round 1 by repeating the pinning, stitching, finger-pressing, and trimming processes.

10. To begin round 2, stitch Purple 2 pieces, positioning them as indicated in the **Block 1 Diagram.** Complete round 2 by adding floral print pieces.

11. Referring to the diagram, continue in this manner until five rounds of patchwork have been added.

12. To complete the block, pin a blue floral corner triangle to one corner of the block. Begin your seam ¼ inch before the printed corner line and extend it ¼ inch beyond the corner line at the end of the seam. Repeat for the remaining corners.

13. Trim the seam allowance on the corner triangles. Lightly glue the corner triangles in place. Leave the paper attached to the wrong side of the block.

14. In the same manner, make four Block 2 blocks, referring to the **Block 2 Diagram** for correct fabric placement.

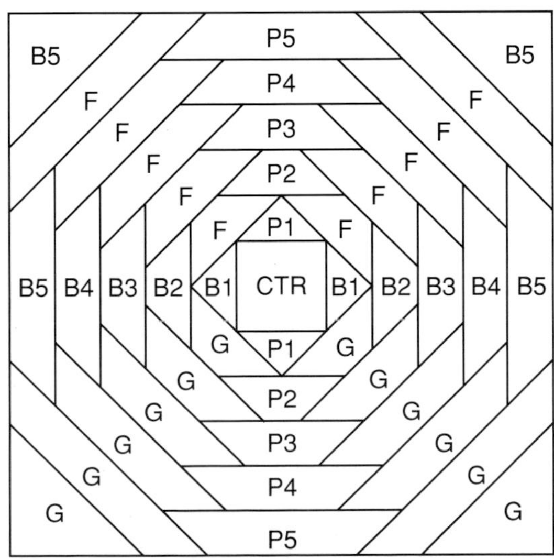

Block 2 Diagram

15. Referring to the **Block 3 Diagram** for fabric placement, make four Block 3 blocks.

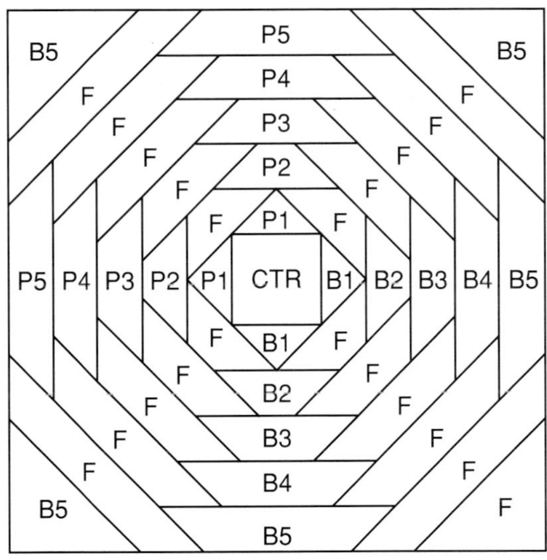

Block 3 Diagram

Assembling the Quilt Top

1. Referring to the photograph on page 56, lay out the nine Pineapple blocks.

2. Join the blocks in three rows with three blocks in each row. To join two blocks, pin them fabric sides together. Use pins to match up the block corners and seam lines. Stitch along the printed seam line.

3. Join the rows.

4. Center and pin a 2½ × 44-inch navy border strip to all four sides of the quilt top. Use the printed guidelines on the blocks as the guideline for your stitching. Miter the border corners. Refer to page 159 for suggestions on how to add borders and miter the border corners.

5. Carefully tear away the paper foundation from the wrong side of the blocks.

Quilting and Finishing

1. Layer the quilt back, batting, and quilt top; baste.

2. Quilt as desired.

3. Using a dressmaker's tape, measure around your piping cord to determine the width to cut the fabric strips to cover the cording. The strips should be wide enough to allow for seam allowances; approximately 1¾ inches should be right. Cut and piece together gold strips to make a strip long enough to cover the cording.

4. Using a zipper foot, encase the cording in the gold strip.

5. Align the raw edges of the cording fabric with the edge of the quilt top. Sewing through all layers, baste the cording to the quilt, overlapping the ends of the cording where they meet.

6. From the binding fabric, make approximately 180 inches of French-fold binding. See page 164 for suggested binding widths and instructions on making and attaching binding.

7. Using a zipper foot, sew the binding to the quilt top, sewing close to the cording. Trim the excess batting and backing, and hand finish the binding on the back side of the quilt.

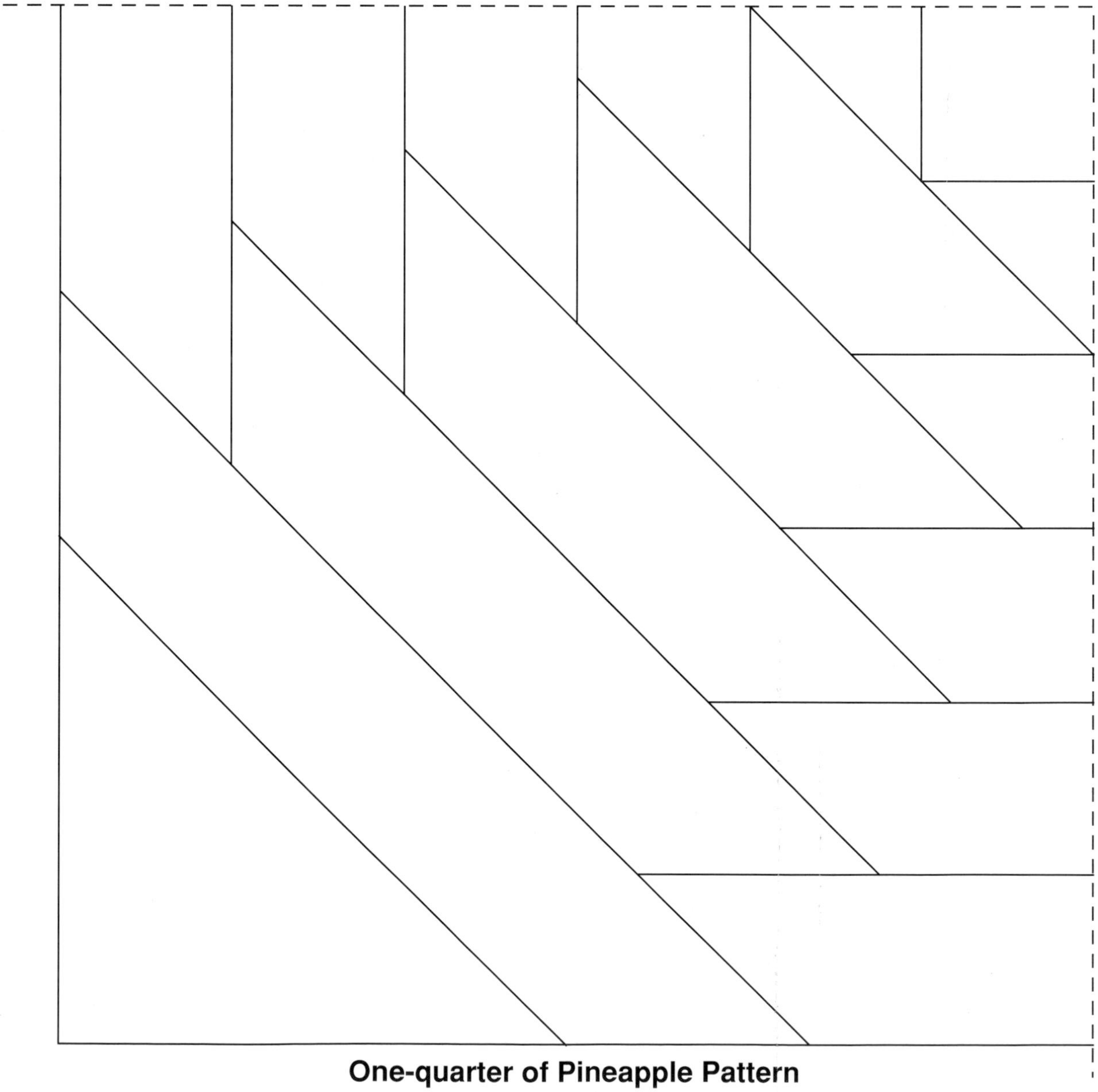

One-quarter of Pineapple Pattern

Brick Wall

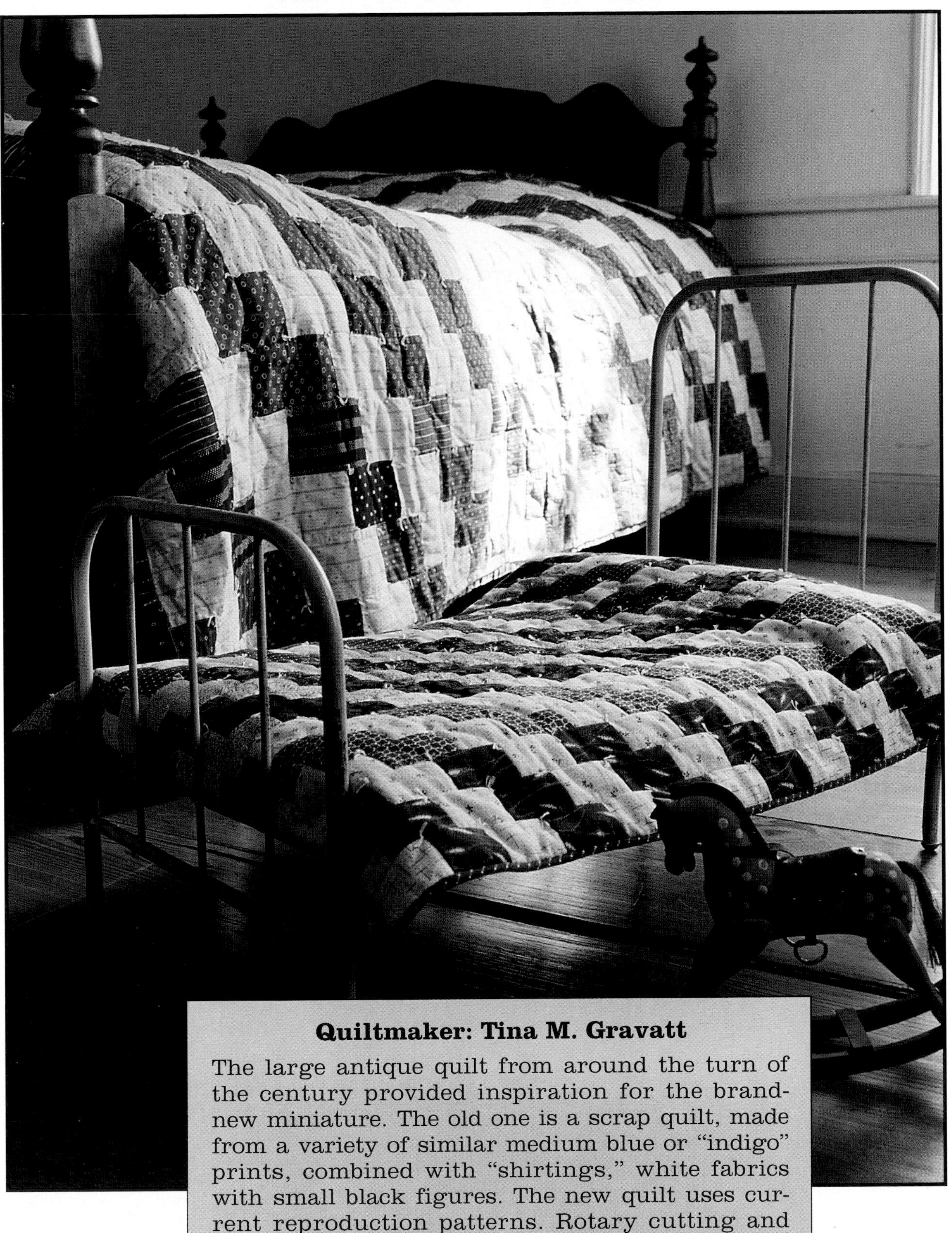

Quiltmaker: Tina M. Gravatt

The large antique quilt from around the turn of the century provided inspiration for the brand-new miniature. The old one is a scrap quilt, made from a variety of similar medium blue or "indigo" prints, combined with "shirtings," white fabrics with small black figures. The new quilt uses current reproduction patterns. Rotary cutting and strip piecing make either project quick and easy to sew. Both are tied rather than quilted.

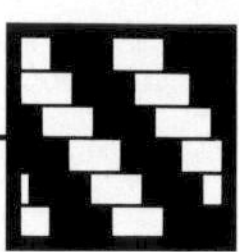

Skill Level: Easy

Size: Finished large quilt is 71½ × 87½ inches

Finished bricks are 2¾ × 5 inches
Finished miniature quilt is 18 × 25⅜ inches
Finished bricks are 1 × 1¾ inches

Fabrics and Supplies for Large Quilt

- ½ yard *each* of seven medium blue print fabrics for patchwork
- ½ yard *each* of seven white-and-black print fabrics for patchwork
- 5½ yards of fabric for quilt back
- ¾ yard of fabric for binding
- Full-size quilt batting (81 × 96 inches)
- Rotary cutter, ruler, and mat
- Cotton or synthetic yarn for tying
- Darning needle

Cutting

All measurements include ¼-inch seam allowances. Instructions given are for quick-cutting the strips for strip piecing.

From each of the blue print fabrics, cut:

- Three 5½ × 44-inch strips

From each of the white-and-black print fabrics, cut:

- Three 5½ × 44-inch strips

Making the Quilt

1. Sew strips together as shown in **Diagram 1,** using one blue print and one white-and-black print strip per set. Make a total of 21 strip sets. Press seams toward the blue fabric strips.

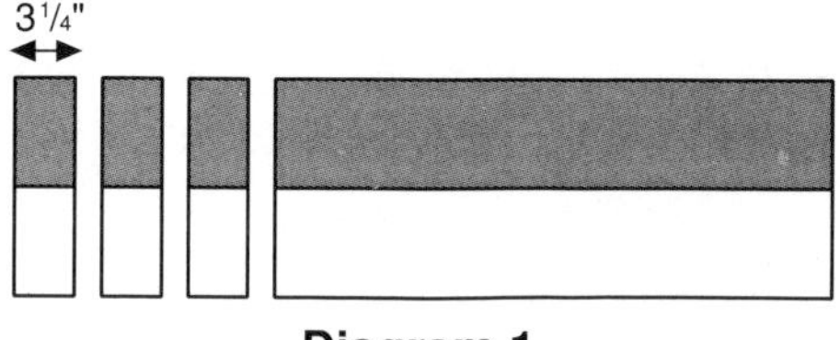

Diagram 1

2. Cut 3¼-inch-wide segments from the strip sets, as shown in the diagram. You should be able to cut 12 or 13 segments from each strip set. You will need a total of 234 segments.

3. Join the cut segments end to end to make 26 long strips of alternating blue and white rectangles, with 9 segments per strip. In the miniature quilt, each long strip is made up of only one blue fabric. In the antique, however, the use of blue fabrics is more random. Decide on the effect you want to create, and piece the strips and segments accordingly.

4. Referring to the **Quilt Diagram** and the photo on page 61, lay out the 26 strips, offsetting the matching color brick rectangles by one-half rectangle as shown. (The heavy lines on the quilt diagram show the layout of the miniature quilt.) Turn strips end for end as needed to position blue or white segments properly. The top and bottom edges of the quilt will be uneven.

5. Before joining the long strips, make positioning marks on the wrong side as described in

Quilt Diagram

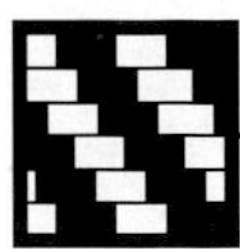

"Making Positioning Marks for Joining Strips" on this page. This ensures that the rectangles will be offset evenly. Join the rows, aligning the positioning marks with the seams. Press the seams in one direction.

6. Trim the uneven top and bottom edges of the quilt.

Finishing

1. Cut the backing fabric into two equal 99-inch lengths and trim the selvages. Divide one piece in half lengthwise. Sew a half panel to each side of the full panel. Press seams away from the center panel.

2. Layer the backing, batting, and quilt top. Use a darning needle and cotton yarn to make ties at corners of seams as desired. See "How to Tie a Comforter" on page 64 for complete directions.

3. From the binding fabric, make approximately 350 inches of French-fold binding. See page 164 for suggested binding widths and instructions on making and attaching binding.

4. Sew the binding to the quilt top. Trim the excess batting and backing, and hand finish the binding on the back side of the quilt.

Fabrics and Supplies for Miniature Quilt

- Six 2¼ × 44-inch medium blue print fabric strips
- Six 2¼ × 44-inch white-and-black print fabric strips
- 1 yard of fabric for quilt back and binding
- Quilt batting, larger than 18 × 25⅜ inches
- Rotary cutter, ruler, and mat
- Cotton or synthetic yarn for tying
- Darning needle

Making the Quilt

1. Sew strips together as shown in **Diagram 2,** using one blue and one white-and-black strip per set. Make a total of 6 strip sets. Press the seams toward the blue fabric strip.

MAKING POSITIONING MARKS FOR JOINING STRIPS

The long strips of rectangular "bricks" are offset by one-half brick from row to row. Before joining rows, make positioning indicators on the wrong side of the fabric at the middle of the white-and-black bricks, as shown in the diagram.

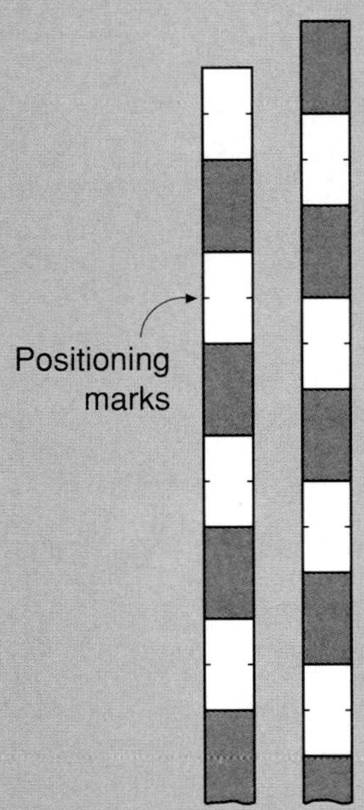

Make indicators either by either measuring and making pencil marks or by folding bricks and making crease marks. If measuring, for the large quilt, lightly mark the bricks 2½ inches away from seams; for the miniature, mark ⅞ inch from seams. Pin rows together before joining them, aligning the marks with the sewn seams to stagger the bricks exactly one-half brick from row to row. ♦

2. Cut 1½-inch-wide segments from the strip sets, as shown in the diagram. You will need 24 segments from each strip set, for a total of 144 segments.

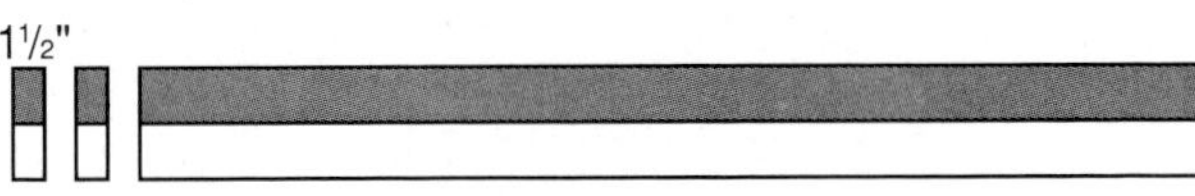

Diagram 2

3. Join the cut segments end to end to make 18 long strips of alternating blue and white rectangles, with 8 segments per strip. In the miniature quilt, only one color brick is used in each strip, and the three same-color strips are placed together in the layout.

4. Referring to the **Quilt Diagram** and the photo on page 61, lay out the 18 strips, offsetting the matching color brick rectangles by one-half rectangle as shown. The heavy lines on the diagram show the layout for the miniature quilt. Turn strips end for end as needed to position blue or white segments properly. The top and bottom edges of the quilt will be uneven.

5. Before joining the long strips, make positioning marks on the wrong side as described in "Making Positioning Marks for Joining Strips" on page 63. This ensures that the segments will be offset evenly. Join the rows, aligning the offset marks with seams. Press the seams in one direction.

6. Trim the uneven top and bottom edges of the quilt.

Finishing

1. Cut a 22 × 30-inch piece of backing fabric.

2. Layer the backing, batting, and quilt top. Use a darning needle and yarn to make ties at corners of seams as desired. See "How to Tie a Comforter" on this page for complete directions.

3. From the binding fabric, make approximately 100 inches of French-fold binding. See page 164 for suggested binding widths and instructions on making and attaching binding.

4. Sew the binding to the quilt top. Trim the excess batting and backing, and hand finish the binding on the back side of the quilt.

HOW TO TIE A COMFORTER

For a tied comforter, choose a stable, synthetic batting designed for tying. Many cotton batts must be quilted at close intervals or the filler will wad up when laundered. For tied comforters, you can use a high-loft batt that provides lots of warmth. Follow the steps below to make sturdy ties.

1. Thread a darning needle with a long length of yarn; don't knot the end. Experiment to see what length yarn works best for you.
2. Make a small stitch at the position for a tie. Be sure the stitch goes through all layers.
3. Pull up the yarn, leaving a 3- to 4-inch-long tail. Do not cut the yarn.
4. Move to the next tie position and make another stitch. Leave a long, loose stitch between the tie positions. Continue to make small stitches at tie positions, rethreading the needle as necessary.
5. Clip the middle of the long, loose stitches.
6. Tie a square knot. Begin by holding the two ends of the yarn in your right and left hands. Wrap the right yarn tail around the left; tighten the half-knot. Complete the knot by wrapping the left tail around the right, as shown in **Diagram 1.** Tighten the knot.

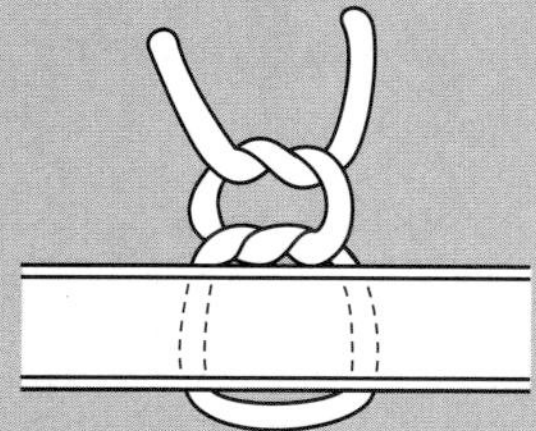

Diagram 1

7. Gather the yarn tails into one hand and clip to the desired length.

Note: If you want a full-looking tie, cut one or two 6-inch-long pieces of yarn and lay them atop the small stitch at each position after the first half of the knot is tied. See **Diagram 2.** Treat the original yarn ends and the added ends as one when completing the square knot, as shown in the diagram. ♦

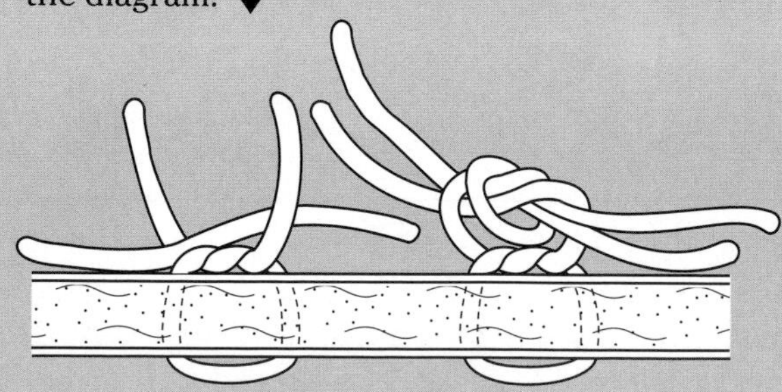

Diagram 2

A Dozen Roses for You

Quiltmaker: Marty Freed

This contemporary appliqué masterpiece is Marty's first appliqué quilt. It follows in the tradition of the red and green appliqué quilts of the mid-nineteenth century. Inspired by the work of Rose Kretsinger, the nine elegant blocks overflow with roses, rosebuds, and woven vines. The quilt is framed with a formal swag and bud border with bows at the border corners.

Skill Level: Intermediate

Size: Finished quilt is 104¾ inches square
Finished block is 20 inches square

Fabrics and Supplies

- 9¼ yards of off-white fabric for blocks, setting squares, side setting triangles, corner setting triangles, and borders
- 3 yards of burgundy fabric for roses, buds, border corners, and binding
- 2½ yards of dark green fabric for vines, leaves, swags, and bows
- 2 yards of medium pink fabric for roses, swags, and bows
- 1 yard of light green fabric for vines
- ½ yard of yellow fabric for rose centers
- ½ yard of light pink fabric for roses and bud centers
- 9¾ yards of fabric for quilt back
- King-size quilt batting (120 inches square)
- Rotary cutter, ruler, and mat
- Plastic-coated freezer paper or template plastic
- Tracing paper
- Black permanent marking pen

Cutting

All measurements include ¼-inch seam allowances. Measurements for the borders are longer than needed; trim them to the exact length when they are added to the quilt top. Instructions given are for quick-cutting the blocks and borders with a rotary cutter and ruler. Read through the tips in "Hand Appliqué" beginning on page 156, and choose the appliqué method you wish for the blocks and borders. Make plastic templates to mark and cut the appliqué pieces or make freezer paper templates. Tips for making and using traditional templates are on page 153.

Patterns for the appliqué pieces begin on page 69. The patterns are finished size; add seam allowances when you cut the pieces from fabric. Using tracing paper, expand the partial patterns for the border swag to full size. For the border corner, trace one pattern A, one pattern B, and one pattern B reverse to create the full corner pattern. Trace the leaf pattern. Trace the rose, bud, and border bud patterns, making a separate template for each of the numbered flower pieces and transferring the numbers to the templates. These numbers indicate the order in which the pieces are appliquéd. In the same manner, trace and label the pattern pieces for the bow.

Before You Begin

To prepare the off-white fabric, first cut a 108-inch-long piece.

From the 108-inch piece of off-white fabric, cut:

- Four 10½ × 108-inch borders

From the remaining off-white fabric, cut:

- Nine 21-inch squares for the appliqué blocks. (Blocks will be trimmed to 20½ inches after the appliqué is complete.)
- Four 20½-inch setting squares
- 8 side setting triangles

  Cut two 29½-inch squares. Cut each square in half diagonally in both directions to make four triangles.
- 4 corner setting triangles

  Cut two 15-inch squares. Cut each square in half diagonally to make two triangles.

From the burgundy fabric, cut:

- 4 border corners
- 72 *each* of pieces R5 and R6 for the roses
- 36 *each* of pieces B1, B3, and B4 for the block buds
- 16 *each* of BB1, BB3, and BB4 for the border buds
- Reserve the remaining fabric for binding

From the dark green fabric, cut:

- Two 20-inch squares to make continuous bias for the vines
- 20 of Swag 1
- 72 leaves
- 4 *each* of Bow 1 and Bow 3
- 4 *each* of Bow 4 and Bow 5
- 4 *each* of Bow 4 reverse and Bow 5 reverse

From the medium pink fabric, cut:

- 20 of Swag 2
- 72 *each* of R1 and R4 for the roses
- 8 of Bow 2

From the light green fabric, cut:
- Two 20-inch squares to make continuous bias for the vines

From the yellow fabric, cut:
- 72 of R3 for the roses

From the light pink fabric, cut:
- 72 of R2 for the roses
- 36 of B2 for the block buds
- 16 of BB2 for the border buds

Preparing the Bias for the Vines

1. Read through the instructions on page 164 for making continuous bias from a square. From each 20-inch square of dark green and light green fabric, cut 1-inch-wide bias. Each square will make a strip of bias approximately 400 inches long.

2. Following the instructions on page 157 for "Making Bias Strips for Stems and Vines," press each long bias strip in thirds. You will need approximately 72 inches of prepared bias for each of the nine blocks.

Appliquéing the Blocks

1. Make a master pattern of the appliqué design to use as a guide for positioning the appliqué pieces on the background blocks. Fold a sheet of tracing paper larger than 20 inches square in half both ways. You will trace one-quarter of the design in each quadrant of the tracing paper to make a full-size drawing of the block, as shown in the **Block Diagram.** The full-size design is printed in two sections: pattern A on page 70 and pattern B on page 71. Aligning the crease lines on the paper with the dotted lines on the pattern, trace **Block Appliqué Pattern A** in one inner corner of the paper. Carefully align it with **Block Appliqué Pattern B** and trace the remainder of the design. Darken the pattern outlines with a permanent marking pen. Repeat in each quadrant of the paper.

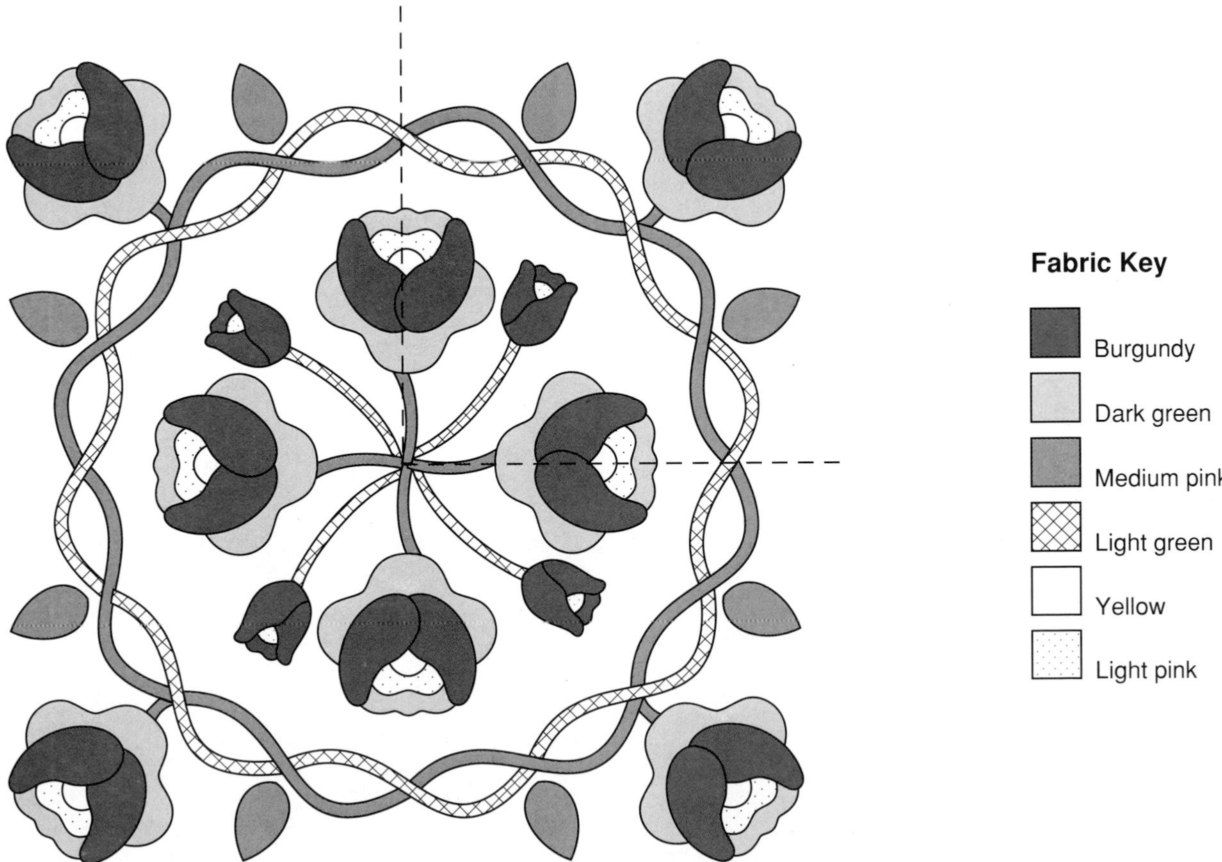

Block Diagram

2. To make one block, begin by folding a 21-inch off-white fabric square in half vertically, horizontally, and diagonally in both directions, and lightly crease. Center the master appliqué pattern under the fabric square, and use a pencil or tailor's chalk to lightly trace the appliqué outlines onto the fabric. (The darkened pen lines should show through the fabric.)

3. Cut two 8-inch-long pieces of light green bias for the bud stems. Position and appliqué these pieces across the center of the block.

4. Position and appliqué the four buds by adding and stitching the pieces in the order indicated on the appliqué patterns.

5. Cut two 4½-inch-long pieces of dark green bias for the flower stems. Position and appliqué these pieces across the center of the block on top of the bud stems.

6. Appliqué the four center roses by adding and stitching the pieces in the order indicated on **Block Appliqué Pattern B.**

7. For the woven vine wreath, cut a bias strip approximately 54 inches long from both the light green and dark green prepared bias. With a running stitch, hand baste the bias strips to the wreath outline, weaving the two colors of bias as you work. Trim off any excess bias, and use the short pieces as stems to connect the outer roses to the vine wreath. Appliqué the bias for the wreath and stems; remove the basting stitches.

8. Position and appliqué the four outer roses by adding and stitching the pieces in the order indicated on the patterns.

9. Position and appliqué eight dark green leaves.

10. When the appliqué is complete, trim any excess off-white background fabric so that the block measures 20½ inches including seam allowances.

11. Repeat to make a total of nine blocks.

Assembling the Quilt Top

1. Referring to the photograph on page 65, lay out the appliqué blocks on point in three rows with three blocks in each row. Add setting squares in the openings between blocks. Position side setting triangles and corner setting triangles around the outer edges.

2. Sew the quilt top together in diagonal rows. Press the seams toward the setting squares and triangles. Join the rows.

Appliquéing and Adding the Borders

1. Using the Swag 1 template, lightly mark positioning guidelines for the five swags along each border, allowing approximately 1 inch between swags. Match the center of the middle swag to the center of the border strip; this ensures that the swags at each end are an equal distance from the ends of the strips. The borders will be trimmed to length in a later step.

2. Position and appliqué all Swag 1 and Swag 2 pieces.

3. For each border bud, position and appliqué the pieces in the order indicated on the **Border Bud Appliqué Pattern.** Appliqué border buds between the swags along the borders.

4. Measure the quilt top (approximately 85¼ inches); cut two borders to this length. Sew the borders to opposite sides of the quilt top.

5. Measure the quilt top including the added borders (approximately 105¼ inches); cut the two remaining borders to this length. Sew the borders to the quilt top.

6. Use the Bow 1 template to mark positioning guidelines for a bow at each border corner.

7. Appliqué a bow at each border corner. Position and appliqué the pieces in the order indicated on the patterns.

8. Appliqué the border corner pieces in position.

Quilting and Finishing

1. Mark quilting designs. On the quilt shown, the setting squares repeat the appliqué design in quilting stitches. Use the appliqué master pattern to trace the appliqué design onto the squares.

The side setting triangles feature the bow design as the quilting design. Trace the bow design on paper, and darken the pattern lines with a permanent marker. Slide the darkened paper pattern under each side setting triangle, and trace the design onto the right side of the fabric.

To personalize her quilt, the quiltmaker traced the hand outline of each person in her family to create the quilting designs for the corner setting triangles. She quilted a heart within each palm and stitched the family member's name.

The borders are quilted with parallel lines spaced 1½ inches apart. All background areas of the blocks and setting pieces are quilted with a diagonal grid of 1-inch squares.

2. Divide the backing fabric into three equal 117-inch lengths. Trim the selvages and sew the pieces together. Layer the quilt back, batting, and top; baste. Trim so that the back is at least 3 inches larger than the quilt top on all sides.

3. Quilt in the ditch around all the appliqué pieces. Quilt all marked designs.

4. From the remaining burgundy fabric, make approximately 430 inches of French-fold binding. See page 164 for suggested binding widths and instructions on making and attaching binding.

5. Sew the binding to the quilt top. Trim the excess batting and backing, and hand finish the binding on the back side of the quilt.

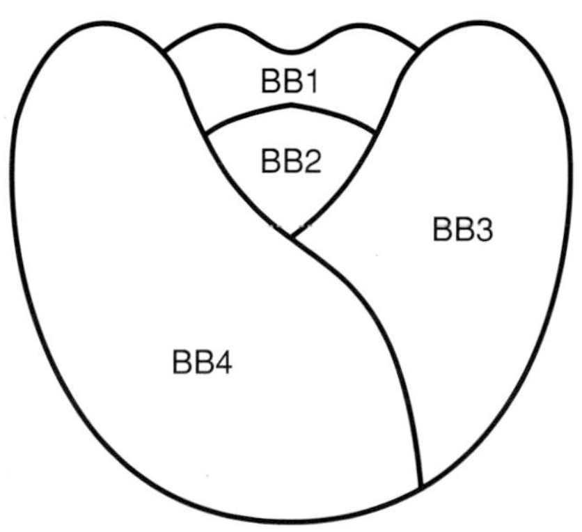

Border Bud Appliqué Pattern

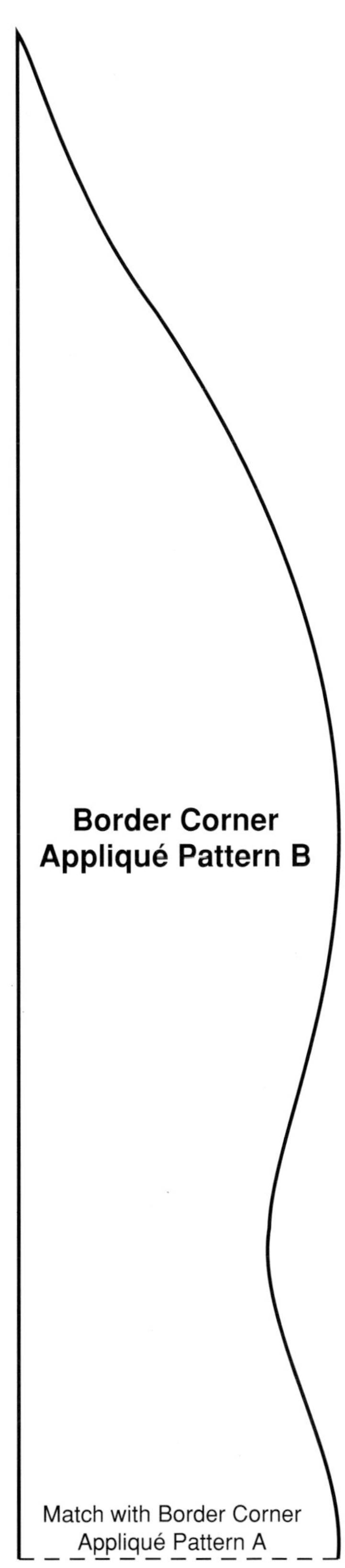

Border Corner Appliqué Pattern B

Match with Block Appliqué Pattern B

Block Appliqué Pattern A

Match with Block Appliqué Pattern B
to complete one-quarter of the block pattern

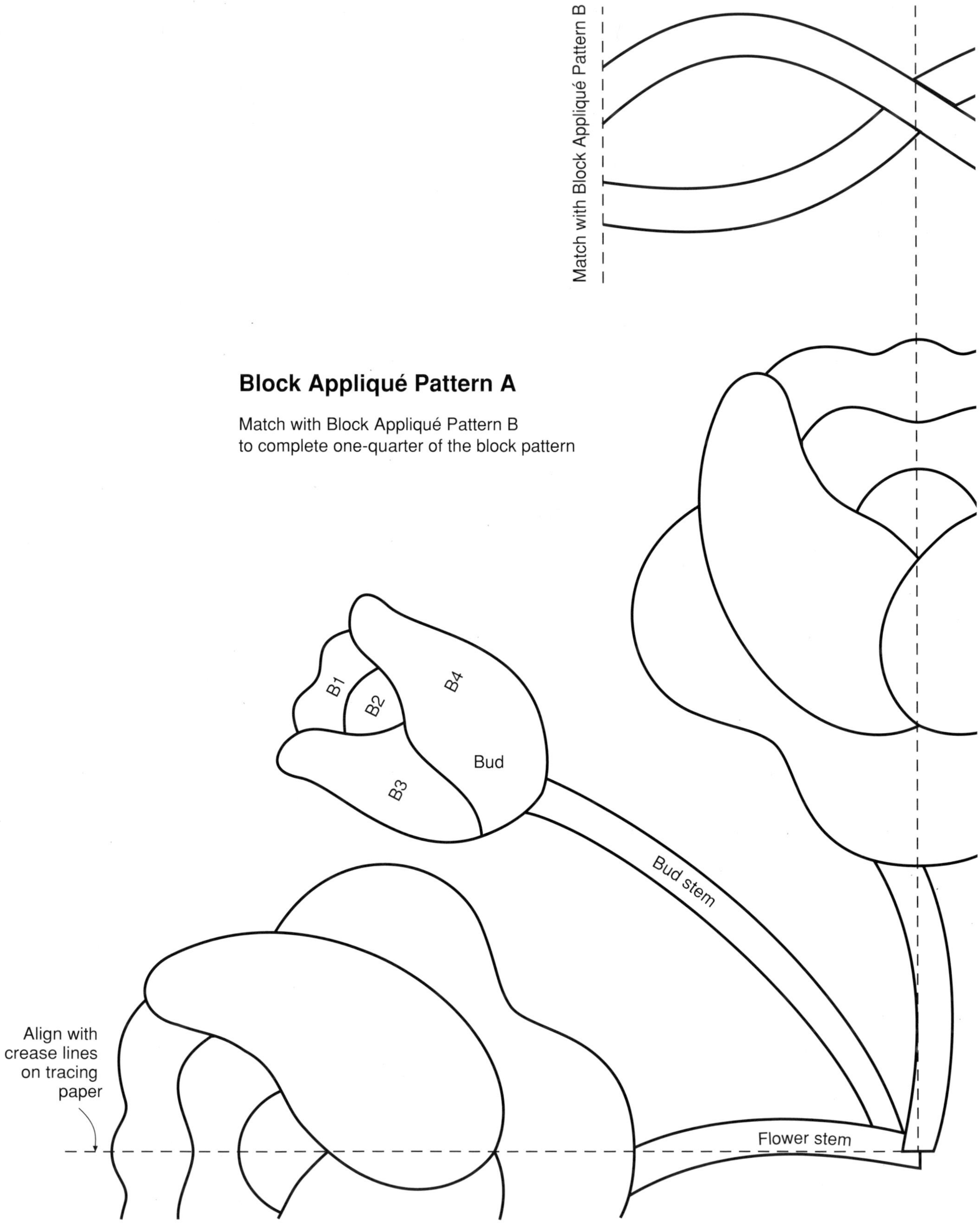

B1

B2

B4

B3

Bud

Bud stem

Align with crease lines on tracing paper

Flower stem

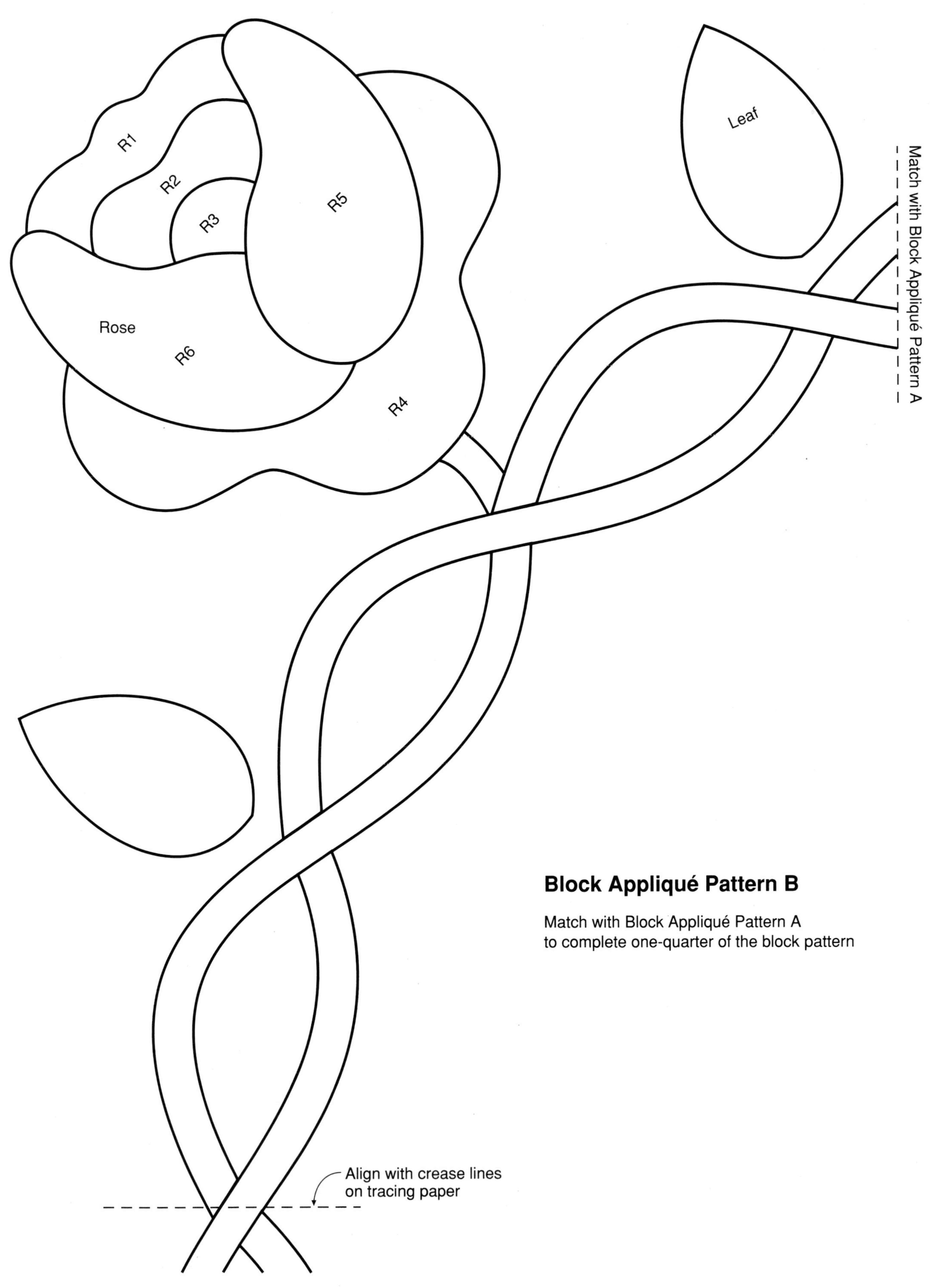

Block Appliqué Pattern B

Match with Block Appliqué Pattern A
to complete one-quarter of the block pattern

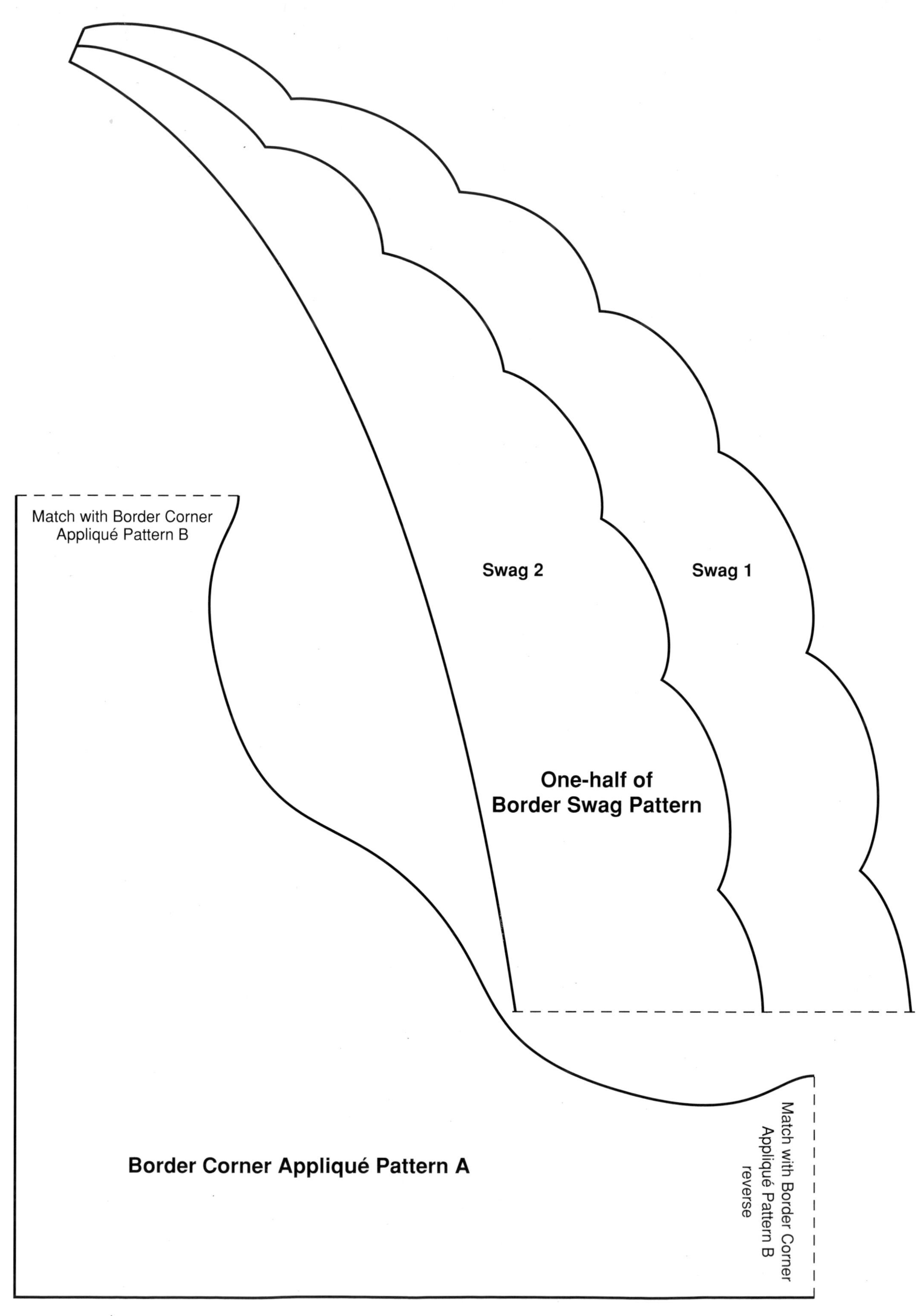
Match with Border Corner
Appliqué Pattern B
Swag 2
Swag 1
One-half of
Border Swag Pattern
Border Corner Appliqué Pattern A
Match with Border Corner
Appliqué Pattern B
reverse

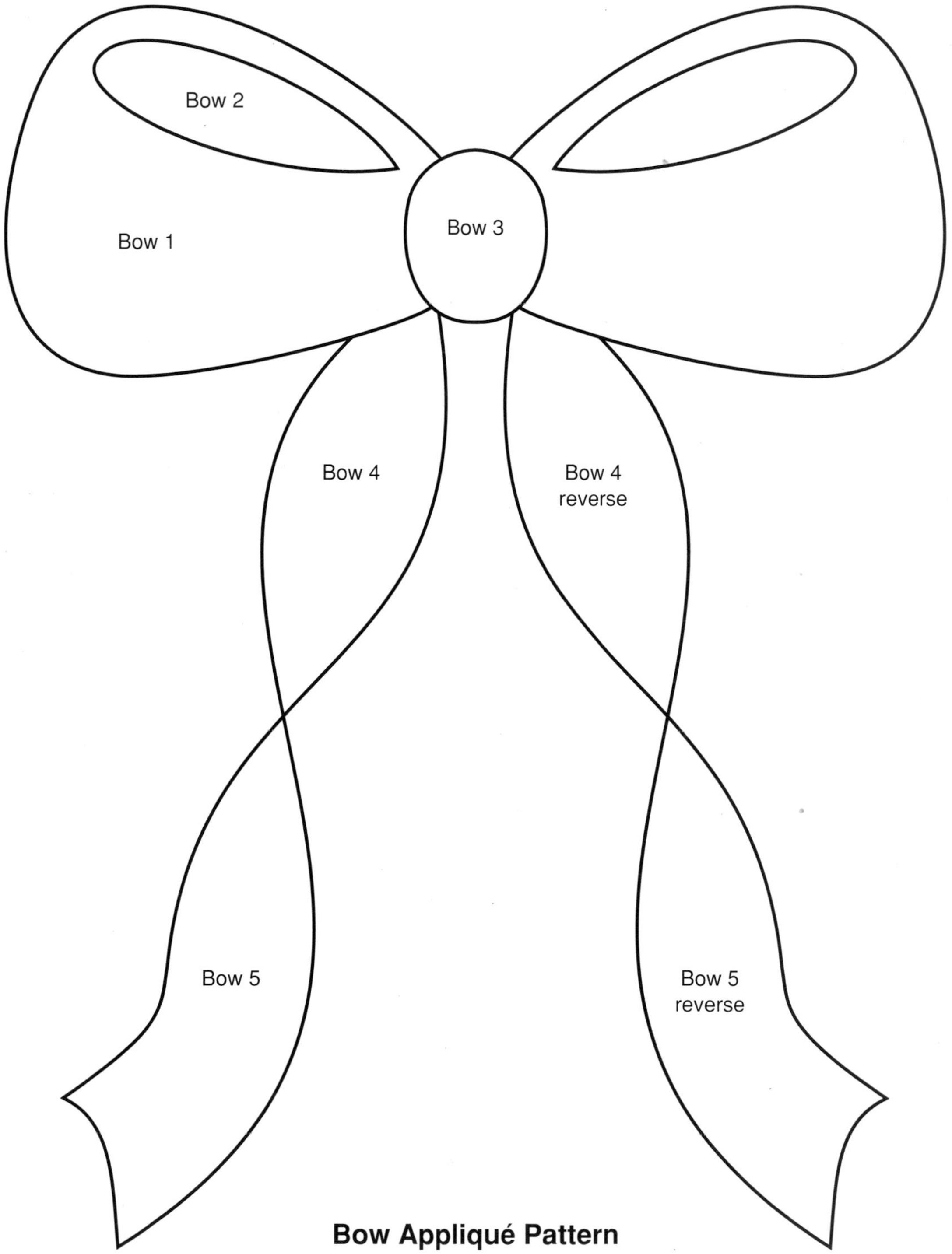

Bow Appliqué Pattern

Special Feature

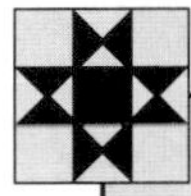

SCRAP QUILTS

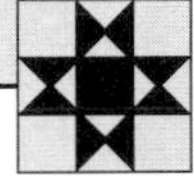

Plaid Spools

Quiltmaker: Kim Baird

A delightful mixture of plaid, print, and solid fabrics works with great success in this bright quilt, perfect for the wall of any dedicated quilter's sewing room. Whether you piece the blocks by hand, as Kim did, or by machine, you'll find the technique given for making corner holes in templates and pivot points on fabric pieces a surefire way to achieve crisp corners for set-in pieces.

Skill Level: Intermediate

Size: Finished quilt is 40 × 44 inches
Finished block is 4 ½ inches square

Fabrics and Supplies

A different plaid fabric was used for each of the 56 blocks in the quilt shown. In approximately half of the blocks, the center A square matches the plaid used for the spool; in the remaining blocks, a solid or print was used for the center square. Many of the solid fabrics used for the background, such as the dark gold, bright yellow gold, bright yellow, and light yellow, were used more than once. When selecting fabrics for each block, choose a plaid and a solid that contrast well with each other. The yardage amounts listed below are generous estimates; only a small amount of fabric is needed for each block.

- ½ yard of plaid fabric for outer border
- ¼ yard of dark green solid fabric for inner border
- 1 ½ yards *total* of assorted solid-color fabrics (dark gold, bright yellow gold, bright yellow, and light yellow) for block background
- Scraps (approximately 6 ½ inches square) of 56 different plaid fabrics for blocks
- Scraps (approximately 2 ½ inches square) of several medium-to-dark solids (olive, brown, navy, rust, teal, royal blue, black, and green) for center A squares on some blocks (optional)
- 1 ½ yards of fabric for quilt back
- ½ yard of solid tan fabric for binding
- Crib-size quilt batting (45 × 60 inches)
- Rotary cutter, ruler, and mat

Cutting

Make templates for A and B using the patterns on pages 78–79. Use a sewing machine needle to make holes in the templates at the corner dots shown on the patterns. Mark around the templates on the wrong side of the fabric; mark the dots on the fabric through the corner holes. The dots will make setting-in the pieces easier.

Instructions given are for quick-cutting the border strips with a rotary cutter and ruler. Border strips will be slightly longer than needed; trim them to the exact length when they are added to the quilt top.

From the plaid border fabric, cut:
- Four 3 ½ × 44-inch strips for outer borders

From the dark green solid fabric, cut:
- Four 1 ¾ × 44-inch strips for inner borders

From the various yellow and gold fabrics, cut:
- 56 pairs of matching B pieces

From the 56 plaid fabrics, cut:
- Two B pieces from each fabric
- 1 A square to match the B pieces for approximately half of the blocks. (For added interest, cut some of the A squares on the bias rather than the straight of grain.)

From the medium and dark solid fabrics, cut:
- A squares for the remaining blocks

Piecing the Blocks

1. For each block, lay out two matching plaid B pieces, a center A square that either matches or contrasts with the plaid B pieces, and two matching solid color B pieces, as shown in the **Block Diagram.**

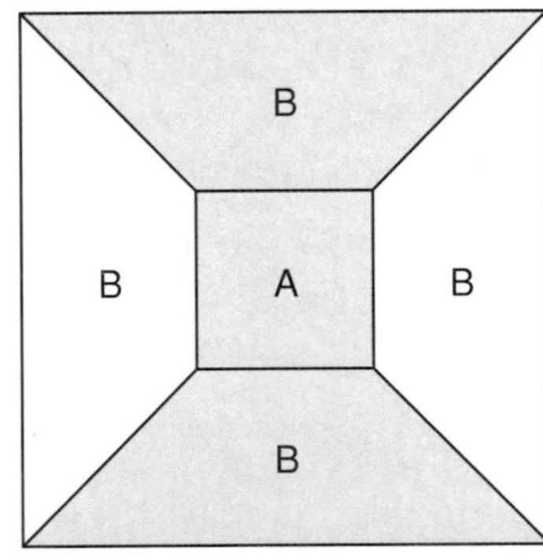

Block Diagram

2. Pin a plaid B piece to one side of the A square, pin-matching at the marked dots. Start stitching at one dot and continue to the end dot, backstitching at the beginning and end of the seam. Do not sew into the seam allowance at either end. In the same manner, pin and join the other plaid B piece to the opposite side of the square.

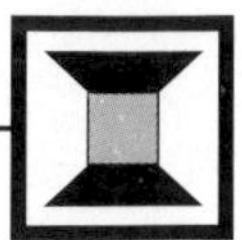

3. Set in each of the two solid B pieces by sewing three separate seams, as indicated in **Diagram 1.** Begin by pin-matching one side of a solid B piece to the adjacent side of the plaid B piece. Stitch from the outside raw edge to the inner dot, backstitching at the beginning and end of the seam; do not stitch into the seam allowance. Pin-match the middle side of the solid B piece to the A square, and stitch from dot to dot. Pin and sew the third seam, stitching from the inner dot to the outside raw edge. Repeat for the other solid B piece. Press the seams away from the center square.

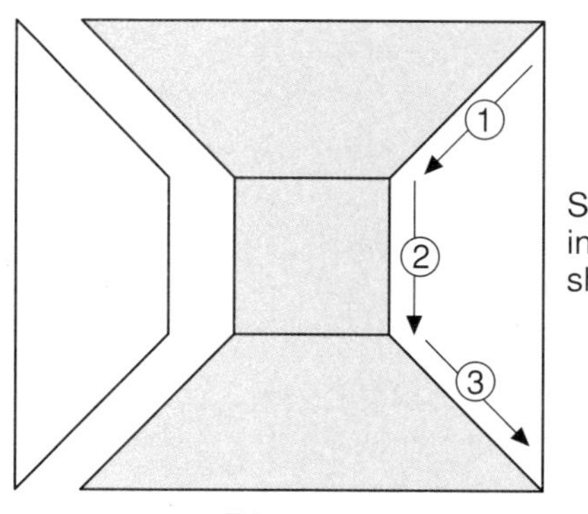

Diagram 1

4. Repeat in this manner to make a total of 56 blocks.

Assembling the Quilt Top

1. Referring to the **Quilt Diagram,** lay out the 56 completed blocks in eight horizontal rows of seven blocks per row. Alternate the direction of the plaid spools from block to block as shown.

2. Join the blocks into rows. Press the seams in alternate directions from row to row. Join the rows.

3. Measure the length of the quilt top (approximately 36½ inches). Trim two of the dark green solid border strips to this length, and sew them to the sides of the quilt top. Measure the width of the quilt top (approximately 34½ inches). Trim and add the two remaining green border strips.

4. Measure the length of the quilt top (approximately 39 inches); trim two plaid border strips to length and add them to the sides of the quilt. Measure the width of the quilt top (approximately 40½ inches); trim the remaining plaid border strips, and add them to the top and bottom.

Quilting and Finishing

1. Mark quilting designs as desired. The blocks in the quilt shown were quilted as illustrated in **Diagram 2.** In addition, a diagonal grid of 1¼-inch squares was quilted in the borders.

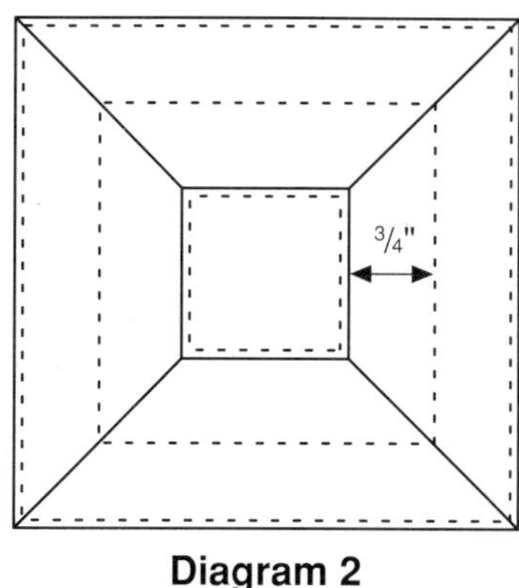

Diagram 2

2. Layer the quilt back, batting, and quilt top; baste. Trim the quilt back so it is approximately 2 to 3 inches larger than the quilt top on all sides.

3. Quilt as desired.

4. From the tan binding fabric, make approximately 175 inches of French-fold binding. See page 164 for suggested binding widths and instructions on making and attaching binding. Make a hanging sleeve for the quilt; see page 167 for instructions.

5. Sew the binding to the quilt top. Trim the excess batting and backing, and hand finish the binding on the back side of the quilt.

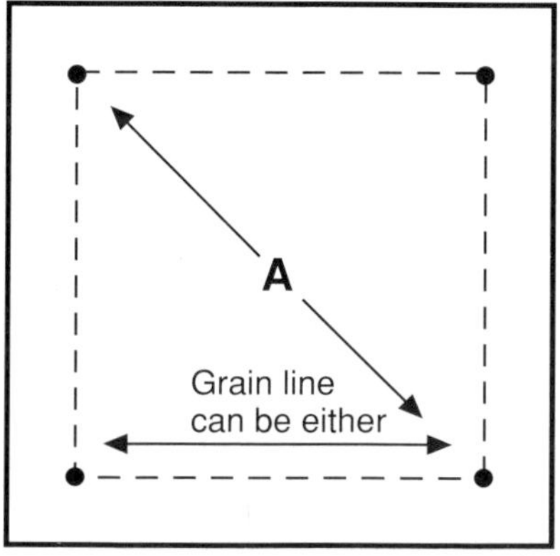

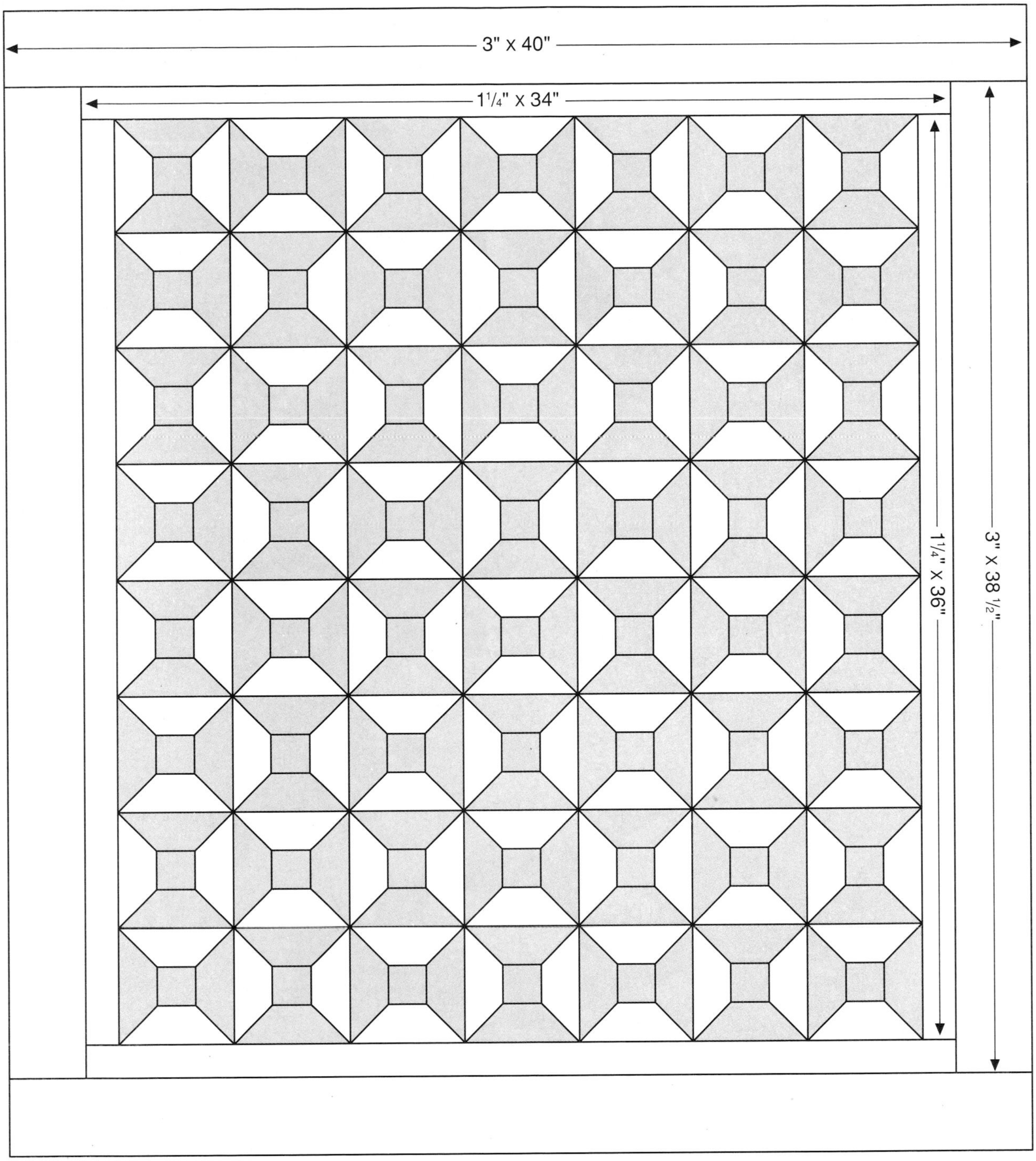

3" x 40"

1¼" x 34"

1¼" x 36"

3" x 38 ½"

Quilt Diagram

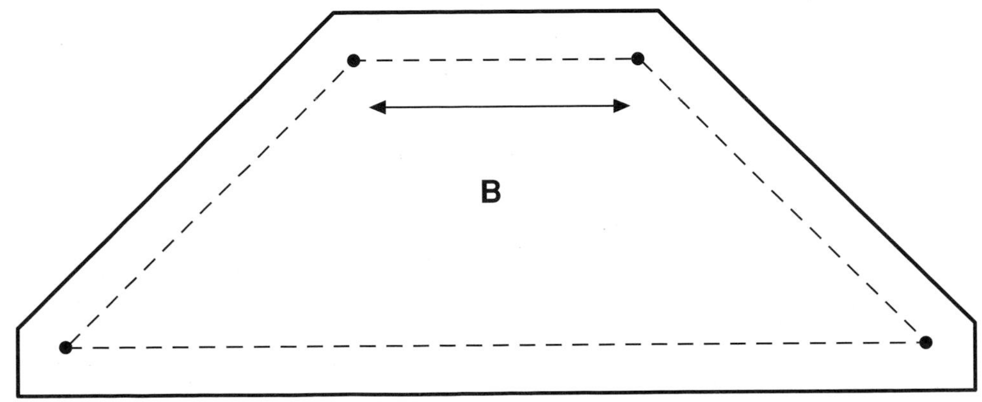

Patchwork Pillows

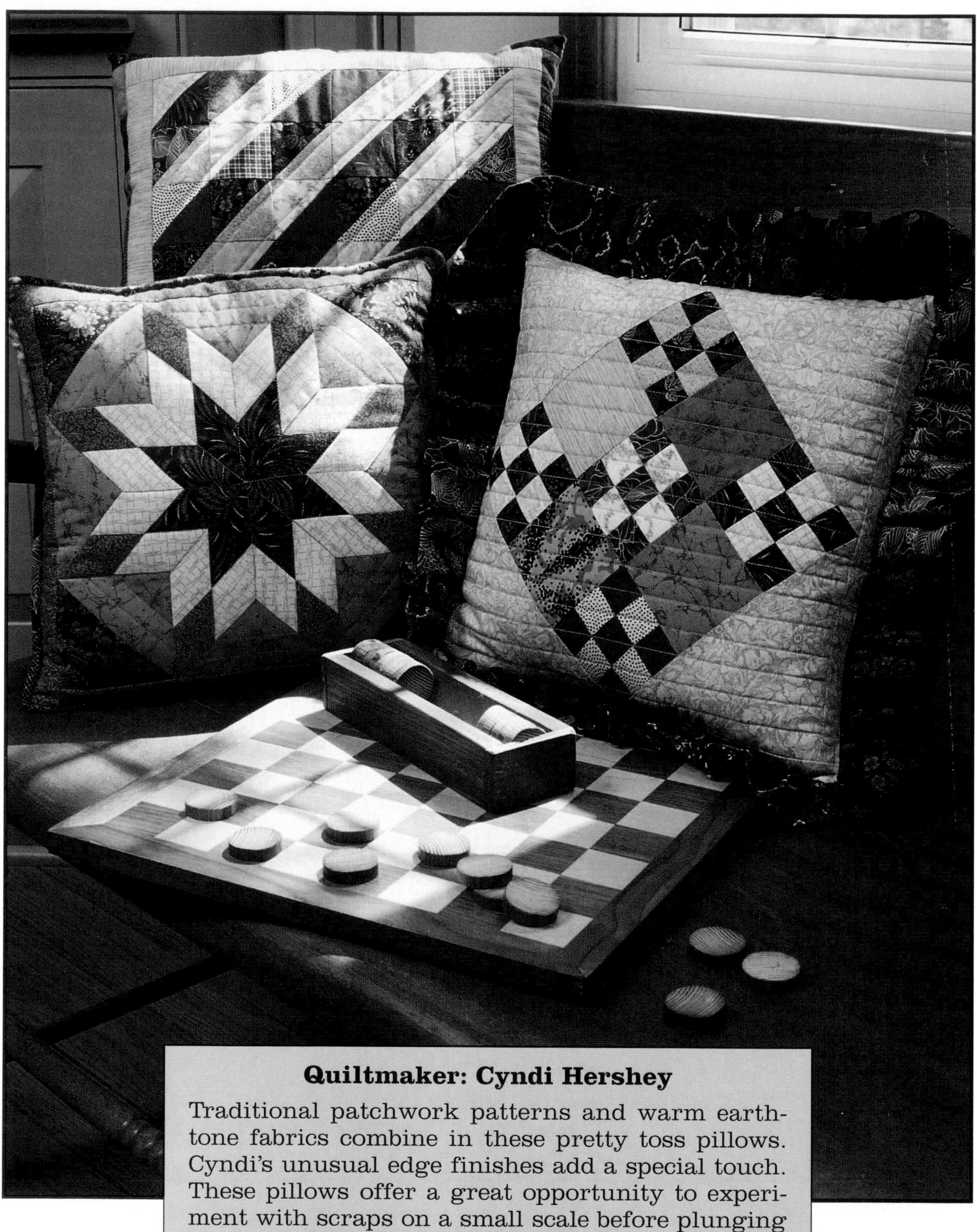

Quiltmaker: Cyndi Hershey

Traditional patchwork patterns and warm earth-tone fabrics combine in these pretty toss pillows. Cyndi's unusual edge finishes add a special touch. These pillows offer a great opportunity to experiment with scraps on a small scale before plunging into a large project. You can build your scrap confidence and make a quick gift at the same time!

Skill Level: Intermediate

Size: Finished Double Nine-Patch Pillow is approximately 20 inches square, including ruffle (14¾ inches without ruffle)
Finished Straight Furrows Pillow is 12 × 16 inches
Finished Morning Star Pillow is 14 inches square

Fabrics and Supplies for the Double Nine-Patch Pillow with Ruffle

- ½ yard of cream print fabric for corner setting triangles, framing strips, and pillow back
- ¼ yard *each* of four dark print fabrics for patchwork and ruffle
- One scrap (approximately 5 inches square) of an additional dark print fabric for patchwork
- Scraps (approximately 5 inches square) of five light print fabrics for patchwork
- Scraps (approximately 4 inches square) of four medium print fabrics for patchwork
- One 18-inch square of quilt batting
- One 18-inch square of muslin for lining
- Polyester fiberfill
- Rotary cutter, ruler, and mat
- Template plastic (optional)

Cutting

All measurements include seam allowances; take ¼-inch seams unless directed otherwise. Instructions are given for quick-cutting the pieces with a rotary cutter and ruler. If you prefer to cut the pieces in the traditional manner, however, make templates for pieces A and B as directed below. Tips for making and using templates are on page 153.

- **A:** 1½-inch square
- **B:** 3½-inch square

From the cream print fabric, cut:
- One 16-inch-square pillow back
- 4 corner setting triangles
  Cut two 7½-inch squares. Cut each square in half diagonally to make two triangles.
- Four 1¾ × 16-inch framing strips

From each of the four dark print fabrics, cut:
- Two 6 × 18-inch rectangles for ruffle
- 5 A squares
  Use Template A
  OR
  Cut five 1½-inch squares.

From the dark print scrap fabric, cut:
- 5 A squares
  Use Template A
  OR
  Cut five 1½-inch squares.

From each of the five light print scrap fabrics, cut:
- 4 A squares
  Use Template A
  OR
  Cut four 1½-inch squares.

From each of the four medium print scrap fabrics, cut:
- 1 B square
  Use Template B
  OR
  Cut one 3½-inch square.

Piecing the Pillow Top

1. Begin by making the five small Nine-Patch blocks. For each small block, lay out five matching dark A squares and four matching light A squares.

2. Referring to the **Fabric Key** and **Diagram 1,** join the nine squares into three rows of three squares per row. Press the seams toward the dark

Fabric Key

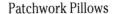

Cream print
Dark print
Light print
Medium print

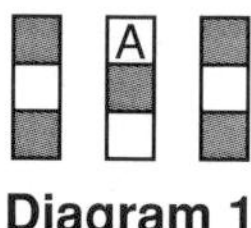

Diagram 1

squares. Join the rows, pressing the seams in one direction. Make a total of five blocks.

3. Lay out the five pieced blocks with the four B squares. Join the blocks and squares to make three rows, as shown in **Diagram 2.** Press the seams toward the B squares. Join the rows.

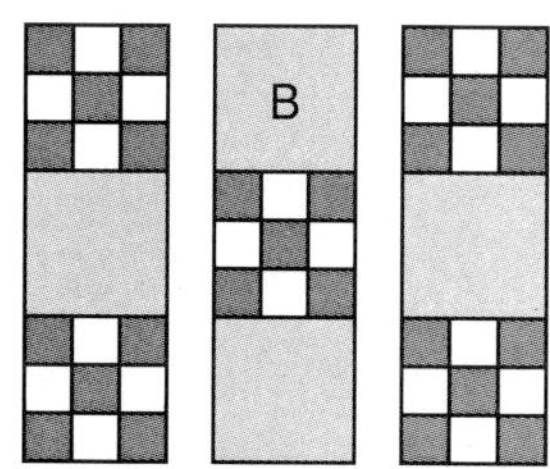

Diagram 2

4. Sew a cream print corner setting triangle to two opposite sides of the completed block. Press the seams toward the triangles. Sew the remaining two cream triangles to the remaining sides of the block; press the seams toward the triangles.

5. Trim two of the 1¾-inch-wide framing strips to the size of the block. Sew the strips to two opposite sides of the squared-off block. Press the seams toward the framing strips.

6. Measure the sides of the block including the framing strips. Trim the two remaining 1¾-inch-wide framing strips to this measurement. Sew them to the remaining two sides of the block to complete the pillow top, as shown in the **Nine-Patch Pillow Diagram.**

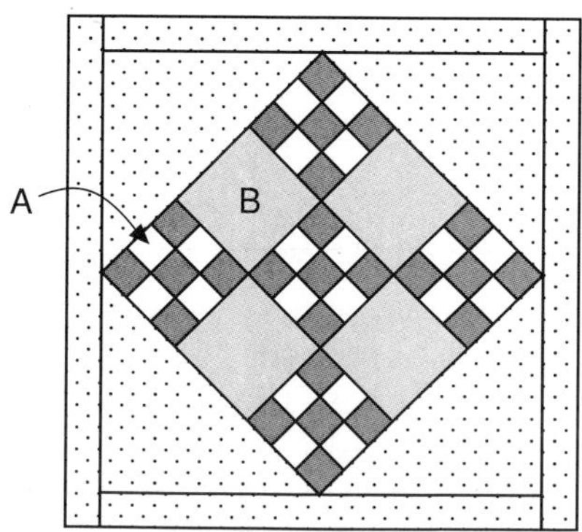

Nine-Patch Pillow Diagram

Quilting the Pillow Top

1. Layer the completed pillow top, the square of batting, and the muslin lining square; baste the layers together.

2. Quilt as desired. The pillow shown was machine quilted with parallel lines approximately ¾ inch apart.

Making the Ruffle and Assembling the Pillow

1. Sew the eight 6 × 18-inch dark print rectangles together end to end, alternating the prints. You will have a long strip 6 inches wide by approximately 140 inches long. Press the seams open.

2. Join the two ends of the strip to make a big loop. Press the strip in half lengthwise, wrong sides together.

3. Machine stitch two lines of large gathering stitches ¼ inch and ⅛ inch in from the raw edge of the ruffle loop.

4. Working with the quilted pillow top right side up, arrange the ruffle loop so that two pieced sections of it will fall on each side of the pillow top. Line up and pin a ruffle seam at the center of each side of the pillow top; line up and pin the remaining ruffle seams close to the corners of the pillow top.

5. Draw up the gathering threads on the ruffle, and pin it to the pillow top, matching raw edges. Space the gathers evenly along the pillow edge, allowing extra fullness at the corners.

6. Machine baste the gathered ruffle to the pillow top with a ¼-inch seam. Pin the folded edge of the ruffle to the pillow top in several places so it won't get caught in the seam when you sew the back on. Trim away excess batting and lining.

7. Pin the pillow top to the back, right sides together. The ruffle will be hidden inside the layers. Sewing from the pillow top side rather than from the pillow back side, machine stitch around the pillow, taking a ⅜-inch seam allowance. Leave a 7½-inch opening along one side for turning and stuffing. Trim the excess backing fabric.

8. Turn the pillow right side out through the opening, and stuff it firmly with polyester filling. Hand stitch the opening closed.

Fabrics and Supplies for the Straight Furrows Pillow

- ½ yard of medium print fabric for border and pillow back
- Scraps (approximately 5 inches square)of 12 dark print fabrics for patchwork
- Scraps (approximately 3 inches square) of 12 light print fabrics for patchwork
- One 20 × 16-inch piece of muslin for lining
- One 20 × 16-inch piece of quilt batting
- Polyester fiberfill
- Rotary cutter, ruler, and mat
- Template plastic (optional)

Cutting

All measurements include ¼-inch seam allowances. The instructions given are for quick-cutting the pieces with a rotary cutter and ruler. If you prefer to cut the pieces in the traditional manner, make a template for the C triangle as directed below. Tips for making and using templates are on page 153.

- **C:** Make a 2⅞-inch square; cut the square in half diagonally.

From the medium print fabric, cut:

- One 12½ × 16½-inch pillow back
- Two 1½ × 14½-inch border strips
- Two 1½ × 8½-inch border strips

From each of the dark print scraps, cut:

- 2 C triangles
  Use Template C
  OR
  Cut one 2⅞-inch square from each fabric. Cut each square in half diagonally to make two triangles.
- Two 1½ × 2½-inch rectangles. Cut two additional rectangles from your favorite scraps.

From the light print scrap fabrics, cut a total of:

- 24 C triangles
  Use Template C
  OR
  Cut one 2⅞-inch square from each fabric. Cut each square in half diagonally to make two triangles.

Piecing the Pillow Top

1. Referring to the **Fabric Key,** join dark and light fabric triangles into 24 pieced-square units like the one shown in **Diagram 3.** Press the seams toward the darker triangle.

Fabric Key

Medium print

Dark print

Light print

C

Diagram 3

2. Referring to the **Straight Furrows Pillow Diagram,** lay out the pieced-square units in six vertical rows of four units per row. Position the fabrics so that the diagonal "straight furrow" stripes are formed as shown in the diagram.

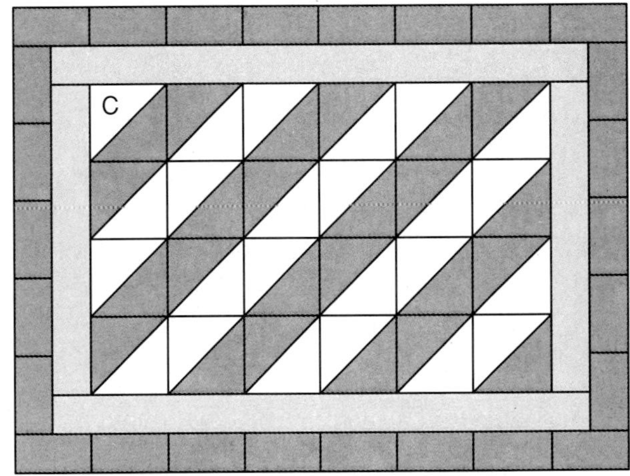

Straight Furrows Pillow Diagram

3. Sew the units together into rows. Press the seams in opposite directions from row to row. Join the rows.

4. Sew the 1½ × 8½-inch medium print fabric border strips to the two short sides of the pieced rectangle. Press the seams toward the border strips. Sew the 1½ × 14½-inch border strips to the two long sides of the rectangle; press the seams toward the strips.

5. Join the dark fabric rectangles in random order to make four pieced border strips. Make two

strips with five rectangles each and two strips with eight rectangles each.

6. Sew the two shorter pieced borders to the two short sides of the pillow top; press the seams toward the borders. Sew the two longer pieced borders to the two long sides of the pillow top; press the seams toward the borders.

Quilting and Finishing the Pillow

1. Layer the completed pillow top, batting, and muslin lining; baste the layers together.

2. Quilt as desired. The pillow shown was machine quilted ¼ inch away from the diagonal seams on the light triangle stripes, as well as in the ditch along the border seams. After quilting, trim excess batting and lining even with the pillow top.

3. Pin the pillow top to the back, right sides together. Using a ¼-inch seam allowance, machine stitch around the pillow, leaving a 7½-inch opening along one side for turning and stuffing.

4. Turn the pillow right side out through the opening, and stuff it firmly with polyester filling. Hand stitch the opening closed.

Fabrics and Supplies for the Morning Star Pillow

- ⅛ yard or scraps of dark green fabric for patchwork
- ⅛ yard or scraps of off-white print fabric for patchwork
- ⅛ yard or scraps of rust print fabric for patchwork and border strips
- Two scraps (approximately 6½ inches square) of gold print fabric for setting triangles
- Two scraps (approximately 4½ inches square) of black print fabric for corner triangles
- Scraps of assorted medium and dark fabrics for covered cording
- One 18-inch square of muslin for lining
- One 14½-inch square of fabric for pillow back
- One 18-inch square of quilt batting
- 1⅔ yards of ⅜-inch-diameter cable cord
- Polyester fiberfill
- Template plastic (optional)
- Rotary cutter, ruler with 45 degree angle line, and mat

Cutting

All measurements include seam allowances; take ¼-inch seams unless directed otherwise. Instructions for making the diamonds are given two ways: You can cut strips for quick-piecing, or make a template for traditional piecing using the pattern on page 86. Tips for making and using templates are on page 153.

If you use templates for D and E , use a needle to make a hole at the corner dots shown on the patterns. Mark around the templates on the wrong side of the fabric, then mark the dot on the fabric through the corner hole. The marked dots will make setting-in the pieces easier.

From the dark green fabric, cut:

- 8 D diamonds
  Use Template D
  OR
  Cut one 1¾ × 44-inch strip.

From the off-white print fabric, cut:

- 16 D diamonds
  Use Template D
  OR
  Cut two 1¾ × 44-inch strips.

From the rust print fabric, cut:

- 8 D diamonds
  Use Template D
  OR
  Cut one 1¾ × 44-inch strip.
- Four 1½ × 15-inch border strips

From the gold print fabric, cut:

- 8 E triangles with the long side of the triangle on the straight of grain
  Use Template E
  OR
  Cut two 6¼-inch squares. Cut each square both ways diagonally to make four triangles.

From the black print fabric, cut:

- 4 E triangles with the leg of the triangle on the straight of grain
  Use Template E
  OR
  Cut two 4⅜-inch squares. Cut each square in half diagonally to make two triangles.

From the assorted scraps, cut:

- 35 D diamonds

  Use Template D

Quick-Piecing the Diamonds for the Star

If you've chosen to piece the diamonds traditionally, skip down to Piecing the Diamonds the Traditional Way.

1. Referring to the **Fabric Key** and **Diagram 4,** make two strip sets using the green, off-white, and rust strips. Press the seams toward the darker fabrics.

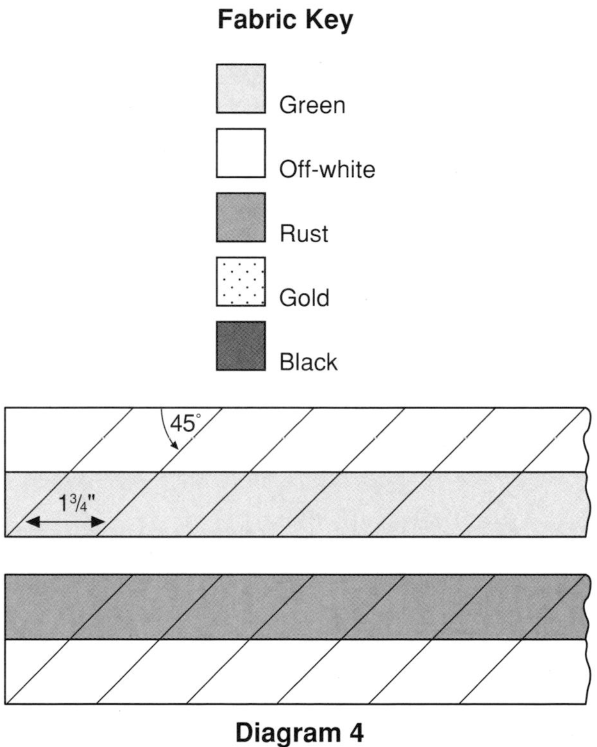

Diagram 4

2. Using the 45 degree angle line on your ruler, cut eight 1¾-inch-wide diamond units from each strip set, as shown in **Diagram 4.**

3. Lay out the diamond units in pairs, as shown in **Diagram 5.** Join the units into sections. You will have eight large diamond sections.

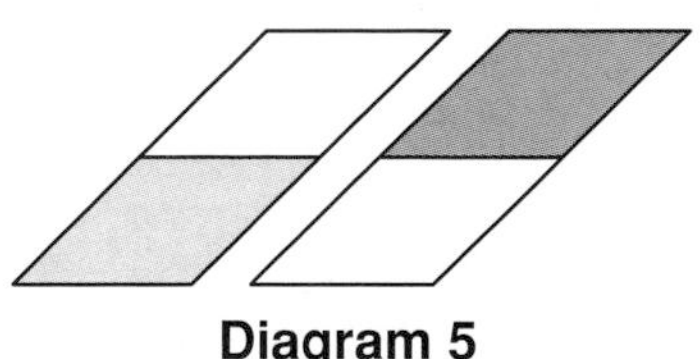

Diagram 5

Piecing the Diamonds the Traditional Way

1. Lay out four D diamonds, as shown in **Diagram 5.** Join the diamonds in pairs. Press the seams toward the darker fabrics.

2. Join pairs to form a larger diamond. Make eight large diamond sections.

Piecing the Star

1. Lay out the large diamond sections and the E triangles, as shown in the **Morning Star Pillow Diagram.** Place the green diamonds toward the center.

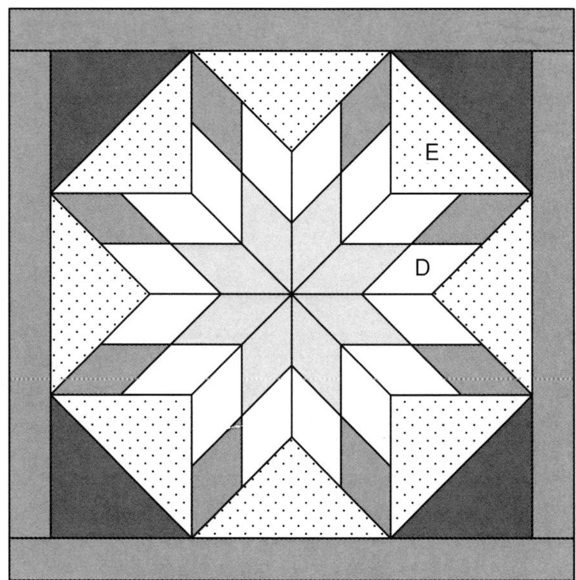

Morning Star Pillow Diagram

2. Referring to **Diagram 6** on page 86, join the large diamond sections in pairs. When joining the diamond sections, begin stitching at the center of the star. Stop stitching exactly ¼ inch from the outside raw edge; do not stitch into the seam allowance on the outside edge of the star.

3. Join the pairs as shown to form two half stars. Stop stitching ¼ inch from the outer edge so that the seams are free at the corners to set in squares and triangles. In the same manner, join the two halves of the star to complete it.

Diagram 6

4. Set four of the gold E triangles into alternate openings around the star. See page 155 for tips on setting-in pieces.

5. Join the black print E triangles and the remaining gold E triangles to form four corner squares. Set a square into each corner, placing the black print triangle to the outside.

Adding the Borders

1. Measure the block, and trim two of the 1½-inch-wide rust print border strips to this size (approximately 12½ inches). Sew the borders to two opposite sides of the completed block. Press the seams toward the borders.

2. Measure the block including the side borders. Trim the two remaining rust strips to this size (approximately 14½ inches), and sew them to the block. Press the seams toward the borders.

Quilting and Finishing the Pillow

1. Mark quilting designs. Layer the completed pillow top, batting, and muslin lining; baste the layers together.

2. Quilt as desired. The pillow shown was machine quilted in the ditch and with parallel lines in the gold triangles. When quilting is complete, trim the excess batting and lining even with the pillow top.

3. Use the 35 diamonds cut from scraps to make the covered cording for the edge. Join the diamonds in random order to make a long strip. Press the seam allowances in one direction.

4. With the wrong side next to the cording, wrap the pieced strip around the cording and baste the raw edges together close to the cording, encasing the cording within the strip.

5. Baste the cording to the front of the pillow top, aligning the raw edge of the encased cording with the raw edge of the pillow top.

6. Pin the pillow top to the back, with right sides facing. Using a ¼-inch seam allowance, machine stitch around the pillow, leaving a 7½-inch opening on one side for turning and stuffing.

7. Turn the pillow to the right side through the opening. Stuff the pillow firmly with polyester filling. Hand stitch the opening closed.

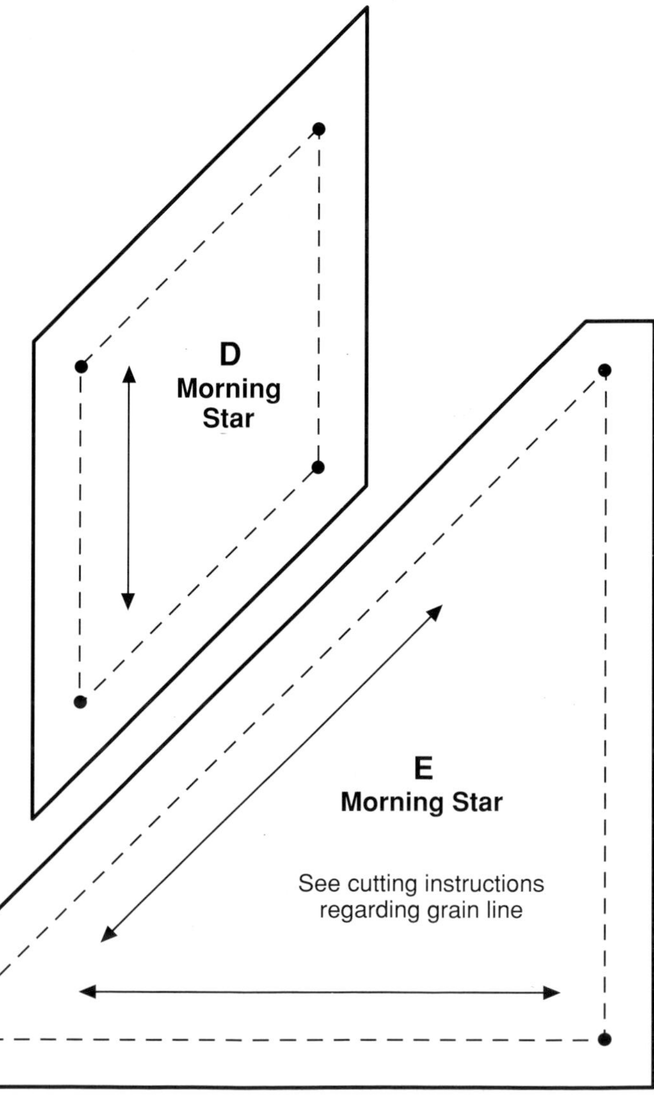

Jim's Scrappy Nine Patch

Quiltmaker: Gloria Greenlee

This wonderful scrap quilt was inspired by an antique quilt discovered in Oklahoma's Heritage Project, which registered pre-1940s quilts. Gloria named the quilt for her husband, who decided while it was still in progress that he wanted to keep it. The quilt offers a great opportunity to use up lots of small fabric scraps in easy Nine-Patch units.

Skill Level: Easy

Size: Finished quilt is 66 × 84 inches

Finished block is 18 inches square

Fabrics and Supplies

- 3 yards of tan print fabric for triangle squares, pieced border, and binding
- 2¼ yards of red print fabric for triangle squares and pieced border
- 1 yard of blue-and-white plaid fabric for middle border
- ⅓ yard of navy blue print fabric for inner border
- Approximately 2¼ yards total of assorted medium fabric scraps
- Approximately 1¾ yards total of assorted light fabric scraps
- Approximately 1¼ yards total of assorted dark fabric scraps
- 5 yards of fabric for quilt back
- Full-size quilt batting (81 × 96 inches)
- Rotary cutter, ruler, and mat
- Template plastic (optional)

Cutting

All measurements include ¼-inch seam allowances. The instructions given are for quick-cutting the pieces with a rotary cutter and ruler. If you prefer to cut the pieces in a traditional manner, make templates for pieces A and B as directed below. Tips for making and using templates are on page 153.

- **A:** 1½-inch square
- **B:** 3⅞-inch square

From the tan print fabric, cut:

- 288 B triangles

  Use Template B

  OR

  Cut fifteen 3⅞ × 44-inch strips; cut each strip into 3⅞-inch squares. You will need 144 squares. Cut each square in half diagonally to make two triangles.
- Reserve the remaining fabric for binding

From the red print fabric, cut:

- 288 B triangles

  Use Template B

  OR

  Cut fifteen 3⅞ × 44-inch strips; cut each strip into 3⅞-inch squares. You will need 144 squares. Cut each square in half diagonally to make two triangles.

From the blue-and-white plaid fabric, cut:

- Eight 3 × 44-inch middle border strips

From the navy blue print fabric, cut:

- Eight 1 × 44-inch inner border strips

From the assorted medium fabric scraps, cut:

- 96 sets of five matching A squares each for the dark Nine-Patch units (480 squares total)

  Use Template A

  OR

  Cut 1½-inch squares.
- 144 sets of four matching A squares each for the light Nine-Patch units (576 squares total)

  Use Template A

  OR

  Cut 1½-inch squares.

From the assorted light fabric scraps, cut:

- 144 sets of five matching A squares each for the light Nine-Patch units (720 squares total)

  Use Template A

  OR

  Cut 1½-inch squares.

From the assorted dark fabric scraps, cut:

- 96 sets of four matching A squares each for the dark Nine-Patch units (384 squares total)

  Use Template A

  OR

  Cut 1½-inch squares.

Piecing the Nine-Patch Units

The blocks in this quilt are made up of dark Nine-Patch units, light Nine-Patch units, and pieced squares. The dark Nine-Patch units use five medium squares and four dark squares; the light Nine-Patch units use five light squares and four medium squares. Refer to the **Fabric Key** throughout the piecing process.

1. To make a dark Nine-Patch unit you will need one set of five matching medium A squares and one set of four matching dark A squares. Sew the squares together into three rows, as shown in **Diagram 1.** Press the seams toward the dark squares.

Fabric Key

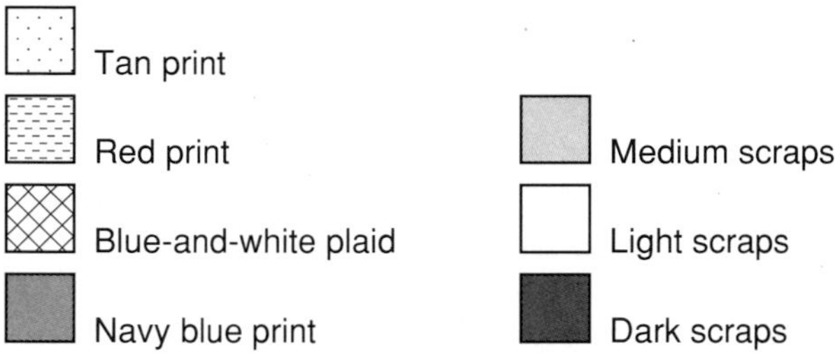

Tan print

Red print

Blue-and-white plaid

Navy blue print

Medium scraps

Light scraps

Dark scraps

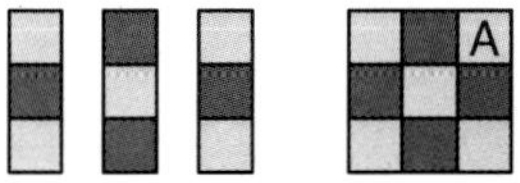

A

Diagram 1
Dark Nine-Patch Units

2. Join the rows. Press the seams away from the center row. Repeat to make 96 of these units.

3. To make a light Nine-Patch unit you will need one set of five matching light A squares and one set of four matching medium A squares. Sew the squares together into three rows, as shown in **Diagram 2.** Press the seams toward the medium squares.

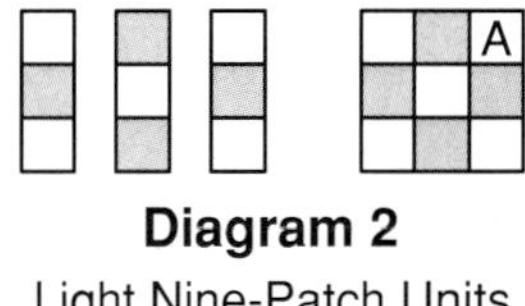

Diagram 2
Light Nine-Patch Units

4. Join the rows. Press the seams away from the center row. Repeat to make 144 of these units.

Making the Pieced-Square Units

1. To make one unit, join a tan print B triangle to a red print B triangle along the long sides to form a square, as shown in **Diagram 3.** Press the seam toward the red print triangle.

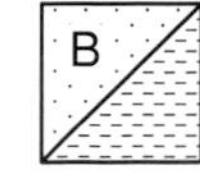

Diagram 3
Pieced-Square Unit

2. Repeat to make a total of 288 of these pieced-square units. You will need 192 units for the blocks and 96 units for the borders.

Piecing the Blocks

1. Each block is made up of four sections like the one shown in **Diagram 4.** To make each section, lay out two dark Nine Patch units, three light Nine Patch units, and four pieced-square units.

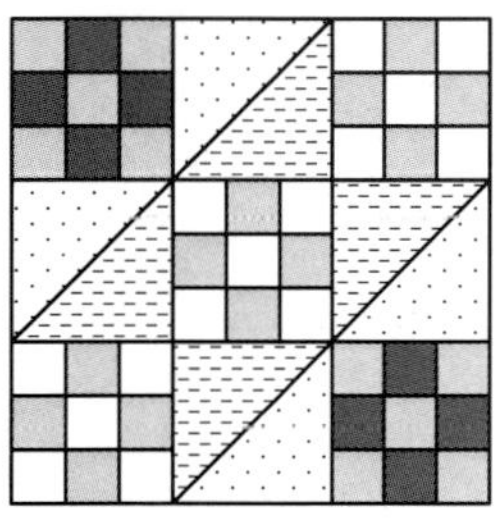

Diagram 4

2. Sew the units together into three rows, as shown in **Diagram 5.** Press the seams toward the pieced-square units. Join the rows, pressing the seams toward the center row. Make 48 of these sections.

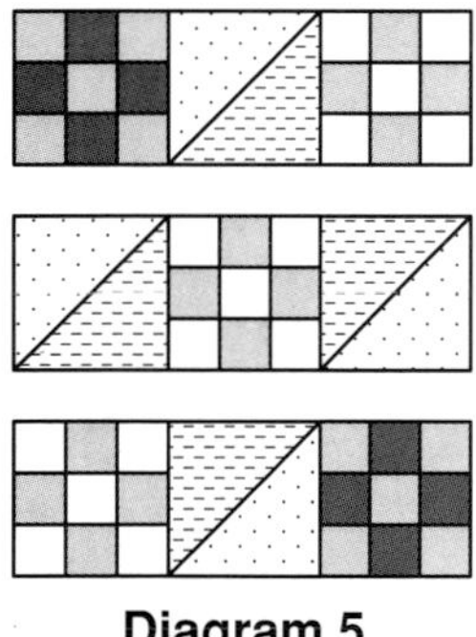

Diagram 5

3. Make 12 blocks by joining sets of four sections, as shown in the **Scrappy Nine-Patch Block Diagram** on page 90. Sew the sections together into two rows, pressing the seams in opposite directions. Join the rows.

Assembling the Inner Quilt Top

1. Lay out the blocks in four horizontal rows with three blocks in each row, as shown in the **Quilt Diagram** on page 91.

2. Sew the blocks together into rows. Press the seams in alternate directions from row to row.

3. Join the rows.

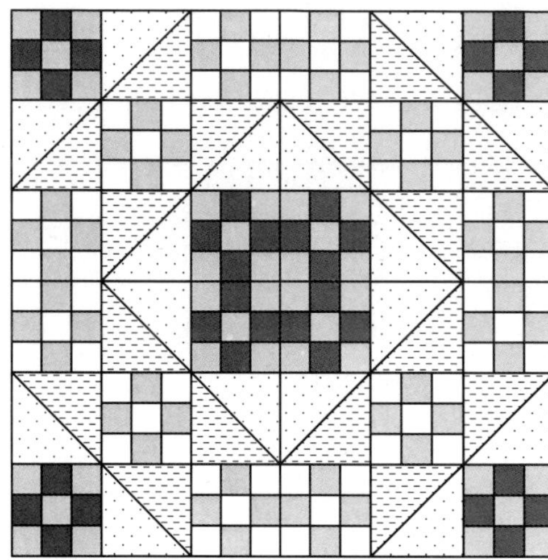

Scrappy Nine-Patch Block Diagram

Adding the Borders

1. Piece four inner borders from the 1-inch-wide navy blue border strips. Join one-and-one-half strips each for the top and bottom borders. Join two-and-one-half strips for each of the side borders.

2. Piece four middle borders from the 3-inch-wide blue-and-white plaid border strips. Join one and one-half strips each for the top and bottom borders. Join two and one-half strips for each of the side borders.

3. Sew the navy blue borders to the corresponding length blue-and-white plaid borders to make four border sets. Press the seams away from the navy blue borders.

4. Place the border sets right sides together with the quilt top, matching centers. Sew the border sets to the quilt, mitering the border corner seams. See page 160 for tips on adding mitered borders to a quilt. The quilt should measure 60½ × 78½ inches, including seam allowances.

5. To make the pieced borders for the sides of the quilt top, sew together 26 pieced-square units for each border, positioning the units as shown in the **Quilt Diagram.** Note that the units change direction in the middle of the strips. Press the seams in one direction. Sew the borders to the sides of the quilt top, pressing the seams toward the blue-and-white plaid borders.

6. To make the pieced borders for the top and bottom of the quilt top, sew together 22 pieced-square units for each border, again referring to the **Quilt Diagram** for correct positioning. Note that the units change direction in the middle of the strips and at the ends. Press the seams in one direction. Sew the borders to the top and bottom edges of the quilt top. Press the seams toward the blue-and-white plaid borders.

Quilting and Finishing

1. Mark quilting designs as desired on the finished quilt top. The pattern for the cable design for the border is provided on this page.

2. Cut the backing fabric into two equal lengths. Trim the selvages, and divide one piece in half lengthwise. Sew a half panel to each side of the full-width panel. Press the seams away from the center panel.

3. Layer the quilt back, batting, and quilt top; baste. Trim the quilt back so it is approximately 3 inches larger than the quilt top on all sides.

4. Quilt all marked designs, and add additional quilting as desired.

5. From the reserved tan print fabric, make approximately 320 inches of French-fold bind-

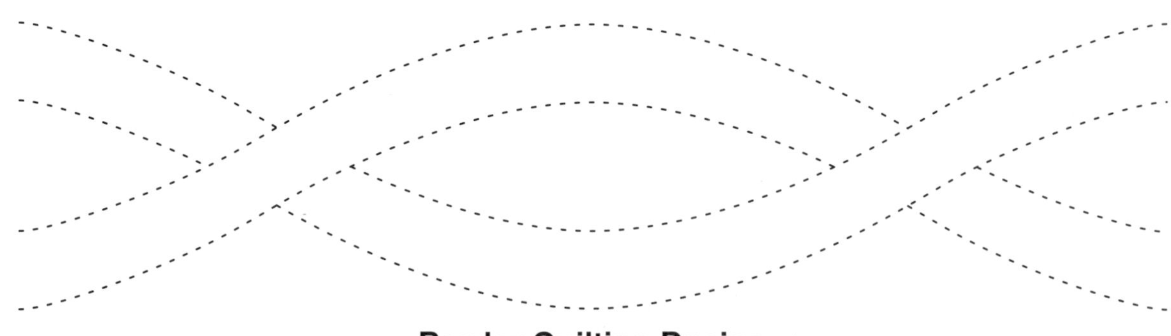

Border Quilting Design

ing. See page 164 for suggested binding widths, instructions, and tips for making and attaching binding.

6. Sew the binding to the quilt top. Trim the excess batting and backing, and hand finish the binding on the back side of the quilt.

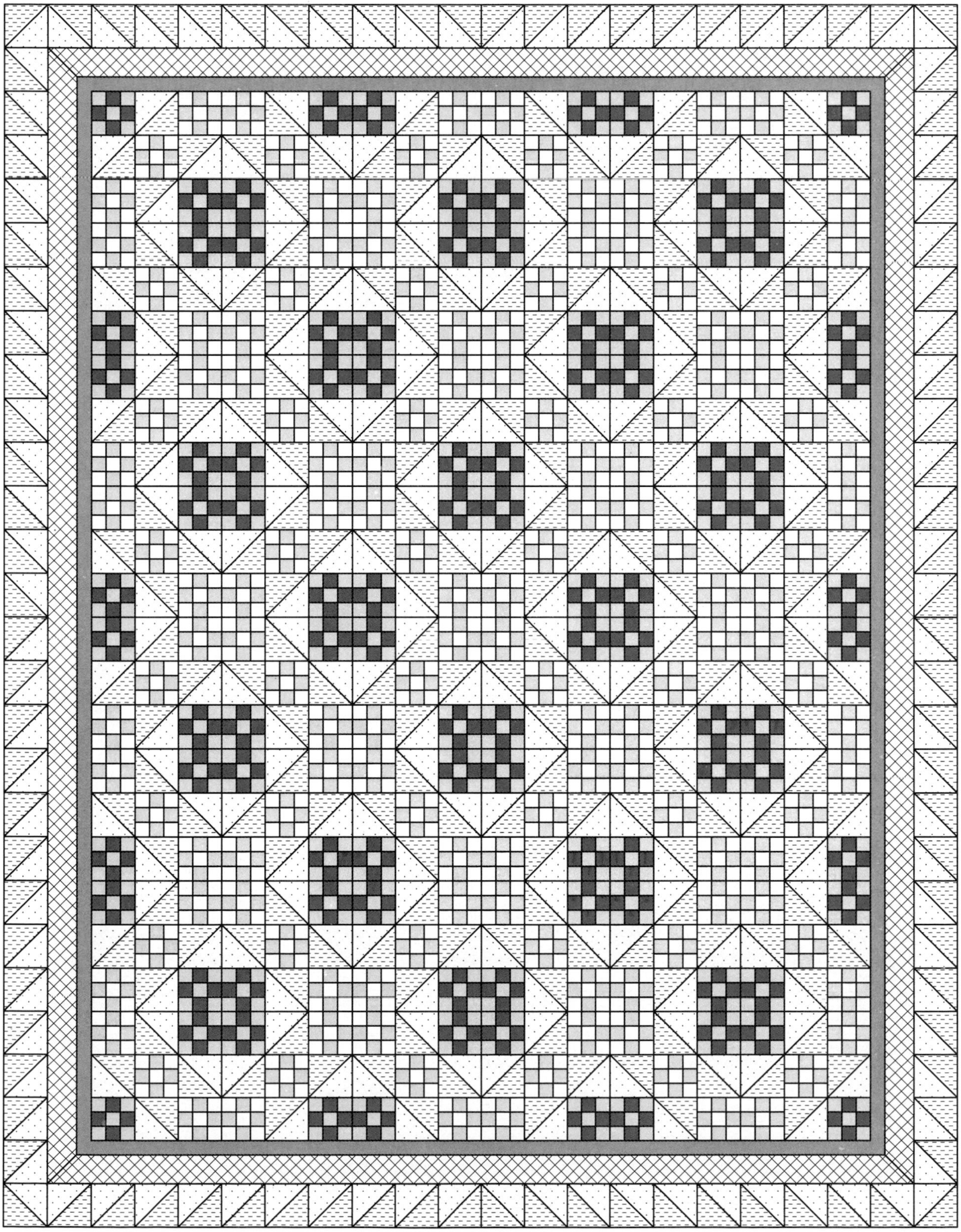

Quilt Diagram

Scrap Baskets

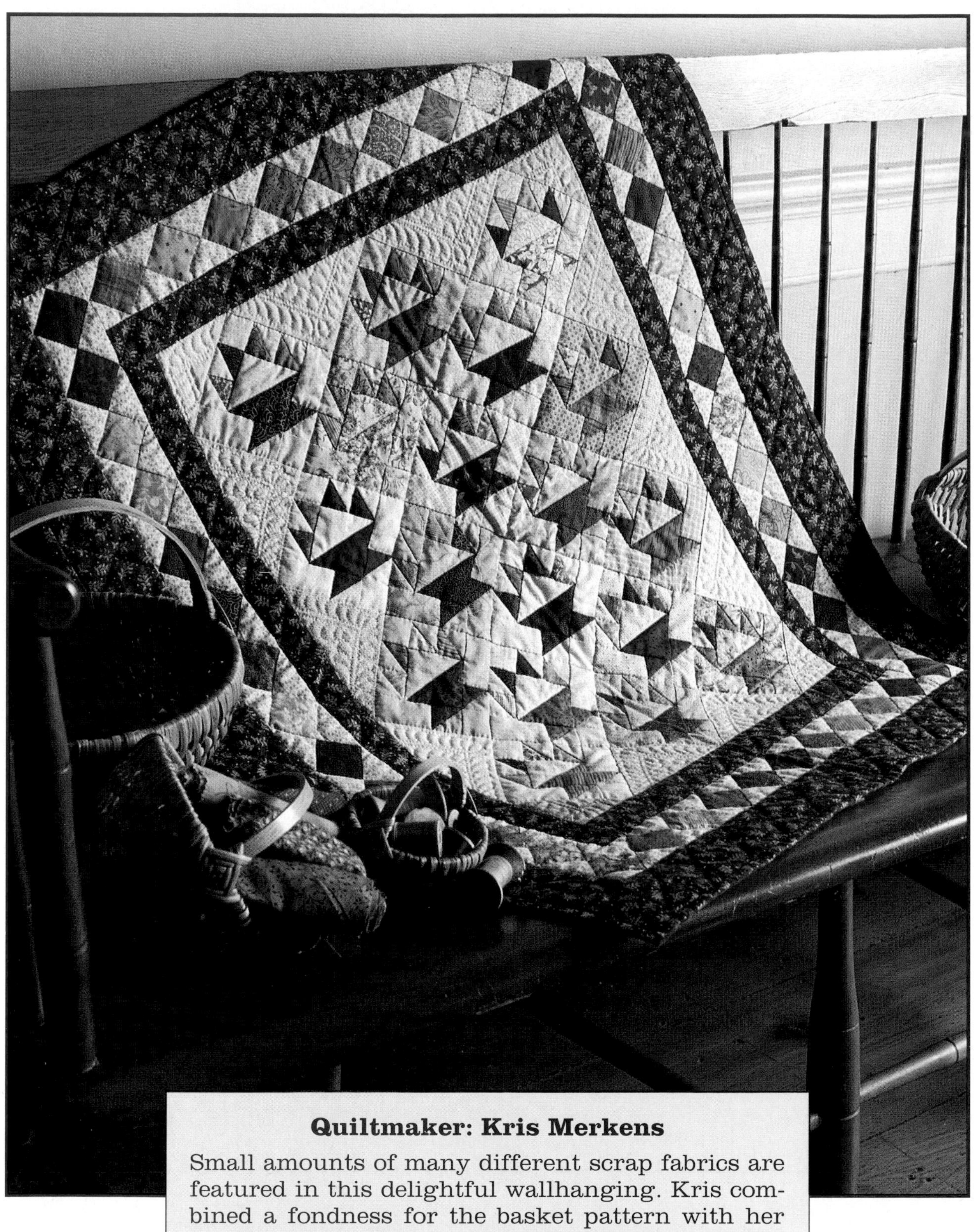

Quiltmaker: Kris Merkens

Small amounts of many different scrap fabrics are featured in this delightful wallhanging. Kris combined a fondness for the basket pattern with her favorite color, blue, to create a small quilt with a real country feeling. Piece the eighteen 4-inch basket blocks by hand, as Kris did, or by machine.

Skill Level: Intermediate

Size: Finished quilt is 28 ¾ × 34 ¾ inches
Finished block is 4 inches square

Fabrics and Supplies

- 1 yard of dark blue print fabric for borders and binding
- ½ yard of cream print fabric for pieced border
- Scraps (approximately 9 inches square) of 18 different cream and beige print fabrics for setting triangles and block backgrounds
- Scraps (approximately 9 inches square) of 18 assorted print fabrics for basket tops. (The colors used in the quilt shown are various dark and medium blues, reds, greens, and browns.)
- 1 yard of fabric for quilt back
- Crib-size quilt batting (45 × 60 inches)
- Rotary cutter, ruler, and mat
- Template plastic (optional)

Cutting

All measurements include ¼-inch seam allowances. Measurements for the borders are longer than needed; trim them to the exact length when they are added to the quilt top. Instructions are given for quick-cutting the pieces with a rotary cutter and ruler. If you prefer to cut the pieces in the traditional manner, make templates using the patterns on page 96. Tips for making and using templates are on page 153.

From the dark blue print fabric, cut:
- Four 3 ¼ × 44-inch outer border strips
- One 1⅞ × 44-inch inner border strip
- Two 1 ½ × 44-inch inner border strips
- Reserve the remaining fabric for binding

From the cream print fabric, cut:
- 84 F triangles
  Use Template F
  OR
  Cut two 3 ⅜ × 44-inch strips; cut each strip into 3 ⅜-inch squares. You will need 21 squares. Cut each square in half diagonally in both directions to make four triangles.
- 16 G triangles
  Use Template G
  OR
  Cut one 2 × 44-inch strip. From the strip, cut eight 2-inch squares. Cut each square in half diagonally to make two triangles.

From each of the 18 cream and beige scrap fabrics, cut:
- 6 A triangles
  Use Template A
  OR
  Cut three 1 ⅞-inch squares. Cut each square in half diagonally to make two triangles.
- 2 B squares
  Use Template B
  OR
  Cut two 1 ½-inch squares.
- 2 D rectangles
  Use Template D
  OR
  Cut two 1 ½-inch × 2 ½-inch rectangles.
- 1 C triangle
  Use Template C
  OR
  Cut one 2 ⅞-inch square. Cut the square in half diagonally to make two triangles. You will have an extra triangle.

From the assorted cream and beige scrap fabrics, cut:
- 10 H setting triangles. (Cut one each from ten fabrics.)
  Use Template H
- 4 I setting triangles. (Cut one each from four fabrics.)
  Use Template I

From each of the 18 assorted print fabrics, cut:
- 2 A triangles
  Use Template A
  OR
  Cut one 1 ⅞-inch square. Cut the square in half diagonally to make two triangles.
- 1 C triangle
  Use Template C
  OR
  Cut one 2 ⅞-inch square. Cut the square in half diagonally to make two triangles. You will have an extra triangle of each fabric.

From the assorted print fabrics, cut:
- 46 E border squares
  Use Template E

OR
Cut forty-six 2-inch squares.

- 72 A triangles for tops of baskets
  Use Template A
  OR
  Cut thirty-six 1⅞-inch squares. Cut each square in half diagonally to make two triangles.

Piecing the Blocks

1. Referring to **Diagram 1,** lay out the A, B, C, and D pieces for one block. Use matching cream or beige print pieces in the background area and matching colored pieces for the basket base portion of the block. Use four different-color A triangles for the top portion of the basket.

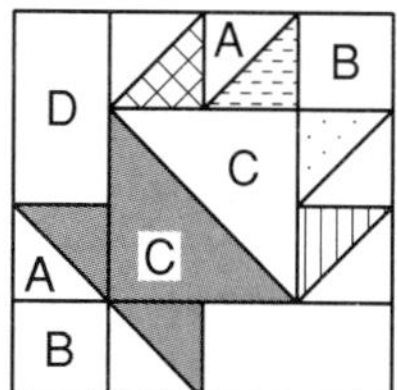

Diagram 1

2. Begin by joining cream and colored A triangles to make the four pieced squares for the top portion of the block. Sew the pieced squares together in pairs, as shown in **Diagram 2.** Press seams toward the darker fabrics whenever possible.

3. Join the two C triangles to make a pieced square. Referring to **Diagram 3** for correct placement, sew a pair of A pieced squares to one side of the C pieced square.

Diagram 2

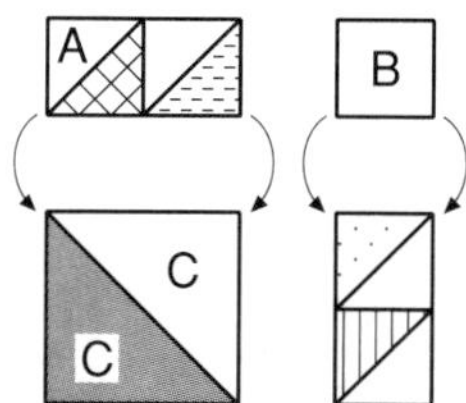

Diagram 3

4. Add a B square to the other pair of A pieced squares to make a strip (again, pay attention to placement). Sew the strip to the side of the Step 3 unit.

5. Join the remaining A triangles to make the two pieced squares for the base portion of the block. Referring to **Diagram 4,** sew the base A pieced squares to the D rectangles.

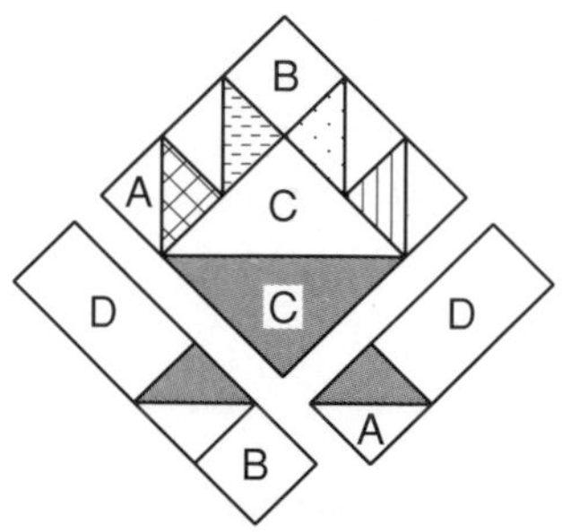

Diagram 4

6. Sew one AD strip to the lower right side of the block, as shown in **Diagram 4.** Sew the remaining B square to the end of the remaining AD strip. Sew the strip to the lower left side of the block to complete it.

7. Repeat to make a total of 18 blocks.

Assembling the Quilt Top

1. Referring to the **Quilt Diagram,** lay out the 18 pieced blocks, the H side setting triangles, and the I corner setting triangles.

2. Join the blocks and setting pieces in diagonal rows. Press the seams in opposite directions from row to row.

3. Join the rows to complete the inner quilt.

Adding the Borders

1. Measure the width of the quilt (approximately 17⅜ inches). Cut two inner border strips to length from the 1⅞-inch-wide dark blue strip. Sew the borders to the top and bottom of the quilt.

2. Measure the length of the quilt (approximately 25¾ inches). Cut the 1½-inch-wide dark blue inner border strips to length, and sew them to the sides of the quilt top.

3. To make the pieced border, sew cream print F triangles to opposite sides of 38 E border squares, as shown in **Diagram 5.**

4. Sew F and G triangles to the eight remaining E squares to make eight corner units, as shown in **Diagram 6.**

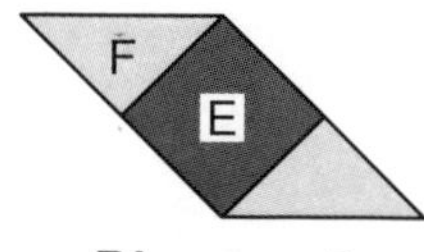

Diagram 5

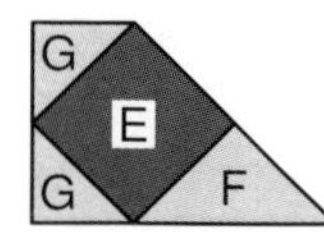

Diagram 6

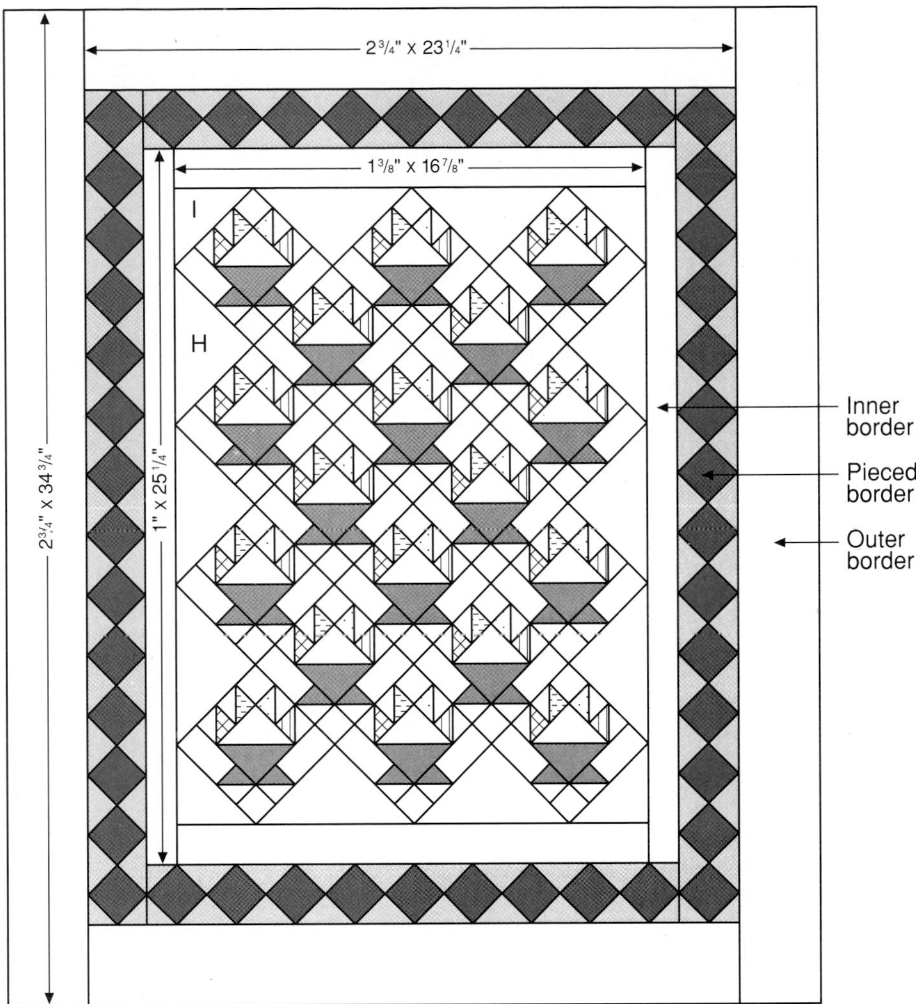

Quilt Diagram

5. Make each top and bottom pieced border by joining seven Step 3 units together to make a strip. Add a Step 4 corner unit to each end of the strip. Sew the pieced borders to the top and bottom of the inner quilt top. Press the seams toward the blue inner borders.

6. Make each side pieced border by joining 12 Step 3 units together to make a strip, and add a Step 4 corner unit to each end. Sew the borders to the sides of the quilt top. Press the seams toward the blue borders.

7. Measure the width of the quilt top (approximately 23⅜ inches). Trim two 3¼-inch-wide dark blue print outer border strips to the width of the quilt. Sew the borders to the top and bottom of the quilt top. Press the seams toward the borders.

8. Measure the length of the quilt top (approximately 34¾ inches). Trim the two remaining 3¼-inch wide outer border strips to the length of the quilt. Sew the strips to the sides of the quilt top. Press the seams toward the borders.

Quilting and Finishing

1. Mark quilting designs. The quilting patterns for the side and corner setting triangles are given on the H and I pattern pieces on page 96.

2. Layer the quilt back, batting, and quilt top; baste. Trim the quilt back so it is approximately 3 inches larger than the quilt top on all sides.

3. Quilt all marked designs, and add additional quilting as desired. On the quilt shown, the basket blocks and the pieced border have quilting in the ditch along the seams. A square grid is quilted in the border.

4. From the reserved binding fabric, make approximately 140 inches of French-fold binding. See page 164 for suggested binding widths and instructions on making and attaching binding.

5. Sew the binding to the quilt top. Trim the excess batting and backing, and hand finish the binding on the back side of the quilt. Add a hanging sleeve to the back. Refer to page 167 for instructions on making and adding a hanging sleeve.

A

B

C

D

E

F

Pattern Piece and Quilting Design

H

I

G

Pattern Piece and Quilting Design

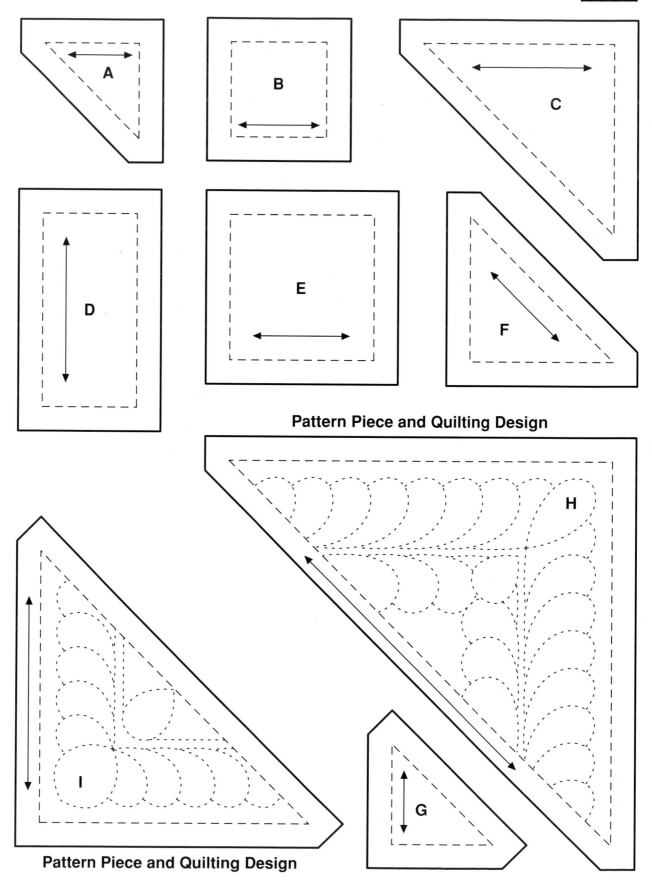

Diamond Charms

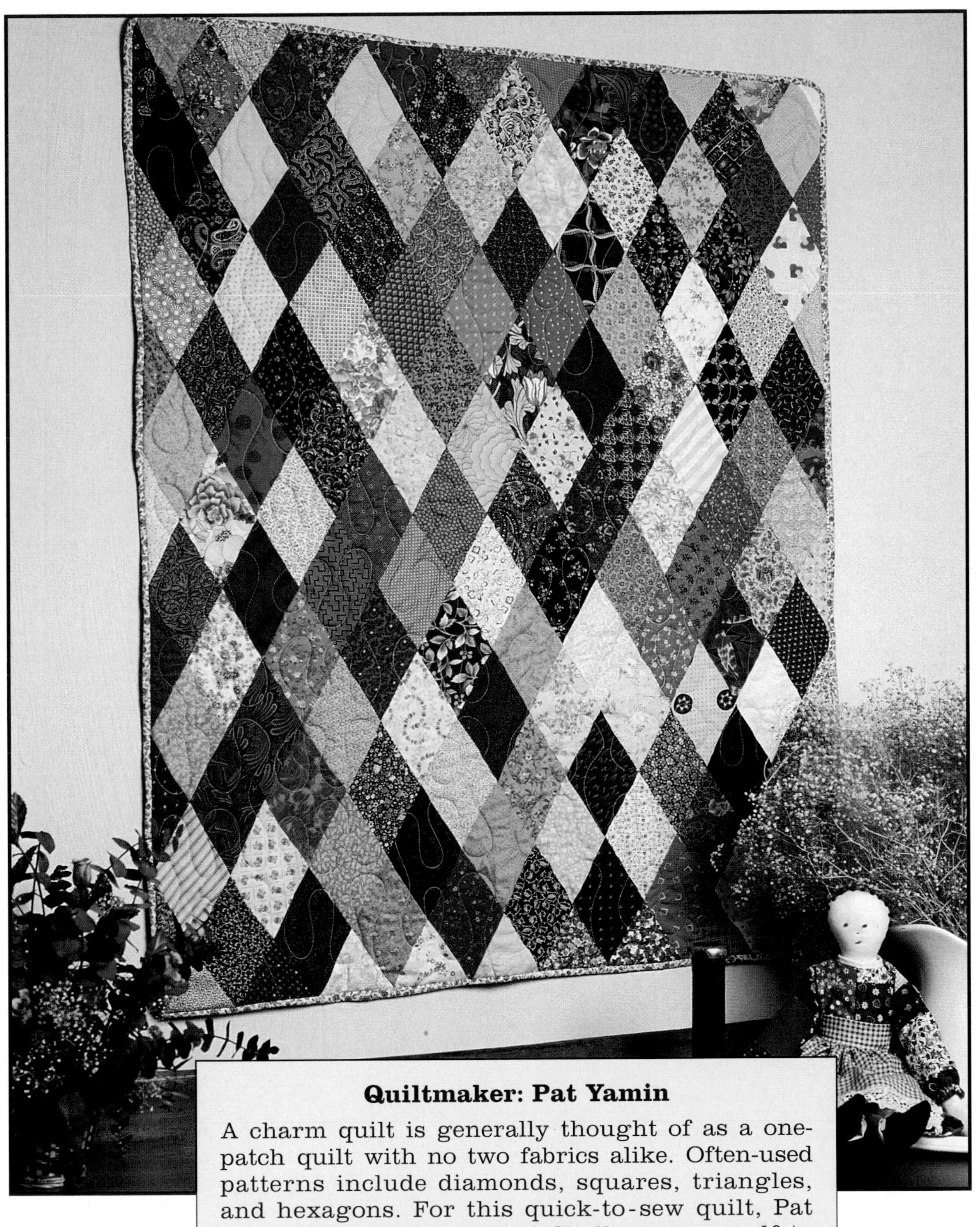

Quiltmaker: Pat Yamin

A charm quilt is generally thought of as a one-patch quilt with no two fabrics alike. Often-used patterns include diamonds, squares, triangles, and hexagons. For this quick-to-sew quilt, Pat used 150 different prints! Challenge yourself to see what you can create without using any fabric twice. Use your scraps and have some fun!

Skill Level: Easy

Size: Finished quilt is approximately 33¼ × 42 inches

Fabrics and Supplies

- 150 scraps (approximately 6½ inches square) of fabric for charm diamonds
- 1¾ yards of fabric for back and binding
- Crib-size quilt batting (45 × 60 inches)
- Rotary cutter, ruler, and mat
- Template plastic

Cutting

All measurements include ¼-inch seam allowances. Make a diamond template using the pattern on page 99. The suggested grain line for cutting is indicated on the pattern piece, but you may disregard it on some pieces of scrap fabric if necessary to make the template fit. Tips for making and using templates are on page 153.

From each scrap fabric, cut:
- One diamond

Piecing the Quilt

1. Lay out the diamonds in a pleasing arrangement, as shown in the photo on page 97.

2. Join the diamonds in diagonal rows as indicated in **Diagram 1.** Press the seams in opposite directions from row to row. Join the rows. The outside edges of the quilt will be uneven.

3. Referring to **Diagram 2,** use a rotary cutter and ruler to trim the outside edges of the quilt top, positioning the ruler so that a ¼-inch seam allowance extends beyond the seams joining the rows.

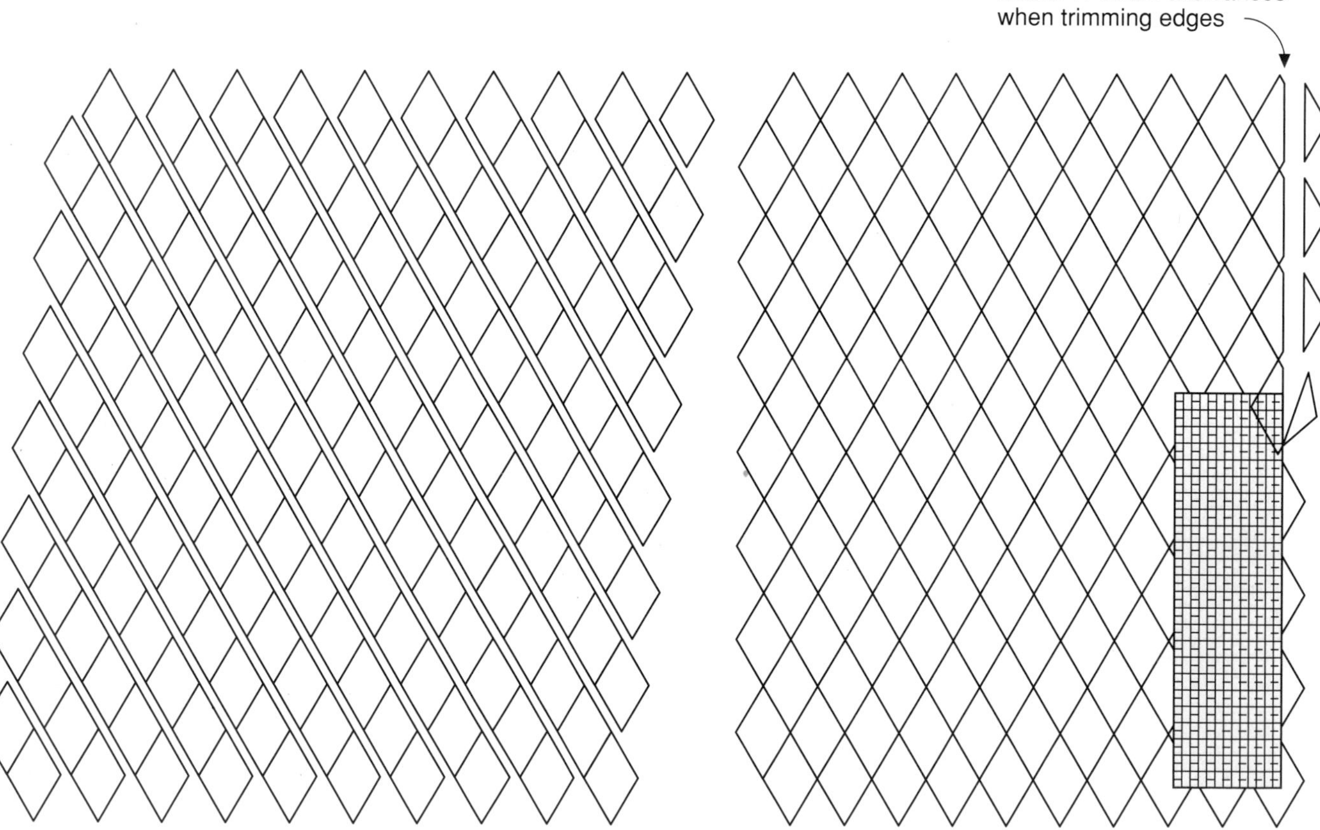
Leave ¼" seam allowances when trimming edges

Diagram 1 **Diagram 2**

Quilting and Finishing

1. Mark quilting designs. The quilt shown was machine quilted with an allover, large-scale "doodle" design.

2. Layer the quilt back, batting, and quilt top; baste. Trim the quilt back so it is approximately 3 inches larger than the quilt top on all sides.

3. Quilt all marked designs, and add additional quilting as desired.

4. From the binding fabric, make approximately 170 inches of French-fold binding. See page 164 for suggested binding widths and instructions on making and attaching binding.

5. Sew the binding to the quilt top. Trim the excess batting and backing, and hand finish the binding on the back side of the quilt.

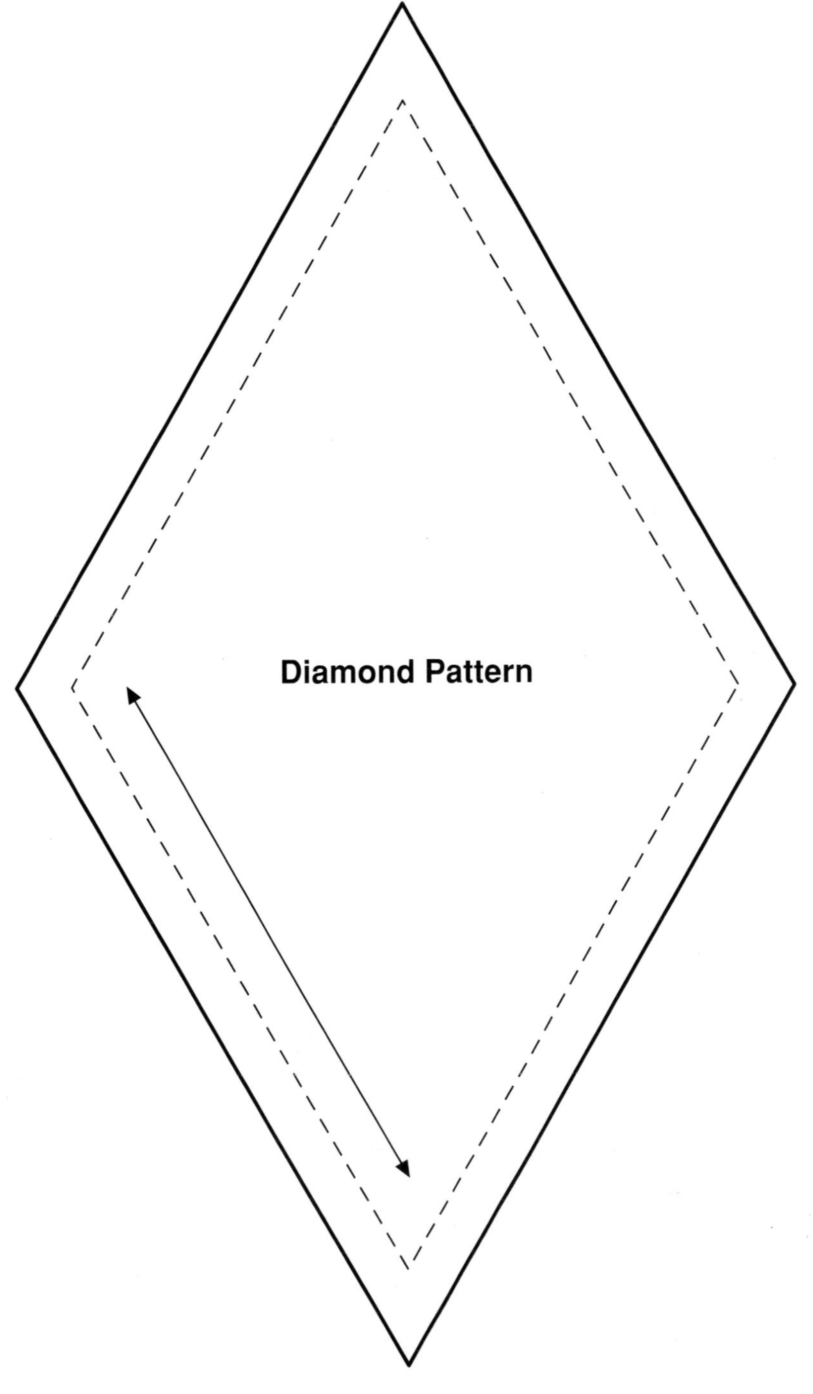

Broken Hearts for Daddy

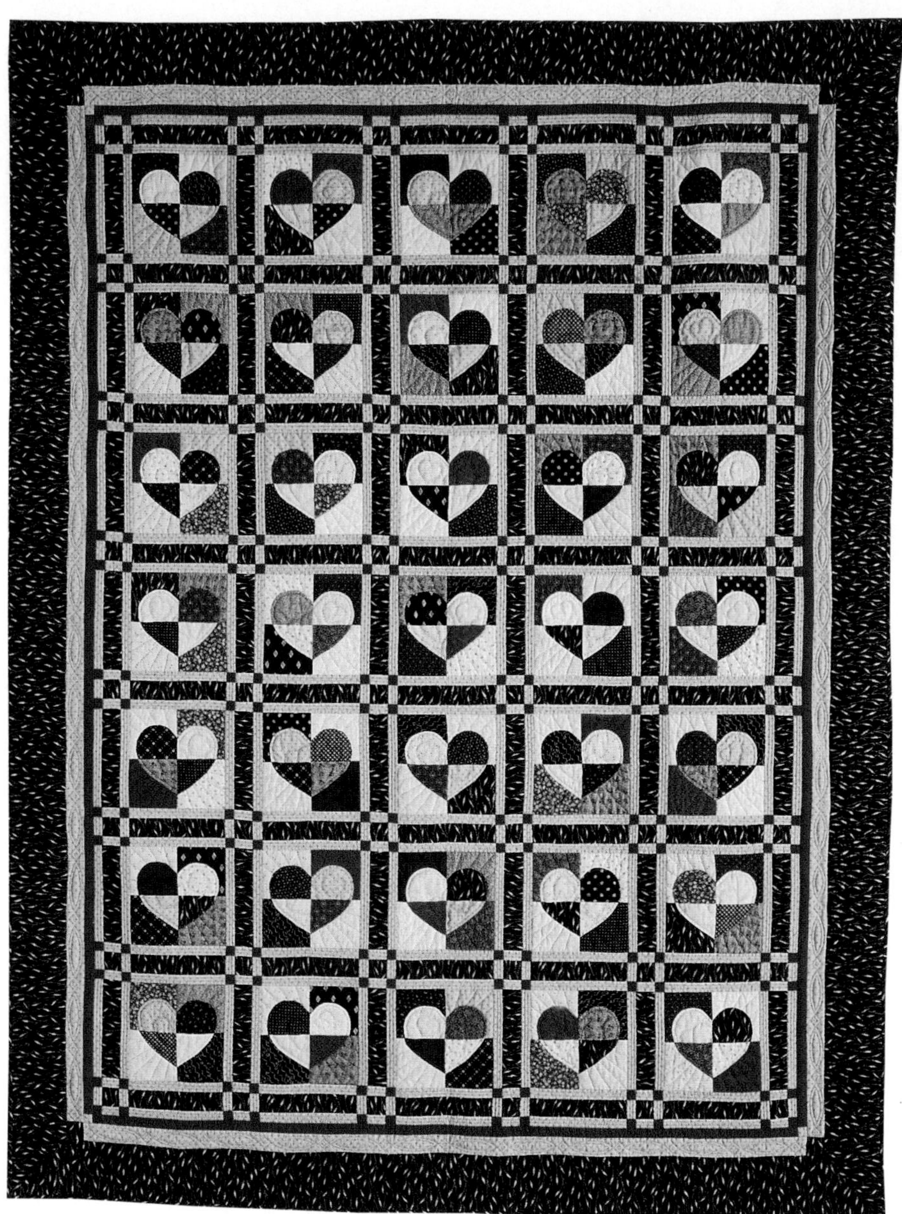

Quiltmaker: Elsie Campbell

Elsie began this quilt shortly after her father's death from a heart attack and named it in honor of his "broken heart." Muted versions of red, white, and blue work well together in this quilt, which calls for both patchwork and appliqué. Quick-cutting and strip-piecing make the delightful sashing treatment easy to construct. The easy heart shape is perfect for freezer paper appliqué.

Skill Level: Easy

Size: Finished quilt is 72 × 94 inches
Finished block is 8 inches square

Fabrics and Supplies

- 3½ yards of navy blue print fabric for outer border, sashing strip sets, and binding
- 2½ yards of taupe print fabric for middle border and sashing strip sets
- 2½ yards total of assorted medium-to-dark red and navy blue print fabrics for blocks
- 2½ yards total of assorted medium-to-light cream, taupe, and blue print fabrics for blocks
- 1 yard of red solid fabric for inner border and sashing strips
- 6 yards of fabric for quilt back
- Full-size quilt batting (81 × 96 inches)
- Rotary cutter, ruler, and mat
- Plastic-coated freezer paper or template plastic

Cutting

All measurements include ¼-inch seam allowances. Measurements for the borders are longer than needed; trim them to the exact length when they are added to the quilt top. Instructions given are for quick-cutting pieces with a rotary cutter and ruler.

The heart shapes will be cut after the squares are joined. Using the pattern on page 105, follow the instructions for freezer paper appliqué given in "Piecing and Appliquéing the Hearts" on page 102, or make a plastic template if you prefer to use traditional cutting and preparation techniques.

From the navy blue print fabric, cut:
- Ten 5 × 44-inch outer border strips
- Twenty-one 2 × 44-inch strips for sashing
- Four 2-inch border corner squares
- Reserve the remaining fabric for binding

From the taupe print fabric, cut:
- Nine 2 × 44-inch middle border strips
- Three 2 × 44-inch strips for sashing
- Forty-two 1¼ × 44-inch strips for sashing
- Four 1½-inch border corner squares

From the medium-to-dark red and navy blue print fabrics, cut:
- Seventy 4½-inch squares for block backgrounds
- Seventy 4-inch squares for hearts

From the medium-to-light cream, taupe, and blue print fabrics, cut:
- Seventy 4½-inch squares for block backgrounds
- Seventy 4-inch squares for hearts

From the red solid fabric, cut:
- Eight 1½ × 44-inch inner border strips
- Six 1¼ × 44-inch strips for sashing

Fabric Key

Navy blue print

Taupe print

Medium-to-dark fabrics

Medium-to-light fabrics

Red

Making the Blocks

For each block, four fabrics are combined for the background, and four other fabrics are combined to make the heart. Choose fabrics that will result in a high degree of contrast between the hearts and the background. In the quilt shown in the photo on the opposite page, the dark fabrics in the background are sometimes in the upper left and lower right positions, and sometimes in the upper right and lower left. **Diagram 1** illustrates the two ways to shade the block.

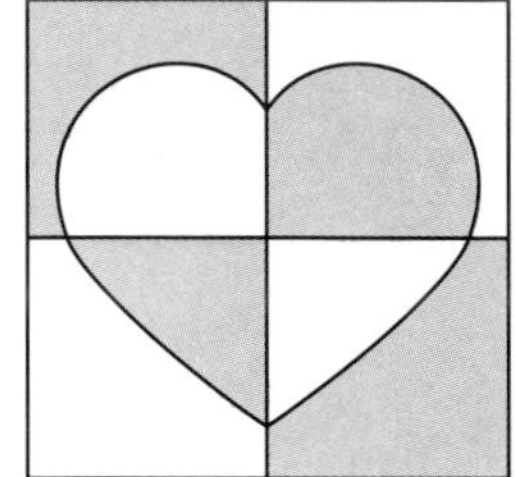

Diagram 1

Piecing the Block Backgrounds

1. Select and lay out four 4½-inch squares, two light and two dark, for one block.

2. Join the squares into two rows of two squares per row, as shown in **Diagram 2.** Press the seams toward the darker squares. Join the rows. The finished block should measure 8½ inches square, including seam allowances.

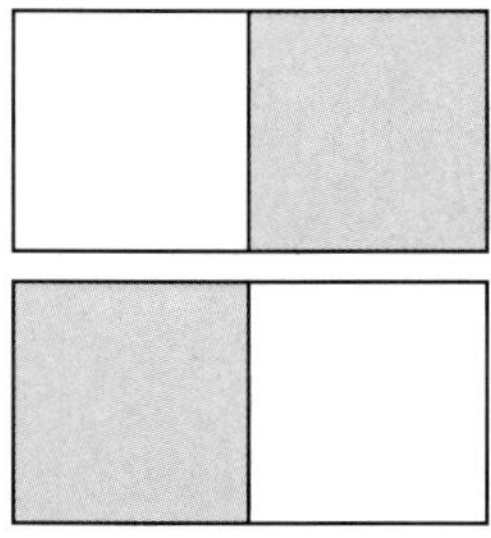

Diagram 2

3. Repeat to make a total of 35 block backgrounds.

Piecing and Appliquéing the Hearts

1. If you are using the freezer paper method, cut a 7-inch square of freezer paper. Trace the heart pattern (including the placement lines) on page 105 onto the smooth (not shiny) side of the paper. Cut out the pattern. If you are using the traditional template method, trace the heart pattern (including the placement lines) onto a sheet of template plastic and cut it out.

2. Select and lay out four 4-inch squares, two light and two dark, for each heart. Make sure the fabrics will contrast well with the block background you designate for each heart.

3. Join the squares into two rows of two squares per row, pressing the seams toward the darker squares. Join the rows. The pieced unit should measure 7½ inches square.

4. Place the freezer paper heart pattern on the *right* side of the pieced square, aligning the placement lines with the seams. Using a dry iron on the wool setting, press the pattern to the fabric. If you are using a template rather than freezer paper, lightly trace the heart shape onto the pieced square.

5. Cut out the heart a scant ¼ inch away from the paper edge or the traced line to form a seam allowance. At the cleft of the heart, remove any stitches that are in the seam allowance so it can be folded under.

6. Pin the heart to the block background, aligning the seams. Appliqué the heart to the background. Turn under the seam allowance with the needle as you stitch, aligning the folded fabric edge with the paper edge or the traced line. After stitching, remove the paper pattern for reuse. See page 156 for tips on appliqué.

7. Turn the block to the wrong side and trim away the background fabric behind the heart, leaving a scant ¼ inch seam allowance.

8. In the same manner, appliqué a heart to each of the 34 remaining background blocks. Make a new freezer paper pattern to replace the original one as it wears out.

Piecing the Sashing

Two different units form the sashing for the quilt. Both units are cut from simple strip sets.

1. Referring to **Diagram 3,** sew a 1¼-inch-wide taupe strip to both sides of a 2-inch-wide navy blue strip. Press the seams toward the navy strip. The strip set should measure 3½ inches wide, including seam allowances. Make a total of 21 of these strip sets.

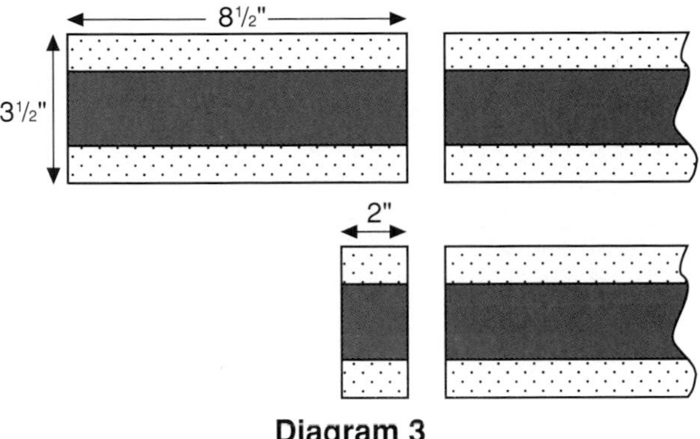

Diagram 3

2. Cut segments from the Step 1 strip sets. First, cut eighty-two 8½-inch-long segments, cutting four from each strip set. (You will have two leftover segments.) These are the sashing units. From the leftover ends of each set, cut a total of forty-eight 2-inch segments. These will be used in the sashing square units.

3. Referring to **Diagram 4,** sew a 1¼-inch-wide red strip to each side of a 2-inch-wide taupe strip. Press the seams toward the red strips. Make a total of three of these strip sets.

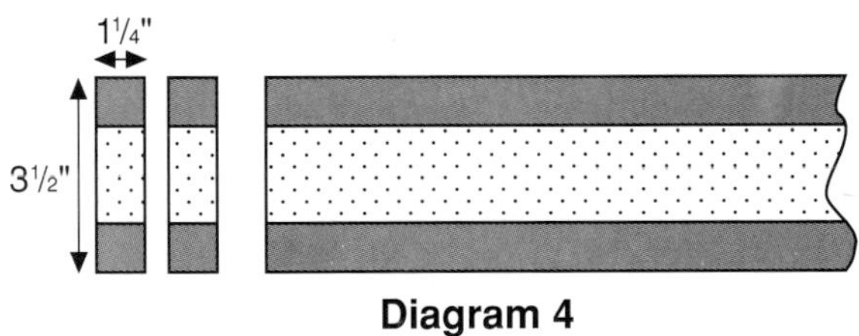

Diagram 4

4. Cut ninety-six 1¼-inch-long segments from the Step 3 strip sets.

5. Make 48 sashing square units by joining one 2-inch Step 2 segment and two Step 4 segments, as shown in **Diagram 5.** Press the seams away from the center section. The finished units should measure 3½ inches square.

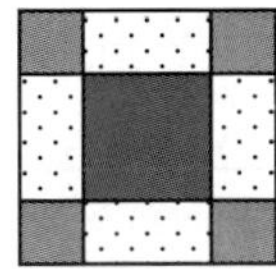
Diagram 5

Assembling the Quilt Top

1. Referring to **Diagram 6,** lay out the heart blocks, sashing units, and sashing square units. Sew the units into horizontal Type A and Type B rows. Type A rows have six sashing square units and five sashing units. Type B rows have six sashing units and five heart blocks. Press the seams toward the sashing units.

2. Join the rows, alternating types.

Adding the Borders

1. Piece four inner borders from the 1½-inch-wide red border strips, joining two strips for each border.

2. Measure the width and length of the quilt top. Trim the borders to these measurements. Sew the side borders to the sides of the quilt, pressing the seams toward the borders. Sew a taupe print corner square to each end of the top and bottom border strips. Press the seams toward the borders. Sew the top and bottom borders to the quilt, again pressing the seams toward the borders.

3. Piece the four middle borders from the 2-inch-wide taupe print border strips. Join two strips for each top and bottom border, and two-and-one-half strips for each side border.

4. Trim and add the taupe borders to the sides of the quilt top in the same manner as the red inner borders. Sew a navy print corner square to each end of the top and bottom border strips before sewing the borders to the quilt. Press the seams toward the taupe borders.

5. Piece the navy print outer borders by joining two 5-inch-wide strips for each top and bottom border, and three strips for each side border. Place the navy border strips right sides together with the quilt top, matching centers. Sew the borders to the quilt, mitering the border corner seams. See page 160 for tips on adding mitered borders to a quilt.

Heart Block

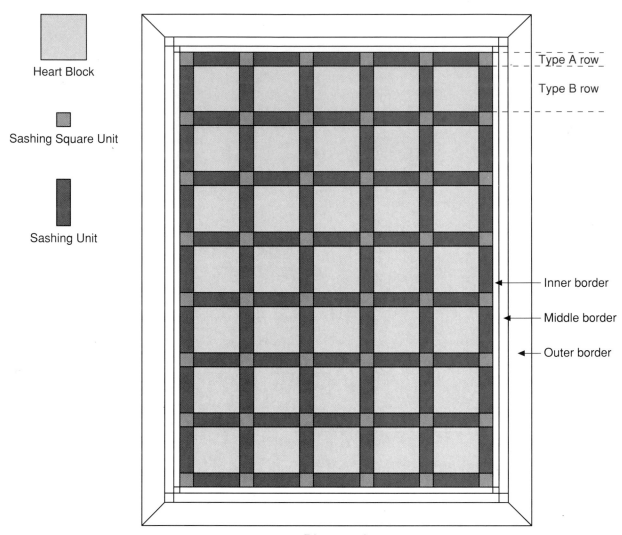

Sashing Square Unit

Sashing Unit

Type A row

Type B row

Inner border

Middle border

Outer border

Diagram 6

Quilting and Finishing

1. Mark quilting designs. On the quilt shown, various-size double hearts in varying positions were quilted within the appliquéd hearts. Patterns for two sizes of double hearts are provided on the opposite page. Straight lines of quilting radiate from the appliquéd hearts in the block background.

2. Cut the backing fabric into two 3-yard pieces and trim the selvages. Divide one of the pieces in half lengthwise. Sew one half to each side of the full-width piece. Press the seams away from the center panel.

3. Layer the quilt back, batting, and quilt top; baste. Trim the quilt back so it is approximately 3 inches larger than the quilt top on all sides.

4. Quilt all marked designs, and add additional quilting as desired.

5. Use the remaining navy blue print fabric to make approximately 350 inches of French-fold binding. See page 164 for suggested binding widths and instructions on making and attaching binding.

6. Sew the binding to the quilt top. Trim the excess batting and backing, and hand finish the binding on the back side of the quilt.

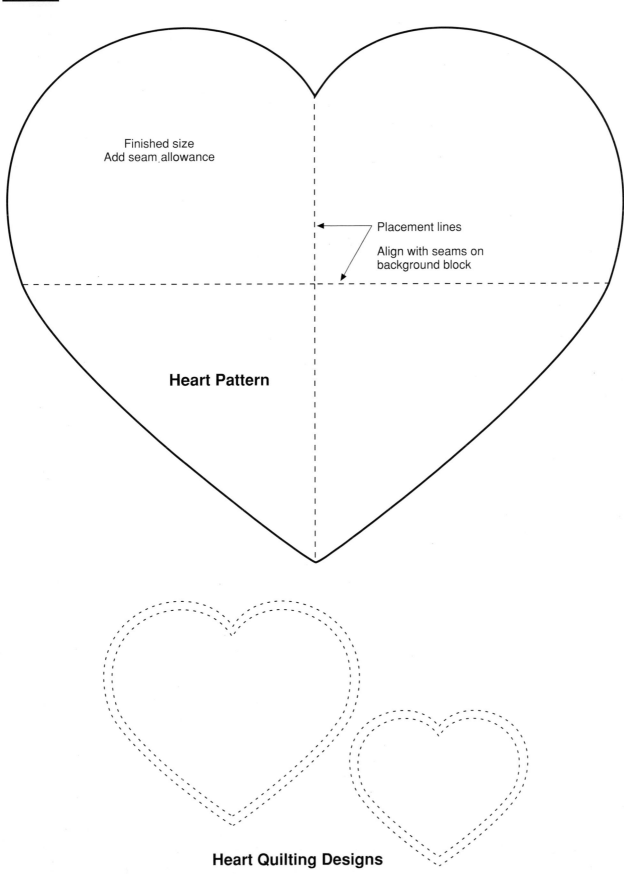

Finished size
Add seam allowance

Placement lines

Align with seams on
background block

Heart Pattern

Heart Quilting Designs

Holidays and Celebrations

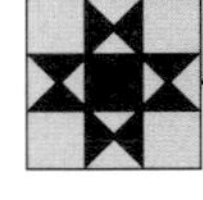

Stars and Stripes Picnic Set

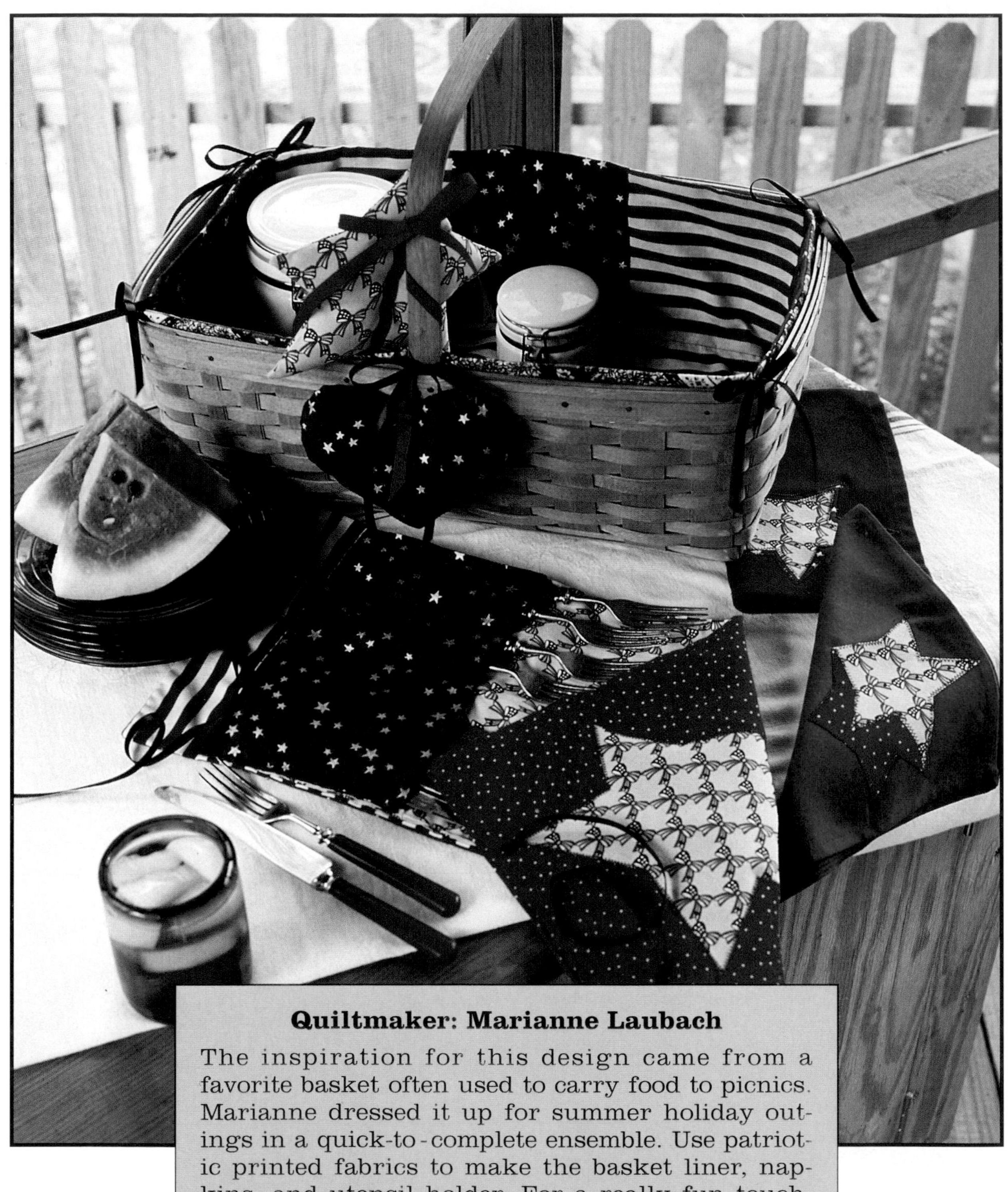

Quiltmaker: Marianne Laubach

The inspiration for this design came from a favorite basket often used to carry food to picnics. Marianne dressed it up for summer holiday outings in a quick-to-complete ensemble. Use patriotic printed fabrics to make the basket liner, napkins, and utensil holder. For a really fun touch, add stuffed heart and star basket accents. Ribbon ties secure the liner and the accents to the basket.

Skill Level: Easy

Size: Liner fits a basket that is approximately 18 inches long, 9½ inches wide, and 6 inches deep
Finished utensil holder is approximately 10 × 23½ inches when open
Finished napkins are 20 inches square

Fabrics and Supplies

- 1 yard of red-and-white striped fabric for liner and utensil holder
- ¾ yard of cotton flannel print fabric for back of basket liner
- ½ yard of blue-and-gold star fabric for liner, utensil holder, and stuffed heart
- ⅓ yard of red print fabric for back of utensil holder
- ¼ yard of patriotic bow print fabric for utensil holder, stuffed star, and appliqué
- 20-inch squares of fabric for napkins
- 10½ × 24-inch rectangle of batting for utensil holder
- Polyester fiberfill for stuffed heart and star accents
- Paper-backed fusible webbing for appliqués
- 5 yards of ¼-inch-wide navy blue satin ribbon for ties
- 1 yard of ⅜-inch-wide dark red grosgrain ribbon for ties

Cutting

All measurements, except appliqués, include ¼-inch seam allowances. Use the pattern pieces on pages 112–113 to make the star appliqués and the stuffed heart and star. Be sure to add seam allowances when cutting out the pieces for the stuffed accents. Follow the directions in "No-Sew Appliqué" on page 116 to prepare, cut out, position, and fuse the appliqués.

From the red-and-white striped fabric, cut:

- One 10½ × 24-inch rectangle for the inside of the utensil holder (cut so the stripes are parallel to the 10½-inch side)
- One 9½ × 18½-inch rectangle for the basket liner (cut so the stripes are parallel to the 18½-inch side)
- Four 6½-inch squares

From the blue-and-gold star fabric, cut:

- One 10½ × 11½-inch rectangle for the utensil holder pocket
- Two 6½ × 9½-inch rectangles
- Two 6½-inch squares
- 2 hearts

From the red print fabric, cut:

- One 10½ × 24-inch rectangle for the back of the utensil holder

From the patriotic bow print fabric, cut:

- One 10½ × 18-inch rectangle for the utensil holder pocket
- 2 large stars. Add ¼-inch seam allowances.

Assembling the Basket Liner

1. Referring to the **Fabric Key** and **Diagram 1** on page 110, sew a 6½ × 9½-inch blue-and-gold rectangle to each short side of the 9½ × 18½-inch red-and-white striped rectangle to make the center panel.

2. Sew a 6½-inch red-and-white striped square to each side of a 6½-inch blue-and-gold square to form one side panel. Repeat to make the other side panel.

3. Sew the two side panels to the two sides of the center panel as shown to complete the liner.

Fabric Key

- Red-and-white striped
- Blue-and-gold star
- Red print
- Bow print

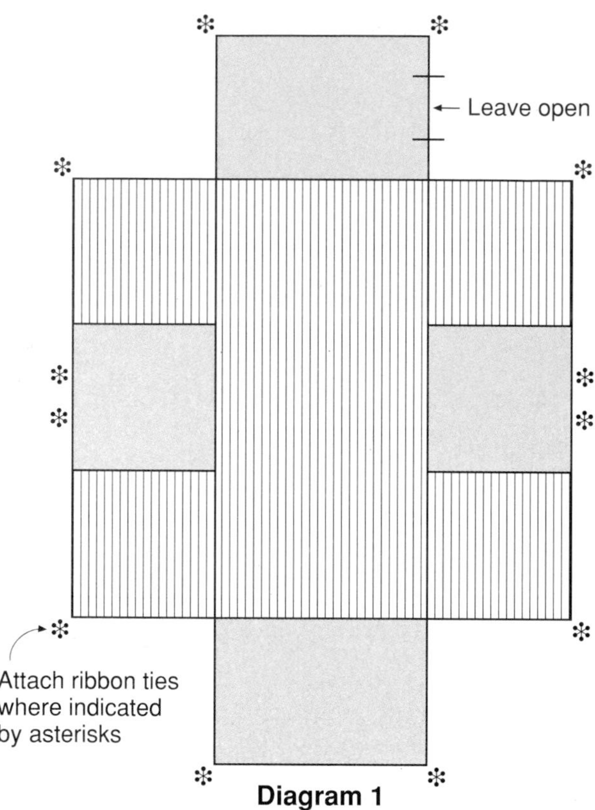

Diagram 1

4. Use the pieced liner as a pattern to cut a liner backing from the cotton flannel. Cut the backing exactly the same size as the pieced liner.

5. Layer the pieced liner right sides together with the cotton flannel liner backing. Using a ¼-inch seam, stitch around the outside edges, leaving one section open for turning, as shown in **Diagram 1.**

6. Clip the seam allowances close to the stitching at the inside corners. Turn the stitched liner right side out through the opening; press. Hand stitch the opening closed.

7. Cut twelve 12-inch lengths of navy blue ribbon to make ties. Tack the ties to the liner backing at the positions indicated by the asterisks on **Diagram 1.**

8. Position the basket liner in the basket. Secure it by bringing the end of the ribbons to the outside of the basket, as shown in **Diagram 2A,** and slipping them through the basket slats at the corners, as shown in **2B.** Tie the ends of the ribbon in a bow. Secure the sides of the liner by tying the ribbons around the basket handle.

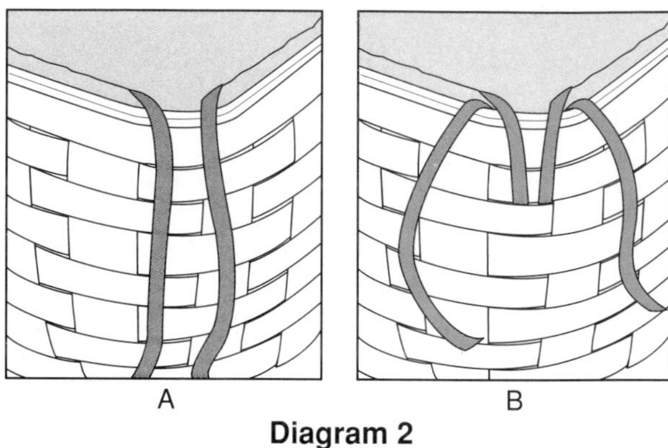

Diagram 2

Assembling the Utensil Holder

1. Lay out the rectangle of batting. Position the 10½ × 24-inch red print rectangle for the back of the holder right side up on top of the batting. Place the 10½ × 24-inch striped fabric rectangle for the inside of the holder on top, wrong side up.

2. Using a ¼-inch seam, stitch around the outside edges, leaving a section at one short end open, as shown in **Diagram 3.**

3. Trim the seam allowances of the batting if necessary to reduce bulk. Turn the holder right side out through the open end. Press the raw edges to the inside at the opening, and topstitch across the end to close the opening.

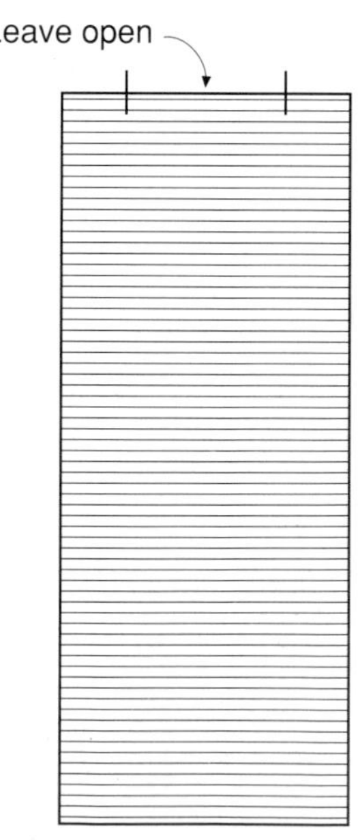

Diagram 3

4. Fold the $10\frac{1}{2} \times 18$-inch bow fabric rectangle in half crosswise with right sides together. Using a $\frac{1}{4}$-inch seam allowance, stitch along the two 9-inch sides, as shown in **Diagram 4.** Clip, turn right side out, and press.

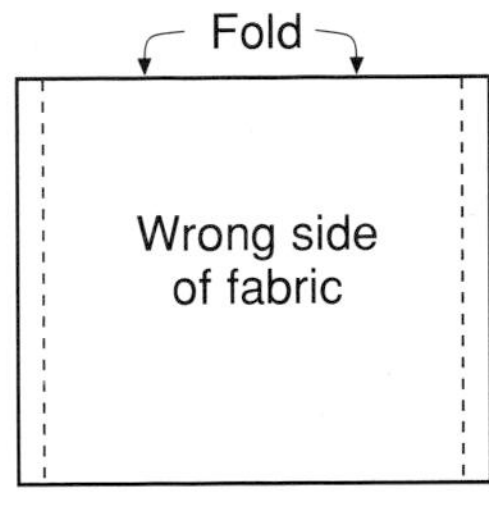

Diagram 4

5. In the same manner, fold the $10\frac{1}{2} \times 11\frac{1}{2}$-inch blue-and-gold rectangle in half right sides together, and stitch along the $5\frac{3}{4}$-inch sides. Turn right side out and press.

6. Position the bow print pocket on the red-and-white striped side of the padded holder, as shown in **Diagram 5.** The top folded edge of the pocket should be approximately $10\frac{1}{2}$ inches down from the end of the holder. Pin in place.

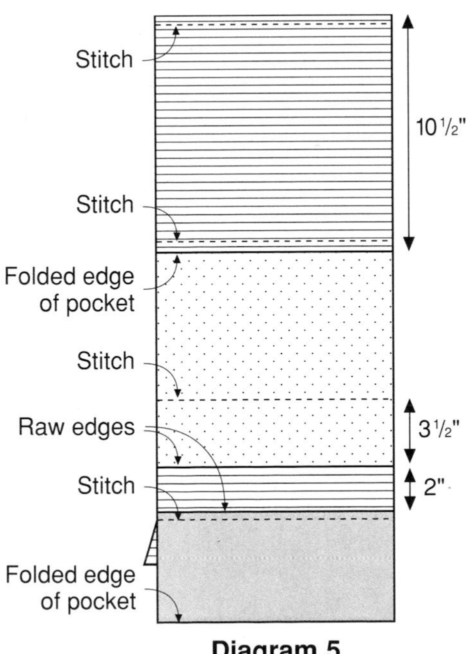

Diagram 5

7. Referring to **Diagram 5,** position the blue-and-gold pocket so that the raw edge is approximately 2 inches from the end of the holder and is facing toward the bow print pocket. The folded edge of the pocket will extend off the end of the holder. Pin in place. You will flip the pocket up into position after stitching.

8. Add four lines of horizontal stitching, as shown in **Diagram 5.** The four places to stitch are: across the top of the holder; just above the folded edge of the bow print pocket; across the lower part of the bow print pocket, approximately $3\frac{1}{2}$ inches from the raw edge; and along the raw edge of the blue-and-gold pocket.

9. Flip the blue-and-gold pocket up so that the folded edge is positioned parallel and closer to the folded edge of the upper pocket. Pin to secure.

10. Add lines of vertical stitching, as shown in **Diagram 6.** First, stitch along the two outside edges to secure the sides of the pockets; then, stitch the divisions on the lower pocket.

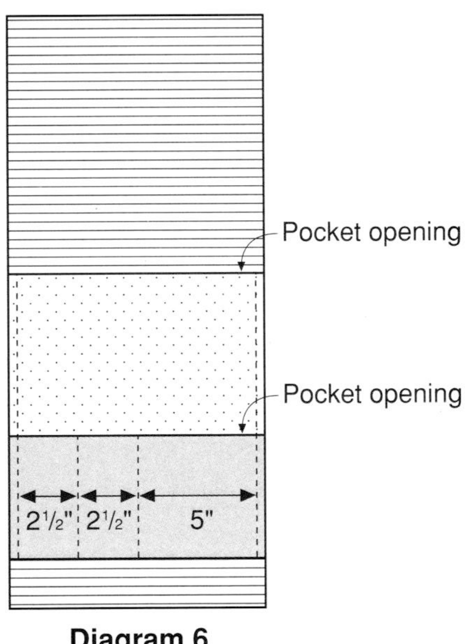

Diagram 6

11. Following the instructions in "No-Sew Appliqué" on page 116, cut out and fuse a large star to the back of the utensil holder. Refer to **Diagram 7** on page 112 for approximate placement of the star. The star pattern is on page 113. After fusing, machine zigzag around the outside edges of the star. Refer to page 158 for instructions on machine appliqué.

12. Cut two 18-inch lengths of navy blue ribbon for ties. Tack one tie at the edge of the bottom flap and one near the corner of the star on the top flap of the holder, as shown in **Diagram 7** on page 112.

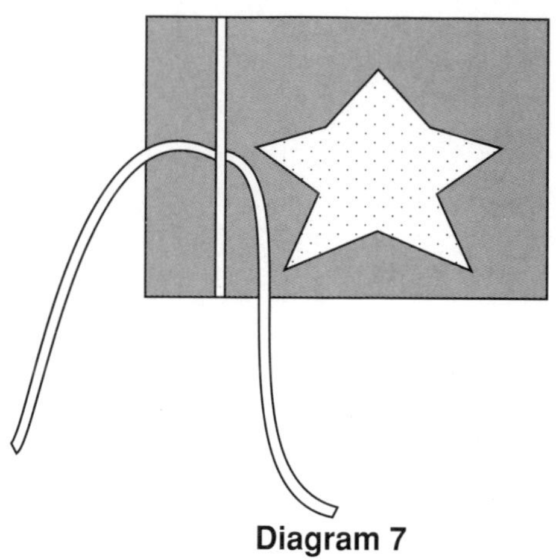

Diagram 7

Making the Napkins

1. For each napkin, either serge the four raw edges or turn and press the edges under and topstitch.

2. Following the instructions in "No-Sew Appliqué" on page 116, cut out and fuse two small star appliqués at one corner of each napkin. The pattern for the appliqué is on the oposite page. After fusing, machine zigzag around the outside edges. Refer to page 158 for instructions on machine appliqué.

Heart Pattern

Making the Heart and Star Accents

1. Use the two hearts and the remaining two large stars to make the stuffed accents. Place the fabrics right sides together and stitch. Leave a 2-inch section open for turning.

2. Clip the inside corners of the star and the cleft of the heart. Turn the pieces right side out through the opening. Press.

3. Stuff the heart and the star with polyester fiberfill. Hand stitch the opening closed.

4. Cut two pieces of red ribbon approximately 18 inches long, and tack one each to the heart and the star to tie them to the basket handle.

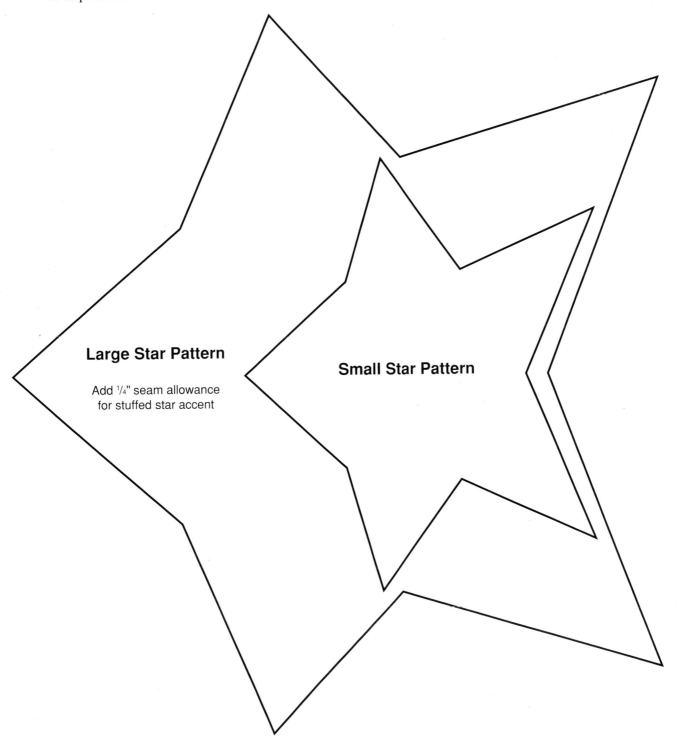

Large Star Pattern

Add 1/4" seam allowance for stuffed star accent

Small Star Pattern

Halloween Mini Quilts

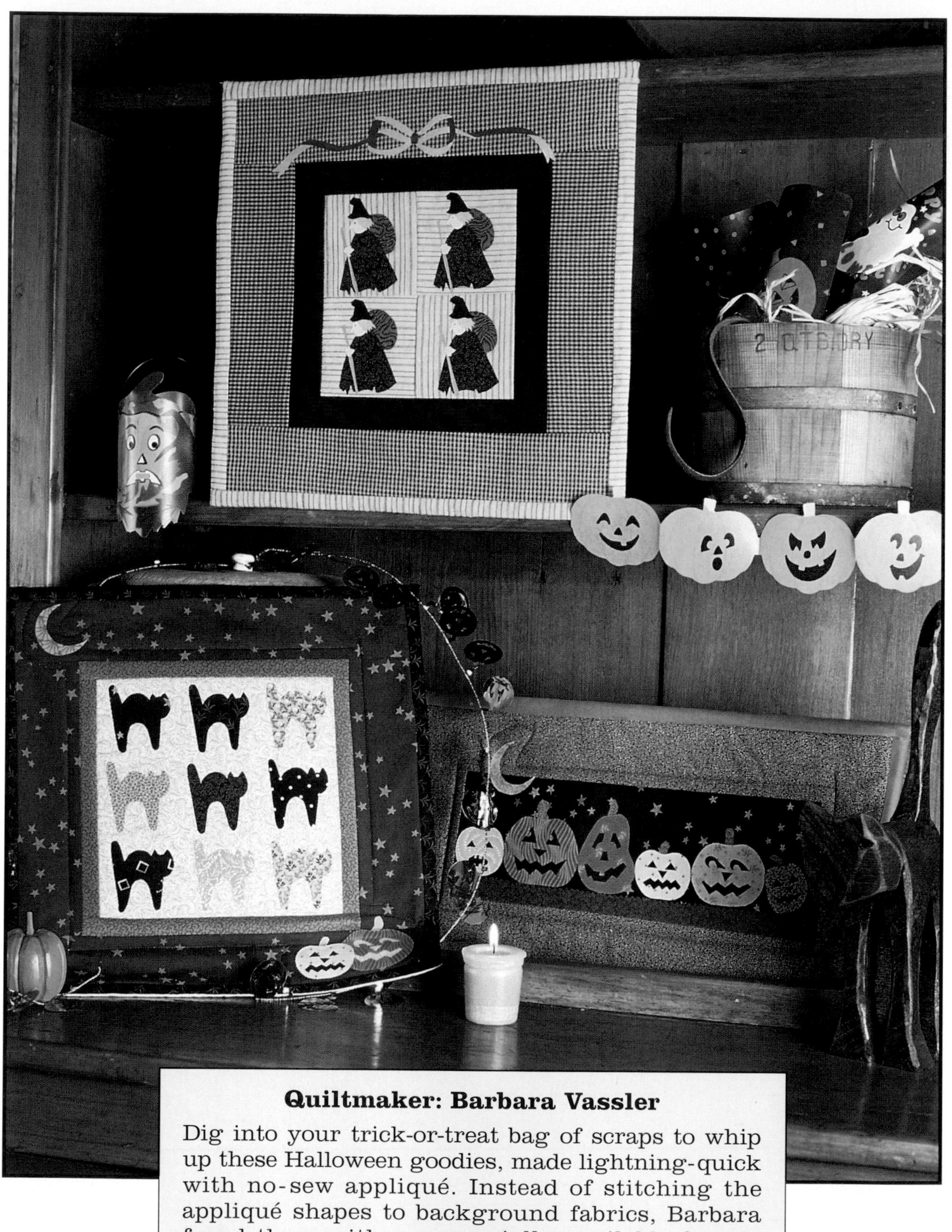

Quiltmaker: Barbara Vassler

Dig into your trick-or-treat bag of scraps to whip up these Halloween goodies, made lightning-quick with no-sew appliqué. Instead of stitching the appliqué shapes to background fabrics, Barbara fused them with commercially available fusible webbing.

Skill Level: Easy

Size: Finished Nine Lives mini quilt is 13½ inches square, including mock binding
Finished All in a Row mini quilt is 9 × 17 inches, including mock binding
Finished Four Witches mini quilt is 14 inches square, including mock binding

Fabrics and Supplies for Nine Lives

- ¼ yard of dark green print fabric for wide border
- ⅛ yard of brown print fabric for inner border
- ⅛ yard of black print fabric for mock binding
- One 8-inch square of beige print fabric for background
- Scraps (approximately 3 inches square) of nine different black or gray print fabrics for cats
- Scraps of orange print fabrics for pumpkins
- Scraps of black, gray, and gold solid fabrics for pumpkin faces, pumpkin stems, and moon
- One 15-inch square of muslin for quilt back
- One 15-inch square of batting
- Paper-backed fusible webbing, such as Wonder-Under
- Rotary cutter, ruler, and mat

Cutting

All measurements, except for appliqués, include ¼-inch seam allowances. Using the pattern pieces on pages 119–120, follow the directions in "No-Sew Appliqué" on page 116 to prepare, cut out, position, and fuse the appliqués. For the pumpkin border appliqués, choose your two favorite designs from the six included on page 119.

From the dark green fabric, cut:
- Two 2½ × 9-inch outer border strips
- Two 2½ × 13-inch outer border strips

From the black and gray print fabrics, prepare fusible appliqués for:
- 9 cats

From the brown print fabric, cut:
- Two 1 × 8-inch inner border strips
- Two 1 × 9-inch inner border strips

From the black print binding fabric, cut:
- Two 1 × 13-inch mock binding strips
- Two 1 × 14-inch mock binding strips

From the scrap fabrics, prepare fusible appliqués for:
- Pumpkins and moon border

Assembling the Mini Quilt

1. Fold and press the background square to create guidelines for positioning the cats. To do so, fold in 2¾ inches on two opposite sides of the square and lightly press; open out. In the same manner, fold in the other two sides and lightly press, being careful not to press out the first creases.

2. Position a cat in each square of the grid, leaving a ¼-inch seam allowance around the outside edge of the background square. Following the instructions in "No-Sew Appliqué" on page 116, fuse the cats in place.

3. Sew the 1 × 8-inch brown print border strips to the sides of the background block. Press the seams toward the strips. Sew the 1 × 9-inch brown border strips to the top and bottom of the block, pressing the seams toward the strips.

4. Sew the 2½ × 9-inch green print border strips to the sides of the block, pressing the seams toward the borders. In the same manner, sew the 2½ × 13-inch green border strips to the top and bottom of the block.

5. Sew the 1 × 13-inch black mock binding strips to the sides of the quilt top; press the seams toward the mock binding. Sew the 1 × 14-

No-Sew Appliqué

Heat-activated fusible webbing, such as Wonder-Under, Aleene's Hot-Stitch, and Heat 'N Bond, make no-sew appliqué fast, easy, and fun. The materials have a paper side to trace the pattern onto and a webbing or film side that bonds the fabric pattern piece onto a background fabric when ironed. Most of the materials are translucent enough to trace onto right from the book page, eliminating the need to make templates.

Follow the manufacturer's directions for the fusible webbing you are using. Note that if you are tracing letters or a design with a definite direction, you must trace it onto the paper side of the material in reverse.

1. Trace the appliqué designs onto the paper side (the smooth side) of the fusible webbing or film.
2. Loosely cut out the shapes, making them slightly larger than the drawn outlines.
3. Following the manufacturer's directions, fuse the webbing or film side of the shapes to the wrong side of the appliqué fabrics.
4. Cut out the appliqués on the drawn lines.
5. Peel off the paper just before positioning the appliqué shapes on the background fabric. When positioning pieces, overlap them as indicated by the dotted lines and/or shaded areas on the pattern pieces.
6. Fuse the design pieces to the background according to the manufacturer's directions. Keep tweezers handy for positioning tiny pieces. ♦

inch black mock binding strips to the top and bottom of the quilt top; press the seams toward the strips. Press the completed block.

6. Referring to the photo on page 114, position and fuse the moon and pumpkin appliqués in the green border.

Finishing

1. Lay the muslin backing square atop the piece of batting. Center the completed quilt top, right side down, on the muslin. Pin the layers together around the edges of the quilt top.

2. Using a ¼-inch seam, sew around the edges, leaving a 5-inch opening at the center of the bottom edge for turning. Trim the corners.

3. Use a rotary cutter and ruler to trim the muslin and batting even with the edges of the quilt top.

4. Turn the mini quilt right side out; press. Hand sew the opening closed.

5. Hand or machine quilt along the border seams and in the border if desired.

Fabrics and Supplies for All in a Row

- ⅛ yard of green print fabric for border
- ⅛ yard of orange solid fabric for mock binding
- Black fabric for background, larger than 4½ × 12½ inches
- Brown print fabric for fence, larger than 1½ × 12½ inches
- Scraps of 6 different orange print fabrics for pumpkins
- Scraps of black, green, and gold fabrics for pumpkin faces, pumpkin stems, and moon
- One 10 × 18-inch piece of muslin for quilt back
- One 10 × 18-inch piece of batting
- Paper-backed fusible webbing, such as Wonder-Under
- Rotary cutter, ruler, and mat
- Pinking shears

Cutting

All measurements, except for appliqués, include a ¼-inch seam allowance. Using the pattern pieces on pages 119–120, follow the directions in "No-Sew Appliqué" on this page to prepare, cut out, position, and fuse the appliqués.

From the green print fabric, cut:

- Two 2½ × 4½-inch border strips
- Two 2½ × 16½-inch border strips

From the orange solid fabric, cut:
- Two 1 × 8½-inch mock binding strips
- Two 1 × 17½-inch mock binding strips

From the black background fabric, cut:
- One 4½ × 12½-inch rectangle

From the various scrap fabrics, prepare fusible appliqués for:
- Pumpkins, stems, faces, and moon

Assembling the Mini Quilt

1. To make the fence, mark a 1 × 12½-inch rectangle on the paper side of the fusible webbing. Loosely cut the rectangle out a little larger than the markings. Fuse to the wrong side of the brown print fence fabric. Cut out along the lines on two short sides and one long side. On the remaining long side, use pinking shears to cut along the line, forming a "picket" edge. With the pieces placed wrong sides together, align the long straight edge of the fence with the edge of the black background rectangle and fuse.

2. Following the instructions in "No-Sew Appliqué" on the opposite page, position the pumpkins along the "fence," keeping them inside the ¼-inch seam allowances on the sides of the background piece. Fuse the pumpkins in place. Position and fuse the jack-o'-lantern faces.

3. Sew the 2½ × 4½-inch green border strips to the short sides of the background rectangle. Press the seams toward the strips. Sew the 2½ × 16½-inch green border strips to the top and bottom of the quilt top; press the seams toward the strips.

4. Sew the 1 × 8½-inch orange mock binding strips to the sides of the quilt top; press the seams toward the strips. Sew the 1 × 17½-inch mock binding strips to the top and bottom of the quilt top; press toward the strips.

5. Position and fuse the border moon appliqué to the quilt top.

Finishing

1. Lay the muslin backing square atop the piece of batting. Center the completed quilt top, right side down, on the muslin. Pin the layers together around the edges of the quilt top.

2. Using a ¼-inch seam allowance, sew around the edges, leaving a 5-inch opening at the center of the bottom edge for turning. Trim the corners.

3. Use a rotary cutter and ruler to trim the muslin and batting even with the edges of the quilt top.

4. Turn the mini quilt right side out; press. Hand sew the opening closed.

5. Hand or machine quilt along the border seams and in the border if desired.

Fabrics and Supplies for Four Witches

- ¼ yard of brown-and-black checked fabric for outer border
- ⅛ yard of orange-and-black striped fabric for background and mock binding
- ⅛ yard of black solid fabric for inner border and witches' hats
- Scraps of light green fabric for hair and border bow
- Scraps of dark green fabric for border bow
- Scraps of black print fabric for witches
- Scraps of gray, brown, and light pink fabrics for sticks, bags, faces, and hands
- One 15-inch square of muslin for quilt back
- One 15-inch square of batting
- Paper-backed fusible webbing, such as Wonder-Under
- Rotary cutter, ruler, and mat

Cutting

All measurements, except for appliqués, include ¼-inch seam allowances. Using the pattern pieces on pages 119–120, follow the directions in "No-Sew Appliqué" on the opposite page to prepare, cut out, position, and fuse appliqués.

From the black-and-brown checked fabric, cut:
- Two 2½ × 8½-inch border strips
- Two 2½ × 12½-inch border strips

From the orange-and-black striped fabric, cut:

- Four 3½-inch background squares
- Two 1½ × 12½-inch mock binding strips
- Two 1½ × 14½-inch mock binding strips

From the black solid fabric, cut:

- Two 1½ × 6½-inch border strips
- Two 1½ × 8½-inch border strips

From the various scrap fabrics, prepare fusible appliqués for:

- Witch and bow pattern pieces. (Refer to **Diagram 1** before cutting the bow pieces.)

Assembling the Mini Quilt

1. Following the fusing instructions in "No-Sew Appliqué" on page 116, position the pieces and fuse one witch to each of the orange-and-black striped background squares, leaving a ¼-inch seam allowance around the outside edge of the squares. Position the witches so that the stripes run vertically on two squares and horizontally on the other two.

2. Stitch the four background squares together in two rows of two squares per row, positioning them so that the direction of the background stripes alternates.

3. Sew the 1½ × 6½-inch black border strips to the sides of the inner quilt. Press the seams toward the strips. Sew the 1½ × 8½-inch black border strips to the top and bottom of the block. Press the seams toward the strips.

4. In the same manner, add the 2½ × 8½-inch black-and-brown checked border strips to the sides. Add the 2½ × 12½-inch strips to the top and bottom. Press the seams toward the strips.

5. Add the 1½ × 12½-inch orange-and-black mock binding strips to the sides. Add the 14½-inch-long strips to the top and bottom.

6. Referring to **Diagram 1,** cut the bow pieces from the light and dark green fabrics. The numbers in the diagram indicate the order in which the pieces are added; the letters indicate whether the piece should be cut from light or dark green fabric. Position and fuse the bow on the top border.

Finishing

1. Lay the muslin backing square atop the piece of batting. Center the completed quilt top, right side down, on the muslin. Pin the layers together around the edges of the quilt top.

2. Using a ¼-inch seam allowance, sew around the edges, leaving a 5-inch opening at the center of the bottom edge for turning. Trim the corners.

3. Use a rotary cutter and ruler to trim the muslin and batting even with the edges of the quilt top.

4. Turn the quilt right side out; press. Hand sew the opening closed.

5. Hand or machine quilt along the border seams and in the border if desired.

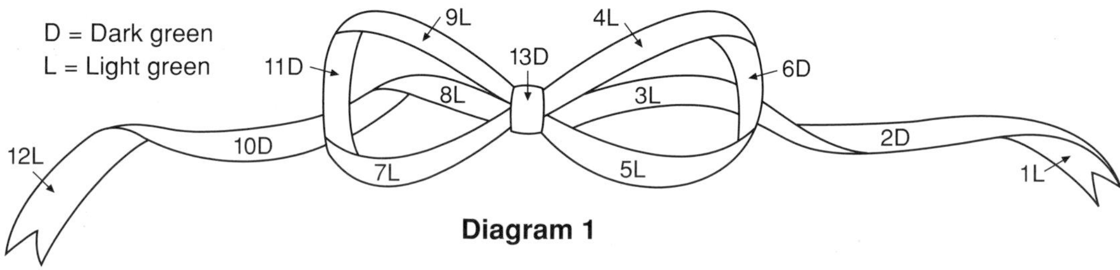

Diagram 1

Pumpkin 1 Pattern

Pumpkin 2 Pattern

Pumpkin 3 Pattern

Pumpkin 4 Pattern

Pumpkin 5 Pattern

Pumpkin 6 Pattern

Moon Pattern

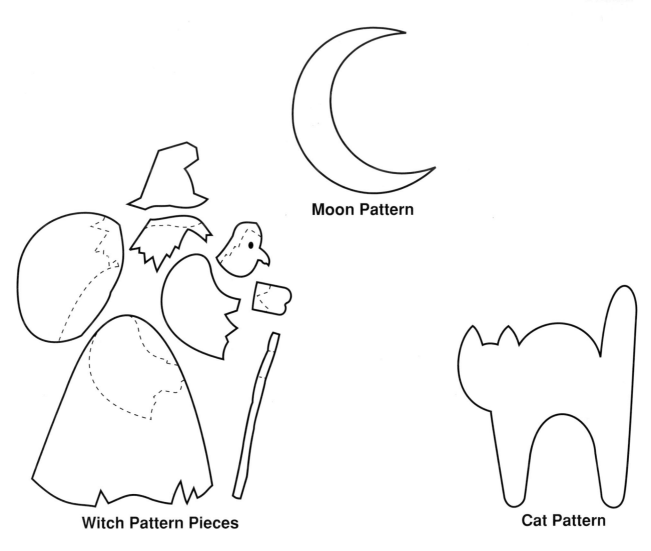

Witch Pattern Pieces

Cat Pattern

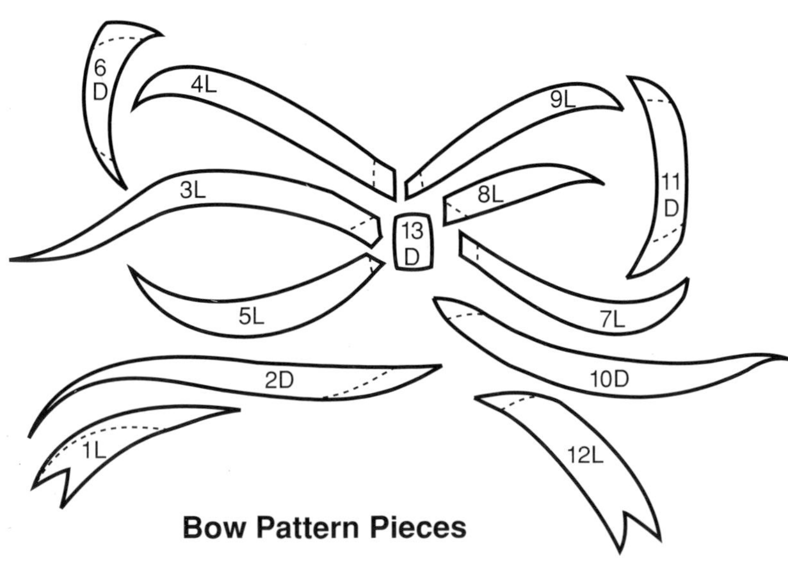

Bow Pattern Pieces

Oak Leaf Wreath

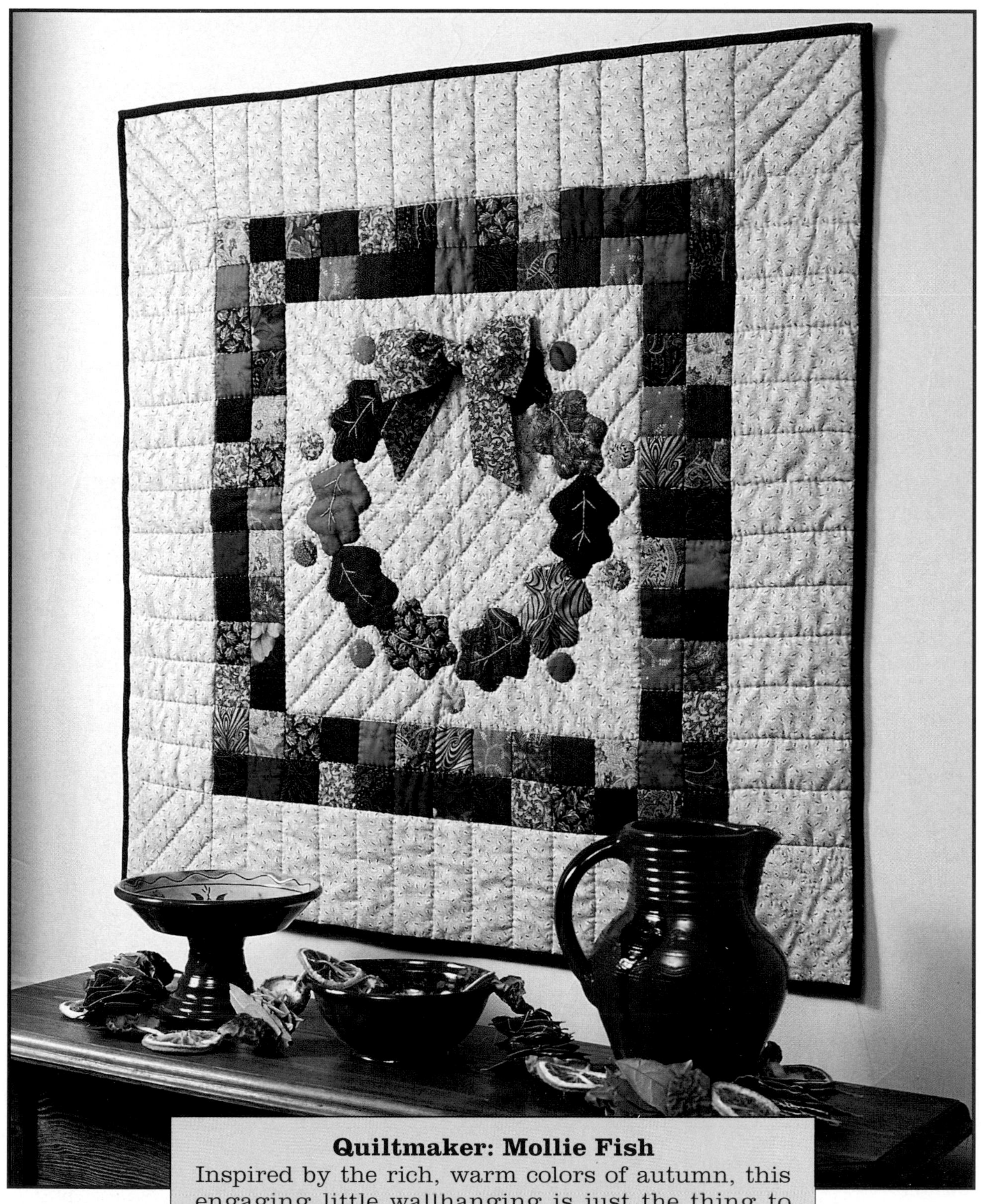

Quiltmaker: Mollie Fish

Inspired by the rich, warm colors of autumn, this engaging little wallhanging is just the thing to welcome the family home for Thanksgiving. Mollie added a bit of embroidery and a three-dimensional bow for a special touch.

Skill Level: Easy

Size: Finished quilt is 27½ inches square
Finished block is 13½ inches square

Fabrics and Supplies

- 1 yard of beige print fabric for block background and outer borders
- Approximately ½ yard *total* of assorted dark and medium print fabric scraps for leaves, berries, bow, and pieced border. (Dark green, brown, taupe, maroon, and beige are among the colors used in the quilt shown.)
- 1 yard of dark brown print fabric for quilt back and binding
- Quilt batting, larger than 27½ inches square
- Rotary cutter, ruler, and mat
- Compass (optional)
- Template plastic or freezer paper
- Index or recipe card
- Embroidery floss

Cutting

All measurements include ¼-inch seam allowances. Measurements for the borders are longer than needed; trim them to the exact length when they are added to the quilt top. The patchwork pieces and borders can be quick-cut using a rotary cutter and ruler.

Make a plastic template for the leaf using the pattern on page 124, or use the freezer paper appliqué method described on page 159. Refer to "Making Crisp Appliqué Circles" on page 37 for a method of making the berries using an index card.

From the beige print fabric, cut:
- Three 4½ × 44-inch border strips
- One 14-inch background square

From the various scrap fabrics, cut:
- 5 leaves and 5 reverse leaves
- Eighty-eight 2-inch border squares
- 9 berries

From one of the scrap fabrics, cut:
- One 3½ × 12½-inch strip for the bow
- One 2½ × 14½-inch strip for the bow tie

Making the Center Block

1. Fold the background square in half both ways to find the center. Using a compass, lightly draw a 9½-inch-diameter circle in the center of the square to use as a placement guideline. If you don't have a compass handy, draw around the outside of a plate or other round object to mark the guideline.

2. Referring to the **Quilt Diagram,** arrange and pin the five leaves and five reverse leaves on the background block to form the wreath, positioning the approximate center of the leaves along the marked guideline.

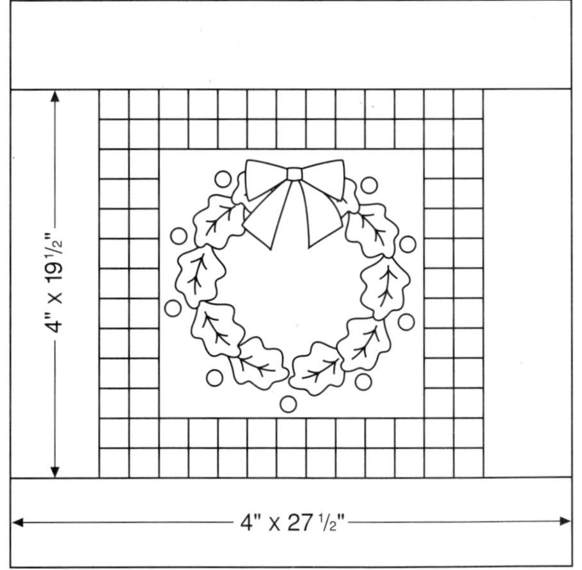

Quilt Diagram

3. Using thread that matches the fabric, appliqué the leaves in place. Begin with the leaves at the bottom of the wreath, and overlap the stem of the previous leaf with each successive one.

4. Using embroidery floss and a chain stitch, stitch the leaf markings from the pattern on page 124 onto the leaves. **Diagram 1** shows a detail of the chain stitch.

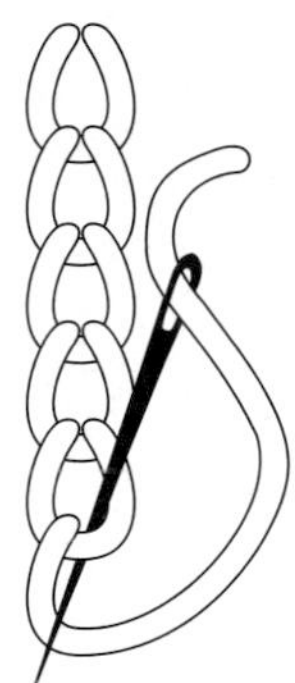

Diagram 1

5. Make the nine berries using the method described in "Making Crisp Appliqué Circles" on page 37. The finished size of the berries is ⅞ inch. Refer to the **Quilt Diagram** for correct placement of the berries on the background. Wait to make and add the three-dimensional bow until the quilt top is complete.

Adding the Borders

1. Sew the 2-inch squares together in pairs, as shown in **Diagram 2,** to make 44 two-square units. Join nine units to form one 14-inch-long border (including seam allowances), as shown in **Diagram 3.** Repeat to make a second identical border.

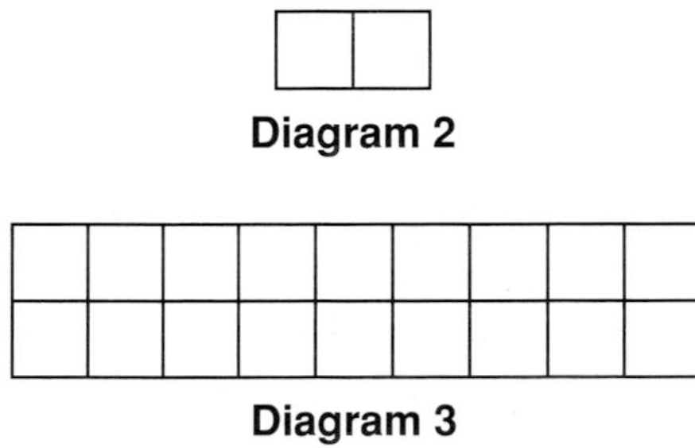

Diagram 2

Diagram 3

2. Sew the borders to the top and bottom of the block. Press the seams toward the block.

3. Join 13 two-square units to form one 20-inch-long border (including seam allowances). Join the remaining 13 units to form a second identical border.

4. Cut two 20-inch-long side borders from one of the 4½ × 44-inch beige print border strips. Sew the beige print borders to the two side pieced borders. Press the seams toward the beige borders. Sew the combination borders to the sides of the quilt top.

5. Measure the width of the quilt top (approximately 28 inches including seam allowances). Trim the two remaining beige print borders to this length. Sew the borders to the top and bottom of the quilt top. Press the seams toward the borders.

Quilting and Finishing

1. Mark quilting designs. The quilt shown has a diagonal grid inside the wreath, diagonal lines to the outside of the wreath, and horizontal and vertical lines in the outer border. In addition, there is outline quilting around the appliqué leaves and in-the-ditch quilting along the seams that join the squares in the border.

2. Cut a piece of backing fabric approximately 34 inches square.

3. Layer the quilt back, batting, and quilt top; baste.

4. Quilt all marked designs, and add additional quilting as desired.

5. From the binding fabric, make approximately 125 inches of French-fold binding. See page 164 for suggested binding widths and instructions on making and attaching binding.

6. Sew the binding to the quilt top. Trim the excess batting and backing, and hand finish the binding on the back side of the quilt. Refer to page 167 for directions on adding a hanging sleeve.

Making and Adding the Bow

1. Referring to **Diagram 4,** fold the 3½ × 12½-inch bow strip in half, bringing the short ends together, with right sides facing. Sew the

short ends together, leaving a ½-inch opening for turning the bow.

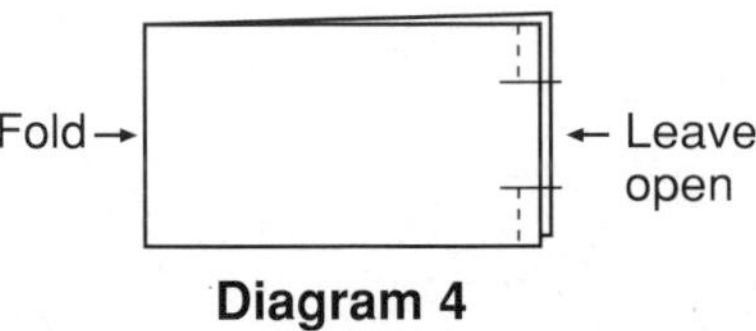

Diagram 4

2. Refold the bow strip so that the seam is centered, as shown in **Diagram 5,** and press. Stitch along the long sides with a ¼-inch seam allowance. Turn the bow right side out through the opening, press, and hand sew the opening closed.

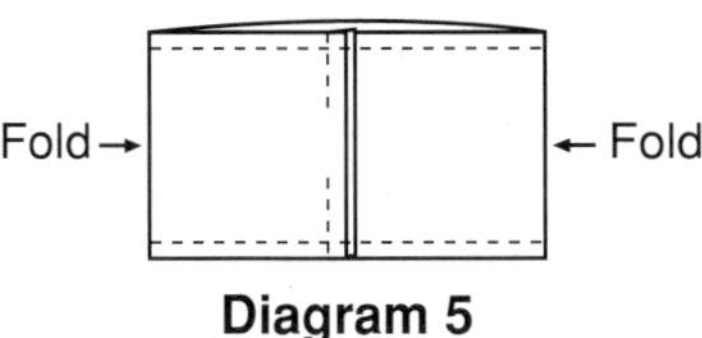

Diagram 5

3. For the tie, fold the 2½ × 14½-inch strip in half lengthwise with right sides facing. Mark angled stitching lines on the short ends, as shown in **Diagram 6.** Stitch along the marked lines and the long raw edges, leaving several inches open for turning, as shown. Turn right side out through the opening, press, and hand sew the opening closed.

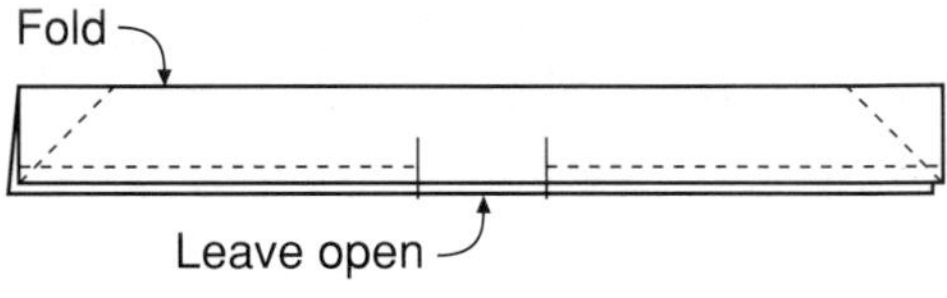

Diagram 6

4. Wrap the finished strip around the center of the bow and tie it. Hand stitch the bow to the top area of the wreath on the quilt.

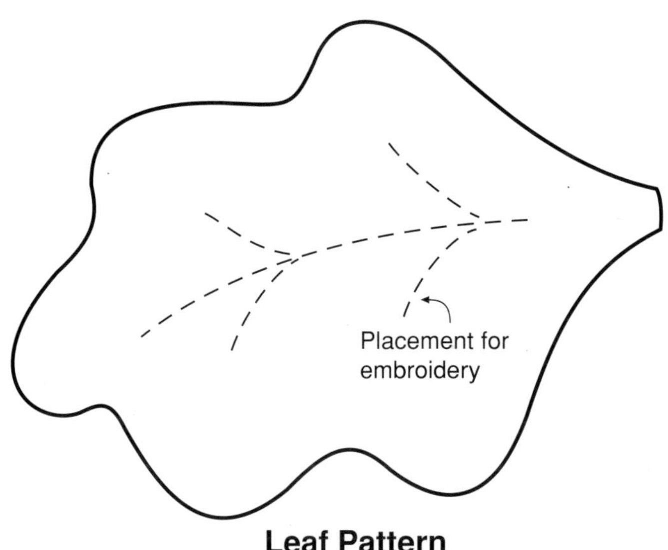

Leaf Pattern

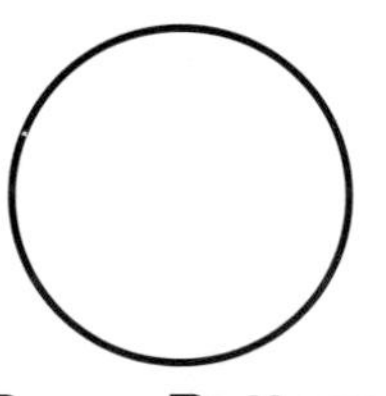

Berry Pattern

Holiday Gift Bags

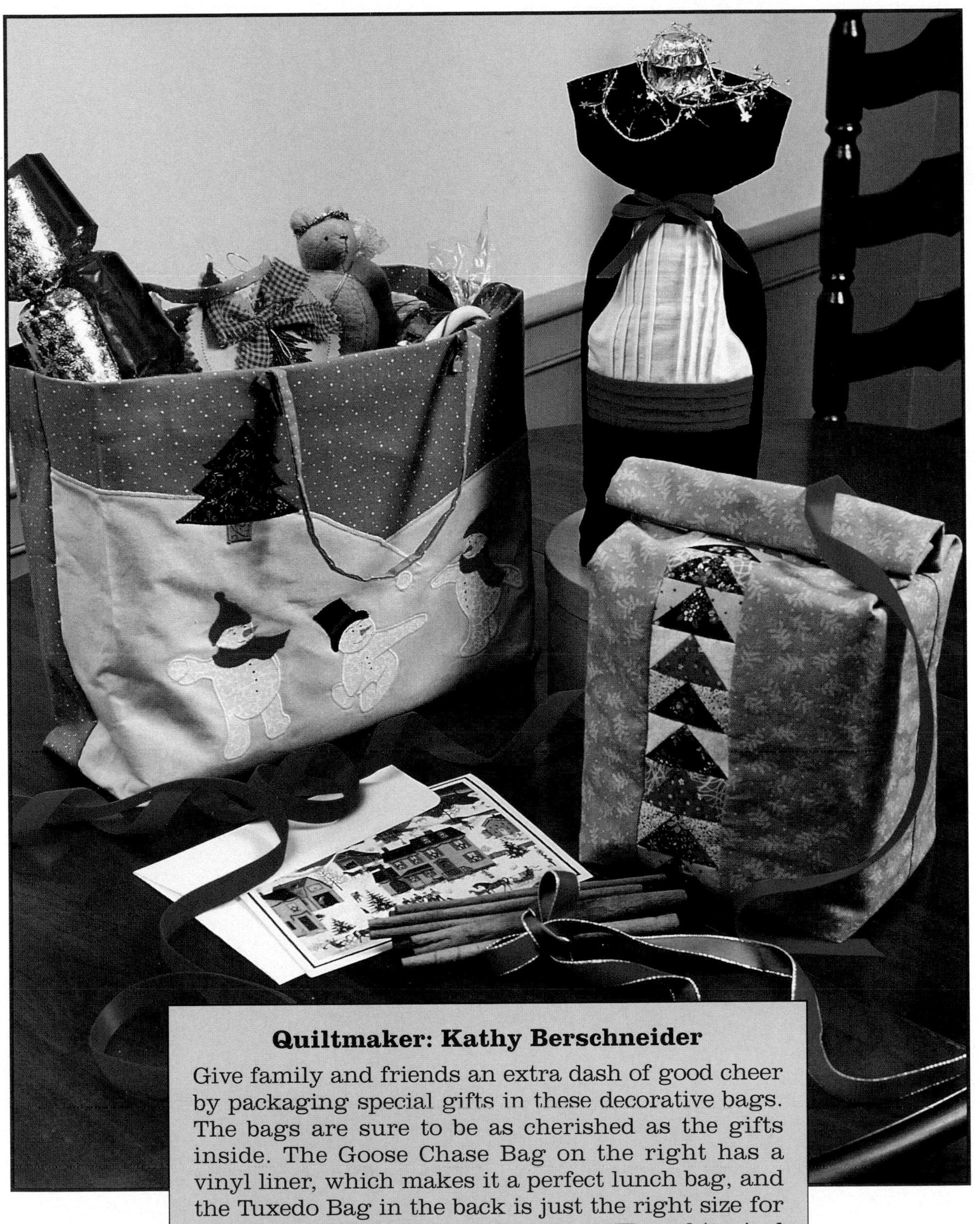

Quiltmaker: Kathy Berschneider

Give family and friends an extra dash of good cheer by packaging special gifts in these decorative bags. The bags are sure to be as cherished as the gifts inside. The Goose Chase Bag on the right has a vinyl liner, which makes it a perfect lunch bag, and the Tuxedo Bag in the back is just the right size for a bottle of wine or sparkling cider. The whimsical Snowmen Bag on the left might be just the thing for a child's gift or an odd-size package.

Skill Level: Easy

Size: Finished Snowmen Bag is approximately 13 inches wides, 11 inches tall, and 4 inches deep
Finished Goose Chase Bag is approximately 6 inches wide, 13 inches tall, and 5 inches deep
Finished Tuxedo Wine Bag is approximately 4 inches wide, 13 inches tall, and 2 inches deep

Fabrics and Supplies for the Snowmen Bag

- ½ yard of blue dot fabric for sky
- ½ yard of lining fabric
- ¼ yard of light gold fabric for ground
- Scraps of green print and brown print fabrics for tree
- Scraps of white, red, and black fabrics for snowmen
- 1 yard of medium weight fusible interfacing
- ¼ yard of paper-backed fusible webbing
- Sewing thread to match appliqué fabrics
- Black and brown fine-point permanent marking pens
- Rotary cutter, ruler, and mat
- Fabric paint (optional)

Cutting

All measurements except appliqué pieces include ¼-inch seam allowances. Using the pattern pieces on pages 129–130, follow the directions in "No-Sew Appliqué" on page 116 to prepare, cut out, position, and fuse the appliqués.

From the blue dot fabric, cut:
- Two 15 × 18-inch rectangles for bag front and back
- Two 1 × 18-inch strips for handles

From the lining fabric, cut:
- Two 14 × 18-inch rectangles

From the light gold fabric, cut:
- One 9 × 18-inch rectangle for bag front

From the various scrap fabrics, prepare fusible appliqués for:
- Tree and snowmen

From the interfacing, cut:
- Two 15 × 18-inch rectangles

Making the Bag

1. Fuse interfacing to the wrong side of the bag front and bag back pieces.

2. Following the manufacturer's instructions, fuse the webbing to the wrong side of the light gold fabric rectangle. Fold the fabric rectangle in half, right sides together. Draw a gentle curve along the top edge of the folded piece, as shown in **Diagram 1.** Trim along the drawn curve and unfold. Trim a little extra along one slope if you want the hills to look a little more natural.

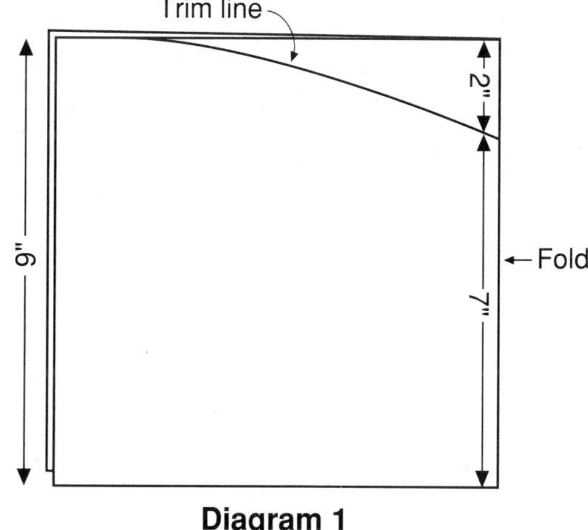

Diagram 1

3. Place the light gold piece right side up on the bag front, matching the bottom and side edges; fuse in place. Using white thread, machine satin stitch along the top curved edge of the gold piece. At the center, extend the stitching down into the gold fabric to create the appearance of a snowdrift.

4. Position the tree and snowman appliqués on the bag front. When you are pleased with the arrangement, fuse the pieces in place.

5. Using thread to match the appliqué pieces, machine satin stitch them in place. Or seal the edges of the pieces with a line of fabric paint. Add faces and buttons with fine-point marking pens.

6. With right sides facing and raw edges aligned, pin the bag front to the bag back. Stitch around three sides, leaving the top edge open, as shown in **Diagram 2.**

7. At one lower corner, fold the bag so that the side and bottom seams are aligned. Pin in

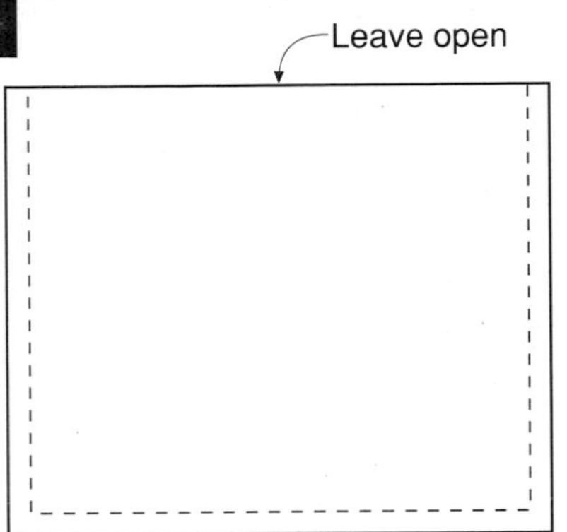

Diagram 2

position. Measure in 2 inches from the corner and draw a stitching line, as shown in **Diagram 3.** The line should extend 2 inches in each direction from the seam. Stitch along the line. Repeat for the other corner. Turn the bag right side out.

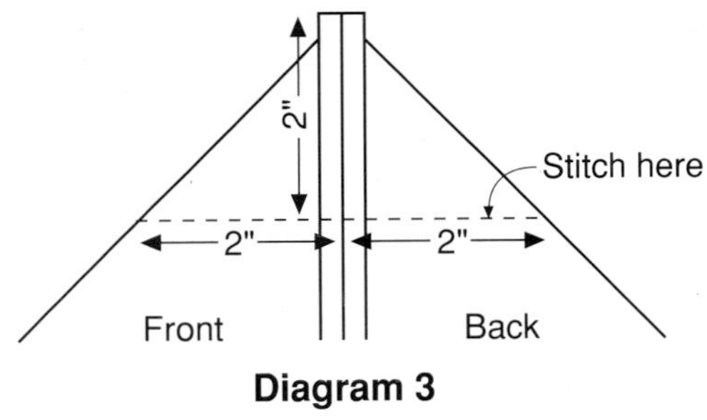

Diagram 3

8. Stitch the lining pieces together, leaving a 4-inch-long opening along one side, as indicated in **Diagram 4.** Stitch the corners of the lining as directed in Step 7.

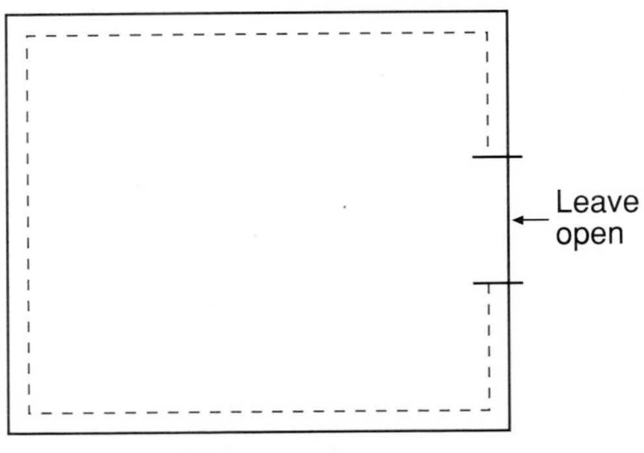

Diagram 4

9. With right sides facing, tuck the bag inside the lining and align the top raw edges. Stitch around the top of the bag. Turn the bag and the lining right side out through the opening in the lining. Tuck the lining inside the bag and hand stitch the opening closed. To keep the lining from shifting, hand tack the bag and lining together at the bottom corners. The top edge of the lining will be approximately 1 inch below the top edge of the bag. Press to create a crisp edge along the top edge of the bag.

10. To prepare one bag handle, fold over ¼ inch along both long sides of a handle strip; press. Fold the strip in half lengthwise and press. Topstitch the edges together. Tie a knot at both ends of the handle strip. Position the ends approximately 3½ inches in from each side of the bag, and stitch the handle to the bag. Repeat for the other handle.

Fabrics and Supplies for the Goose Chase Bag

- ½ yard of tan print fabric for bag and lining
- Scraps of assorted off-white print fabrics for patchwork
- Scraps of red, navy, and black print fabrics for patchwork
- ⅛ yard of ¾-inch-wide tan Velcro
- Two 12½-inch squares of clear vinyl for bag liner
- Rotary cutter, ruler, and mat
- Template plastic (optional)

Cutting

All measurements include ¼-inch seam allowances. Instructions given are for quick-cutting the pieces with a rotary cutter and ruler. If you prefer to cut the pieces in the traditional manner, make templates for pieces A and B as directed below. Tips for making and using templates are on page 153.

- **A:** Make a 3¼-inch square; cut the square in half diagonally in both directions.
- **B:** Make a 1⅞-inch square; cut the square in half diagonally.

From the tan print fabric, cut:

- Two 5½ × 16½-inch rectangles for bag front
- Three 12½ × 16½-inch rectangles for bag back and lining

From the assorted off-white fabrics, cut:

- 32 B triangles

  Use Template B

  OR

  Cut sixteen 1⅞-inch squares. Cut each square in half diagonally to make two triangles.

From the red, navy, and black fabrics, cut a total of:

- 16 A triangles
  Use Template A
  OR
  Cut four 3¼-inch squares. Cut each square diagonally in both directions to make four triangles.

Assembling the Bag Front

1. Make a Goose Chase unit by sewing a B triangle to each short side of an A triangle, as shown in **Diagram 5.** Press the seams away from the A triangle. Repeat to make 16 units.

2. Join the units into a long strip, checking to see that all the A triangles are pointing in the same direction. Press the seams toward the A triangles.

3. Sew a 5½ × 16½-inch bag front piece to each side of the Goose Chase strip, as shown in **Diagram 6.** Press the seams away from the strip.

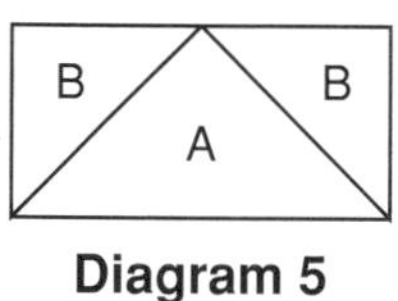

Diagram 5

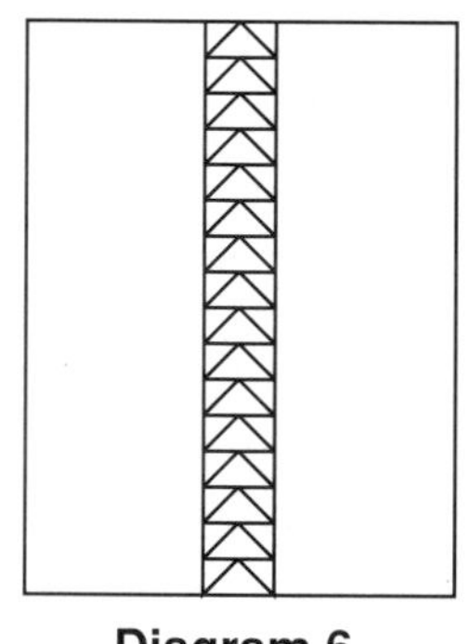

Diagram 6

Making the Bag

1. With right sides facing and raw edges aligned, pin the bag front to the bag back. Stitch them together along three sides, leaving the top edge open, as shown in **Diagram 2** on page 127.

2. At one lower corner, fold the bag so that the side and bottom seams are aligned; pin. Measure in 2½ inches from the corner and draw a stitching line, as shown in **Diagram 3** on page 127. The line should extend 2½ inches in each direction from the seam. Stitch along the line. Repeat for the other corner. Turn the bag right side out.

3. Stitch the lining pieces together, leaving a 4-inch-long opening along one side, as indicated in **Diagram 4** on page 127. Stitch the corners of the lining as directed in Step 2.

4. With right sides facing, tuck the bag inside the lining and align the top raw edges. Stitch around the top of the bag. Turn the bag and the lining right side out through the opening in the lining. Tuck the lining inside the bag and hand stitch the opening closed. Hand tack the bag and lining together at the bottom corners.

5. Cut two 1-inch-long pieces of Velcro. On the bag front, position each Velcro piece so that the long top edge is 2½ inches down from the top of the bag and the short inner edge is ½ inch away from the edge of the patchwork strip. Stitch the pieces in place. Stitch the matching pieces of Velcro along the top edge of the bag back.

6. To make the liner, stitch the two vinyl squares together along three sides. Stitch the lower corners as directed in Step 2. Slip the liner inside the bag. Leave the liner unattached so that it can be removed and the bag can be laundered.

Fabrics and Supplies for the Tuxedo Bag

- ½ yard of black fabric for bag and lining
- Scraps of white and red fabrics
- ½ yard of ¼-inch-wide red satin ribbon
- Rotary cutter, ruler, and mat
- Template plastic

Cutting

All measurements include ¼-inch seam allowances. The instructions given are for quick-cutting the bag pieces with a rotary cutter and ruler, and using templates for the patchwork tuxedo shirt and cummerbund. Make templates from patterns C and D on page 130. Make a template for E as directed below. Tips for making and using templates are on page 153.

- **E:** 1½ × 5¼-inch rectangle

From the black fabric, cut:

- Three 6¾ × 14¼-inch rectangles for bag back and lining
- Two 1¼ × 14¾-inch strips for bag front
- Two 5¼-inch squares for bag front
- One D and one D reverse triangle

From the white fabric, cut:

- One 5 × 8-inch rectangle for shirt

From the red fabric, cut:

- One 2½ × 8-inch rectangle for cummerbund

Piecing the Bag Front

1. Fold the white fabric rectangle in half crosswise and crease. Working on the right side of the fabric, use a pencil or other removable marker to lightly mark four crease lines, each ½ inch apart, on each side of the center crease. See **Diagram 7.** These will form the tucks in the tuxedo shirt.

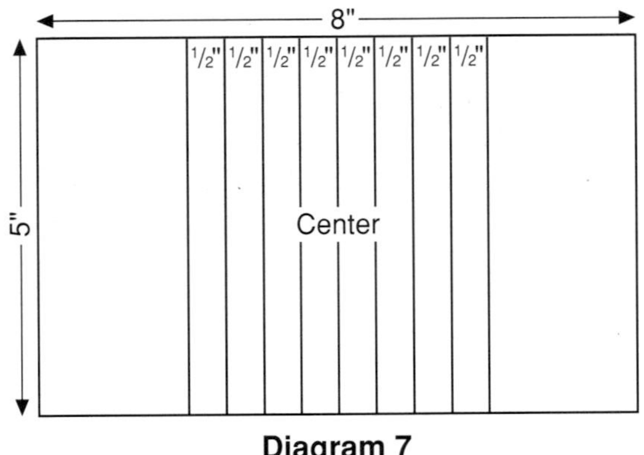

Diagram 7

2. With wrong sides facing, fold the fabric along the first crease line. Sew along the crease to form the first tuck, keeping the line of stitches ⅛ inch from the fold. Repeat to make four tucks on each side of the center. Press toward the center.

3. Using template C, cut the shirt from the tucked white fabric. Center the template on the fabric with the tucks running parallel to the grain line on the template.

4. Stitch a black D triangle to each side of the shirt piece to complete the rectangle. Press the seams toward the triangles.

5. To make the cummerbund, fold the red fabric rectangle in half lengthwise and crease it. Working on the right side of the fabric, lightly mark a crease placement line ½ inch away on each side of the center crease, as shown in **Diagram 8.**

6. Fold the fabric along the crease lines, and stitch three ⅛-inch-deep tucks along the strip. Press all the tucks to one side.

7. Cut an E rectangle from the prepared red fabric. Place the template so that the tucks are parallel to the long edge of the template.

8. Aligning the raw edges, stitch the cummerbund to the lower edge of the shirt unit.

9. Sew 5¼-inch black squares to the top

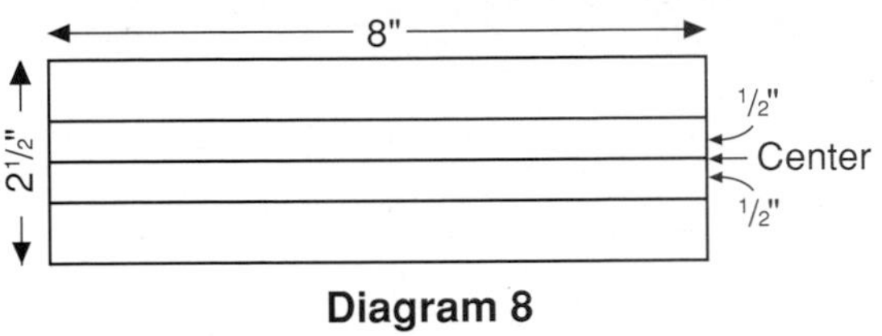

Diagram 8

and bottom of the shirt/cummerbund unit. Press the seams toward the black fabric.

10. Sew a 1¼ × 14¾-inch black strip to each side of the pieced unit. Press toward the strips.

Making the Bag

1. With right sides facing and raw edges aligned, pin the bag front to the bag back. Stitch around three sides, leaving the top edge open, as shown in **Diagram 2** on page 127.

2. At one lower corner, fold the bag so that the side and bottom seams are aligned. Measure in 1 inch from the corner and draw a stitching line, as shown in **Diagram 3** on page 127. The line should extend 1 inch in each direction from the seam. Stitch along the line. Repeat for the other corner. Turn the bag right side out.

3. Stitch the lining pieces together, leaving a 4-inch-long opening along one side. Stitch the corners of the lining as directed in Step 2.

4. With right sides facing, tuck the bag inside the lining and align the top raw edges. Stitch around the top of the bag. Turn the bag and the lining right side out through the opening in the lining. Tuck the lining inside the bag and hand stitch the opening closed. Hand tack the bag and lining together at the bottom corners.

5. Tack the center of the ribbon to the center of the bag back approximately 4 inches from the top of the bag.

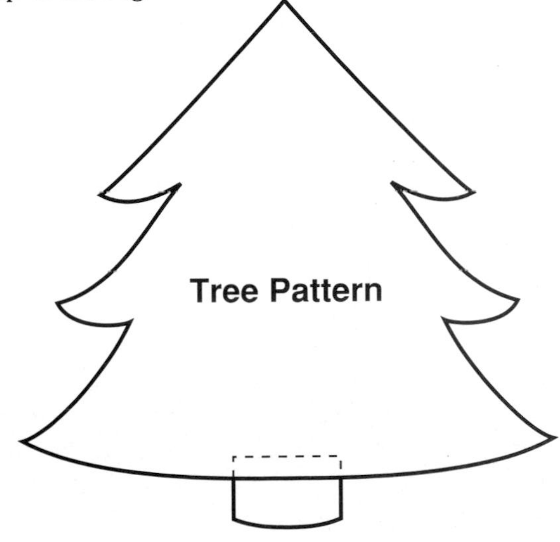

Snowman 2 Pattern
Snowman 3
Pattern
Snowman
1 Pattern
C
D

Christmastime

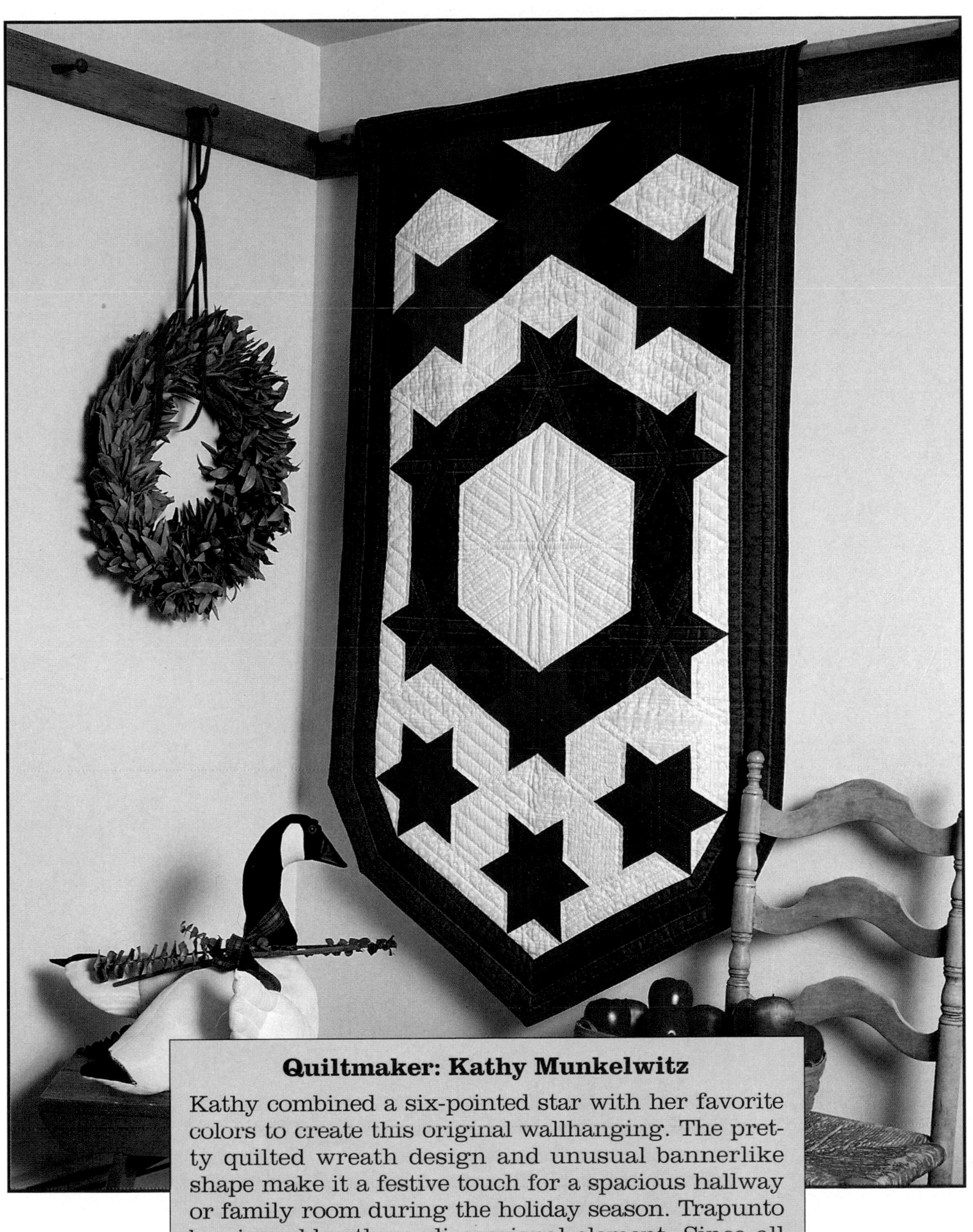

Quiltmaker: Kathy Munkelwitz

Kathy combined a six-pointed star with her favorite colors to create this original wallhanging. The pretty quilted wreath design and unusual bannerlike shape make it a festive touch for a spacious hallway or family room during the holiday season. Trapunto berries add a three-dimensional element. Since all the pieces must be set in, this is an ideal project for hand piecers and accomplished machine piecers.

Skill Level: Intermediate to Challenging

Size: Finished quilt is approximately 36½ × 64 inches

Fabrics and Supplies

- 1½ yards of dark green lengthwise-striped fabric for patchwork stars and border
- 1½ yards of printed muslin for blocks
- ½ yard of medium red print fabric for blocks
- ½ yard of dark red print fabric for blocks
- ½ yard of green print fabric for blocks
- ¼ yard of red solid fabric for berries and unfilled piping
- 2 yards of fabric for quilt back
- ½ yard of dark green solid fabric for binding
- Quilt batting, larger than 36½ × 64 inches
- Template plastic
- Polyester fiberfill for stuffing berries

Cutting

All measurements include ¼-inch seam allowances. Make templates for the berry and pieces A through F using the patterns on pages 135–136. Use a sewing machine needle to make holes in the templates at the corner dots, where seam lines meet and pieces will be set in. Mark around the templates on the wrong side of the fabric. Mark dots on the fabric pieces through the corner holes.

From the green striped fabric, cut:

- Four 4½ × 54-inch border strips. From one of the strips, cut two 20-inch-long G borders and one 10-inch-long H border. From a second strip, cut one 40-inch-long J border and one 10-inch-long H border. The remaining two strips will be used full length as I borders.
- 30 A diamonds. (Cut the pieces so that the stripe is running the long way through the center of the diamond. All four sides of the diamond will be on the bias.)

From the printed muslin fabric, cut:

- 9 A diamonds
- 11 B diamonds
- 10 C hexagons
- 2 D triangles
- 4 E pieces
- 8 F pieces

From the medium red print fabric, cut:

- 24 A diamonds

From the dark red print fabric, cut:

- 26 A diamonds

From the green print fabric, cut:

- 10 C hexagons
- 4 F pieces

From the red solid fabric, cut:

- Five ¾ × 44-inch piping strips
- 18 berries

Piecing the Inner Quilt

When joining pieces, pin-match the seams at the marked dots. Stitch from one dot to the next dot without sewing in the seam allowances. Backstitch at the beginning and the end of the seam. If machine sewing, remove the work from the machine after sewing each seam. Whenever possible, press seam allowances toward the darker fabrics.

1. Referring to the **Fabric Key** and **Diagram 1,** lay out all the pieces for the inner quilt.

Fabric Key

- Green striped
- Printed muslin
- Medium red print
- Dark red print
- Green print

2. Piece the center muslin star. Begin by constructing two segments with three A dia-

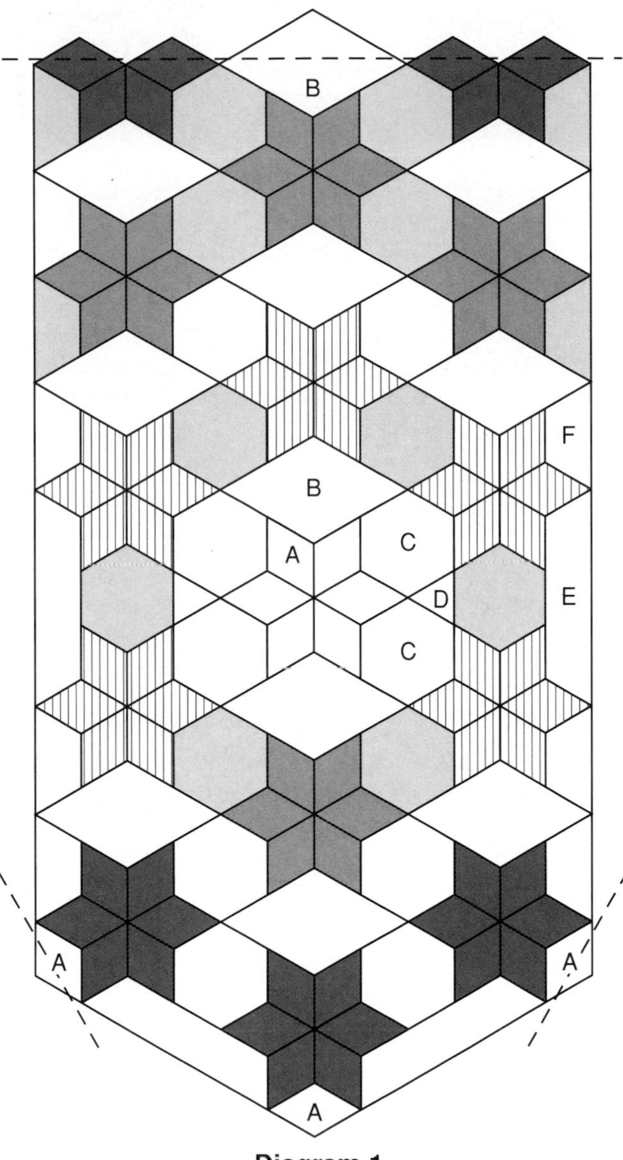

Diagram 1

monds per segment. Join the two segments to complete the star, as shown in **Diagram 2.**

3. Set in two muslin C hexagons at the bottom of the star, as shown in **Diagram 3.** Sew a muslin D triangle to one side of a muslin C hexagon as shown; set in to one side of the center

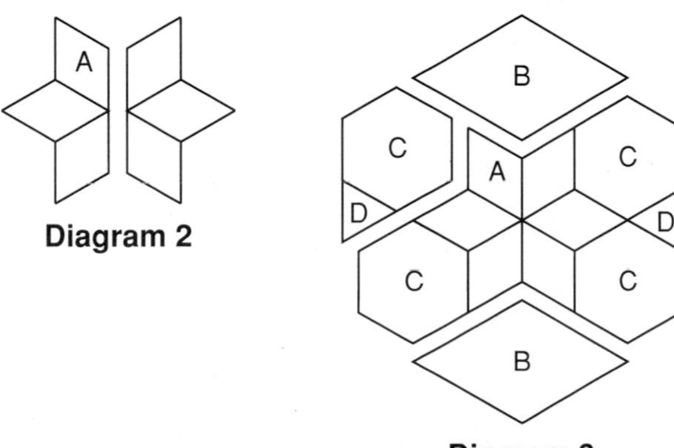

Diagram 2

Diagram 3

star. Repeat with a C hexagon and D triangle on the opposite side. Set in muslin B diamonds at the top and bottom of the star.

4. In the same manner as for the muslin star, make five stars using the 30 green striped A diamonds. Make four stars using the medium red print A diamonds. Using the dark red print diamonds, make three full-size stars and two half stars, as shown in **Diagram 4.**

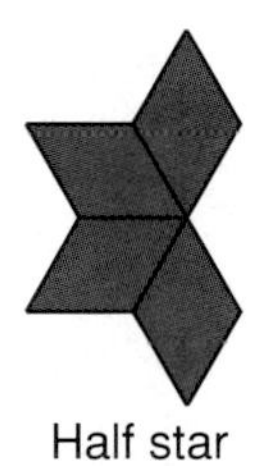

Half star

Diagram 4

5. Referring to **Diagram 1,** add the five green striped stars, one medium red print star, and six green print C hexagons to the center unit, forming the wreath. Start with the green striped star at the top and alternate hexagons and stars, setting-in the pieces one by one around the center unit. Be sure to place the medium red print star at the bottom.

6. Building out from the center wreath, add muslin diamonds, hexagons, and the E and F pieces next. Add the remaining medium red print stars, the dark red print stars, and the other pieces to complete the inner quilt. The top edge of the quilt will be uneven because of the half-stars and the top center B diamond.

Adding the Borders

1. Trim the uneven top edge of the quilt top. To trim, place a see-through acrylic ruler so that a ¼-inch seam allowance extends beyond the points of the pieces. Draw a line and cut with scissors, or cut with a rotary cutter.

2. Trim the lower edges of the quilt top, as shown in **Diagram 1.** Place the ruler on the muslin diamonds so that a ¼-inch seam allowance extends beyond the points of the dark red print stars; trim.

3. Referring to **Diagram 5,** center and sew the striped borders to the quilt top. Begin and

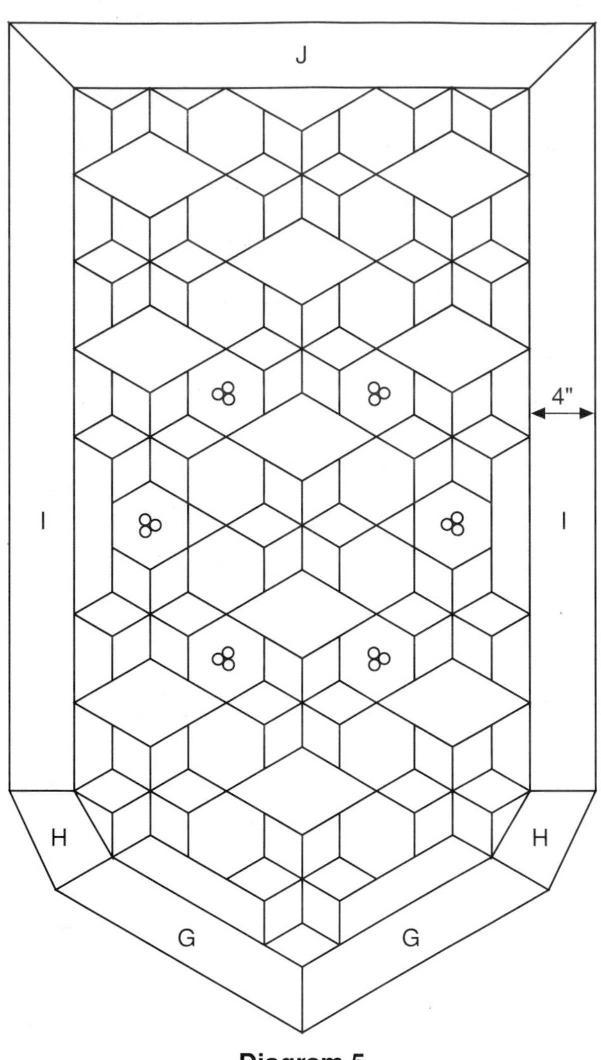

Diagram 5

end stitching ¼ inch from the ends of the borders; backstitch seams to secure.

4. Join the borders with mitered seams. Turn under the end of one border at an angle and appliqué the angled edge to the adjacent border. Repeat until all borders are joined. Trim the excess border fabric on the back side, leaving ¼ inch for seam allowance. Press the miter seams in one direction. Press the border seams toward the borders.

Adding the Trapunto Berries

1. Using a spool, a coin, or a template made from the pattern on the opposite page, draw finished-size (⅞-inch-diameter) berry placement circles on the green print hexagons in the center wreath. Refer to **Diagram 5** for placement.

2. Using thread that matches the fabric, run a gathering thread around each of the 18 red fabric circles, about ⅛ inch to the inside of the raw edge. Keep the stitches tiny and even. When you reach the starting point, pull the thread, gathering the circle slightly.

3. Tuck a small amount of loose polyester stuffing into one circle; pull on the thread again to gather the fabric tightly around the filling. Backstitch to secure and leave the thread attached. Repeat for each berry.

4. Position a stuffed berry on a placement circle. Appliqué the berry in place, aligning the folded edge with the placement line. Repeat for each berry.

Quilting and Finishing

1. Mark quilting designs as desired. The quilt shown has straight-line quilting on the muslin pieces and additional quilting ¼ inch away from the patchwork seam lines, in the ditch next to the stuffed berries, and along the lines of the striped fabric.

2. Layer the quilt back, batting, and quilt top; baste. Trim the quilt back so that it is approximately 3 inches larger than the quilt top on all sides.

3. Quilt all marked designs, and add additional quilting as desired.

4. To make the unfilled piping, press the ¾-inch-wide red strips in half lengthwise, *wrong* sides together. For each of the seven sides of the quilt, cut a pressed strip that is approximately 1 inch longer than the side. Pin the strips to the quilt top, placing raw edges even with the quilt edges and overlapping the strip ends at the corners.

5. From the binding fabric, make approximately 190 inches of French-fold binding. See page 164 for suggested binding widths and instructions on making binding.

6. With right sides together and raw edges aligned, place the quilt binding on top of the piping and quilt top. Stitch through all layers, being careful to keep the stitching straight since it determines the width of the piping. Miter the binding at the corners, as described on page 166.

7. Trim the excess batting and backing, and hand finish the binding on the back side of the quilt. See page 167 for instructions on making and adding a hanging sleeve.

F

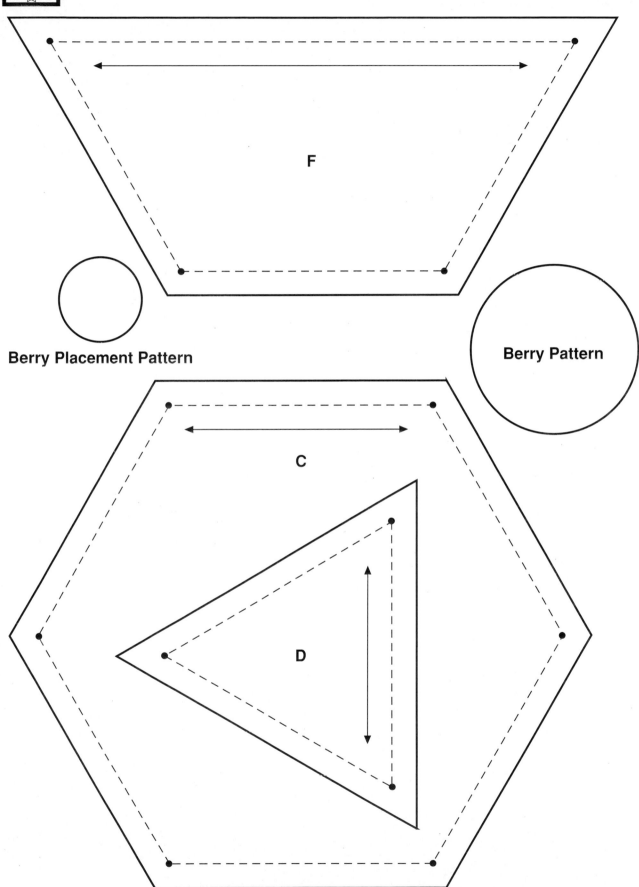

Berry Placement Pattern

Berry Pattern

C

D

One-half of E

Place on fold

A

One-half of B

Place on fold

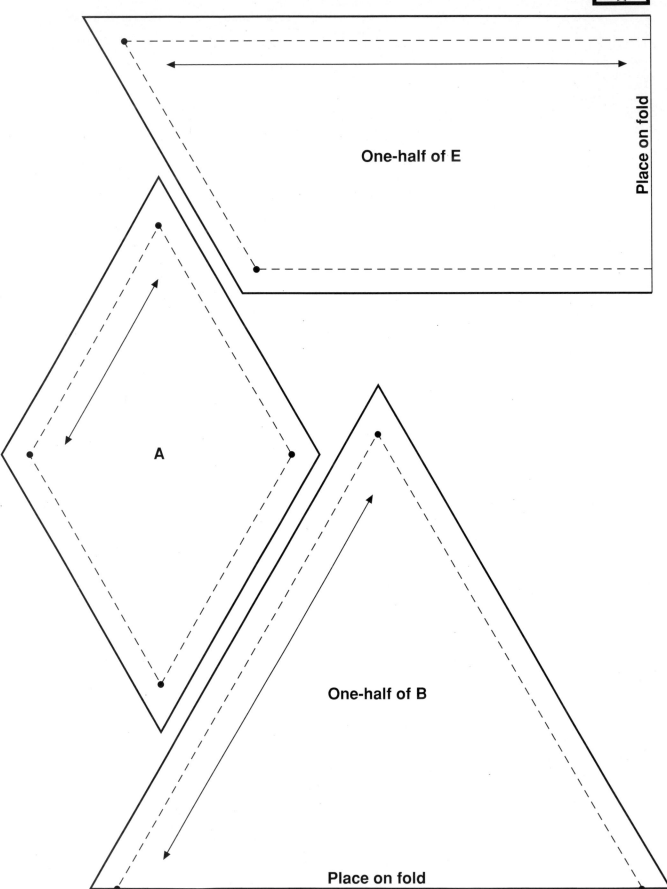

Crazy Quilt Stockings

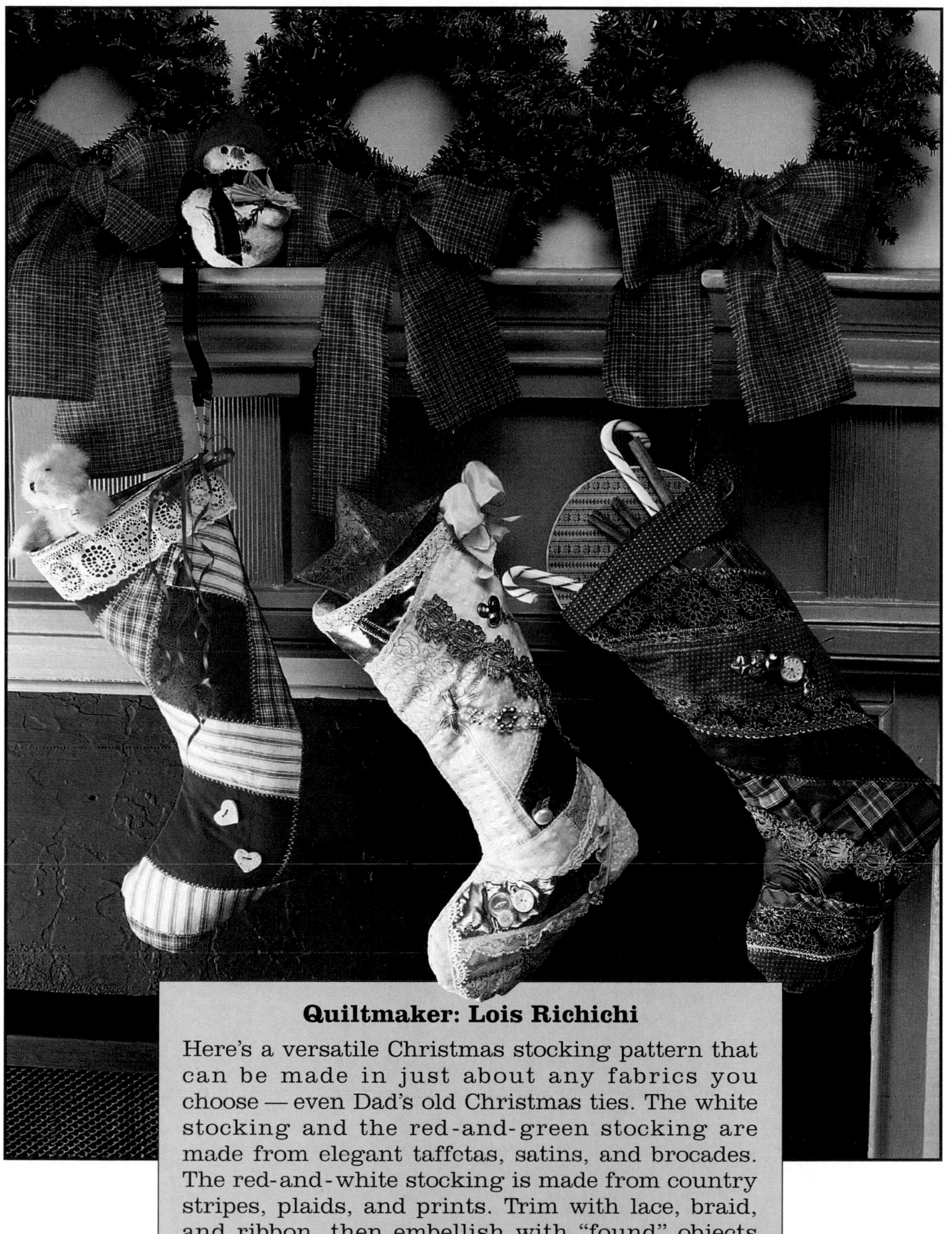

Quiltmaker: Lois Richichi

Here's a versatile Christmas stocking pattern that can be made in just about any fabrics you choose — even Dad's old Christmas ties. The white stocking and the red-and-green stocking are made from elegant taffetas, satins, and brocades. The red-and-white stocking is made from country stripes, plaids, and prints. Trim with lace, braid, and ribbon, then embellish with "found" objects such as old buttons, charms, and other jewelry.

Skill Level: Easy

Size: Stockings are approximately 16 inches long

Fabrics and Supplies for the Red-and-White Stocking

- ½ yard of fabric for lining and stocking back
- Scraps or ⅛ yard *each* of three different red fabrics to coordinate with the lining/backing fabric
- ½ yard of polyester fleece
- ½ yard of 2-inch-wide pregathered lace for stocking top
- White machine embroidery thread
- Metallic machine embroidery thread (optional)
- 3 yards of ⅛-inch-wide red satin ribbon for bow
- Scraps of lace, ribbon, braid, and other trims
- 2 ceramic heart buttons and 1 Santa button (optional)

Cutting

Using a large sheet of tracing paper, trace the stocking pattern on pages 141–142, carefully matching the pieces. The pattern includes ¼-inch seam allowances. Unless directed otherwise, use a ¼-inch seam and sew all pieces with right sides facing. Before tracing and cutting out the stocking pieces, decide which direction your finished stocking will point. The directions that follow result in a stocking that points to the left.

From the lining/backing fabric, cut:

- 3 stocking shapes (2 pointing left and 1 pointing right)
- One 2 × 5-inch rectangle for the stocking hanging tab

From the fleece, cut:

- 2 stocking shapes (1 pointing left and 1 pointing right)

Making the Stocking Front

1. Working on a fleece stocking shape with the toe pointing to the left, pin a fabric scrap approximately in the center of the stocking, as shown in **Diagram 1.** The right side of the fabric scrap should be facing up.

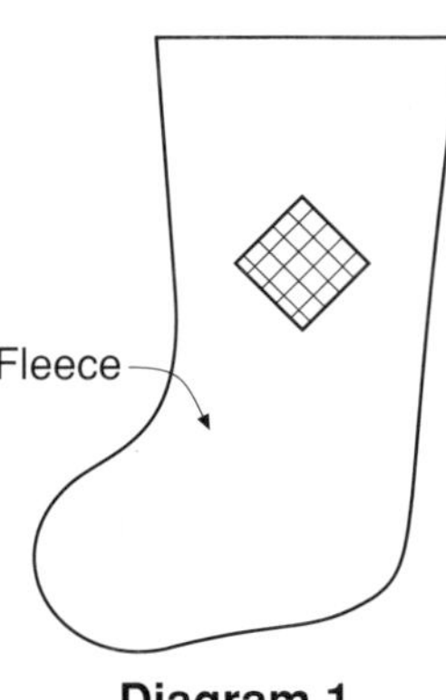

Diagram 1

2. With right sides together, place a second fabric scrap on top of the first piece, as shown in **Diagram 2.** Align the pieces along one raw edge and sew through all layers.

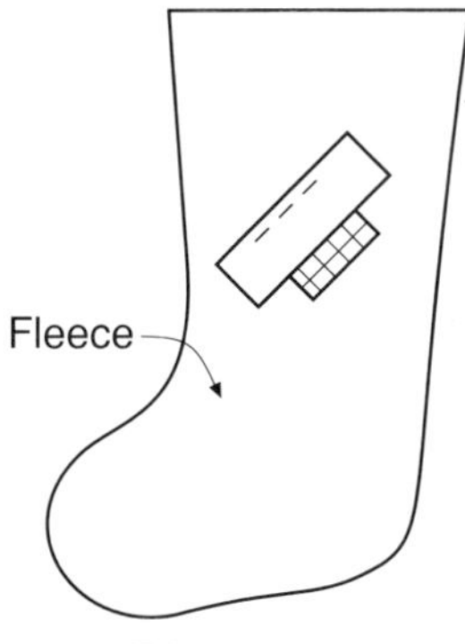

Diagram 2

3. Open out the second fabric piece and finger press the seam. Trim the edges to create the shape desired, as shown in **Diagram 3.**

4. In a similar manner, continue to add pieces until the entire fleece stocking is covered with fabric. Don't worry if some of the pieces extend beyond the edge of the stocking shape.

5. Stay stitch around the edge of the stocking shape. Trim any excess fabric scraps that extend beyond the edge of the fleece.

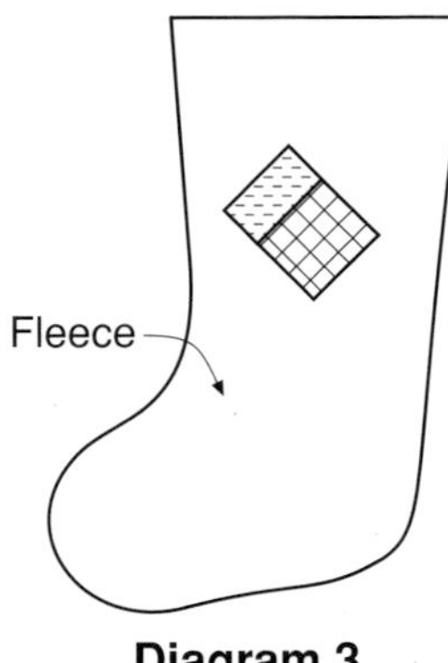

Diagram 3

6. Using a decorative machine embroidery stitch, such as a feather stitch, stitch along all seams that join fabric pieces and cover any raw edges of pieces.

7. Referring to the photograph on page 137, stitch buttons and other "found" objects in place as desired.

Assembling the Stocking

1. Place the wrong side of a right-pointing stocking on top of the remaining fleece stocking. This will become the stocking back. Machine stay stitch around the perimeter of the stocking.

2. Fold under and press ¼ inch along both long edges of the hanging tab piece. Fold tab in half lengthwise with wrong sides facing. Topstitch the long edges together.

3. With right sides facing, sew the stocking front to the stocking back, leaving the top of the stocking open. Clip curves and turn right side out. Baste the hanging tab to the top edge of the stocking back seam.

4. Place the stocking lining pieces right sides together. Sew the pieces together, leaving the top open and leaving an area on the back edge open for turning, as indicated on the pattern. Wait to turn the stocking lining right side out.

5. Slip the stocking inside the stocking lining; right sides should be facing and the hanging tab should be between the stocking and the lining. Stitch around the stocking top. Turn the stocking and the lining right side out through the opening in the back edge of the lining. Hand stitch the opening in the lining closed. Tuck the lining inside the stocking. Topstitch around the stocking top.

Finishing

1. Topstitch the lace trim around the stocking top.

2. Cut the red ribbon into three 1-yard pieces. Hold the three ribbons together as though they were one piece and tie a bow. Tack the bow to the top of the stocking.

Fabrics and Supplies for the White-and-Gold Stocking

- ½ yard of fabric for lining and stocking back
- Scraps or ⅛ yard *each* of three white-on-white or white-and-gold print or striped fabrics to coordinate with the stocking back fabric
- ⅛ yard of gold tissue lamé
- ⅛ yard of woven fusible interfacing to stabilize the lamé
- ½ yard of polyester fleece
- ½ yard of ½-inch-wide pregathered lace for stocking top
- ¾ yard of gold-trimmed ½-inch-wide ivory satin ribbon for bow
- Gold metallic machine embroidery thread
- Scraps of lace, ribbon, gold braid, and other trims
- Buttons

Making the Stocking

Refer to the directions given in "Cutting" on the opposite page to cut the stocking pieces from the lining/backing fabric and the fleece.

1. Using a press cloth, fuse the interfacing to the wrong side of the gold lamé to stabilize it and to help prevent fraying.

2. Using the gold lamé and the white-on-white and white-and-gold fabrics, make the stocking front and assemble the stocking by following the instructions given in "Assembling the Stocking" on page 139.

3. Topstitch the lace along the stocking top.

4. Tie a ribbon bow and tack it to the stocking top.

Fabrics and Supplies for the Red-and-Green Stocking

- ½ yard of fabric for lining and stocking back
- Approximately five worn-out men's neckties or ¼ yard *each* of five "fancy" fabrics such as taffeta, satin, or brocade
- ½ yard of polyester fleece
- Scraps of lace, ribbon, braid, and other trims
- Gold and multicolor metallic machine embroidery threads
- Gold charms and buttons

Making the Stocking

Refer to the directions given in "Cutting" on page 138 to cut the stocking pieces from the lining/backing fabric and the fleece.

1. Cut a piece approximately 17 inches long from the narrow end of one necktie, and set it aside to decorate the top of the stocking. Open the seams on the old neckties and remove any interfacing. If you are not using old ties, cut 2-inch-wide strips from the assorted fabrics.

2. Working on a left-pointing fleece stocking piece, pin a length of necktie across the fleece at an angle, as shown in **Diagram 4.**

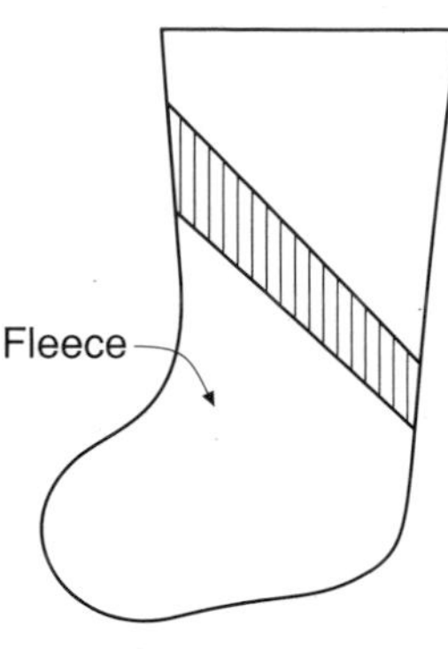

Diagram 4

3. With right sides facing and raw edges aligned along one side, pin a second length of tie atop the first. Stitch through all layers. Open out the second piece and finger press the seam, as shown in **Diagram 5.**

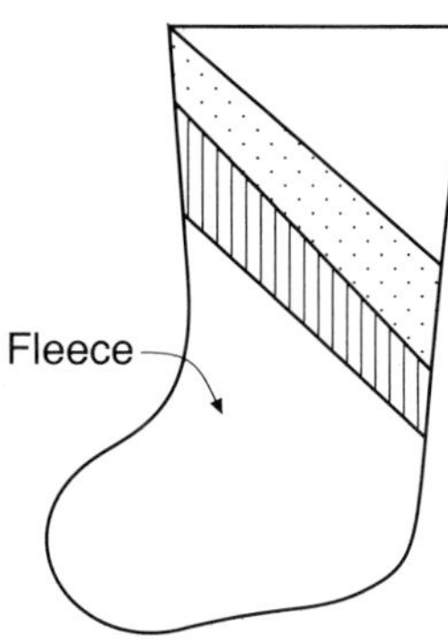

Diagram 5

4. Continue in this manner until the fleece is covered with fabric. Topstitch around the perimeter of the stocking; trim any excess fabric.

5. Complete the stocking according to the directions given in "Assembling the Stocking" on page 139.

6. Topstitch the reserved length of necktie along the top edge of the stocking. Sew a gold button to the pointed edge of the tie piece.

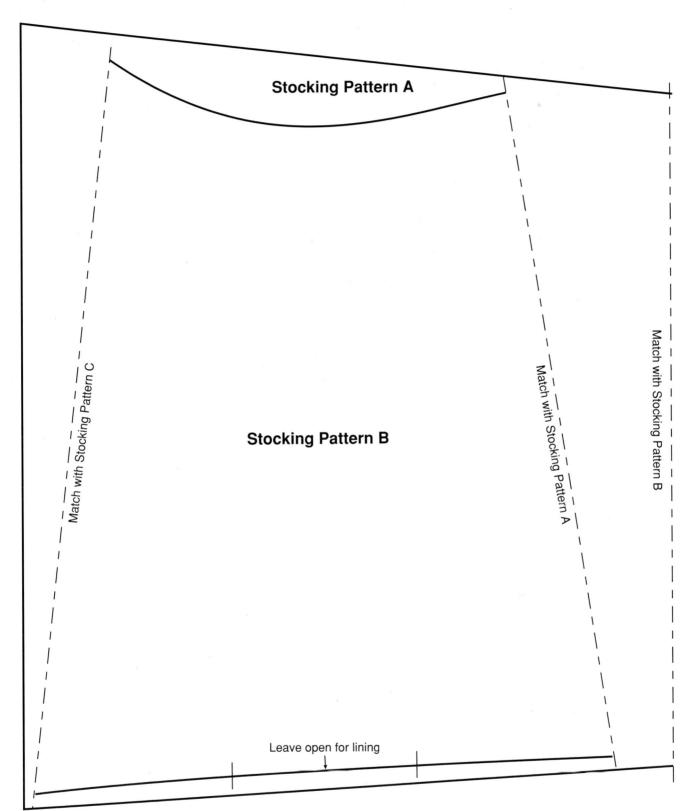

Stocking Pattern A

Match with Stocking Pattern C

Stocking Pattern B

Match with Stocking Pattern A

Match with Stocking Pattern B

Leave open for lining

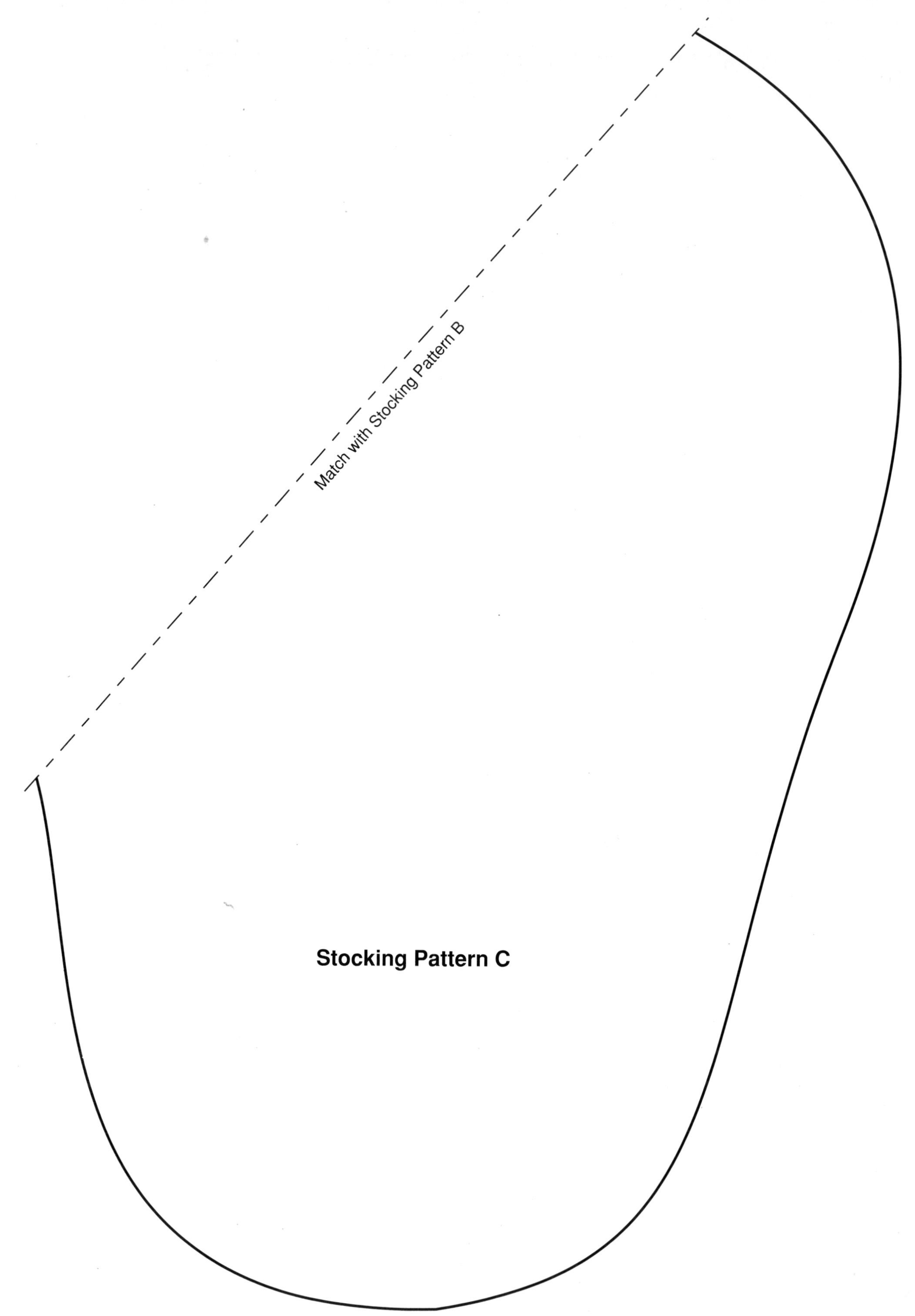
Match with Stocking Pattern B
Stocking Pattern C

Stepping Stones

Quiltmaker: Kathy Munkelwitz

Two traditional patchwork blocks alternate in an original setting to create this quilt. Special sashing strips, contrasting sashing squares, and shared fabrics make the blocks seem to flow together. Setting and corner triangles that are variations of one of the blocks continue the flow of the pattern to the edge of the border. Kathy designed this quilt with lots of open spaces for quilting.

Skill Level: Intermediate

Size: Finished quilt is approximately 81 ½ × 107 inches

Finished block is 16 inches square

Fabrics and Supplies

- 4 yards of dark green solid fabric for blocks and sashing strips
- 3 ¼ yards of red solid fabric for blocks, sashing squares, and borders
- 1 ¾ yards of red floral print fabric for blocks
- 1 ¾ yards of cream floral print fabric for blocks
- 1 ¼ yards of medium green print fabric for blocks and sashing strips
- 1 yard of dark green-and-white dot fabric for blocks
- ¾ yard of green-and-black floral print fabric for block centers
- ¼ yard of red dot fabric for side setting triangles
- 7 ½ yards of fabric for quilt back
- 1 yard of dark green print fabric for binding
- King-size quilt batting (120 inches square)
- Rotary cutter, ruler, and mat
- Template plastic (optional)

Cutting

All measurements include ¼-inch seam allowances. Measurements for the borders are longer than needed; trim them to the exact length when they are added to the quilt top. Instructions given are for quick-cutting the pieces with a rotary cutter and ruler. If you prefer to cut the pieces in the traditional manner, make templates using pattern C on page 149 and the dimensions listed below. Tips for making and using templates are on page 153.

- **A:** 2 ½-inch square
- **B:** 2 ½ × 4 ½-inch rectangle
- **D:** Make a 2 ⅞-inch square; cut the square in half diagonally.
- **E:** 4 ½-inch square
- **F:** 6 ½-inch square
- **G:** Make a 6 ⅞-inch square; cut the square in half diagonally.
- **H:** Make a 4 ⅞-inch square; cut the square in half diagonally.
- **I:** Make a 5 ¼-inch square; cut the square in half diagonally both ways.

From the dark green solid fabric, cut:

- 192 D triangles
  Use Template D
  OR
  Cut seven 2 ⅞ × 44-inch strips. Cut the strips into 2 ⅞-inch squares. You will need 96 squares. Cut each square in half diagonally to make two triangles.
- 34 F squares
  Use Template F
  OR
  Cut six 6 ½ × 44-inch strips. Cut the strips into 6 ½-inch squares.
- 28 triangles
  Use Template G
  OR
  Cut three 6 ⅞ × 44-inch strips. Cut the strips into 6 ⅞-inch squares. You will need 14 squares. Cut each square in half diagonally to make two triangles.
- Forty-eight 2 ½ × 16 ½-inch sashing strips

  Cut three 16 ½ × 44-inch strips. Cut the strips into 2 ½ × 16 ½-inch rectangles.

From the red solid fabric, cut:

- Four 3 ¼ × 117-inch strips for borders
- 175 A squares
  Use Template A
  OR
  Cut four 2 ½ × 117-inch strips. From the strips, cut 2 ½-inch squares.

From the red floral print fabric, cut:

- 56 D triangles
  Use Template D
  OR
  Cut two 2 ⅞ × 44-inch strips. Cut the strips into 2 ⅞-inch squares. You will need 28 squares. Cut each square in half diagonally to make two triangles.
- 48 C and 48 C reverse pieces
  Use Template C

OR
Cut sixteen 2½ × 44-inch strips. You will cut them into C pieces later.

From the cream floral print fabric, cut:

- 96 D triangles

  Use Template D
  OR
  Cut four 2⅞ × 44-inch strips. Cut the strips into 2⅞-inch squares. You will need 48 squares. Cut each square in half diagonally to make two triangles.
- 48 C and 48 C reverse pieces

  Use Template C
  OR
  Cut sixteen 2½ × 44-inch strips. You will cut them into C pieces later.

From the medium green print fabric, cut:

- 192 A squares

  Use Template A
  OR
  Cut twelve 2½ × 44-inch strips. Cut the strips into 2½-inch squares.

From the dark green-and-white dot fabric, cut:

- 96 B rectangles

  Use Template B
  OR
  Cut eleven 2½ × 44-inch strips. Cut the strips into 2½ × 4½-inch rectangles.

From the green-and-black floral fabric, cut:

- 18 E squares

  Use Template E
  OR
  Cut two 4½ × 44-inch strips. Cut the strips into 4½-inch squares.
- 10 H triangles

  Use Template H
  OR
  Cut one 4⅞-inch-wide strip. From the strip, cut five 4⅞-inch squares. Cut each square in half diagonally to make two triangles.
- 4 I triangles

  Use Template I
  OR
  Cut one 5¼-inch square. Cut the square in half diagonally in both directions to make four triangles.

From the red dot fabric, cut:

- 40 D triangles

  Use Template D
  OR
  Cut two 2⅞ × 44-inch strips. Cut the strips into 2⅞-inch squares. You will need 20 squares. Cut each square in half diagonally to make two triangles.

Piecing the Blocks

Two different but similar blocks alternate in this quilt. Shared fabrics help the flow of the design across the quilt. You will need 12 of Block 1 and 6 of Block 2. Refer to the **Fabric Key** and the diagrams for correct color placement.

Fabric Key

Dark green
Medium green print
Red
Dark green-and-white dot
Red floral print
Green-and-black floral print
Cream floral print
Red dot

Block 1

1. Referring to **Diagram 1,** sew red and medium green print A squares together into four-patch units. Make two rows of two squares each; join the rows. Repeat to make 48 of these units.

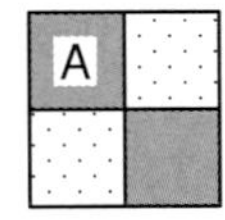

Diagram 1

2. Sew a green-and-white dot B rectangle to one side of each of the 48 Step 1 units, as shown in **Diagram 2** on page 146. Press the seams toward the B rectangles. Sew a red A square to one end of each of the 48 remaining B rectangles. Sew the AB units to the larger units. Press the seams toward the B rectangles.

3. To cut the C pieces, divide the 2½-inch-wide red floral print strips into eight pairs. Position the pairs with right sides facing and raw edges aligned. Trim one end of a set of

paired strips at a 45 degree angle. Cut C pieces by making cuts parallel to the 45 degree cut at 3¼-inch intervals, as shown in **Diagram 3.** Repeat to cut C pieces from the remaining pairs of strips. You'll need a total of 48 pairs of C pieces. Cut the sixteen 2½-inch-wide cream print strips in the same manner, and set them aside to be used in Block 2.

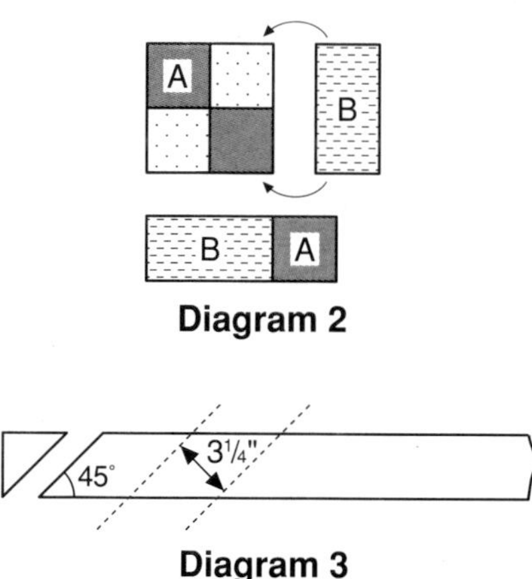

Diagram 2

Diagram 3

4. Referring to **Diagram 4** for correct placement, sew a dark green D triangle to one end of each red floral C piece. Sew a cream floral D triangle to each opposite end, as shown. Press the seams away from the C pieces. Repeat for all 48 C pieces. In the same way, add triangles to the ends of the red floral C reverse pieces, as shown in the diagram.

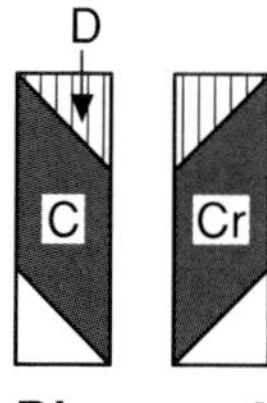

Diagram 4

5. Sew the two Step 4 units together, as shown in **Diagram 5.** Press the seams to one side. You will have 48 completed units.

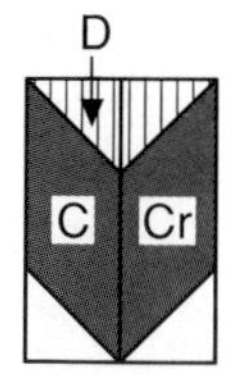

Diagram 5

6. Referring to **Diagram 6,** lay out the units for one Block 1. Join the units into rows, pressing the seams in alternate directions from row to row. Join the rows. Repeat to make 12 Block 1 blocks.

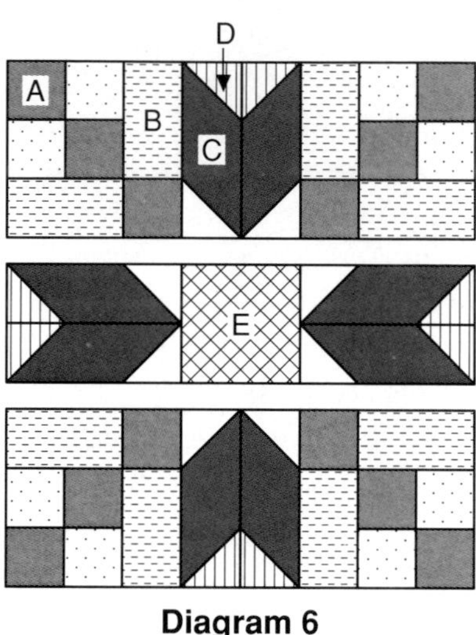

Diagram 6

Block 2

1. Referring to **Diagram 4** and Step 4 on this page, make 24 pieced units using dark green D triangles, cream floral C pieces, and red floral D triangles. Press the seams away from the C pieces. In the same way, make 24 units using the cream floral C reverse pieces.

2. Referring to **Diagram 5** and Step 5 on this page, sew the C and C reverse units together. You should have 24 completed units.

3. Referring to **Diagram 7,** lay out the pieces for one Block 2. Join the pieces in rows, pressing

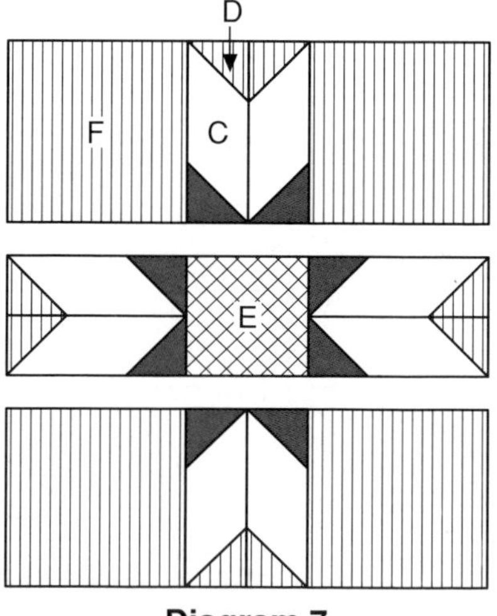

Diagram 7

the seams in alternate directions from row to row. Join the rows. Repeat to make six Block 2 blocks.

Piecing the Side Setting Triangles

1. Using dark green D triangles, cream floral C pieces, and red dot D triangles, make 20 pieced C units in the same manner as for the blocks. Make 20 pieced C reverse units. Sew the units together.

2. Sew a dark green F square to the left side of ten of the Step 1 units, as shown in **Diagram 8.** Sew a dark green G triangle to the right side of the units, as shown. Press the seams away from the pieced units.

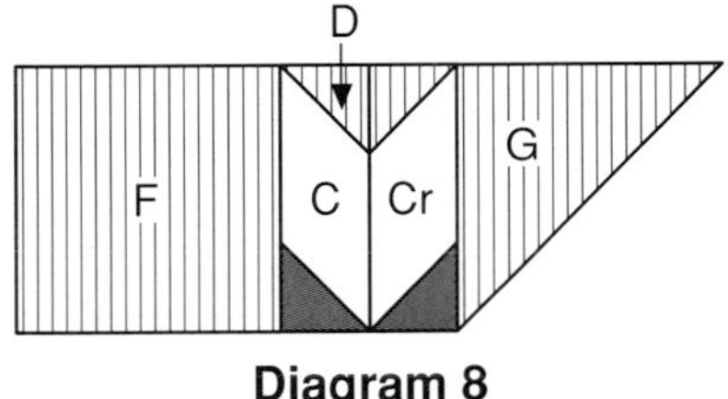

Diagram 8

3. Sew a green-and-black floral H triangle to the short side of the remaining ten units, as shown in **Diagram 9.** Press the seams away from the pieced units.

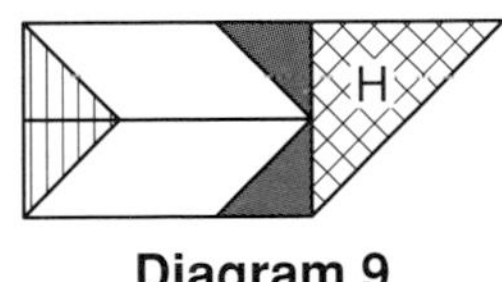

Diagram 9

4. Sew the Step 2 sections and the Step 3 sections together as shown in the **Side Setting Triangle Diagram.** Add a dark green G triangle to the bottom of each joined section. You should have ten side setting triangles.

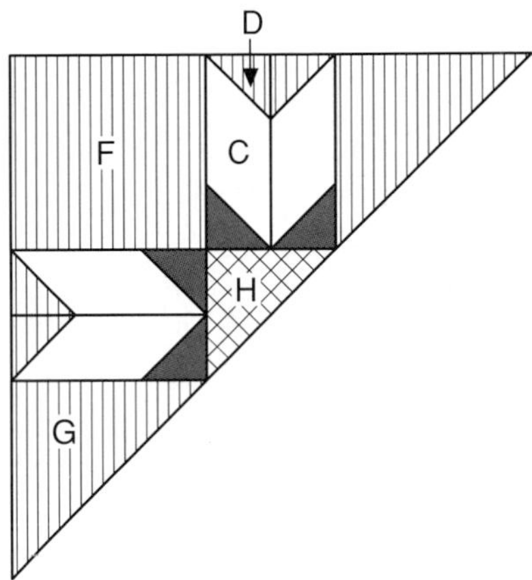

Side Setting Triangle Diagram

Piecing the Corner Setting Triangles

1. Referring to **Diagram 4,** make four pieced C units using dark green D triangles, cream floral C pieces, and red floral D triangles. In the same manner, make four C reverse units. Sew the units together.

2. Sew a green print I triangle to one end of the pieced C units, as shown in **Diagram 10.**

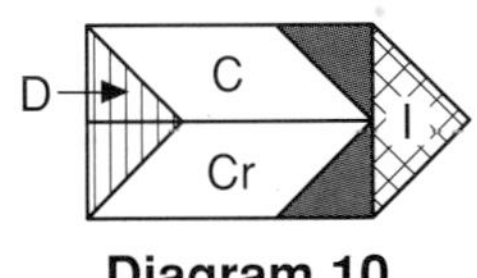

Diagram 10

3. Sew a dark green G triangle to each side of the Step 2 units. The completed units should look like the one shown in the **Corner Setting Triangle Diagram.**

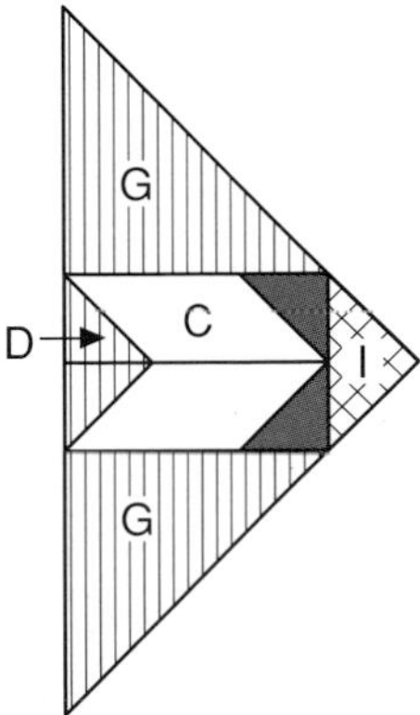

Corner Setting Triangle Diagram

Making the Pieced Sashing Strips

1. To make one pieced sashing strip, pin a medium green print A square to the end of a sashing strip, with right sides together and aligning the raw edges. Repeat with a second A square at the other end of the strip. Stitch diagonally across the A squares from corner to corner, sewing through both layers, as shown in **Diagram 11.**

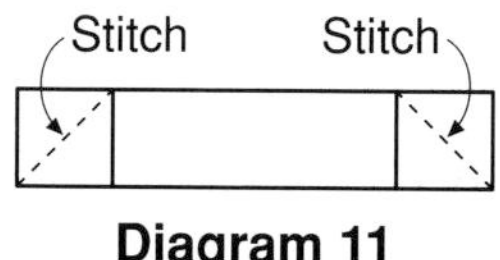

Diagram 11

2. Trim off the excess fabric at the corners of the strip, as shown in **Diagram 12A,** leaving ¼-inch seam allowances. Open out the green triangles, as shown in **12B;** press the seams toward the green triangles.

3. Repeat to make 48 pieced sashing strips.

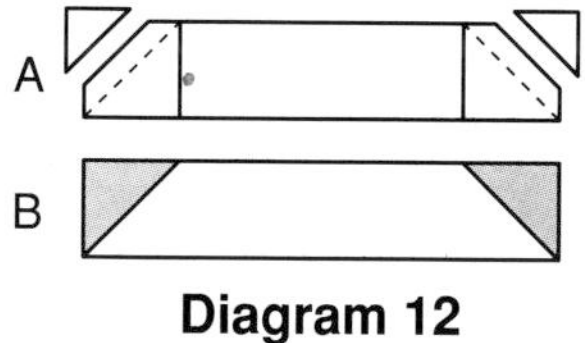

Diagram 12

Assembling the Quilt Top

1. Referring to the **Quilt Diagram,** lay out Blocks 1 and 2, sashing strips, red A squares, side setting triangles, and corner setting triangles. Pay attention to the placement of the sashing strips; make sure the direction of the green triangles matches the diagram.

2. Sew the pieces together in diagonal rows. In the rows with blocks, press the seams toward the blocks. In rows of sashing, press the seams toward the sashing squares, not the strips.

3. Join the block rows and sashing strips. Press the quilt top.

4. Measure the length and width of the quilt top. Place the red border strips right sides together with the quilt top, matching centers. Sew the borders to the quilt, mitering the border corner seams. See page 160 for complete instructions on adding mitered borders to a quilt.

Quilting and Finishing

1. Mark quilting designs. A cable design for the border is on the opposite page.

2. Divide the backing fabric crosswise into three 2½-yard pieces and trim the selvages. To piece the quilt back, sew the three pieces together along the long sides. The seams will run crosswise across the quilt.

3. Layer the quilt back, batting, and quilt top; baste. Trim the quilt back so it is approximately 3 inches larger than the quilt top on all sides.

4. Quilt all marked designs, and add additional quilting as desired.

5. From the binding fabric, make approximately 400 inches of French-fold binding. See page 164 for suggested binding widths and instructions on making and attaching binding.

6. Sew the binding to the quilt top. Trim the excess batting and backing, and hand finish the binding on the back side of the quilt.

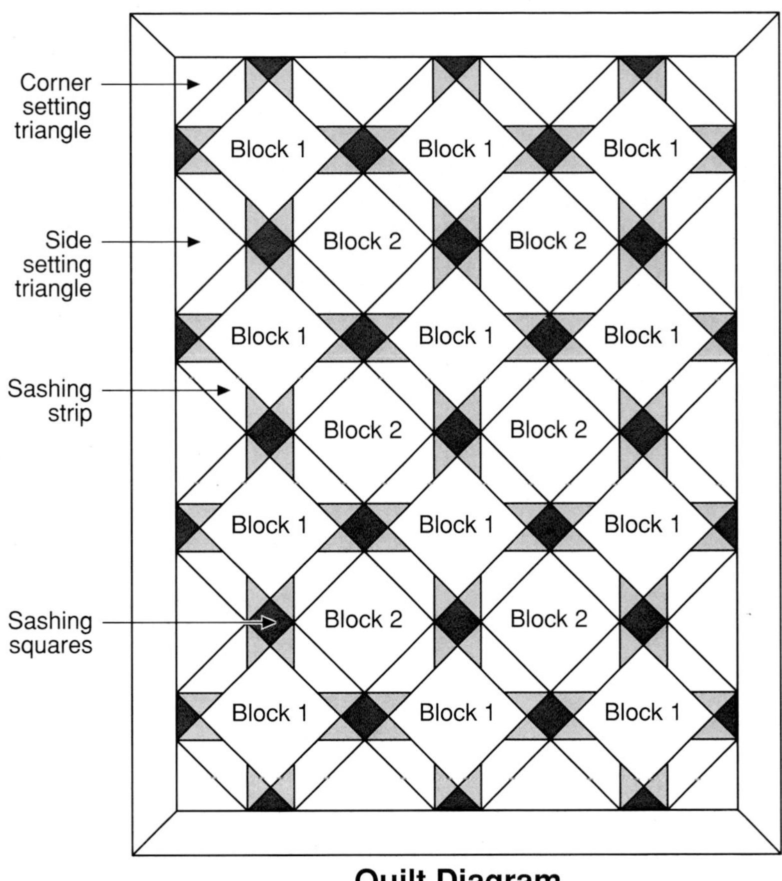

Quilt Diagram

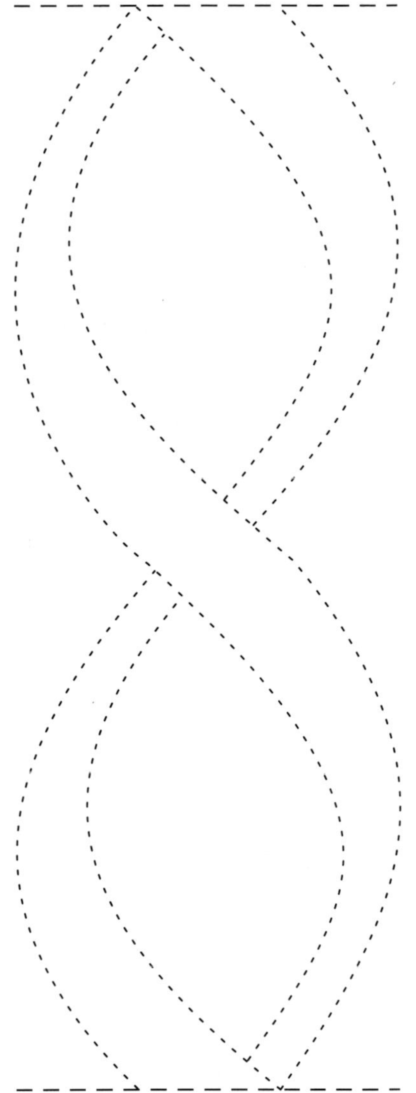

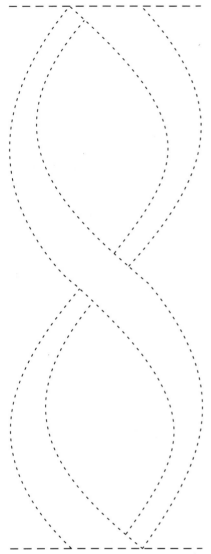

Border Quilting Design

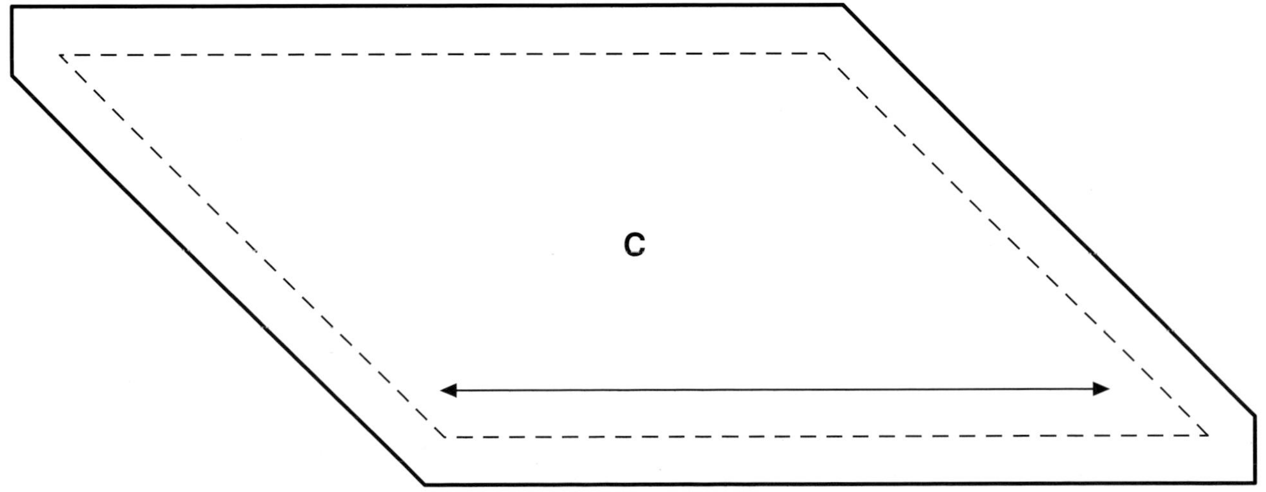

Tips and Techniques

In this chapter you'll find detailed descriptions of general quiltmaking techniques, as well as hints and tips designed to make your quiltmaking successful and fun. Take a few moments to read this chapter from start to finish and become familiar with what's here. Not only will you find it easier to complete the projects in this book, you'll also learn some helpful pointers that can apply to any quilt you make.

Supplies to Have on Hand

"Quiltmaking Basics" below describes the supplies you'll need to get started on the projects in this book. "Quiltmaking Time-Savers" describes quilting tools that you may want to work with. They are readily available at quilt shops and fabric stores and through mail-order catalogs. A few of the projects also require specialized supplies; those supplies are listed with the projects.

Quiltmaking Basics

- **Needles.** Use *sharps* for hand sewing and appliqué and *betweens* for hand quilting. For both sharps and betweens, the larger the number, the smaller the needle. The general rule is to start with larger-size needles and move to smaller ones as you gain experience. Experiment with different sizes to see which are most comfortable in your hand and the easiest to manipulate through the fabric.
- **Straight pins.** Do not use pins that have become burred or rusted; they may leave marks in your fabric. Long (1½-inch) pins with glass or plastic heads are easy to work with, especially when pinning layers.
- **Scissors.** If you are cutting your fabric with scissors, use a good, sharp pair of dressmaker's shears. Use these only on fabric. You should also have a pair of small, sharp embroidery scissors for trimming threads and seam allowances, and a pair of general scissors for cutting paper and template plastic.
- **Iron and ironing board.** Careful pressing is important for accurate piecing. To save steps and increase efficiency, keep your ironing board and iron close to your sewing area.
- **Sewing machine.** Keep it clean and in good working order.
- **Template plastic or cardboard.** Templates are rigid master patterns used to mark patchwork and appliqué shapes on fabric. Thin, semitransparent plastic, available at quilt and craft shops, is ideal, although poster-weight cardboard can also be used.
- **Thread.** Always use good-quality thread. For sewing, use either 100 percent cotton or cotton-covered polyester. For quilting, use special quilting thread.

Quiltmaking Time-Savers

- **Rotary cutter and cutting mat.** For greater speed and accuracy, you can cut all border strips and many other pieces with a rotary cutter instead of scissors. You must always use a specially designed cutting mat when working with a rotary cutter. The mat protects the work surface and helps to grip the fabric to keep it from slipping. An all-purpose cutting mat size is 18 × 24 inches. See page 152 for tips on using the rotary cutter.
- **See-through ruler.** The companion to the rotary cutter and mat is the see-through plastic ruler. It comes in several sizes and shapes; a useful size to have on hand is a 6 × 24-inch heavy-duty ruler that is marked in inches, quarter-inches, and eighth-inches and has a 45 degree angle line for mitering. Also handy is a 12 × 12-inch ruled plastic square.
- **Plastic-coated freezer paper.** Quilters have discovered many handy uses for this type of paper, which is stocked in grocery stores with other food-wrapping supplies. Choose a quality brand, such as Reynolds.

About Fabric

Since fabric is the most essential element in a quilt, what you buy and how you treat it are

important considerations. Buy the best that you can afford; you'll be far happier with the results if you work with good-quality materials. Read through this section for additional tips on selecting and preparing fabric.

Selecting Fabrics

The instructions for each quilt include the amount of fabric you will need. When choosing fabrics, most experienced quilters insist on 100 percent cotton broadcloth, or dress-weight, fabric. It presses well and handles easily, whether you are sewing by hand or machine.

If there is a quilt shop in your area, the sales staff there can help you choose fabrics. Most home-sewing stores also have a section of all-cotton fabrics for quilters. If you have scraps left over from other sewing, use them only if they are all-cotton and all of similar weight.

Gaining Color Confidence

Deciding on a color scheme and choosing the fabrics can seem daunting to a beginner. You can take some of the mystery out of the process by learning the basics of color theory. Consult books on color theory, or seek out a class at a local quilt shop. Learn how helpful a color wheel can be. Your color confidence will grow as you learn the basics and then experiment with different combinations.

Purchasing Fabrics

The yardages given for projects in this book are based on 44/45-inch-wide fabrics. These yardages are adequate for both the template and rotary-cutting methods. They have been double-checked for accuracy and always include a little extra. Be aware, however, that fabric is sometimes narrower than the size listed on the bolt, and that any quilter, no matter how experienced, can make a mistake in cutting. It's wise to buy an extra half yard of each fabric just to be safe.

CHOOSING THE RIGHT COMBINATIONS

When selecting fabrics for a project, keep in mind that color is not the only consideration. Value (the lightness or darkness of a color) and scale (the size of the print) are also important. If you can, do this simple test while you're still at the fabric store. Place your chosen fabrics in a stack so that they're all visible. Stand a few feet away from the stack and squint at the fabrics. This will help you to see if you have enough variety of scale and if the colors work together. ❖

Preparing Fabrics

For best results, prewash, dry, and press fabrics before using them in your quilts. Prewashing allows shrinkage to occur and removes finishes and sizing, softening the cloth and making it easier to handle. Washing also allows colors to bleed before light and dark fabrics are combined in a quilt. Keep in mind, however, that prewashing might remove the lovely finish from chintz and polished cotton. If you want to use these fabrics, save them for wallhangings or other items that won't need to be laundered.

Using your automatic washer, wash fabric in warm water and a mild detergent. Dry on a medium setting in your dryer or outdoors on a clothesline. It's a good idea to get in the habit of washing all your fabrics as soon as you bring them home, even if you don't plan to use them right away. Then, when you are ready to use a fabric, you won't have to wonder whether it's been washed.

While prewashing is best, some quilters prefer the crispness of unwashed fabric and feel they can achieve more accurate machine-sewn patchwork by using fabric right off the bolt. Some machine quilters like to use unwashed fabric, then wash the project after quilting and binding so the quilt looks crinkled and old-fashioned. The risk in washing after stitching is that colors may bleed.

SETTING DYE WHEN COLORS BLEED

While most fabrics today are colorfast, some, especially reds and purples, may bleed. To test for colorfastness, soak a scrap in warm water. If the color bleeds, set the dye by soaking the whole piece of fabric in a solution of three parts cold water to one part vinegar. Rinse the fabric several times in warm water. If it still bleeds, don't use it in your quilt. ❖

Cutting the Fabric

The cutting instructions for each project follow the list of fabrics and supplies. To make the book as easy to use as possible,

the cutting instructions appear two ways. Quilters who prefer the traditional method of making templates and scissor-cutting individual pieces will find full-size patterns or directions for making templates. For quilters who prefer to rotary cut, quick-cutting directions speed things along. You may want to try a combination of techniques, using scissors and templates for pattern pieces and the rotary cutter for straight pieces like borders and bindings. Experiment and see what works best for you.

For some projects there are no patterns. In these cases, you will either measure and cut squares, triangles, and rectangles directly from the fabric, or you will sew strips together into strip sets and then cut them into special units to combine with others.

Although rotary cutting can be faster and more accurate than cutting with scissors, it has one disadvantage: It does not always result in the most efficient use of fabric. In some cases, the quick-cutting method will result in long strips of leftover fabric. Don't think of these as wasted bits of fabric; just add them to your scrap bag for future projects.

Tips on Rotary Cutting

- Keep the rotary cutter out of children's reach. The blade is extremely sharp!
- Make it a habit to always slide the blade guard into place as soon as you stop cutting.
- Always cut *away* from yourself.
- Square off the end of your fabric before measuring and cutting pieces, as shown in **Diagram 1.** Place a ruled square on the fold, and place a 6 × 24-inch ruler against the side of the square. Hold the ruler in place, remove the square, and cut along the edge of the ruler. If you are left-handed, work from the other end of the fabric.
- When cutting strips or rectangles, cut on the crosswise grain, as shown in **Diagram 2,** unless instructed otherwise. Strips can then be cut into squares, as shown.
- Check strips periodically to make sure the fabric is square and the strips are straight. Your strips should be straight, not angled. (See **Diagram 3.**) If your strips are not straight, refold the fabric, square off the edge, and begin cutting again.
- Cut triangles from squares, as shown in **Diagram 4.** The project directions will tell you whether to cut the

THE BEST TOOL FOR THE JOB

Rotary cutters are available in several sizes and styles and from several different manufacturers. The large, heavy-duty size is best for cutting several layers at one time. The small cutter is ideal for cutting around thick plastic templates; it is easy to control around curves and points. There are even models that are designed to reduce strain on joints and muscles—great for quilters with arthritis or carpal tunnel syndrome. The sales staff at your local quilt shop or fabric store can help you determine which rotary cutter will meet your needs. ❖

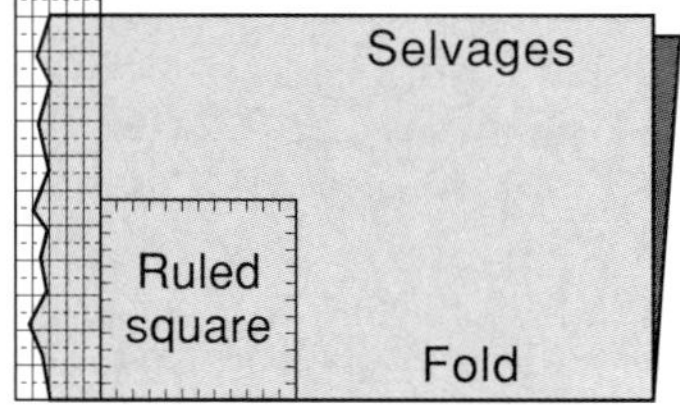

***Diagram 1:** Square off the uneven edges of the fabric before cutting the strips.*

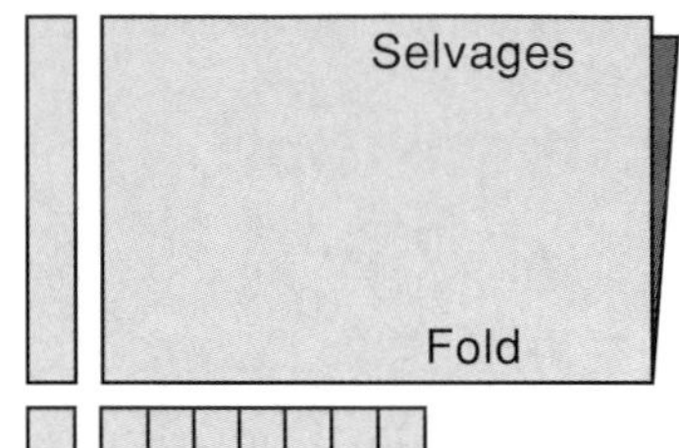

***Diagram 2:** Cut strips or rectangles on the crosswise grain. Cut the strips into squares.*

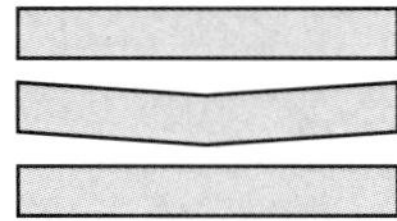

***Diagram 3:** Check to see that the strips are straight. If they are angled, refold the fabric and square off the edge again.*

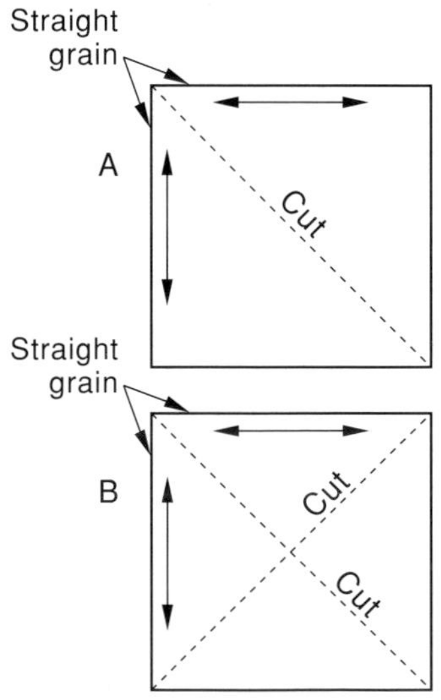

***Diagram 4:** Cut two triangles from a square by making one diagonal cut (A). Cut four triangles from a square by making two diagonal cuts (B).*

square into two triangles by making one diagonal cut **(Diagram 4A)** or into four triangles by making two diagonal cuts **(Diagram 4B).**

CUTTING PIECES FROM STRIPS

When cutting squares or rectangles from fabric strips, speed up the process by cutting several layers of fabric at one time. A rotary cutter with a large blade will easily cut through six to eight layers of cotton fabric. Fold the strips in half crosswise so that they are approximately 22 inches long. Keeping raw edges aligned, stack three or four strips atop each other (making six or eight layers of fabric). Make cross-grain cuts through the stacked fabric. ❖

Making and Using Templates

Many of the patterns in this book are printed full size, with no drafting required. For most of the pieced projects, you will have the option of either making templates and cutting fabric pieces individually or using a rotary cutter to quick-cut them.

Thin, semitransparent plastic makes excellent, durable templates. Lay the plastic over the book page, carefully trace the patterns onto the plastic, and cut them out with scissors. To make cardboard templates, transfer the patterns to tracing paper, glue the paper to the cardboard, and cut out the templates. Copy identification letters and grain lines onto your templates. Always check your templates against the printed pattern for accuracy.

The patchwork patterns in the book are printed with double lines: an inner dashed line and an outer solid line. If you intend to sew your patchwork by hand, trace the inner dashed line to make finished-size templates. Cut out the templates on the traced line. Draw around the template on the wrong side of the fabric, as shown in **Diagram 5,** leaving ½ inch between lines. The lines you draw are the sewing lines. Then mark the ¼-inch seam allowances before you cut out the fabric pieces.

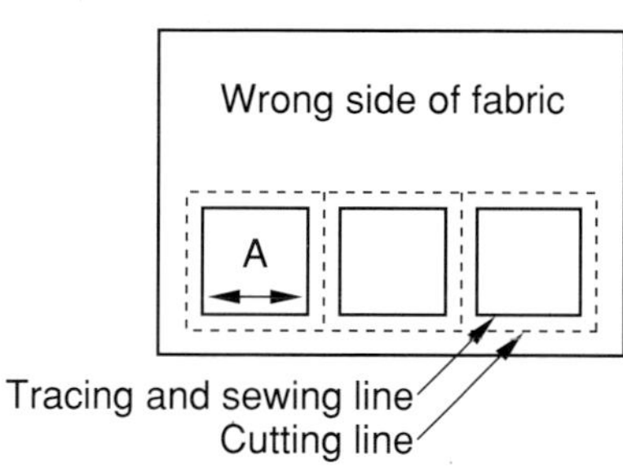

Diagram 5: *If piecing by hand, mark around the template on the wrong side of the fabric. Cut it out, adding ¼-inch seam allowances on all sides.*

If you plan to sew your patchwork by machine, use the outer solid line and make your templates with seam allowances included. Draw around the templates on the wrong side of the fabric, as shown in **Diagram 6.** The line you draw is the cutting line. Sew with an exact ¼-inch seam for perfect patchwork.

Patterns for appliqué pieces are finished size and are printed with only a single line. Draw around templates on the right side of the fabric, as shown in **Diagram 7,** leaving ½ inch between pieces. The lines you draw will be your fold-under lines, or guides for turning under the edges of the appliqué pieces. Then add scant ¼-inch seam allowances as you cut out the pieces.

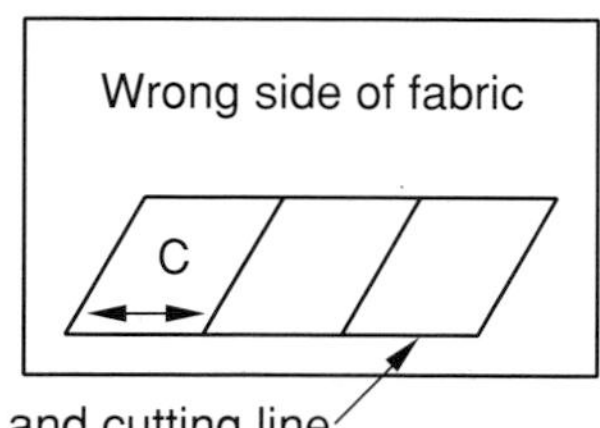

Diagram 6: *If piecing by machine, use templates with seam allowances included.*

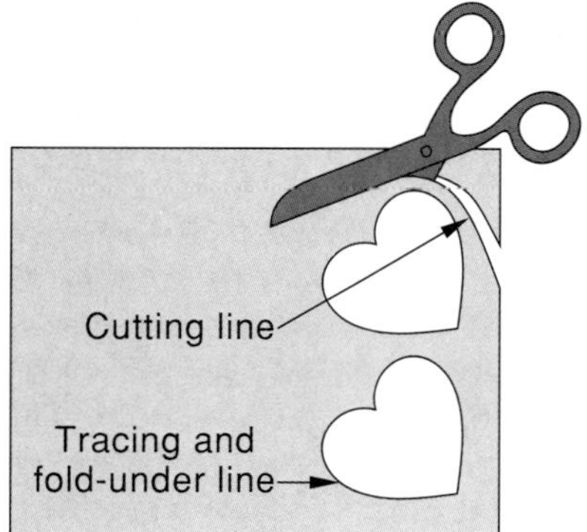

Diagram 7: *Draw around the templates on the right side of the fabric for appliqué pieces. Add seam allowances as you cut out the pieces.*

Tips on Piecing

The standard seam allowance for piecing is ¼ inch. For precise patchwork, where the pieces always meet exactly where they should, you must be vigilant about accurate seam allowances. Some sewing machines come with a handy seam allowance guide marked alongside the feed dogs. On other machines, the distance from the needle to the outside of the presser foot is ¼ inch. (Measure your machine to be sure this is accurate.) On

machines that have no built-in guides like these, you can create your own. Measure ¼ inch from the needle and lay down a 2-inch-long piece of masking tape. Add layers of tape on top of the first one until you have a raised edge against which you can guide your fabric, automatically measuring the ¼-inch seam allowance.

When assembling pieced blocks, keep in mind these basic rules: Combine smaller pieces to make larger units, join larger units into rows or sections, and join sections to complete the blocks. If you follow these rules, you should be able to build most blocks using only straight seams. Setting-in pieces at an angle should only be done when necessary. (Pointers on setting-in appear on the opposite page.)

Lay out the pieces for the block right side up, as shown in the project diagram, before you sew. For quilts with multiple blocks, cut out and piece a sample block first to make sure your fabrics work well together and to make sure you have cut out the pieces accurately.

Hand Piecing

For hand piecing, use finished-size templates to cut your fabric pieces. Join the pieces by matching marked sewing lines and securing them with pins. Sew with a running stitch from seam line to seam line, as shown in **Diagram 8,** rather than from raw edge to raw edge. As you sew, check to see that your stitching is staying on the lines, and make a backstitch every four or five stitches to reinforce and strengthen the seam. Secure the corners with an extra backstitch.

Diagram 8: *Join the pieces with a running stitch, backstitching every four or five stitches.*

When you are crossing seam allowances of previously joined smaller units, leave the seam allowances free rather than stitching them down. Make a backstitch just before you cross, slip the needle through the seam allowance, make a backstitch just after you cross, and then resume stitching the seam. (See **Diagram 9.**) When the block is finished, press the seam allowances toward the darker fabrics.

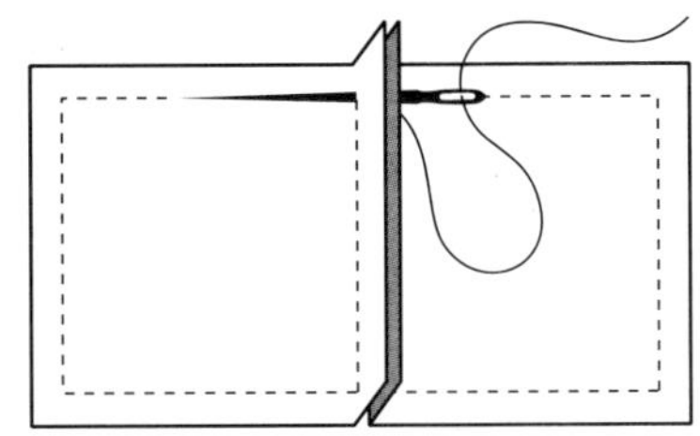

Diagram 9: *When hand piecing, leave the seam allowances free by slipping through without stitching them down.*

Machine Piecing

For machine piecing, cut the fabric pieces using templates with seam allowances included or use a rotary cutter to quick-cut. Before sewing a block, sew a test seam to make sure you are taking accurate ¼-inch seams. Even 1/16 inch of inaccuracy can result in a block that is not the right size. Adjust your machine to sew 10 to 12 stitches per inch. Select a neutral-color thread that blends well with your fabrics.

Join the pieces by sewing from raw edge to raw edge. Press seams before crossing them with other seams. Since the seam allowances will be stitched down when crossed with another seam, you'll need to think about the direction in which you want them to lie. Press the seam allowances toward darker fabrics whenever possible to prevent them from shadowing through lighter ones. For more information on pressing, see page 156.

In many quilts, you need to sew a large number of the same size or shape pieces together to create units for the blocks. For a bed-size quilt, this can mean a hundred or more squares, triangles, or rectangles that need to be stitched together. A timesaving method known as assembly-line piecing can reduce the drudgery. Run pairs of pieces or units through the sewing machine one after another without cutting the thread, as shown in **Diagram 10.** Once all the units you need have been sewn, snip them apart and press.

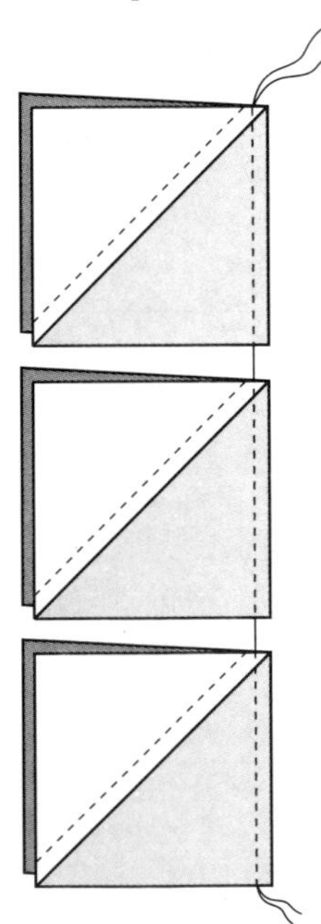

Diagram 10: *Feed the units through the machine without cutting the thread.*

Setting-In Pieces

Not all patchwork patterns can be assembled with continuous straight seams. An example is the Plaid Spools wallhanging on page 76. The background pieces must be set into the angled openings created by the plaid spool pieces. Setting-in calls for precise stitching as you insert pieces into angles, as shown in **Diagram 11.** In this example, pieces A, B, and C are set into the angles created by the four joined diamond pieces.

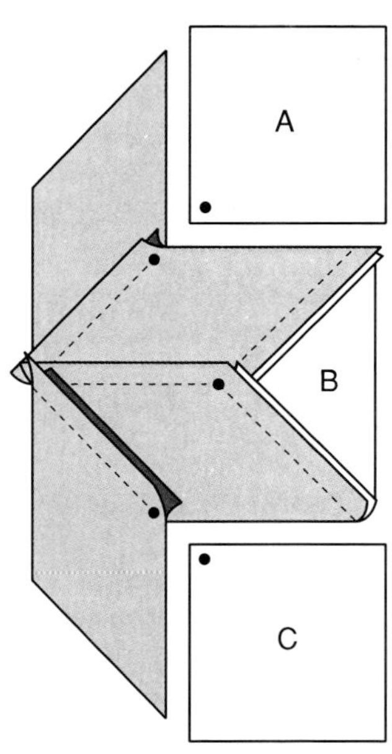

Diagram 11: *Setting-in calls for careful matching of points and precise stitching. Here, pieces A, B, and C are set into the angles created by the four joined diamonds.*

Setting-In by Hand

With hand sewing, setting-in pieces is simple. Following the directions on page 153, make finished-size templates. Trace around the templates, then mark the ¼-inch seam allowances before you cut out the pieces.

1. Pin the piece to be set in to one side of the angle, right sides together, matching the corners exactly.

2. Starting ¼ inch from the outside edge and working toward the corner, stitch along the seam line, as shown in **Diagram 12.** Knot the thread at the corner and clip it.

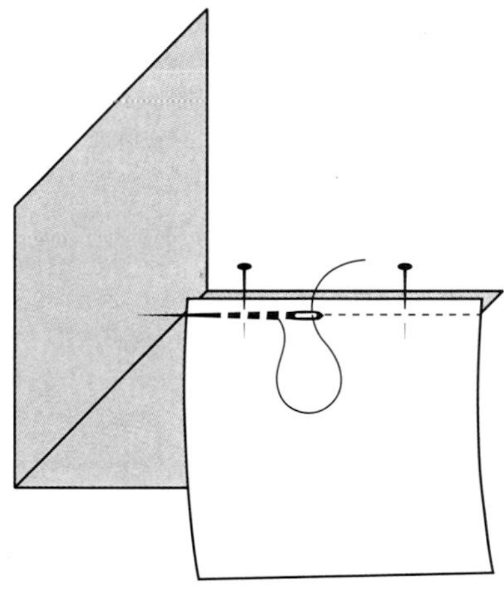

Diagram 12: *Pin the pieces right sides together and stitch from the outside into the corner.*

3. Bring the adjacent edge up and pin it to the other side of the angle, as shown in **Diagram 13.** Hand stitch the seam from the corner out, stopping ¼ inch from the edge at the end of the marked seam line.

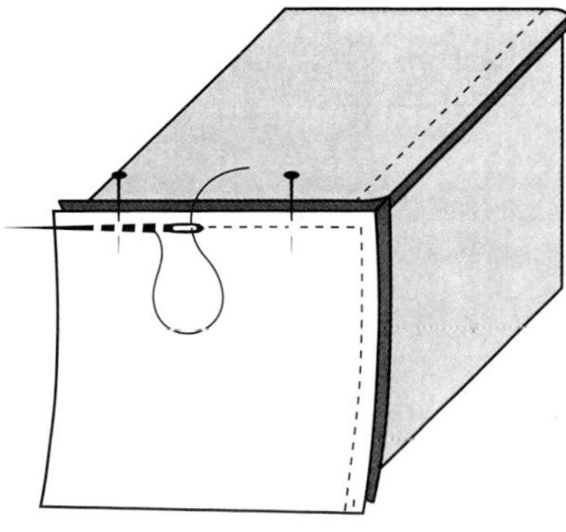

Diagram 13: *Pin the adjacent edge to the other side of the angle and stitch from the corner to the outside.*

Setting-In by Machine

If you are setting-in pieces by machine, make special templates that will allow you to mark dots on the fabric at the points where pieces will come together. By matching dots on the pattern pieces as they meet at the angle, you can be sure of a smooth fit. To make these templates, first mark the sewing lines, then use a large needle to pierce a hole at each setting-in point. (See **Diagram 14.**) As you trace the templates onto the wrong side of the fabric, push the tip of the pencil through each of these holes to create a dot. Mark all corners of each pattern piece; this allows you to turn the piece to adjust color or pattern placement.

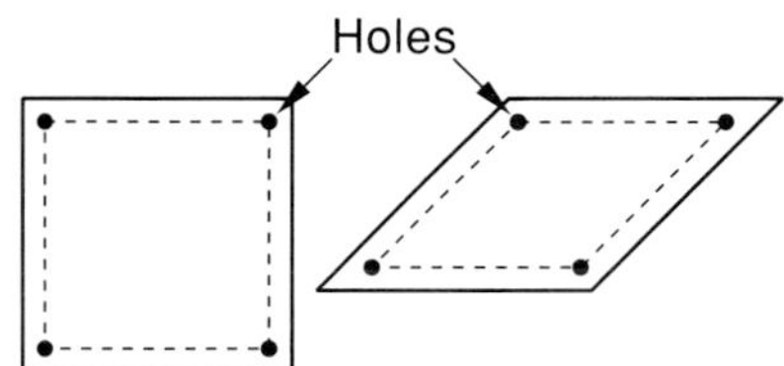

Diagram 14: *For setting-in pieces by machine, make templates with holes at the setting-in points.*

1. Pin a piece to one side of the angle with right sides together, matching the dots. Beginning and ending the seam with a backstitch, sew from the raw edge into the corner. Stop the stitching exactly on the marked corner dot; don't allow any stitching to extend into the seam allowance. (See **Diagram 15.**)

2. Remove the work from the sewing machine to realign the pieces for the other side of the seam. Swing the other side of the angled piece up, match the dots, and pin the pieces together.

3. Sew from the corner dot to the outside edge to complete the seam, again backstitching at the

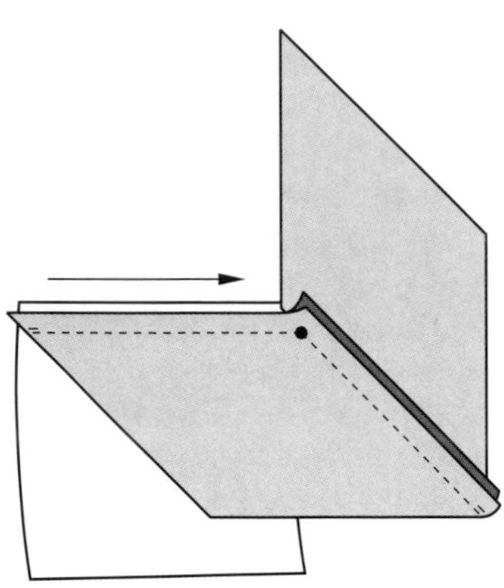

Diagram 15: *Pin the piece to one side of the angle, matching dots. Stitch from the edge into the corner.*

beginning and the end. (See **Diagram 16.**) Press the seams toward the set-in piece.

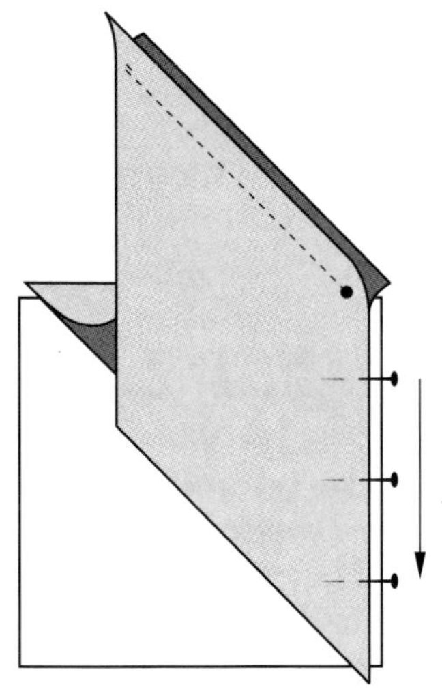

Diagram 16: *Matching dots, pin the piece to the other side of the angle. Stitch from the corner out to the edge.*

Pressing Basics

Proper pressing can make a big difference in the appearance of a finished block or quilt top. Quilters are divided on the issue of whether a steam or dry iron is best. Experiment to see which works best for you. For each project, pressing instructions are given as needed in the step-by-step directions. Review the list of guidelines that follow to brush up on your general pressing techniques.

- Press a seam before crossing it with another seam.
- Press seam allowances to one side, not open.
- Press seams of adjacent rows of blocks, or rows within blocks, in opposite directions. The pressed seams will abut as the rows are joined, producing precise intersections. (See **Diagram 17.**)

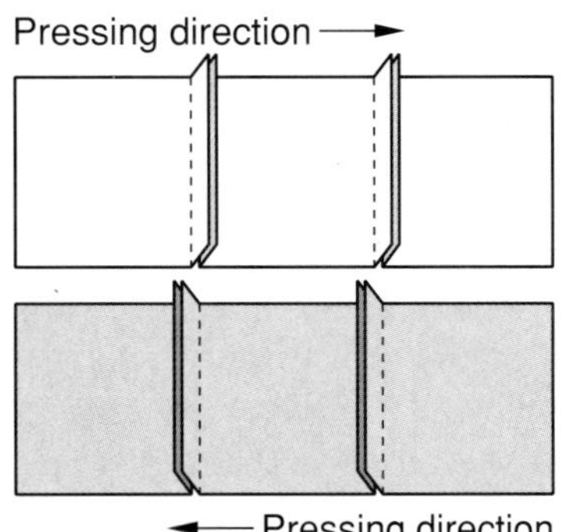

Diagram 17: *Press the seams of adjacent rows in opposite directions. When the rows are placed right sides together to be joined, the pressed seams will abut.*

- Press, don't iron. Bring the iron down gently and firmly on the fabric from above; don't rub it over the surface of the patchwork.
- Avoid pressing appliqués on the right side after they have been stitched to the background fabric. They are prettiest when slightly puffed, rather than flat. To press appliqués, turn the piece over and press very gently on the back side of the background fabric.

PRESSING TOWARD THE LIGHT

Whenever possible, press seams toward darker fabrics to avoid show-through on the front of the quilt. If you must press toward the lighter fabric, be sure to trim the seam allowance of the darker fabric so that it will be hidden behind the seam allowance of the lighter fabric. ❖

Hand Appliqué

Several of the quilts featured in this book include beautiful appliqué, sometimes in combination with patchwork. The true tests of fine appliqué work are smoothly turned, crisp edges and sharp points; no unsightly bumps or gaps; and nearly invisible stitches.

Depending on your personal preference, there are two popular techniques that can help you achieve flawless appliqué. In the basting-back method, the seam allowances are turned under and basted in place before the appliqué pieces are stitched to the background fabric. In needle-turn appliqué, the appliqué pieces are pinned in position and the seam allowances are turned under and stitched in place as you go.

For either method, use thread that matches the appliqué pieces, and stitch the appliqués to the background fabric with a blind hem or appliqué stitch, as shown in **Diagram 18.** Invest in a package of long, thin size 11 or 12 needles marked *sharps.* Make stitches ⅛ inch apart or closer, and keep them snug.

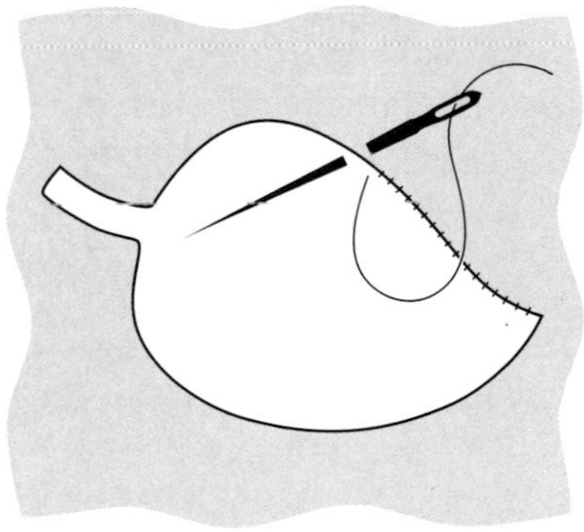

Diagram 18: *Stitch the appliqués to the background with a blind hem stitch. The stitches should be nearly invisible.*

When constructing appliqué blocks, always work from background to foreground. When an appliqué piece will be covered or overlapped by another, stitch the underneath piece to the background fabric first.

Basting Back Method

1. Make finished-size cardboard or plastic templates. Mark around the templates on the right side of the fabric to draw fold-under lines. Draw lightly so the fold-under lines are thin.

2. Cut out the pieces a scant ¼ inch to the outside of the marked lines.

3. For each appliqué piece, turn the seam allowance under, folding along the marked line, and baste close to the fold with white or natural thread. Clip concave curves and clefts before basting. (See **Diagram 19.**) Do not baste back edges that will be covered by another appliqué.

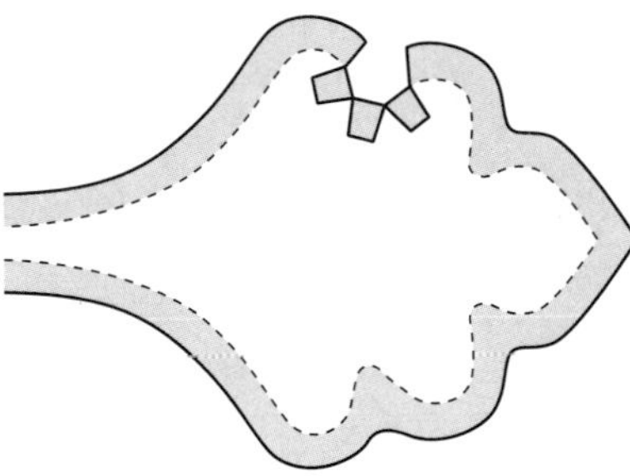

Diagram 19: *Clip any concave curves, then baste back the seam allowances.*

4. Pin the appliqués in place and stitch them to the background fabric. Remove the basting after the pieces are stitched down.

Needle-Turn Method

1. For this method, use plastic or cardboard templates to mark finished-size pieces. Mark lightly on the right side of the fabric.

2. Cut out the pieces a generous ⅛ inch larger than finished size.

3. Pin the pieces in position on the background fabric. Use the tip and shank of your appliqué needle to turn under ½-inch-long sections of seam allowance at a time. As you turn under a section, press it flat with your thumb and then stitch it in place.

Making Bias Strips for Stems and Vines

Fabric strips cut on the bias have more give and are easier to manipulate than strips cut on the straight grain. This makes them ideal for creating beautiful curving stems and vines and twisting ribbons. Bias strips enhance several of the projects in this book, including the Blossoms and Buds (page 35) and Midnight Rainbows (page 45) wallhangings. The instructions for the quilts include directions for cutting bias strips the proper width.

Cut bias strips with your rotary cutter using the 45 degree angle line on your see-through ruler. Straighten the left edge of your fabric as described on page 152. Align the 45 degree angle line on your ruler with the bottom edge of the fabric, as shown in **Diagram 20A,** and cut along the edge of the ruler to trim off the corner. Move the ruler across the fabric, cutting parallel strips in the needed width, as shown in **20B.** Once the strips are cut, prepare them for appliqué by following the steps below.

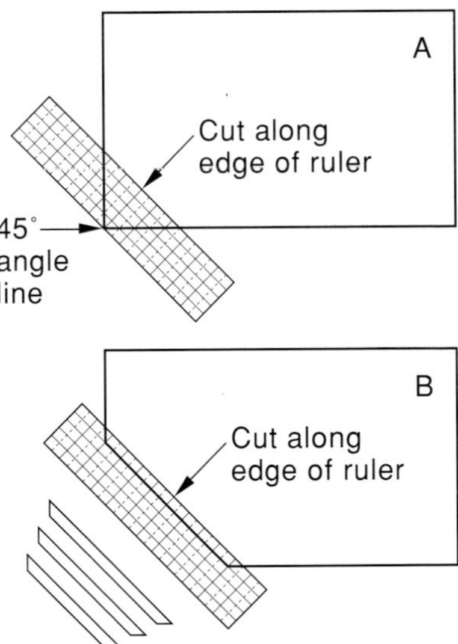

Diagram 20: *Use the 45 degree angle line on your see-through ruler to trim off the corner of the fabric (A). Then move the ruler across the fabric, cutting parallel strips of the width needed (B).*

For strips that are cut ¾ inch or wider (to finish ¼ inch wide or

more), prepare them by folding and steam pressing in thirds as follows.

1. Place the bias strip wrong side up on the ironing board.

2. Use the tip of the iron to fold over the first third of the fabric, as shown in **Diagram 21A.**

3. Fold over the other raw edge and press, making sure it does not extend beyond the first fold, as shown in **21B.**

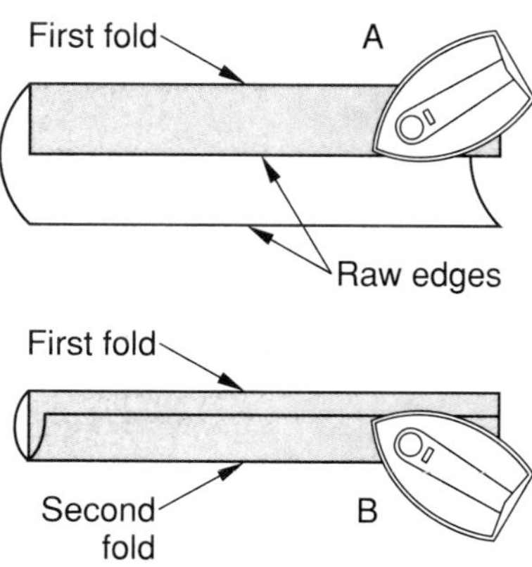

Diagram 21: *Using the tip of the iron, fold over the first third and press (A). Fold over the second third and press (B), making sure the raw edge does not extend beyond the first fold.*

4. Turn the folded strip over and press once more.

5. Baste the prepared strip in position and appliqué it in place, stitching along both folds. For curved bias strips, such as on the Midnight Rainbows wallhanging on page 45, appliqué the inner curve first, then the outer curve.

For very thin stems that finish ¼ inch or less, cut the bias strips slightly less than four times the finished width. For example, for strips that are 3⁄16 inch wide finished, cut them slightly less than ¾ inch wide. Then prepare the strips as follows.

1. Fold the strip in half, wrong sides together, and press.

2. Fold in half again and press to form a center guideline.

3. Lightly draw a placement line on the background fabric.

4. Place the raw edges of the folded strip along the placement line. Using thread that matches the appliqué fabric, stitch the strip to the background, sewing with a small running stitch through the pressed guideline. (See **Diagram 22.**)

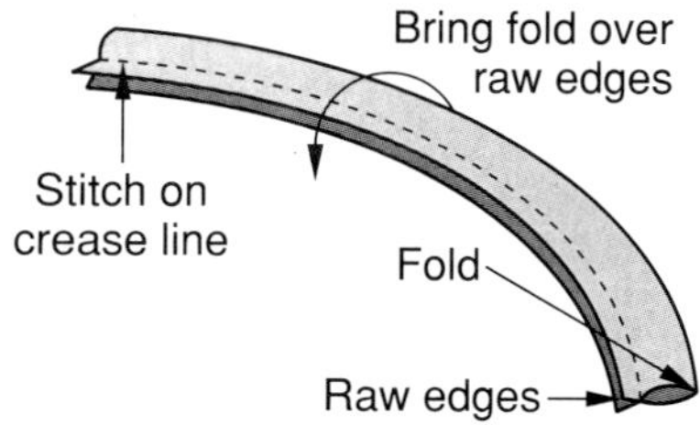

Diagram 22: *Baste along the pressed guideline, then bring the folded edge over to cover the raw edges and appliqué in place.*

5. Bring the folded edge over to cover the raw edges, trimming the raw edges as needed. Appliqué the fold in place.

Narrow bias strips can also be made using metal or plastic bars called bias bars or Celtic bars. These bars are available in quilt shops and through mail-order catalogs. You could also make your own using thin cardboard. The bar should be equal to the required finished width of the bias strip. Cut a fabric strip wide enough to wrap around the bar and to allow for ⅛-inch seam allowances. Fold the strip in half lengthwise, wrong sides facing, and using a ⅛-inch seam allowance, sew the long raw edges of the strip together. Insert the bar into the tube. Center the seam along the bar and press. Continue to slide the bar along the tube, pressing as you go. Remove the bar and press the strip one more time.

Machine Appliqué

Machine appliqué is ideal for decorative projects and home accessories like the Holiday Gift Bags on page 125 and the Stars and Stripes Picnic Set on page 108. It's a quick-and-easy way to add appliqué pieces to projects that you don't want to spend a lot of time hand stitching. Plus, machine appliqué stands up well to repeated washings, so it's great for items like place mats and clothing.

Satin stitch machine appliqué can be done on any sewing machine that has a zigzag stitch setting. Use a zigzag presser foot with a channel on the bottom that will allow the heavy ridge of stitching to feed evenly. Match your thread to the appliqué pieces. Set your machine for a medium-width zigzag stitch and a very short stitch length. Test stitch on a scrap of fabric. The stitches should form a band of color and be ⅛ to 3⁄16 inch wide. If necessary, loosen the top tension slightly so that the top thread is barely pulled to the wrong side.

1. To prepare the appliqué pieces, use Wonder-Under or a similar paper-backed fusible webbing, following the manufacturer's instructions. For most products, the procedure is the same: Trace the appliqué shapes onto the paper side of the webbing and roughly cut out the designs. See **Diagram 23.**

2. Using an iron set on Wool, fuse the webbing onto the wrong side of the fabrics you have chosen for appliqués. Cut out the pieces along the tracing lines, as shown in **Diagram 24,**

allowing approximately ¼ inch underlap on adjacent pieces within a design. Peel off the paper backing, position the pieces on the background fabric, and fuse in place.

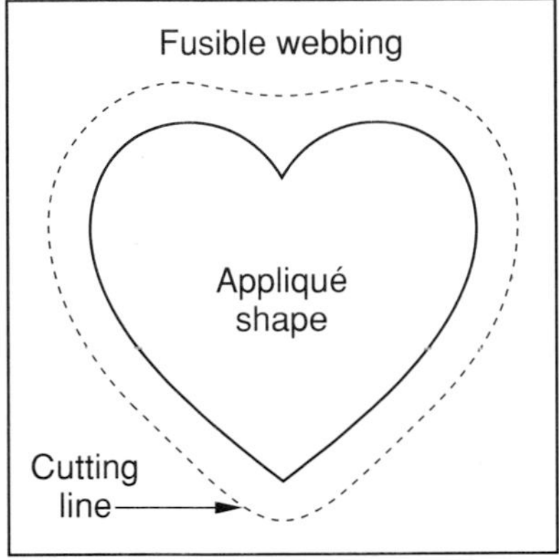

Diagram 23: *Trace the appliqué shape onto the paper side of the webbing and roughly cut out the design.*

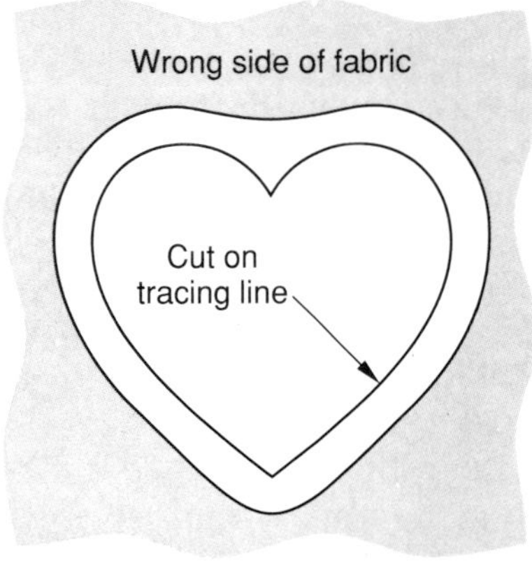

Diagram 24: *Fuse the webbing onto the wrong side of the fabric and cut along the tracing line.*

3. Stabilize the background fabric by pinning a sheet of typing paper or commercial stabilizer such as Tear-Away to the wrong side of the background fabric in the areas where you will be stitching.

4. Machine satin stitch around the edges of the appliqué pieces, covering the raw edges. Change thread colors to match the pieces. When stitching is complete, carefully tear away the stabilizer from the wrong side.

FREEZER PAPER STABILIZER

Plastic-coated freezer paper, which is available in grocery stores or quilt shops, makes a convenient and inexpensive stabilizer for machine appliqué. Cut a sheet of freezer paper slightly larger than the area you need to stabilize. Using a dry iron set on Wool, lightly press the shiny side of the paper to the wrong side of the background fabric. Remove the paper after stitching is complete. ❖

Assembling Quilt Tops

To assemble a quilt that is comprised of rows of blocks, such as Bleeding Heart on page 14, refer to the quilt diagram or photograph and lay out all the pieced or appliqué blocks, plain blocks, and setting pieces right side up, positioned as they will be in the finished quilt.

Pin and sew the blocks together in vertical or horizontal rows for straight-set quilts and in diagonal rows for diagonal-set quilts. Press the seams in opposite directions from row to row. Join the rows, abutting the pressed seam allowances so the intersections will be accurate.

To keep a large quilt top manageable, join rows into pairs first and then join the pairs, rather than add each row to an increasingly unwieldy top.

When pressing a completed top, press on the back side first, carefully clipping and removing hanging threads; then press the front, making sure all the seams are flat.

Tips for Successful Borders

For most of the quilts in this book, directions for adding the appropriate borders are included with the instructions for that quilt. Here are some general tips that can help you with any quilt you make.

- Cut borders to the desired finished width plus ½ inch for seam allowances. Always cut border strips several inches longer than needed, just to be safe. (Cutting instructions for borders in this book already include seam allowances and extra length.)
- Before adding borders, measure your completed inner quilt top. Measure through the center of the quilt rather than along the edges, which may have stretched from handling. Use this measurement to determine the exact length of your borders. This is an important step; if you don't measure first and simply give the edge of the quilt as much border as it "wants," you may end up with rippled edges on your quilt. Measuring and marking your borders first will allow you to make any necessary adjustment or ease in any fabric that may have stretched along the edge.

- Measure and mark sewing dimensions on the ends of borders before sewing them on, and wait to trim off excess fabric until after sewing.
- Fold border strips in half crosswise and press lightly or mark with a pin to indicate the center. Align this mark with the center point along the quilt side when pinning on the border.
- Press border seam allowances away from the center of the quilt.

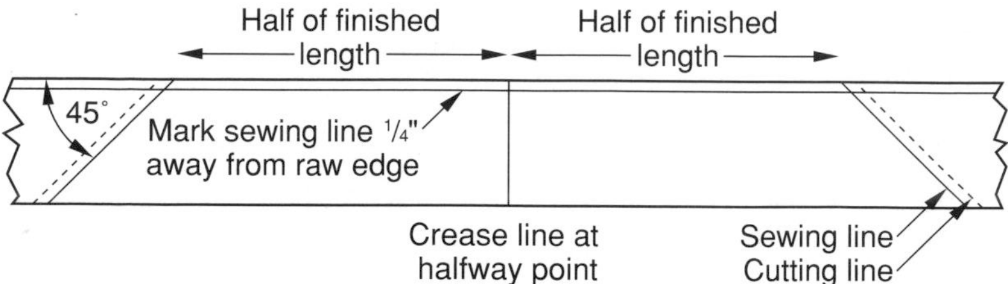

Diagram 25: *Mark the border strips for mitering before sewing them to the quilt top.*

Mitered Borders

Mitered borders add a wonderful professional touch to your quilt and are not hard to master if you keep in mind a few basics.

1. Start by measuring your finished quilt top through the center to determine the length the borders should be.

2. If you have multiple borders that are to be mitered, find and mark the center of each border strip. Match the centers, sew the strips together, and treat them as one unit.

3. With a ruler and pencil, mark a ¼-inch sewing line along one long edge of the border strip. For a multiple border, mark the inner strip that goes next to the quilt. Fold the strip in half crosswise and press lightly to mark the halfway point.

4. Starting at the halfway point, measure out in each direction to one-half of the desired finished border length, and make a mark on the sewing line.

5. Use a ruler that has a 45 degree angle line to mark the miter sewing line. Referring to **Diagram 25,** draw a line from the end mark made in Step 4 to the outer edge of the border strip. Mark a cutting line ¼ inch to the outside of the sewing line, but don't trim until after the border is sewn to the quilt top.

6. Pin the marked border strip to the quilt top, matching the crease at the halfway point to the center side of the quilt. Position the end marks on the border strip ¼ inch in from the raw edges of the quilt top. Repeat for all remaining borders.

7. Stitch the borders to the quilt top, starting and stopping at the end marks exactly ¼ inch from each end. Backstitch to secure the stitching. Press the seams away from the quilt top.

8. To sew the miters, fold the quilt diagonally, right sides together, and align the marked miter lines on adjacent borders. Stitch from the inner corner mark to the outer raw edge.

9. Check the accuracy of your miter, then trim the excess seam allowance.

Quilting Designs

Exquisite quilting is often the element that makes a quilt truly special. Even a simple quilt can be set apart by the fine workmanship demonstrated by small, even stitches. While some quilts lend themselves to very simple quilting patterns, such as outline quilting, others are beautifully accented by cables, feathers, and floral designs. Suggestions for quilting designs are included with many of the project instructions. You can duplicate the design the quiltmaker used, create your own, or choose one of the many quilting templates available at quilt shops and through mail-order catalogs.

Some quilting needs no design template. Outline quilting simply follows the seams of the patchwork. It can be in the ditch, that is, right next to the seam, or it can be ¼ inch away from the seam. In-the-ditch quilting needs no marking. For ¼-inch outline quilting, you can work by eye or use ¼-inch-wide masking tape as a guide. These and other straight lines can also be marked lightly with a pencil and ruler.

Another type of quilting that needs no marking is called echo quilting. It consists of lines of quilting that outline appliqués in concentric rings or shapes. The lines are generally spaced about ½ inch apart.

In contrast to outline and echo quilting, which need no marking, quilting designs, such as the floral and geometric designs for the quilt titled A Dozen Roses for You (page 65), should be marked before the quilt top is layered with batting and backing. How you mark depends on whether your fabric is light or dark.

Marking Light Fabrics

If your fabric is a light color that you can see through, such as muslin, you can place the pat-

tern under the quilt top and easily trace the quilting design onto the fabric. First, either trace the design out of the book onto good-quality tracing paper or photocopy it. If necessary, darken the lines with a black fine-point permanent marker. If the pattern will be used many times, glue it to cardboard to make it sturdy. Place the pattern under the quilt top and carefully mark the designs on the fabric, making a thin, continuous line that will be covered by the quilting thread. Use a silver quilter's pencil or a mechanical pencil with thin (0.5 mm) medium (B) lead.

Marking Dark Fabrics

Use a white or silver pencil to mark quilting designs on dark fabrics. Mark from the top by drawing around a hard-edged quilting design template. To make simple quilting templates, trace the design onto template plastic and cut around the outer edge. Trace around the template onto the fabric, then add inner lines by eye.

You may be able to place the pattern underneath the fabric to trace it if you place the pattern and the fabric on a light box while marking. The light shining through the paper and fabric will allow you to see the pattern outline through even the darkest fabrics. A glass-topped coffee table or dining room table makes an excellent light box area. Take the lampshade off a small lamp and place the lamp under the table. Tape your pattern to the tabletop, place the fabric on top of the pattern, and trace the pattern onto the fabric.

FABRIC MARKERS FOR DARK FABRICS

Several commercial markers are available for marking quilting designs on medium and dark fabrics. White or silver quilter's pencils, soapstone pencils, tailor's chalk pencils, and chalk dispensers all work well on many fabrics. An inexpensive marker that you probably have around the house is a small sliver of hand soap. Experiment to see which markers show up best on the fabrics you are using. ❖

Quilt Backings

For each of the projects in this book, the materials list includes yardage for the quilt back. For wallhangings that are narrower than 44 inches, simply use a full width of yardage cut several inches longer than the quilt top. For the wider wallhangings and most of the bed quilts, the quilt backing must be pieced.

Whenever possible, piece quilt backings in two or three panels with the seams running parallel to the long side of the quilt. Backs for quilts such as Broken Hearts for Daddy (page 100) and Jim's Scrappy Nine Patch (page 87), which are narrower than 80 inches wide, can easily be pieced this way out of two lengths of yardage. Divide the yardage in half crosswise. Then, to avoid having a seam down the center of the quilt back, divide one of the pieces in half lengthwise. Sew a narrow panel to each side of a full-width central panel, as shown in **Diagram 26.** Be sure to trim the selvages from the yardage before joining the panels. Press the seams away from the center of the quilt.

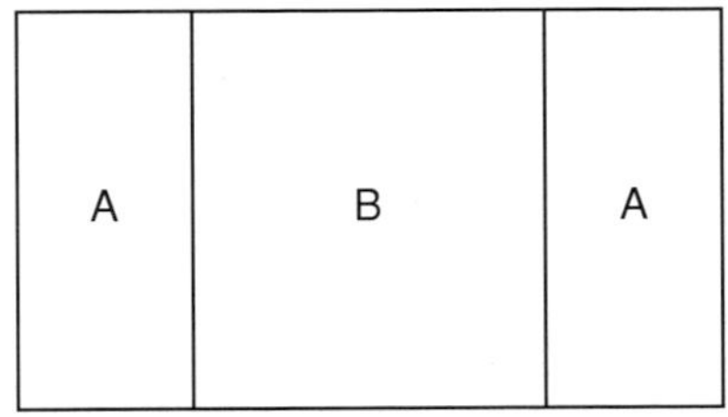

Diagram 26: *Divide the yardage in half crosswise; divide one of the pieces in half lengthwise. Sew one of those halves to each side of the full-width piece, as shown.*

For some quilts, you may make more sensible use of your yardage by piecing the back so that the seams run parallel to the short side of the quilt, as shown in **Diagram 27.** As an example, the Double Irish Chain quilt (page 9) is 82 × 102 inches. To have the seams run parallel to the long side of the quilt, you

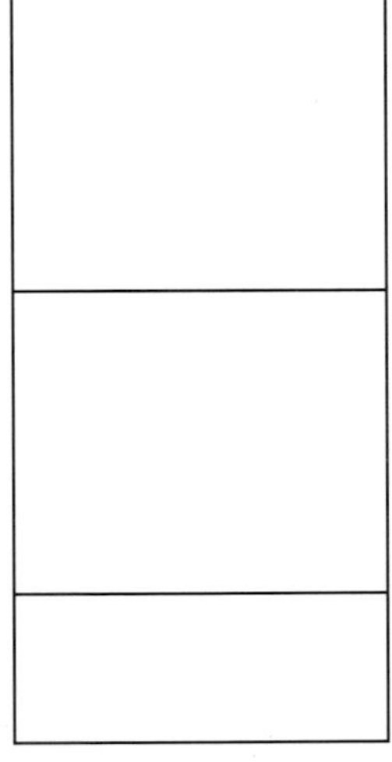

Diagram 27: *Divide the yardage crosswise into three equal panels. Sew the three full-width panels together side by side. Layer the backing, batting, and quilt top with the seams running parallel to the short side of the quilt top, as shown. Trim the excess from one panel as needed.*

would need three panels that are each 3 yards long, for a total of 9 yards of fabric. However, if the seams run parallel to the short side of the quilt, you'd need three panels that are 2½ yards long, for a total of 7½ yards of fabric.

To prepare the backing, divide the yardage crosswise into three panels. Trim the selvages and sew the full-width panels together along their long sides. In the example of the Double Irish Chain, you would need two full-width panels and approximately one-half of the third panel, but wait to trim the third panel until after you have layered the backing with the batting and quilt top. The finished quilt backing should look like the one shown in **Diagram 27.**

SEAMLESS QUILT BACKS

To eliminate seams on a quilt back, purchase fabric that is wider than your quilt top. Many fabric stores and quilt shops carry extra-wide cotton fabrics to use as quilt backs. Muslin and other basic colors are often available in 90- or 108-inch widths. ❖

Types of Quilt Batting

Quilters generally spend a lot of time selecting the fabrics for their quilts, but often not enough time choosing the batting they will use. When purchasing batting for your quilt, take the time to read the manufacturer's literature and think about the intended use of your quilt. Also, talk to experienced quilters about their favorite batting. Experiment with different battings to find which type works best for you. No matter what kind you use, before layering the batting with the quilt backing and top, unfold it and allow it to relax for several hours, or tumble it in the clothes dryer for a few minutes with no heat to remove sharp folds.

Polyester Batting

One hundred percent polyester batting, though lightweight, is very durable and warm. It launders without shrinking and needles easily for hand quilting. One disadvantage of polyester batting is the bearding that often occurs: The fibers migrate through the fabric of the quilt top, creating a fuzzy look. Many polyester battings are bonded, or coated, to reduce bearding. Unfortunately, the bonding makes the batting a little more difficult to needle. Polyester batting comes in many different lofts, which makes it suitable for everything from quilted clothing and home accessories to puffy, tied comforters.

Cotton Batting

All-cotton battings are popular with quilters who like a very flat, old-fashioned look, though some hand quilters think cotton is harder to needle. Unlike polyester, cotton fibers do not beard. At one time, all-cotton batting had to be quilted at very close intervals (¼ to ½ inch) to prevent lumping and migration of the fibers during washing. Some modern cotton battings can be laundered even when quilting is several inches apart. Note that cotton battings will shrink when washed. This is desirable for some quilters who want to create an antique look; the shrinking batting wrinkles the fabrics around the lines of quilting, instantly creating the look of an old quilt.

Cotton/Polyester Blends

Another option is to use a cotton/polyester blend batting, which combines the low-loft sculpted look of cotton with durability. This type of batting is easier to needle than the cotton and can be quilted at greater intervals. The fibers are bonded, or coated, to reduce bearding. Some quilters prefer to presoak this type of batting to break down the coating and make the needling easier. Follow the manufacturer's recommendations for pretreating.

Other Options

Keep in mind, too, that batting is not the only option. Cotton flannel gives quilts a flat look that can be ideal for miniature quilts that would be overpowered by a very puffy batting. Quiltmakers have also used wool and silk battings.

A dark-color batting is a good choice for quilts with dark or black backgrounds. The dark fibers would be far less noticeable than white fibers if they were to migrate through the quilt top.

Layering and Basting

Once your quilt top is complete and marked for quilting, your batting is purchased, and your backing is prepared, you are ready to assemble and baste together the layers. Whether you plan to hand or machine quilt, the layers must be assembled securely so that the finished quilt will lie flat and smooth.

Follow the procedure below for successful layering. If you plan to quilt by hand, baste with thread. If you will be machine quilting, use safety pins. Thread basting does not hold the layers securely enough during machine quilting. The thread is also more difficult to remove when quilting is completed.

For best results when basting large quilts, work at two or three banquet-type tables at a community center, library, or church basement. The next best thing is a large, clear area on the living room floor. Whatever surface you work on, make sure it is completely free of dust and dirt before laying the quilt back on it.

Layering

1. Fold the quilt back in half lengthwise and press to form a centerline. Place the back, wrong side up, on the basting table. Position the pressed centerline at the middle of the table. To keep the backing taut, use masking tape at the corners or clamp it to the table with large binder clips from a stationery store.

2. Fold the batting in half lengthwise and lay it on the quilt backing, aligning the fold with the pressed centerline. Open out the batting; smooth and pat down any wrinkles.

3. Fold the quilt top in half lengthwise, right sides together, and lay it on the batting, aligning the fold with the center of the batting. Unfold the top; smooth it out and remove any loose threads. Make sure the backing and batting are at least 2 inches larger than the quilt top on all four sides.

Thread Basting

For hand quilting, use a long darning needle and white sewing thread to baste the layers together, making lines of basting approximately 4 inches apart. Baste from the center out in a radiating pattern, or make horizontal and vertical lines of basting in a lattice fashion, using the seams that join the blocks as guidelines.

Pin Basting

For machine quilting, use 1-inch-long safety pins to secure the layers together, pinning from the center out approximately every 3 inches. Be careful not to place the pins where you intend to quilt. You may need as many as 1,000 pins to pin baste a queen-size quilt.

Quilting

All of the full-size quilts in this book are hand quilted, but some of the smaller projects are machine quilted. The Patchwork Pillows (page 80), Oak Leaf Wreath wallhanging (page 121), and Blossoms and Buds wallhanging (page 35) are machine quilted. Whether you will be stitching by hand or by machine, the tips that follow can help with your quilting.

Hand Quilting

- Use a hoop or frame to hold the quilt layers taut and smooth during quilting.
- Use short quilting needles, called *betweens,* in either size 9 or size 10.
- Use quilting thread rather than regular sewing thread.
- Start with a length of quilting thread about 18 inches long. This is long enough to keep you going for a while, but not so long that it tangles easily.
- Pop the knot through the fabric at the beginning and end of each length of thread so that no knots show on the quilt front or back. To do this, insert the needle through the top and batting about 1 inch away from where you will begin stitching. Bring the needle to the surface in position to make the first stitch. Gently tug on the thread to pop the knot through the top and bury it in the batting, as shown in **Diagram 28.**

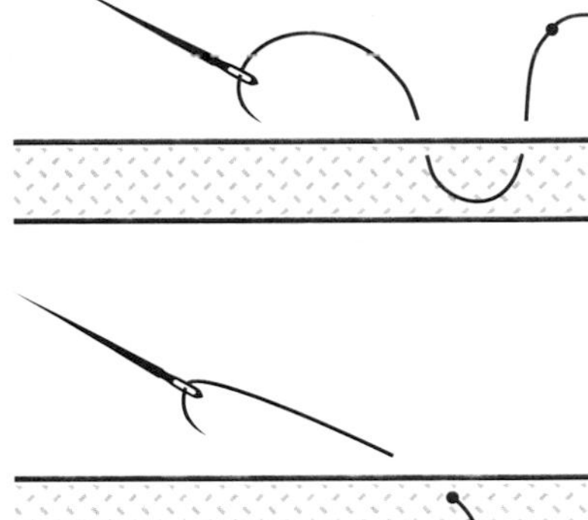

Diagram 28: *Insert the needle through the top and batting, and gently tug on the thread until the knot pops through the fabric.*

- Quilt by making running stitches, about $\frac{1}{16}$ to $\frac{1}{8}$ inch long, through all three layers. Try to keep the stitches straight and even.
- Thread several needles with quilting thread before you begin, and keep them handy while you work. Then you won't have to stop and thread a needle every time you finish a length of thread.

Machine Quilting

- Use a walking foot (also called an even feed foot) on your sewing machine for quilting straight lines. Use a darning or machine embroidery foot for free-motion quilting.

- To secure the thread at the beginning and end of a design, take several short stitches.
- For free-motion quilting: Disengage the sewing machine feed dogs so you can manipulate the quilt freely as you quilt. (Check your sewing machine manual to see how to do this.) Choose continuous-line quilting designs so you won't have to begin and end threads as frequently as with interrupted designs. Guide the marked design under the needle with both hands, working at an even pace so stitches will be of a consistent length.

Making and Attaching Binding

The most common edge finish for quilts is binding, cut either on the bias or on the straight of grain. Bias binding has more give, which makes it ideal for quilts that have curves or points along the outside edges. Use the yardage reserved for binding to make the type of binding you prefer. Some projects in this book are finished without binding. Directions for those finishes are included with the projects.

French-fold binding, also called double-fold binding, is recommended for bed quilts. The bias or straight grain binding strip is folded in half, and the raw edges are stitched to the edge of the quilt on the right side. The folded edge is then brought to the back side of the quilt, as shown in **Diagram 29,** and hand stitched in place. French-fold binding is easier to apply than single-fold binding, and its double thickness adds durability. The strips for this type of binding are cut four times the finished width plus seam allowances. As a general rule, cut the strips 2 inches wide for quilts with thin batting such as cotton and 2¼ inches wide for quilts with thicker batting. The project directions in this book specify French-fold binding, and the fabric yardages are based on that type of binding.

The amount of binding needed for each project is included with the finishing instructions. Generally, you will need the perimeter of the quilt plus 10 to 12 inches for mitering corners and ending the binding. Three-quarters to 1 yard of fabric will usually make enough binding to finish a large quilt.

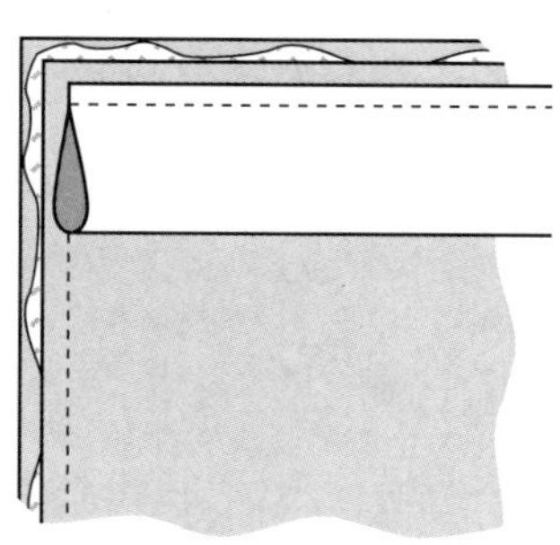

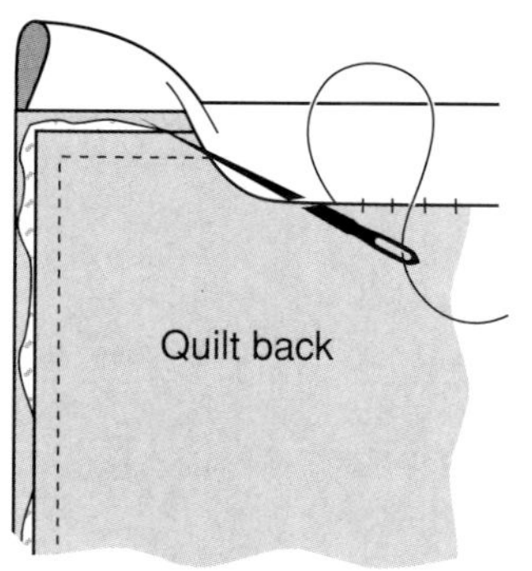

Diagram 29: For French-fold binding, fold the strip in half and stitch it to the quilt front. Bring the folded edge to the back of the quilt and hand stitch it in place.

Follow the instructions below to make continuous-cut bias binding or to join straight strips for continuous straight-grain binding. Unless the project directions tell you otherwise, sew the binding to the quilt as described below, mitering the binding at the corners.

Making Continuous-Cut Bias Binding

Continuous-cut bias binding is cut in one long strip from a square of fabric that has been cut apart and resewn into a tube. You must first determine the size of the square you will need. To make approximately 400 inches of 2- or 2¼-inch-wide French-fold binding, enough to bind most bed quilts, start with a 30-inch square. If you don't have enough fabric for one large square, use several smaller squares. To estimate the number of inches of binding a particular square will produce, use this formula:

Multiply the length of one side by the length of another side. Divide the result by the width of binding you want.

Using a 30-inch square and 2¼-inch binding as an example: 30 × 30 = 900 ÷ 2¼ = 400 inches of binding.

Seven Steps to Continuous-Cut Binding

1. Once you have determined the size you need, measure and cut a square of fabric.

2. Fold the square in half diagonally and press lightly. Cut the square into two triangles, cutting on the fold line.

3. Place the two triangles, right sides together, as shown in **Diagram 30.** Sew the pieces together, taking a ¼-inch seam. Open out the two pieces and press the seam open. The resulting piece should look like the one shown in **Diagram 31.**

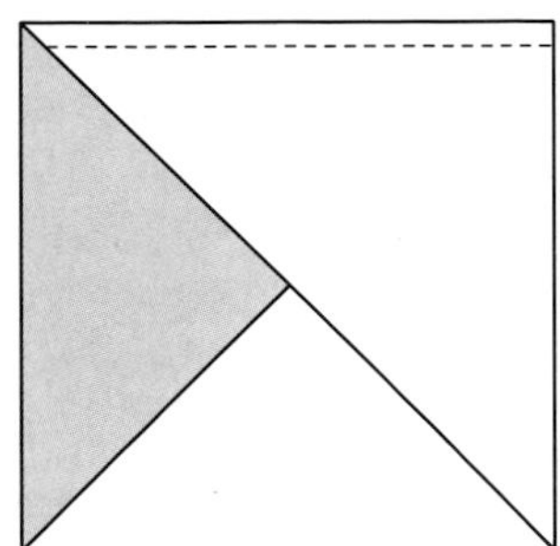

Diagram 30: *Place the triangles right sides together as shown and stitch.*

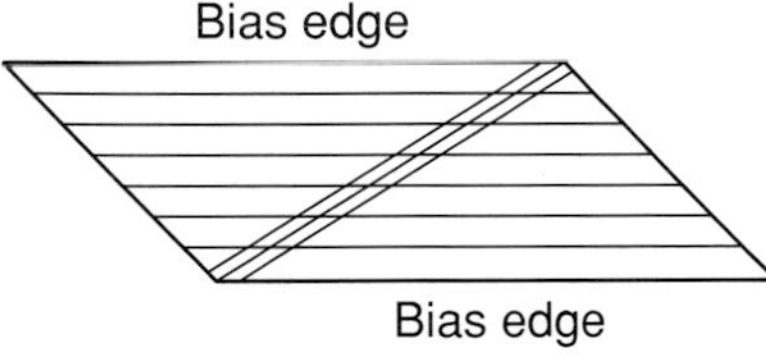

Diagram 31: *Open out the two pieces and press the seam open. On the wrong side, mark cutting lines parallel to the bias edges.*

4. Referring to **Diagram 31,** mark cutting lines on the wrong side of the fabric in the desired binding width. Mark parallel to the bias edges.

5. Fold the fabric right sides together, bringing the two non-bias edges together and offsetting them by one strip width, as shown in **Diagram 32.** Pin the edges together, creating a tube, and sew, taking a ¼-inch seam. Press the seam open.

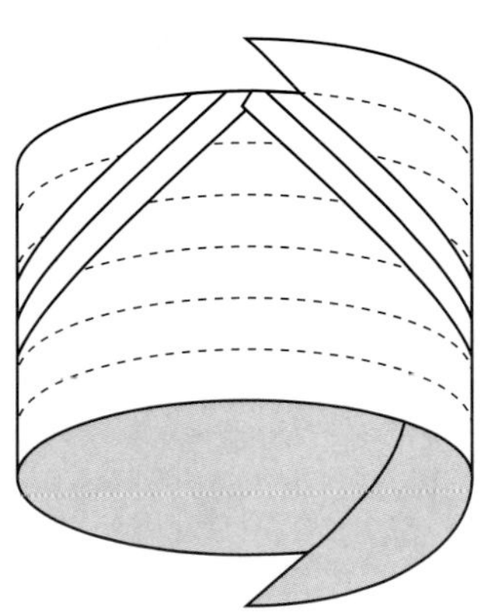

Diagram 32: *Bring the non-bias edges together, offsetting them by one strip width. Sew the edges together to create a tube.*

6. Cut on the marked lines, as shown in **Diagram 33,** turning the tube as you cut one long bias strip.

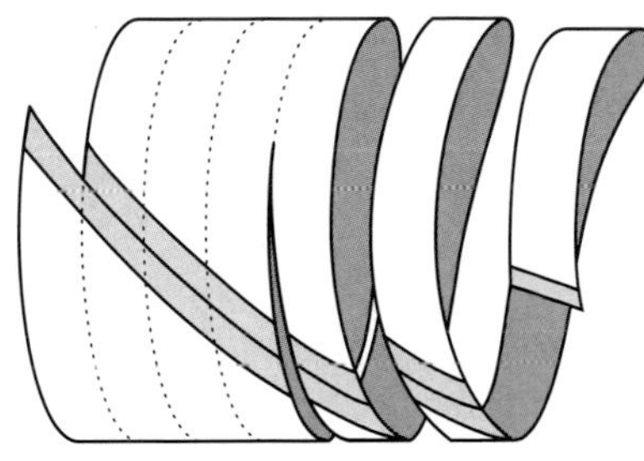

Diagram 33: *Turning the tube as you go, cut along the marked lines to make one long bias strip.*

7. To make French-fold binding, fold the long strip in half lengthwise, wrong sides together, and press.

Straight-Grain Binding

Straight-grain binding is a little easier to prepare than bias binding. Simply cut strips across the grain of the fabric and sew them together end to end to get the required length. Although it doesn't have the same flexibility as bias binding, it works just fine for quilts with straight edges.

Simple Straight-Grain Binding Method

1. Refer to the project instructions for the amount of binding the quilt requires. Estimate and cut the needed number of strips. When possible, cut straight strips across the width of the fabric rather than along the length so they are slightly stretchy and easier to use.

2. Join the strips, as shown in **Diagram 34.** Place them right sides together, with each strip set in ¼ inch from the end of the other strip, as shown. Sew a diagonal seam. Trim the excess fabric, leaving a ¼-inch seam allowance. Continue adding strips until you have the length needed. For French-fold binding, fold and press the long strip in half lengthwise, wrong sides together.

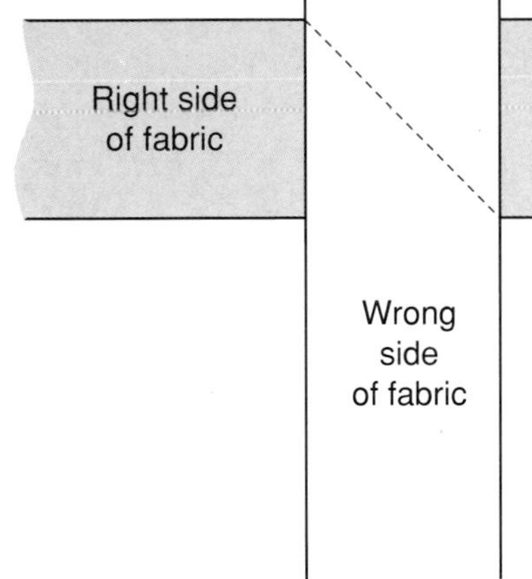

Diagram 34: *Place the strips right sides together, positioning each strip ¼ inch in from the end of the other strip. Join with a diagonal seam.*

Preparing a Quilt for Binding

Wait to trim excess batting and backing until after the binding is stitched to the top of the quilt. If the edges of the quilt are uneven after quilting, use a ruler and pencil to mark a placement line for the binding, as close as possible to the raw edges of the quilt top. This will give you a guideline against which you can align the raw edge of the binding strip. For best results, use a ruled square to mark the placement lines at the corners.

If you have a walking foot or an even feed foot for your sewing machine, use it in place of the regular presser foot when sewing on the binding. If you do not have a walking foot, thread baste around the quilt along the edges to hold the layers firmly

together during binding and to avoid puckers.

Attaching the Binding

1. Once you have made your binding strips (using either the continuous-cut bias or straight-grain strip method), you must prepare them so they can be attached to the quilt. If you are using French-fold binding, fold the long strip in half lengthwise, wrong sides together, and press. If you are using single-fold binding, you must fold over ¼ inch along one long side of the strip and press.

2. Begin attaching the binding in the middle of a side, not in a corner. Place the binding strip right sides together with the quilt top, with the raw edges of the binding strip even with the raw edge of the quilt top (or the placement line if you have drawn one).

3. Fold over the beginning raw edge of the binding approximately 1 inch, as shown in **Diagram 35.** Securing the stitches with a backstitch, begin sewing ½ inch away from the fold. Sew the binding to the quilt, stitching through all layers, ¼ inch away from the raw edge of the binding.

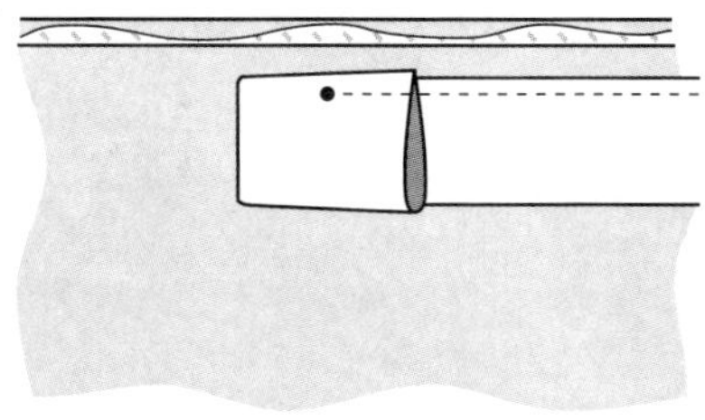

Diagram 35: *Fold the raw edge back about 1 inch, and begin stitching ½ inch from the fold. Backstitch to anchor the stitching.*

4. When approaching a corner, stop stitching exactly ¼ inch away from the raw edge of the corner. Backstitch and remove the quilt from the sewing machine, clipping threads.

5. Fold the binding up and away from the corner, as shown in **Diagram 36A,** forming a 45 degree angle fold.

6. Fold the binding strip back down and align the raw edges with the adjacent side of the corner, as shown in **36B.**

7. Begin stitching the next side at the top edge of the quilt, as shown in **36B.** The fold created in the fabric is essential; it provides the fullness necessary to fit around the corners as you fold the binding to the back side of the quilt. Miter all four corners in this manner.

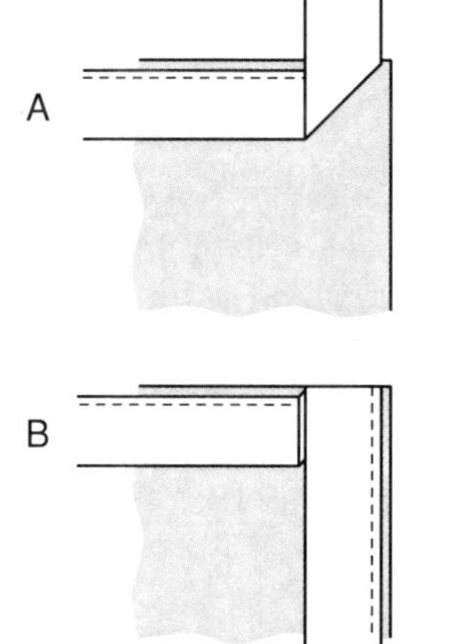

Diagram 36: *Stop stitching ¼ inch from the corner and fold the binding up at a 45 degree angle (A). Fold the binding strip back down, align the raw edges with the side of the quilt top, and stitch the binding in place (B).*

8. As you approach the point where you began, overlap the folded-back beginning section with the ending section. Sew across the fold, as shown in **Diagram 37,** allowing the ending section to extend approximately ½ inch beyond the beginning.

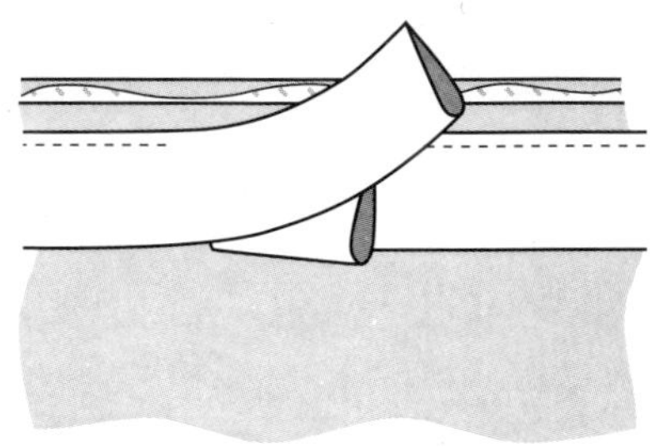

Diagram 37: *Cross the beginning section with the ending section, overlapping them about ½ inch.*

9. Trim away the excess batting and backing, using scissors or a rotary cutter and a ruler. Before you trim the whole quilt, trim a small section and turn the binding to the back of the quilt to determine the right amount of excess to trim. The binding will look best and wear longer if it is filled rather than hollow.

10. Turn the binding to the back of the quilt and blindstitch the folded edge in place, covering the machine stitches with the folded edge. Finish the miters at the corners by folding in the adjacent sides on the back of the quilt and placing several stitches in the miter, as shown in **Diagram 38.** Add several stitches to the miters on the front in the same manner.

If adding a hanging sleeve, follow the directions on the opposite page to make and attach the sleeve before turning and finishing the binding.

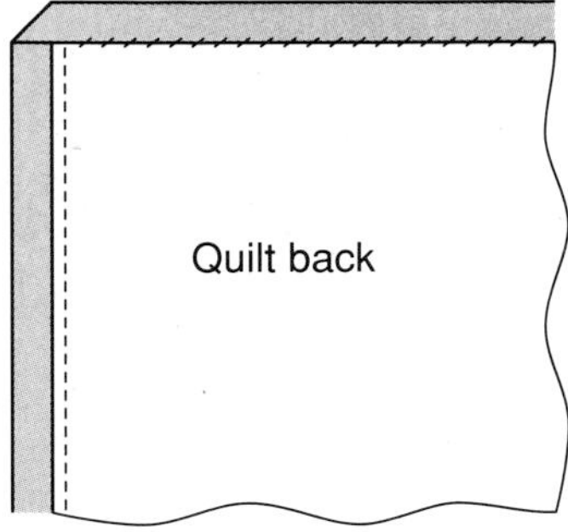

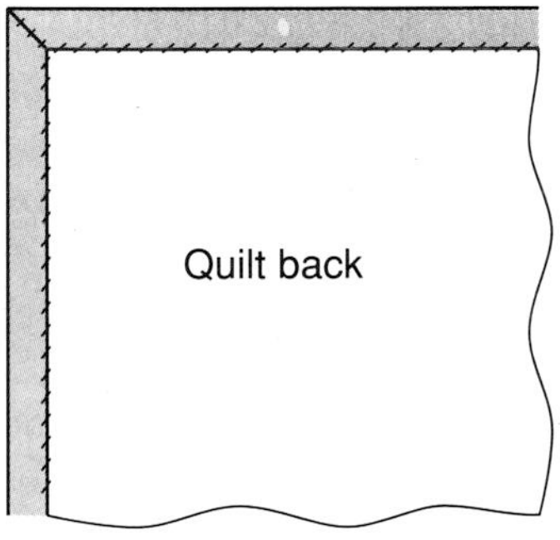

Diagram 38: Blindstitch the binding in place on the quilt back. Fold in the adjacent corner and stitch along the miter.

Adding a Hanging Sleeve

If you plan to display your quilt, either at home or at a quilt show, you will certainly need to add a hanging sleeve to the back.

The best way to prepare any of the wallhangings in this book for display is to add a hanging sleeve when you are binding the quilt. A rod or dowel can be inserted in the sleeve and supported by nails or hooks on the wall. Many quilters put hanging sleeves on bed quilts as well so that their work can be exhibited at quilt shows. Use the following procedure to add a 4-inch-wide hanging sleeve, which can accommodate a 2-inch-diameter dowel or pole.

SIGNING YOUR QUILT

Once your quilt is complete, be sure to sign and date it. If the backing is muslin, use a permanent pen and write the information right on the fabric. Or write on a muslin label and stitch it to the back.

Some quiltmakers like to embroider their names and the date on their quilts. Others sign with short verses or dedications. If the quilt is made as a gift, you may want to note the recipient's name and the occasion. Be creative! Give your quilt the perfect finishing touch. ❖

1. Cut a strip of muslin or other fabric that is 8½ inches wide and 1 inch shorter than the width of the finished quilt.

2. Machine hem the short ends. To hem, turn under ½ inch on each end of the strip and press. Turn under another ½ inch and stitch next to the pressed fold.

3. Fold and press the strip in half lengthwise, wrong sides together, aligning the two long raw edges.

4. Position the raw edges of the sleeve to align with the top raw edges on the back of the quilt, centering the sleeve on the quilt. The binding should already be sewn on the front, but not turned to the back of the quilt. Pin the sleeve in place.

5. Machine stitch the sleeve to the back of the quilt, stitching from the front by sewing on top of the stitches that hold the binding to the quilt.

6. Turn the binding to the back of the quilt and hand stitch it in place so that the binding covers the raw edge of the sleeve. (See **Diagram 39.**) When turning the binding on the edge with the sleeve, you may need to trim away more batting and backing in order to turn the binding more easily.

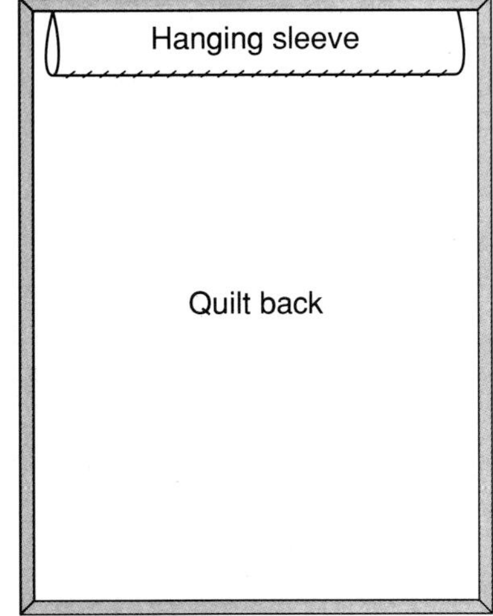

Diagram 39: Stitch the raw edge of the sleeve to the top of the quilt. Bring the binding to the back of the quilt and hand stitch it in place, covering the top raw edge of the sleeve. Then, hand stitch the bottom edge of the sleeve to the quilt back.

7. Hand stitch the bottom loose edge of the sleeve in place, being careful not to sew through to the front of the quilt.

Directory of Quilt Shows

Because the dates and locations for many quilt shows change from year to year, and because there are new shows being added to the calendar all the time, it is impossible to provide a complete and current listing. The shows listed here are national in scope and therefore generally have fixed locations and dates. Write to the addresses provided for exact dates and complete information.

American Quilter's Society National Quilt Show and Contest
Paducah, Kentucky
Date: Generally the last week in April
Mailing address:
American Quilter's Society
P.O. Box 3290
Paducah, KY 42002-3290

The Great American Quilt Festival
New York City
Date: Generally in early May
Mailing address:
Museum of American Folk Art
Quilt Connection
61 West 62nd Street
New York, NY 10023

International Quilt Festival
Houston, Texas
Date: Generally the last week in October
Mailing address:
International Quilt Festival
14520 Memorial Drive #54
Houston, TX 77079

Mid-Atlantic Quilt Festival
Williamsburg, Virginia
Date: Generally the last week in February
Mailing address:
c/o David M. & Peter J. Mancuso, Inc.
P.O. Box 667
New Hope, PA 18938

National Quilting Association
The date and location change each year for the NQA show, though it is always held during the summer.
Mailing address:
National Quilting Association
P.O. Box 393
Ellicott City, MD 21041-0393

Pacific International Quilt Festival
San Francisco, California
Date: Generally the second week in October
Mailing address:
P.I.Q.F.
c/o David M. & Peter J. Mancuso, Inc.
P.O. Box 667
New Hope, PA 18938

Quilters' Heritage Celebration
Lancaster, Pennsylvania
Date: Generally the first week in April
Mailing address:
Quilters' Heritage Celebration
P.O. Box 503
Carlinville, IL 62626

Silver Dollar City's National Quilt Festival
Branson, Missouri
Date: Generally late August or early September
Mailing address:
Special Events Department
Silver Dollar City, Inc.
West Highway 76
Branson, MO 65616